Atheism?

Atheism?

A Critical Analysis

Stephen E. Parrish

WIPF & STOCK · Eugene, Oregon

ATHEISM?
A Critical Analysis

Copyright © 2019 Stephen E. Parrish. All rights reserved. Except for brief quotations in critical publications or reviews, no part of this book may be reproduced in any manner without prior written permission from the publisher. Write: Permissions, Wipf and Stock Publishers, 199 W. 8th Ave., Suite 3, Eugene, OR 97401.

Wipf & Stock
An Imprint of Wipf and Stock Publishers
199 W. 8th Ave., Suite 3
Eugene, OR 97401

www.wipfandstock.com

PAPERBACK ISBN: 978-1-5326-7266-8
HARDCOVER ISBN: 978-1-5326-7267-5
EBOOK ISBN: 978-1-5326-7268-2

Scripture quotations are from The Holy Bible, New King James Version, copyright © 1982 by Thomas Nelson, Inc.

Permission has been granted by the Editor of *Philosophia Christi* to republish parts and revisions of, "Theism, Naturalism, and Worlds," which first appeared in *Philosophia Christi* 18:2 (2016) 433-50. Additional information is available at www.epsociety.org.

Manufactured in the U.S.A.

To my dear daughters:
Sarah,
Rebekah,
Mary

And to the memory of
Elaine Elness
my encouraging mother-in-law

Contents

Acknowledgements | xv

Preface | xvii

Introduction | 1
    Worldviews · 1
        Naturalism · 4
        Theism · 8

Chapter 1: **The Issues** | 16
    What is Religion? · 16
    Political Religions and Ideology · 22
    What is Science? · 25
        History of Science · 26
        Science is not a Worldview · 27
        Conflict between science and religion? · 27
        Scientism · 28
            Scientific Method · 29
            Strong Scientism · 30
            Weak Scientism · 30
        Reason · 30
        Discovering Truth · 30
        Science cannot be a worldview · 31
            Implications · 31
        Science is not identical with materialism · 32
        Materialism does *not* own science · 32
    What is Reason? · 33
        The Argument and the Ambiguity · 34
        Logic and the senses · 35

viii CONTENTS

        Plausibility Structure · 35
        Using Reason to Judge Worldviews · 38
        Worldviews and Plausibility Structures · 39
        Neutrality in Worldviews? · 39
            Naturalism is not neutral · 40
            Naturalism is not the "default" position · 41
            Naturalism's "God of the gaps" argument · 42
            Methodological Naturalism · 42
        Discovering or Dismissing the Truth · 43
What is Faith? · 44
        Reason to Have Faith · 45
        Reason vs. Faith? · 46
        Belief Without Reason? · 47
        Rationalization vs. Evidence · 47
        Belief · 48
        Deciding for Faith? · 49
            On Authority? · 49
            Based on Worldviews? · 50
            For No Reason? On Blind Faith? · 50
            Fodder for the Atheists · 51
        Faith Commitment and the Work of the Holy Spirit · 51
        Faith in Which Worldview? · 51
            Circularity · 52
            Getting around circularity · 53
            Perception and Plausibility Structures · 54
            Testing Worldviews · 55
                Consistency · 55
                Correspondence with facts and Justifiability · 55
                Transcendental Test · 55
            Verification or Falsification of Ideas · 55
The Questions To Be Answered · 56
        The Mystery of Existence · 56
        The Mystery of Consciousness · 57
        The Mystery of Values and Evil · 57
        Answering the Questions · 58
        The Big Question · 58

Chapter 2: The Competing Theories of Existence | 59

    What is the Mystery of Existence? · 59
        What is Ultimate Reality? · 59
    Defining the Concept of God · 60
        Concepts of God · 60
        Criteria for a "god" · 62
            Person · 62

Other characteristics · 64
  Power over the laws of nature · 64
  What about Hitler's God? · 65
  The "One" or Absolute · 68
  What about Spinoza's "God"? · 69
  Panentheism · 71
 Summary of Concepts of God · 71
The God of Classical or Perfect Being Theism · 72
 Omniscient · 73
 Omnipotent · 74
 Omnipresent · 75
 Necessarily Existent · 75
  Possible Worlds · 75
  God, a Necessary Being · 76
 Omnibenevolent · 78
 Incomprehensible · 78
  Literally vs Moderately Incomprehensible · 79
  Analogical vs Univocal Knowledge of God · 79
 Transcendent · 81
 Immanent · 82
 Infinite · 82
 Sovereign · 82
 Trinity · 83
 Simplicity · 83
Atheism · 87
 Distinction between Atheism and Agnosticism · 88
 The Burden of Proof · 89
 Is Everyone an Atheist Of Sorts? · 91
Naturalism · 93
 The Universe(s) · 94
 Materialism/Physicalism · 95
 Dualism · 95
  Objects and Properties · 95
 Naturalism and Atheism · 96
 Naturalism vs Theism · 96
 Concrete vs Abstract Objects · 96
 Putting it all together · 98
  Faith Commitment · 98
Ultimate Reality · 99

Chapter 3: **The Universe: Its Existence and Order** | 102

 Foundational Questions · 103
  Possible Worlds—What Could Have Been · 103
  Chance or Necessity? · 105

   Brute Fact Theory · 105
   Necessary World Theory · 106
   Necessary Deity Theory · 106
    Atheist's Challenges · 107
 Necessary Deity Theory Examined · 108
  Why must the Necessary Cause be a Deity? · 108
  Does Everything in the Universe Need a Cause? · 109
  Doesn't God Need a Cause? · 109
  Why Does God Exist? · 110
 Brute Fact Theory Examined · 111
  Possible Worlds · 112
  Possible Worlds Cannot Contain Contradictions · 114
  By Chance · 115
  The Odds · 116
  What About the Laws of Physics? · 120
  Why Do Things Remain in Existence? · 121
   Two Possibilities for Contingent Beings · 121
    For No Reason At All · 121
    Due to a Reason External to Itself · 125
 Necessary Universe Theory Examined · 125
  Option 1—The Universe Itself is Necessary · 126
  Option 2—Something Emanates the Universe · 128
   The Plotinian One · 128
   The God of Spinoza · 129
   Oppy's Explanation · 130
  Modal Realism · 131
  Caused by Abstract Entities? · 133
 Summary · 135

Chapter 4: **The Existence of the Mind** | 137

 The Nature of "Persons" · 138
  Physical Objects · 138
  What about the "Conscious"? · 138
   The Physicalist (Materialist) View · 139
   The Dualist View · 139
 Dualists · 139
 Materialists · 140
 Consciousness · 141
 Types of Materialism · 141
  Mysterianism · 142
  Eliminativism · 142
  Identity Theory · 142
  Supervenience Theory · 143
  Functionalist Materialism · 143

- Realization Materialism · 143
- Two Major Groupings · 144
  - Reductive Materialism · 144
  - Non-reductive Materialism · 144
- Problems with Materialism · 145
  - Problem One: The *Existence* of Consciousness · 145
    - Relationship Between the Brain and Consciousness · 146
    - Consciousness an Illusion? · 147
    - Intentionality · 148
    - The Fundamental Problem · 148
  - Problem Two: Are Consciousness and the Brain Identical? · 149
  - Problem Three: The Causal Closure of the Physical · 151
    - Consciousness Becomes Useless · 152
      - Belief Becomes Irrelevant? · 152
      - Beliefs Have Nothing To Do With Reality? · 153
      - The Upshot · 154
  - Problem Four: The Relationship Between the Mental and the Physical · 154
    - The Brain · 155
    - The Mental World · 155
    - The Relationship Between Brain and Thought · 156
  - Problem Five: Free Will · 158
    - Libertarian Free Will · 159
    - Compatibilism · 159
    - Free Will is Incompatible with Materialism · 159
    - Agent Causation · 161
- Theistic Dualism · 161
- Objections to Dualism · 162
  - Objection One: How Do Mind and Matter Interact? · 162
  - Objection Two: The Pairing Problem · 162
  - Objection Three: "Ectoplasm" · 163
  - Other Objections: Based on Presuppositions and Assumptions · 163
  - A Better Answer · 163
  - Oppy's Objection · 164
- Summary of the Mind-Body Problem · 166

Chapter 5: **Value Part 1: Ethics** | 168

- Metaethics · 169
  - What are Ethical Truths Like (if they exist)? · 169
- Ethical Truths' Characteristics · 170
  - Necessity—Necessarily True · 170
  - Universal · 170
  - Person Related · 171
- Ethical Theory Categories · 171
  - Strong Realism (ethics discovered) · 172

Weak Realism (ethics derived) · 172
Anti-Realism (ethics invented) · 173
Axioms · 174
The Law of Non-Contradiction · 175
The Case for Strong Ethical Realism · 176
The Awful Consequences Argument · 176
Wired to Believe in Morality · 178
Mode of Being · 179
Arguments Against Ethical Realism · 181
The Argument from Strangeness · 181
The Argument from Ethical Relativity · 183
What about Weak Realism? · 184
The Explanatory Gap · 185
In the View of Utilitarianism · 185
In the View of Kantianism · 186
In the View of Any Consequentialist Theory · 186
Attempts to Found Ethics on Human Nature · 187
Rationality? · 187
Human Nature · 189
Cultural Influences · 189
Sinnott-Armstrong's Moral System · 190
The Weaknesses of Weak Realism · 191
Non-Moral Choice · 191
Prudence · 191
A Matter of the Will · 191
Not a Categorical Imperative · 192
Which is the Best Theory of Strong Ethical Realism? · 192
Impersonal · 192
Personal · 193
The Euthyphro Objection · 194
Secure Grounding · 195
Love · 195

Chapter 6: **Value Part 2: Beauty and Evil** | 197

Beauty · 197
The Problem of Evil · 200
Moral Evil vs Natural Evil · 202
Logical Argument *vs* Evidential Argument · 202
The Logical Argument Fails · 203
The Evidential Argument · 203
Defense *vs* Theodicy · 203
Attempted Solutions · 204

Free Will Defense · 204
Soul Making Defense · 204
Natural Law Defense · 205
Understanding God's Purpose · 205
Austere Theism · 206
Natural Evil · 209
Solution to the Problem of Evil? · 211
The Problem of Evil and Theism *vs* Naturalism · 211
True Morality · 212
The "Odds" Question · 213
Summary of the Problem of Evil · 214

Chapter 7: Conclusion | 216

Questions—Set 1: About *Existence* · 217
Existence Question A: *Why?* · 217
Theism's Answer to *Why?* · 217
Naturalist Atheism's Answer to *Why?* · 217
Existence Question B: Why *Remain?* · 218
Theism's Answer to *Remaining* · 218
Naturalist Atheism's Answer to *Remaining* · 218
Existence Question C: Why *Orderly?* · 218
Theism's Answer to *Orderliness* · 218
Naturalist Atheism's Answer to *Orderliness* · 219
Questions—Set 2: About *Consciousness, Minds, Rationality, Intentionality, and Free Will* · 219
Consciousness Questions · 219
Theism's Answer for *Consciousness* · 219
Naturalist Atheism's Answer for *Consciousness* · 219
Mind Questions · 219
Theism's Answer for *Minds* · 220
Naturalist Atheism's Answer for *Minds* · 220
Rationality Questions · 220
Theism's Answer to *Rationality* · 220
Naturalist Atheism's Answer to *Rationality* · 220
Intentionality Questions · 221
Theism's Answer to *Intentionality* · 221
Naturalist Atheism's Answer to *Intentionality* · 221
Questions of *Free Will* · 221
Theism's Answer to *Free Will* · 221
Naturalist Atheism's Answer to *Free Will* · 222
Questions—Set 3: About *Value* · 222
Value Question A: Why *Morality?* · 222

             Theism's Answer to *Morality* · 222
             Naturalist Atheism's Answer to *Morality* · 222
         Value Question B: Why *Beauty*? · 222
             Theism's Answer for *Beauty* · 223
             Naturalist Atheism's Answer for *Beauty* · 223
         Value Question C: *The Problem of Evil* · 223
             Theism's Answer to *the Problem of Evil* · 223
             Naturalist Atheism's Answer to *the Problem of Evil* · 223
     Summary: The Greater Explanatory Power · 224
         Why is naturalism so popular? · 224
             The Problem of Evil · 224
             Science and a false claim of its ownership · 225
         Naturalism is no utopia · 226

Appendix 1: **Atheism and Ideology** | 227

     History of the Coming of Atheism in the West · 227
         Ancient Times · 227
         Middle Ages · 228
         Renaissance and Enlightenment · 228
         Darwin · 229
         Secular Worldviews · 229
         From Theistic to Political "Religions" · 230
         Minimizing Religion · 231
         Blind Faith · 232
         The Shoe is on the Other Foot · 233
         Atheism is Ungrounded · 233
     The Central Paradox of Naturalist Atheism · 234
         The Rise of Atheistic Worldviews · 234
         Authority · 235
         Meaning · 235
         Human Nature · 236
     The Secularization Thesis · 238
     Utopia · 239
         Utopianism · 241
     Conclusion · 244

Appendix 2: **Social Effects of Atheism** | 246

Bibliography | 253

Index | 277

Acknowledgements

FIRST, I WOULD LIKE to thank my wife, Dr. Elenn' Parrish, who had the idea for a book like this in the first place and encouraged me in its production. She has been a great help at every stage, especially in editing, wherein she turned my writing into something more intelligible.

I also want to acknowledge the late Elaine Elness, my wife's mother, who drove down from Duluth, Minnesota to Livonia, Michigan, near Detroit, in order to carefully check the notes, quotes, and bibliography. Sadly, she did not live to see the final product.

I would also like to thank Concordia University Ann Arbor, for giving me a semester sabbatical, allowing me more time to work on this project.

Also needing mention are J. W. Wartick and Dave Andersen, who helped in research and reading the manuscript.

Finally, I would like to thank Gary Habermas, Angus Menuge, and J. P. Moreland for their support.

Preface

> That man is the product of causes which had no prevision of the end they were achieving, that his origin, his growth, his hopes and fears, his loves and his beliefs, are but the outcome of accidental collocations of atoms; that no fire, no heroism, no intensity of thought and feeling can preserve an individual life beyond the grave; that all the labors of the ages, all the devotion, all the noonday brightness of human genius, are destined to extinction in the vast death of the solar system, and that the whole temple of man's achievement must inevitably be buried beneath the debris of a universe in ruins—all these things, if not quite beyond dispute, are yet so nearly certain that no philosophy which rejects them can hope to stand. Only within the scaffolding of these truths, only on the firm foundation of unyielding despair, can the soul's habitation henceforth be safely built.
>
> BERTRAND RUSSELL[1]

> I want atheism to be true and am made uneasy by the fact that some of the most intelligent and well-informed people I know are religious believers. It isn't just that I don't believe in God and, naturally, hope that I'm right in my belief. It's that I hope there is no God! I don't want there to be a God; I don't want the universe to be like that.
>
> THOMAS NAGEL[2]

IN MY EXPERIENCE, THE general attitude in academia in the twentieth and twenty-first centuries is reflected in these words of Nagel, much more so

---

1. Russell, "Free Man's Worship," 116.

2. Nagel, *Last Word*, 130. Nagel goes on to say, "My guess is that the cosmic authority problem is not a rare condition and that it is responsible for much of the scientism and reductionism of our time." Nagel, *Last Word*, 131.

than in those of Russell. The most popular philosophy held in the halls of higher learning in the western world today is some form of *naturalism*—the idea that all that exists is the natural universe and the things in it. This belief is usually combined with some form of materialism, which is basically the idea that all that exists is matter and energy. As can be seen from the quotations above, this philosophy is also atheistic; in it, Ultimate Reality is the physical universe itself, not a personal God of any sort.

Nagel's attitude has never made any sense to me. Without God, human beings exist for no purpose, being the unplanned result of evolution in a physical universe, and (almost always) there is no hope for an afterlife. I realize that in some sense, the removal of God allows for human autonomy—human beings are not subordinate to anyone or anything else. On this view, we make our own rules. This self-focused concept is very attractive to many people.

However, this belief seems to me to be false. Given atheism, there is no God to whom we owe obedience. But, since human beings are, given naturalism and physicalism, only material objects, and since the behavior of material objects is governed by the laws of physics, then in a real sense, human beings are not autonomous after all. They are ruled by these laws, and therefore everything they do would be dictated by these laws and the physical situation.[3] Human beings, thus, can never be truly autonomous because they are finite, contingent beings who necessarily exist in a world they didn't make, and indeed made them.

The major justification for believing in naturalist atheism is that it has within itself the resources to explain reality, and therefore there is no need to think that God exists. In this book, I attempt to show that despite its immense popularity in academia and elsewhere, naturalist atheism fails to deliver that elucidation of reality. It simply does not have the resources, I will argue, to explain much of anything.[4]

The Debate

The debate over the existence of God has often been along these general lines: The theist is expected to prove, or at least give a strong argument to

---

3. In short, I think that consistent materialists should be hard determinists. This will be explained in chapter 5.

4. Along these lines John Foster writes, "The fact that we cannot make sense of the corporealist view of the subject, and that we can achieve a satisfactory version of the Cartesian alternative only if we accept the existence of God, is simply a further indication of the bankruptcy of atheism." Foster, "Subjects of Mentality," 97.

show, that God exists. If, however, the argument does not convince the naturalist, then it is held to be unsuccessful. Naturalism is held, though this is often unstated, to be the *default position*. No proof is required of naturalism—it was taken as the beginning of any investigation, with the burden of proof squarely held to be on the theist, the believer in God.

This position has been under attack for the last few decades. For example, Alvin Plantinga has argued that theism can be properly basic, that one *can* rationally hold to it without having any argument at all.[5] In this book I take a different tack. I ask what the reasons are for thinking that naturalism is true. Does naturalism provide an adequate explanation of the world we live in? To cut the suspense, the answer I will give is an emphatic, "No."

My approach will be almost entirely philosophical, rather than scientific. A great deal of ink has been used on what can be called science/religion issues: specifically, debates about evolution and the apparent fine-tuning of the laws of the universe. Though these are interesting and important issues, my focus will be elsewhere. Specifically, what are the *philosophic reasons* for thinking naturalism true or false? Does philosophical naturalism deserve the popularity it now has? In addition, I will also spend some time in appendices to show the destructive impact of naturalism in world history and society.

Besides debunking the myth that naturalist atheism is the default position on interpreting reality, this book presents a definite position that stands solidly in contrast to atheism. This is not mere theism, but perfect being theism, in which God is a personal being. This philosophy, I will argue, can, unlike naturalism, explain reality as it is.

The initial notion for writing this book came from three others. One is Arthur Balfour's *Theism and Humanism*,[6] wherein the two systems are compared. The next is Gordon Clark's *A Christian View of Men and Things*,[7] which does the same thing. Both books take the theistic side of things, whereas the third book doesn't. This is Graham Oppy's *The Best Argument Against God*.[8]

The Importance of the Debate

It is important to note that this book is not meant primarily for professional philosophers: it is written in the hope that others also will read it. By others,

5. See Plantinga and Wolterstorff, *Faith and Rationality*.
6. Balfour, *Theism and Humanism*.
7. Clark, *Christian View*.
8. Oppy, *Best Argument against God*.

I mean people who are interested in these issues, and the impact they have on the world. The issues are too vital to be left to only just a comparatively small number of professionals to think about.

In bringing these thoughts alive I will first have to define some terms and cover some topics that are relevant to the subject. To that end, I also address a couple of issues, such as the National Socialist concept of God, that have had much more discussion on the internet than they have among scholars.

There are two basic reasons for critiquing a concept: the first is that the concept is intrinsically worth examining; the other, that even though the concept may not be worthwhile, it may be influential, and thus should be debunked. It is my hope that this book will help in the rejection of a false philosophy, that I believe has been extraordinarily destructive.

For the rest of the book, atheism and naturalism will be held to be the same: indeed, these terms will be interchangeable, unless otherwise specified. There are other versions of atheism available, but the vast majority of atheism in the western world today is of the naturalist variety, and it is to this version that I primarily address.

Introduction

> As he [man] thinks in his heart, so is he.
>
> Proverbs 23:7

Throughout history the world has been strongly divided about matters of fundamental beliefs and values, and this is especially true now. The most fundamental divisions have been between different worldviews, which we shall here briefly examine.

Worldviews

Worldviews are descriptions of reality at its most basic level. A worldview is the way that persons look at reality as a whole. A worldview contains both the most fundamental beliefs that one has and is also the structure of the totality of one's beliefs. All other beliefs that one has are fitted into the structure of the worldview that is held. A worldview can be considered as being analogous to a large box containing many smaller boxes. The smaller boxes can be thought of as being one's beliefs on politics, religion, economics, gardening, football, or whatever else. Since the various worldviews all differ from one another, the big boxes which represent them will have different shapes, and the smaller boxes will be shaped in different ways and sizes from each other.

All the worldviews give answers to the same basic questions. These include: what is ultimate reality; what is it composed of; why does it exist; what is truth; what is beauty; what are human beings like; are there objective values; how should we live (if there is any way in which we *should* live); what is wrong with the world and what should be done about it; and so on? In short, worldviews attempt to give answer to the most basic questions that there are. Every one of them is, in a sense, a narrative, or story about how things are and why they are the way they are.

Though there are many different worldviews, they may be grouped into a few basic categories. The two most popular categories of worldviews in the West today may be called *naturalism* and *theism*. Put simply, *naturalism* is the concept that the physical universe exists on its own; there is nothing beyond it that is its cause.[1] It is therefore, ultimate reality.[2] In contrast, *theism*, or more explicitly *monotheism*, is the theory that there is one God, that this God is the ultimate reality, and that our physical universe and anything else that exists, are dependent upon him.[3] Looked at one way, naturalism and theism differ at every fundamental point—and they are in many ways opposites, so that people with different worldviews are mentally living in different worlds.

Two people may be neighbors and have many of the same beliefs and values. They may work at the same kind of job, vote for the same party, root for the same sports teams, and have the same hobbies. However, suppose that one is a naturalist and the other a theist. Though they may share many different beliefs regarding life in the world, they will also differ radically in basic beliefs. The naturalist will usually believe that the universe is all that there is, that it is entirely made of physical things like matter and energy, as are human beings, and that there is no afterlife. The theist will usually believe that God is the ultimate being, that the universe is dependent upon God, that there is an immaterial aspect to human beings, and that there is an afterlife. As far as fundamental beliefs go, there are different universes that exist next door to each other.[4]

---

1. I am leaving out here the issue of abstract entities, which will be looked at below.

2. Naturalism is the prevalent philosophy in academia today, though it has roots in ancient times. Philosophical naturalism has as a corollary that there is no transcendent God. The vast majority of naturalists in academia today are atheists. Books that specifically defend a naturalistic worldview include: Nielsen, *Naturalism Without Foundations*; Papineau, *Philosophical Naturalism*; Rundle, *Why There is Something*; Ryder, *American Philosophical Naturalism*; Shook and Kurtz, *Future of Naturalism*; Post, *Faces of Existence*; and Vitzhum, *Materialism*. The ancient classic text expositing and defending naturalism is Lucretius, *On Nature*. A book containing many essays on naturalism, mostly by naturalists, is Clark, *Blackwell Companion to Naturalism*. For a critique of naturalism, see Craig and Moreland, *Naturalism*.

3. Theism is also an ancient theory. In the most general terms, virtually all cultures have been theistic, though the concept of God has varied greatly. Most philosophers in the West until recent times were theists. Books that put forth the basics of theism in various ways are extremely numerous, and include Morris, *Anselmian Explorations*, and *Concept of God*; Nash, *Concept of God*; Wood, *God*; and Parrish, *God and Necessity*. These books all concentrate on the concept of God itself, as it is the central idea in any theistic worldview.

4. See Sire, *Universe Next Door*.

Other worldviews include *polytheism* and *pantheism*. In *polytheism*, there are many gods rather than one. However, these gods are usually conceived of as existing within the physical universe, and so may be a form of naturalism, though unusual in this day and age. *Pantheism*, like polytheism has many different variants, but usually considers that the "God" and the universe is one thing. This pantheistic God is usually considered to be impersonal. There are also some forms of polytheism that are variants of pantheism wherein the different gods and goddesses are simply held to be expressions of the pantheistic ultimate being.

Theism, simply defined as the belief in gods or God, seems to have always existed. In many early studies of religion, it was often assumed that belief in gods arose out of animism, the belief that inanimate objects in fact have souls or minds. The presumption continued with animism's developing into polytheism, the belief in many gods, and from that, the rising of monotheism, the belief in one God. However, in contrast, some have argued that monotheism is the original religion of mankind. This later position has been recently developed and defended at length.[5] At any rate, undoubtedly monotheism is a very old and widespread idea.

Naturalism in its broadest sense is also an old belief, because many of the ancients were both polytheists and naturalists. That is, they believed both in gods and in the natural world's being the totality of reality. They could believe this because for them, the gods were beings existing in the natural world. This was true not only of the ancient Greeks gods like Zeus and Hera, who were supposed to live on top of Mount Olympus, but also of the ancient philosophers like the stoics, whose god was a material being who filled the natural world.[6] Though the Stoics were monotheists, at least believing in one ultimate God, they also believed their God existed within the universe, and indeed was spread throughout its totality, and thus can also be considered a variant of pantheism. The difficulty with which lines can be drawn among the different positions will be discussed below.

Let's take the differences between these two popular views more systematically.

---

5. On this, see Corduan, *In the Beginning God*.

6. On the Stoics, see for example Clark, *Selections from Hellenistic Philosophy*, 50–105, and *Ancient Philosophy*, 205–27. The Stoics seemed to conceive of God as impersonal, but personal notions of God were also present. See More, *Christ the Word*, 282–84.

Naturalism

According to the standard naturalist narrative, the universe can basically be described as follows: What exists is the physical universe. Per some scientific theorizing, there may be physical universes other than the one that we inhabit. However, all may be considered part of one reality—one possible world, as philosophers say.[7] Naturalism purports that our universe has either always existed in some form or other, or else came into existence from nothing, uncaused by anything else. Most scientists now believe that the universe, at least in its present condition, came into existence in the Big Bang. It is thought that either the Big Bang is the beginning of physical reality or else came from some earlier stage of physical reality or some other prior existing universe. Most atheists today, at least in Western civilization, are naturalists. It is thus to naturalist forms of atheism that I will pay the most attention.

In this theory, there is no other, non-physical concrete reality (such as a personal God) that caused the universe to come into existence, and which maintains it, that is, that keeps it in existence. Thus, given naturalism, the physical universe is in some sense ultimate reality.

Naturalists usually see the universe as composed by *purely* physical things. That is, the universe and everything in it are composed of things that are studied by physicists. These include space, time, energy, and matter in all their many forms. This view often goes under the title of *materialism* or *physicalism*. Materialism and physicalism do not necessarily have the exact same meaning, but for the purposes of our discussion here, the two terms will be used interchangeably. Naturalists usually believe human beings to be themselves entirely physical. However, some naturalists are dualists.[8] This term will be explained below in greater detail, but for now what I mean by it is, briefly put, dualists hold that human beings are made of two different kinds of things: the body which is material, and the mind or soul, or else simply the person's conscious thoughts, which are immaterial. Still, the typical naturalist will believe in some form of physicalism or materialism.

According to naturalism, all the things in the universe that now exist—galaxies, stars, planets, mountains, seas, trees, animals, and people, all came into existence from other things in the universe. That is, they evolved in some way or another from previous things, including living things. Humans are the final product (so far) from other living creatures in a long line of descent, ultimately the first living creature, which is thought to be a primitive

---

7. See chapter 2, footnote 32 for more discussion of possible worlds.
8. See for example, Levine, "Naturalism and Dualism," 209–19.

one-celled organism of some sort. The first primitive one-celled organisms themselves came into existence from non-living matter, in some manner or other by chance and the laws of physics. Thus, for naturalism, all the living creatures that exist or have existed are themselves the product of unguided evolution. The important point here is not evolution per se, because many theists also accept an evolutionary account of things; *rather it is that all of this happened without design or purpose.*

Indeed, the aspect that I wish to emphasize here about the naturalist story is that in this scenario, there is nothing that guides the universe and the development of everything in it. There are different descriptions of why the laws of nature are what they are, or why the universe came into existence, or how it turned out the way that it did, but given naturalism, none of them include a designer. So, with *naturalism, reality is ultimately impersonal.* Persons, whatever they are thought of as being, are themselves the rather odd products of an impersonal, unguided, and unplanned evolution. The implications for human beings from all of this are that we human beings both individually and collectively are in some sense accidental. In naturalism, selves, mind, consciousness, and reason all developed from non-mind, non-consciousness, and non-rational physical things, ultimately by chance and the laws of nature.

Consciousness is thus considered to be a product of blind evolution. Given physicalism, a certain arrangement of matter in a brain somehow caused consciousness to come into existence. Further, since most naturalists are also physicalists, either a person's thoughts are in some way or other identical with the physical brain, or else related to the brain in the same way that wetness is related to water or is realized in the brain. In some views, consciousness is held not to exist as such. Every conscious aspect of the mind is thus *reducible* in one way or another, to matter and energy, as is everything else in the universe. There are some materialists who argue for what is called a non-reductive form of materialism. However, even they must hold that mind ultimately in some way reduces to matter, even if we cannot see how it does. If they were to deny this, then they would not be materialists, but dualists.

The above description has several implications. One of these is that for the vast majority of naturalists there is no life after death. This follows from the other beliefs. If human beings and other animals are merely products of time, matter, and chance, there seems to be no reason why they should or even could survive death. If we are purely physical beings, then when the body dies, there is nothing else left to survive. And if there is no god of any sort, there is nothing that could somehow recreate us. So, this life is all there is. In the shape of this worldview box, it follows that any good that human beings have are in this world, in this life. Any happiness that we can achieve is also only of this world and can only be achieved by our own efforts.[9]

Since for naturalists what exists is the physical universe, *science*, especially the natural sciences, is extremely important. After all, if everything that exists is purely physical, then the physical sciences are telling us about ultimate reality. Sometimes naturalists call their view the "scientific" worldview, because science is that area of study that shows to us what reality is like. I consider this somewhat misleading, as science can and has been done by theists, and pantheists, too, for that matter. Some theists have argued that science is more consistent with theism than naturalism.[10] The claim that is sometimes made, that naturalism has sole ownership of science, goes against the facts. Indeed, it was theists who largely developed science.[11]

Postmodernism, a kind of philosophy that has been much discussed the last few decades, may be considered, in several respects at least, to be a naturalistic rejection of the pre-eminence of science. Many, if not most postmodernists, are naturalists, but they reject the view that science is the only or best way to discover the nature of reality. Postmodernism may best be thought of as a kind of skepticism, wherein all reality can only be known from different limited perspectives, and not with a God's eye view that sees everything in relation to everything else.[12]

Interestingly, there are some other concepts that many naturalists hold to that do not seem to flow from naturalism itself. In the metaphor of boxes, these small boxes don't seem to fit the large worldview shape. One of these is the belief in "natural goodness," or at least the inborn moral neutrality of human beings. This is the notion that people are by nature good and are only corrupted by society. With this idea, there was a rejection of inborn character traits in humanity, a denial of human nature; there was an initial "blank slate." These beliefs do not automatically arise from naturalism, but nonetheless are quite widely held. I think that the motivation for holding this is, to some extent, a reaction and rejection to the Christian doctrine of original sin—that human beings are sinful by nature.[13] It should be noted that the blank slate

---

9. "No deity will save us; we must save ourselves," states *Humanist Manifesto II*.

10. Plantinga, *Where the Conflict*.

11. Hannam, *God's Philosophers*.

12. For the philosophic background on postmodernism, see for example Schroeder, *Continental Philosophy*, 206–344. See also Gairdner, *Book of Absolutes*.

13. "The concept of original sin is the common opponent against which all the different trends of the philosophy of the Enlightenment join forces. In this struggle Hume is on the side of English deism, and Rousseau of Voltaire; the unity of the goal seems for a time to outweigh all differences as to the means of attaining it." Cassirer, *Philosophy of Enlightenment*, 141. On the history of the idea of human perfectibility see Passmore,

view of humanity and its denial of an innate human nature, has been under attack from science in the last few decades.[14]

However, naturalists often hold to more beliefs than the above. Naturalists are often also humanists, or secular humanists. If *naturalism* is a theory about the *nature of reality*, *secular humanism* is a theory about what human beings *ought to do in this reality*. Although it is possible to be a secular humanist without being a philosophical naturalist and atheist (one could be an agnostic or a theist who thinks that God exists but is irrelevant to what we should do in the world), most secular humanists are naturalists.[15] A secular humanist is a person who holds both that society ought to be reformed to make it much better than it is, and that God either does not exist, or is unknowable, or is at least irrelevant to our concerns here on earth.

Ethically, naturalists are often either what I will call *weak realists* or *antirealists*.[16] What I mean by this is that they hold that there are no ethical truths that exist apart from human beings. Rather, ethics is something that either comes from our human nature as rational beings, or else is something we invent to make our lives, individually or collectively, go better. For naturalists, there are no commandments given to us by God, for the obvious reason that in their minds there is no God. Whatever happiness we can achieve is therefore up to us.

For naturalists who are humanists, there is a kind of salvation to be sought, though quite a different one from the one which theists usually believe. For humanists, salvation is not the forgiveness of sin, but is a perfect or at least much better society, which is achievable through politics. *Utopianism*—the notion that we can create heaven on earth—is thus included in several versions of naturalism.[17]

In truth, though, utopianism does not easily fit with other things that naturalists believe. For if human beings are merely the product of billions of years of unplanned evolution, purely from mutation and natural selection,

---

Perfectibility of Man. For a study of Enlightenment Utopianism, see Becker, *Heavenly City*.

14. Steven Pinker, *Blank Slate*. Gairdner gives a list of universal human character traits in *Book of Absolutes*, 314–34. For a philosophical refutation of the blank slate, see McGinn, *Inborn Knowledge*.

15. For an introduction to secular humanism, see the various Humanist Manifestos, and Kurtz, *In Defense*.

16. See Ritchie, *From Morality*, for a more complete description. There are exceptions. For two recent atheistic defenses of realism, see for example Enoch, *Taking Morality Seriously*; and Wielenberg, *Robust Ethics*.

17. Regarding Utopia, see Molnar, *Utopia*; Jean and Isaac, *Coercive Utopians*; Goldberg, *Liberal Fascism*; Lasky, *Utopia and Revolution*; and Muravchik, *Heaven on Earth*,11.

to be hunter gatherers, it is difficult to see why we would now be naturally good beings who can create on our own a perfect (or nearly perfect) society.[18] Be that as it may, vast amounts of energy have disastrously gone into attempts to create a heaven on earth.[19]

Attempts to do this started long ago but began in earnest with the French revolution.[20] In the twentieth century, Marxist communism was the main source of utopian thinking, though there have been others. It should be noted, however, that one can be a naturalist and not be a humanist, though humanism can be defined very broadly. A naturalist could, for example, be a nihilist, and hold that there are no real values, and that the flourishing of human beings is not important.

Theism

In contrast to naturalism stands the other major narrative about the nature of reality in the western world. This is called *theism*, which literally means *godism*. Though there are many different concepts of God, the one that has been the most popular in western civilization is *Monotheism*; that God is the ultimate reality and is *perfect*. Indeed, a variation of this view is called perfect being theology.[21] According to this theory, the ultimate, foundational reality is God.[22] God is both immaterial and personal. Though there are many different theistic theories as to how God relates to the physical universe, all of them stand in contrast to the various naturalistic theories. In theism, God created the universe, and has guided and/or planned its development over time. Because in theism God is the ultimate being, all other concepts and things that exist must be eventually understood in terms of their relationship to God.

18. On the notion that human beings are naturally good, see Kinneging, *Geography*, 39–52.

19. On the philosophical background for this, see Shafarevich, *Socialist Phenomena*; Heller, *Cogs*; and Heller and Nekrich, *Utopia in Power*. Whittaker Chambers wrote on the appeal of revolutionary utopianism, "It is the vision of man's mind replacing God as the creative intelligence of the world. It is the vision of man's liberated mind, by the sole force of its rational intelligence, redirecting man's destiny and reorganizing man's life and the world. It is the vision of Man, once more the central figure of the Creation, not because God made man in His image, but because man's mind makes him the most intelligent of the animals." Chambers, *Witness*, 9.

20. Billington, *Fire in the Minds*; Schama, *Citizens*; Winik, *Great Upheaval*; and Voegelin, *From Enlightenment*.

21. On this see Rogers, *Perfect Being Theology*, and Nagasawa, *Maximal God*. See also Hill, *Divinity*.

22. On this, see especially Parrish, *God and Necessity*.

In theism, consciousness is an essential property of God. This is to say that since God is a personal being, he is intrinsically conscious—that is just the way that he is. According to many or most theists, human beings are not purely physical beings, but are also composed of an immaterial soul, or self, though this has come under attack in recent years. Thus, typically theists are *dualists* of one kind or other. They believe that humans are composed of two different kinds of "stuff," the material and the conscious. To be immaterial in this sense is to be conscious or capable of being conscious, and not to be explained in terms of any physical kinds of things. Since in most theistic systems, God is immaterial, and per many theists human beings are made in the image and likeness of God, it is not surprising that human beings are also considered partly immaterial.[23]

This concept of God is far from the only one in existence. Western philosophy began in ancient Greece, then moved on to other parts of the ancient world, such as Rome and Egypt.[24] When it began, was it naturalistic or theistic? In a way, it was both. The reason I can say this is that the concept of God had by these first Greek philosophers was different than the theism that I described above. As was mentioned above, the Greeks usually either believed in finite gods who existed within the natural universe (as in popular Greek religion), or, as was the case with some philosophers, held that god was a physical being whose "body" permeated the entire universe. This example shows, among other things, that defining the concept of god to cover all beliefs is no easy thing. This will be explored more in chapter 2.

Most of the ancient Greek philosophers believed in some sort of god. Even among the atomists, who were the early forebears of modern philosophical materialism, there was a belief in gods—though ones who had nothing to do with us.[25] The other major Greek philosophers all seemed to believe in a god, though sometimes this god was identified with the universe

---

23. For a discussion of being made in the image of God, see Collins, *Did Adam and Eve*, 93–100. For biblical defenses of mind/body dualism, see Moreland, *Soul*; and Cooper, *Body, Soul*.

24. For good introductions to ancient philosophy, see Adamson, *Classical Philosophy*, and *Philosophy Hellenistic and Roman*.

25. Frederick Copleston describes the atomist theology thusly, "The gods are anthropomorphically conceived, for they too are composed of atoms—even if of the finest atoms and possessing only ethereal or quasi-bodies—and are divided sexually: they are like to mankind in appearance and breathe and eat as we do . . . The wise man, therefore, does not fear death—for death is mere extinction—nor the gods—for they are unconcerned with human affairs and exact no retribution." Copleston, *History of Philosophy, vol. 1, part II*, 150.

itself. Both Plato and Aristotle seemed to accept the notion of a supreme God, though again, one different from the Christian tradition.[26]

With the coming of Christianity, philosophy was then impacted by an alternate view, quite alien to the Greeks. This view of God was quite different from that of the pagans. For one thing, the Bible teaches *creation ex nihilo*, creation out of nothing.[27] The ancient pagans believed in a universe that had always existed, and thus was ultimate along with god, or else was where the gods existed, along with everything else.

The religious, ethical, social, and political implications of theism partly depend upon which concept of God is believed. Different ideas of what God is like and what God wants vary greatly from religion to religion. What one religion teaches about God, thus, may be quite different from what another religion teaches.

Salvation for theists is usually thought of quite differently than for naturalists. Theistic systems usually have some concept of life after death. Though there are many varying conceptions, salvation is to be thought of as being saved from sins or bad karma. How this salvation is to be achieved varies widely, but a major part of most theistic systems is salvation.

However, just because most theistic systems have the concept of some sort of afterlife, that does not automatically mean that all theists are uninterested in conditions here on earth. Some are, and some are not. Gnosticism, a group of religions which existed in the early years of the Christian era, differed from each other on many things. However, one thing that they all seemed to believe is that this physical world and matter are inherently evil, created by an evil god, and that people should be able to escape it and go to a purely spiritual reality wherein the good god dwelt. For them, trying to improve the world was hopeless.[28]

---

26. Regarding God, Copleston writes of Plato, "Plato says that it is a mistake to suppose that any of the predicates we are acquainted with apply to the 'king of the universe,' and in his sixth letter he asks his friends to swear an oath of loyalty 'in the name of the God who is captain of all things present and to come, and of the Father of that captain and cause.'" Copleston, *History of Philosophy*, vol. I, part I, 203. About Aristotle theology, Copleston writes, "God, for example, exists necessarily, and that which exists necessarily must be fully actual: as the eternal Source of movement, of the reduction of potentiality to act, God must be full and complete actuality, the Unmoved First Mover." Copleston, *History of Philosophy*, vol. 1, part II, 53. God for Aristotle, is a conscious being in the sense that he knows some things.

27. See Copan and Craig, *Creation*.

28. On Gnosticism see for example, Finegan, *Myth and Mystery*, 217–59; and van den Broek and Hanegraaf, *Gnosis and Hermeticism*. A couple of books on the influence of Gnosticism today are Jones, *Gnostic Empire Strikes Back*; and Voegelin, *Science, Politics*.

On the other hand, some religions, such as Christianity, have taught that the physical world, although marred, is basically good because it is the creation of a good God, and that therefore Christians have a responsibility to improve it. Britain's outlawing of the slave trade in the early nineteenth century, for example, was driven by evangelicals.[29]

For about one thousand years, almost all philosophers in the western part of the Eastern Hemisphere were either Christian, Jewish, or Muslim, and they were all monotheists—believers in one God supreme over everything. However, beginning in early modern times an intellectual revolt began in Europe against Christianity. At first it was not atheistic, but as time went on, it became so. In the 1700s, during the enlightenment, full-fledged atheism, naturalism, and materialism took root.[30] It grew rather quickly, fed by influences like Darwin's theory of evolution. By the late 1800s, if not earlier, naturalism became the standard view among many intellectuals and was seeping down into general society.[31]

At present, philosophical naturalism is the received view in academia, and any other area in society is influenced by it. Society, especially in Europe but also America, has become highly secularized. Many academics today, including the majority of philosophers, are either atheists or agnostics. This is not to say that theism is dead at a scholarly level. Indeed, during the last few decades, there has been a revival of Christian philosophy. And most people, at least in America, still have some belief in God. Yet, in most academic circles, naturalism is not only widely accepted but almost taken for granted. A common attitude is that although it might be all right to be religious in one's private life, when it comes to scholarly, academic work, the truth of philosophical naturalism is to be presupposed.[32] Indeed, in much of academia,

---

29. See for example Hochschild, *Bury the Chains*. On a life of one of the men who played a major role in ending the slave trade, see Hague, *William Wilberforce*.

30. A classic (and very positive) history of the Enlightenment is found in Gay's, *Enlightenment: Rise of Modern Paganism*, and *Enlightenment: Science of Freedom*. It should be noted that according to Stanley G Payne, "Fascist ideas have often been said to stem from opposition to the Enlightenment or the 'ideas of 1789,' when in fact they were a direct by-product of aspects of the Enlightenment, derived specifically from the modern, secular, Promethean concepts of the eighteenth century." Payne, *History of Fascism*, 8. For a response to some of the ideas of the enlightenment, see Ward, *Redeeming the Enlightenment*.

31. Several books on the growth of philosophical naturalism and atheism in the modern world are de Lubac, *Drama*; Buckley, *Origins*; Vitzhum, *Materialism*; Neusch, *Sources of Modern Atheism*; and Taylor, *Secular Age*. For recent developments, see LeDrew, *Evolution of Atheism*.

32. See Smith, "Metaphilosophy of Naturalism," 196. Smith goes on to say that this consensus began to unravel in philosophy beginning in the late 1960's, starting with the work of Alvin Plantinga with the publication of his book *God and Other Minds*.

there is prejudice against theism, and especially orthodox Christian beliefs. This prejudice is not universal, but it is widespread.

One more point to be made here: atheism is sometimes compared as a rival to theistic worldviews like Christianity. However, this is wrong. *Atheism is not by itself a worldview*. Atheistic worldviews like *Marxism* or *secular humanism* are worldviews in which atheism is an important component. Atheism is the opposite of theism, not the opposite of a theistic worldview like Christianity. The opposite of Christianity is an atheistic worldview like Marxism, of which atheism is only one part, albeit a central and important one. Theism by itself is not a worldview either, but only an important part.

To sum up, in naturalism, reality is ultimately physical and impersonal. In theism, reality is ultimately conscious and personal. Also, for naturalism, the physical universe is considered to exist uncaused,[33] while in theism, there is a deeper level of reality, which is God that is the cause of the existence of the universe. Therefore, the two systems or narratives contradict each other at the most fundamental points. There is, of course, also a great deal of overlap between the systems. Both naturalism and theism are attempting to give a description of the universe in which we live, and an explanation of why what exists does exist.

For example, the laws and constants of nature seem to be the same everywhere. The speed of light in a vacuum seems to be 186,282 miles per second everywhere and at every time. Naturalists think that this existence and nature of the physical universe is either a *brute fact* (has no ultimate cause or explanation for its existence in the manner that it exists) or else that it is somehow *necessary*, or some combination of both. Theists believe this orderliness is the result of God's choosing to create a world with these laws and constants, and of his keeping them the same throughout space and time.

We have visited briefly the definitions of some overarching concepts. Other more common terms will also be explored. These include words such as religion, science, God, and others. Though often used in ordinary and scholarly discussions alike, they are often left with only a rather vague definition which is inadequate to the purpose at hand. Further, the concepts are not only vague, but different contradictory definitions of them have been given. There is quite a bit of confusion, and I believe that this confusion has led to a good deal of muddled thinking in public discussions. Since they are relevant to the topic, below I will try to show what I will mean by them, and the implications of this.

---

33. Except for a few philosophers who think that abstract entities cause the universe to exist.

All of this is a build up to important questions—questions that should be of interest not only to philosophers, but also to everyone. It is to these questions that I will spend most of the rest of the book exploring. The most fundamental of these questions are the following: "Why does the universe exist as it is instead of in some other manner, or not at all?" "Why persons, including the essential traits of consciousness, reason, and subjectivity, exist in a world made up mainly of unconscious entities like atoms, rocks and stars?" "What are values, and why do people find things to be moral or immoral, and beautiful or ugly?" I will attempt to show that the different worldviews give radically different answers to these (and other) questions mainly because they start out by accepting radically different presuppositions; which is to say, they make different assumptions about what the nature of reality is ultimately like.

It is this very difference in the presuppositions that the opposed worldviews have that allows for argumentation as to which is the most coherent explanation, and which gives the best account of why reality exists in the manner that it does. The details of the worldview that follow from theses presuppositions are entailed by the basic beliefs of the worldview.

One last point needs to be emphasized here. All this talk about *worldview* is not about pure theory. Why does it matter? Because *whatever is the reigning worldview of a culture at a particular time will be the most significant mold of the institutions, morals, and mores of that culture.* This is not to say that cultures, like individuals, are ever completely consistent in what they think and do, or that there are no other influences in them than the reigning worldview. Nonetheless, the reigning worldview in a society will have a great impact upon what is done in that society.

Ideas have consequences.[34] The inner logic of the nature of any worldview will come to be spelled out in the cultures which affirm it. Alternate versions of naturalist atheism may be very different from each other, as may be different versions of theism. This is a major reason why cultures differ from one another. For example, countries with a Christian heritage are quite different from Islamic ones even though monotheism is the basis for both worldviews.[35]

The alternate concepts of God are also a major reason why western civilization has changed so much in the last few centuries. The worldview of most of the elite in the west has shifted from Christianity to various versions of secularist naturalism. Since Christianity and the different secularisms are radically different worldviews, the cultures that they produce will

---

34. Weaver, *Ideas*.
35. See for example Schmidt, *Great Divide*; and Darwish, *Wholly Different*.

inevitably be different. Indeed, the history of the western world, and, even the whole world, especially ever since the time of the Enlightenment and the French revolution, has been to a large extent the history of a shift from a religious or Christian way of thinking about things to a secular one.[36] The rights and wrongs of these changes due to a change in worldviews can be, and are being, debated, but that there has been a great change in society is undeniable.

For example, if everyone in the West had still held to a Christian view of things, the whole history of Marxist communism would never have happened, and the world would be a radically different place than it is today. With no communism, there might not have been a second world war, or the cold war that followed it. There might have been world wars, but they would have been different wars, fought for different purposes.

This book is thus mainly about theism and naturalist atheism. It is an examination of their basic ideas, the implications of these ideas, and how the implications can help us to discover the truth or falsity of them. It is the contention of this author that theism can sustain and explain existence, knowledge, value (both ethical and aesthetic), and the worth of the individual, whereas naturalism in the final analysis can do none of these.[37]

Again, it is not just naturalism and theism that have different impacts. The fact that Europe and America are the way that they are, while North Africa and Western Asia are quite different, can be traced largely to the fact that historically they had different versions of theism—Christianity on the one hand, and Islam on the other—which were influential in their development. A major reason why Christian and Islamic societies were and are so different is because although they both profess a belief in a God, their ideas about what God is like are quite different from each other.[38] For example, with Christianity, human beings are regarded as being made in God's image, whereas for Islam the nature of human beings in this regard may not be as clear. This will be explored in the section below on God.

Similarly, such civilizations as China and India were and are the way that they are because of the fundamental beliefs (worldviews) that were and

---

36. For a history of the relation of religion, politics, and secularism in Europe, especially in politics since the French Revolution to the present, see Burleigh, *Earthly Powers*, and *Sacred Causes*. For a summary of cultural change, see Ehlke, *Like a Pelting Rain*.

37. In this respect, I agree with Balfour when he writes, "My desire has been to show that all we think best in human culture, whether associated with beauty, goodness, or knowledge, requires God for its support, that Humanism without Theism loses more than half its value." Balfour, *Theism and Humanism*, 143.

38. Gordon H. Clark writes, "The source of all contrasts between paganism and Christianity is the difference in their concepts of God." Clark, *Thales to Dewey*, 183.

are held in them.[39] Even seemingly small differences can have major effects. With this point in mind, I shall turn to understanding some key concepts that are essential to the issues being discussed.

---

39. For an interesting look at the way that different civilizations thought about the rise of modern science, specifically the way they thought about telescopes, see Huff, *Intellectual Curiosity*. A study on how theism supported and promoted the rise of science is Torrance, *Divine and Contingent Order*.

Chapter 1

The Issues

IN ANY INVESTIGATION, IT is important to understand the meaning of the words that are crucial to the study. So, this beginning chapter of the book will attempt to define what some important words mean, such as *religion, science, faith, theism,* and *naturalism*. I have already explained, in a way, the last two terms, but here I will attempt to see if a more rigorous definition can be given. One thing that will emerge from this discussion is just how difficult it is to define these terms with any degree of exactitude, and how many different ideas there are that go into each. We will see just how much the discussion depends upon the *meaning* of the terms that are being used, or on their precise definitions. Nevertheless, as should be obvious, it is important for the discussion that we know what we are talking about.

What is Religion?

> Religion is the sigh of the oppressed creature, the heart of a heartless world, just as it is the spirit of spiritless conditions. It is the opium of the people.[1]
>
> KARL MARX

> Men despise religion; they hate it, and fear it is true.[2]
>
> BLAISE PASCAL

Religion is one of those words that are commonly used, and that generally everyone thinks they know what they mean, but *Religion* is, in fact, a term

---

1. Marx, *Contributions*, 39. For something of a response, see Aron, *Opium*. For a recent study of how utopianism appeals to intellectuals, see Sesardić, *When Reason*.

2. Pascal, *Pensées*, No. 187, 52. An interesting and useful discussion of the nature of religion and science is found in Koperski, *Physics of Theism*, 11–57.

very difficult to define with any exactitude. If an ordinary person were to say what religion is, perhaps they would say that it is belief in God or gods, belief in life after death, and includes things like worship, prayer and the like. This definition might seem natural to one living in Western civilizations (and to others), but there are difficulties with such a definition. There are several different concepts of religion, and though there is often an overlap, there are also contradictions between the different concepts.[3]

Some of the problems involved with the definition of religion are these. First, not everything generally recognized as religion, such as Theraveda Buddhism, has a belief in God.[4] Second, even for religions like Christianity that do hold to a belief in God there is much more to these religions than just beliefs. Belief is very important, of course, but there are also such things as rituals, community, and devotion. It is possible to believe in God and not be religious in some of these other senses of the word. Aristotle believed in the existence of a God, but apparently did not worship or pray to him. Aristotle's God had more to do with physics and philosophy than with what is commonly thought of as religion.[5] Third, there is a question of how the concept of religion is to be understood in relationship to the concept of worldview, that is, with all the other concepts that are in that particular worldview.

On the other hand, some things that are not in themselves generally considered to be religions have aspects that seem religious. For example, take Marxism, or at least certain versions of it. Marxism, with its philosophy of dialectical materialism, attempts to give a description of the fundamental nature of reality. Further, many of its believers were extremely devoted to it.[6] Indeed, they were devoted to it to such an extent that they were willing to both die and kill large numbers of people for it.[7] That there are similarities of Marxism to Christianity has often been noted, even though Marxism is militantly atheistic. Instead of God the Creator, Marxists believe that all happens because of the dialectical movement of matter. Instead of the fall of mankind

---

3. For a discussion of these points, see Cavanaugh, *Myth*, 15–56.

4. "The teachings of Theraveda Buddhism typically are understood as being incompatible with belief in a Creator God or a Supreme Being." Yandell and Netland, *Buddhism*, 29–30. This is not to say that there are no gods at all in it. "Traditional Buddhist cosmology includes many levels of heavens and hells, inhabited by gods, demigods, humans, animals, ghosts, and hell beings." Netland, *Christianity and Religious Diversity*, 76. See also Keown, *Buddhism*.

5. "[T]here is no indication that Aristotle ever thought of the First Mover [God] as an object of worship, still less as a Being to Whom prayers might profitably be addressed." Copleston, *History of Philosophy*, vol.1, part II, 59.

6. A close comrade of Lenin said of him, "[F]or Vladimir Ilyich Marxism was not a conviction, but a religion." Sebestyn, *Lenin*, 138.

7. For one documentation of this, see Courtois, et al, *Black Book of Communism*.

into sin, Marxists believe that capitalism, and indeed private property, is the reason for the suffering in the world. Instead of Christ's saving the world,[8] the party and working class are given the role of saving mankind. And instead of heaven, the Marxist believes in a perfect classless society of communism after the revolution has swept away private property, marriage, and religion. For them, a fundamental belief is that there will be a sort of heaven on earth, but one created by human beings, not God.[9]

In several ways, Marxism may be the antithesis of what is normally considered to be religion, thus the enemy of all religion. However, looked at it from another angle, it mimics a particular religion—Christianity—to such an extent that some consider it to be a religion, or at least a *quasi* or *ersatz* religion.[10]

A similar problem can be seen with other definitions of religion. For example, it can be seen in the concept of an afterlife. The problem is that it is possible, however unusual, to believe in an afterlife without attaching anything else considered religious to that belief. One could believe in an afterlife but not in a god or have any rituals or devotions regarding it and not attach any devotion to the idea. Some ancient Greeks had a belief in a sort of afterlife, but it was just the survival of a shade of a human being, and not something to be looked forward to.

Some scholars believe that the early Jews had no clear belief in an afterlife; apparently at least the Sadducees didn't believe in an afterlife, or at least in a resurrection.[11] Further, Buddhists, though they believe in reincar-

---

8. Regarding the modern obsession with saving the world, or parts of it anyway, Allan Chapman writes, "So 'saving' people, especially distant strangers and those quite outside one's own sphere of natural family or group-culture concern, for reasons of pure altruism, is very much a legacy of the Christian heritage . . . For what, one might argue, secularists with a passion for saving are doing is trying to turn *themselves* into saviours." Chapman, *Slaying the Dragons*, 218.

9. On the nature of Marxism see Lee, *Communist Eschatology*. Of course, the basic primer of Marxism is *The Communist Manifesto*, which is much shorter. For writings by the founders of Marxian communism on religion see *Marx and Engels on Religion*. For an attempt to differentiate Marxism from utopianism (quite unsuccessfully in my opinion), see Engels, *Socialism*.

10. On this, see Voegelin, "Ersatz Religion," 83–114. Writes Harold Netland, "In the mid-twentieth century there was considerable debate over whether Marxism or Communism should be understood as a religion." Netland, *Christianity*, 29.

11. Writes F. F. Bruce, "[T]he Sadducees denied the doctrine of bodily resurrection, and rejected the belief in a spirit-world of angels and demons . . . " Bruce, *Book of Acts*, 453. Paul Barnett states, "Moreover, their Saducean theology was about the 'here and now' with a this-worldly eschatology of the first five books of the Bible. They did not espouse the Pharisaic and apocalyptic doctrine of the resurrection of the body and universal judgment at the end of history." Barnett, *Jesus and the Rise*, 140. John Cooper writes, "Intertestamental Judaism includes diverse perspectives on eschatology

nation, in a sense do not have a clear notion of an afterlife. This is because they do not believe in an enduring self—a self that lasts or persists over time.[12] They think that there is no abiding self even for our life now; rather, there is only a succession of mental states, one following the other. According to one view, the duration of these states is so short that sixty-five of them happen "while a strong man snaps his fingers."[13]

Other examples of this could be given. There are different concepts, all ordinarily tied to what is commonly conceived to be religion, but which upon examination do not seem to be necessarily religious in all senses of the word. Some people claim to be Christians, or members of some other theistic religion, and yet though they believe, perhaps quite sincerely, in God and other doctrines of their religious denomination, from the way that they live it seems that their real devotion is to something else, such as politics, making money, or even a hobby like golf or football.

There seems to be no single standard universally accepted definition of what religion is, one that fits all the possible cases. Rather, there are several concepts, some of which may be contradictory to each other at some points. In short, we have here a similar situation to Wittgenstein's observation of games—there is no one definition that fits all, but rather a group of things, all with family resemblance to each other.[14] As this discussion has indicated, trying to give a precise definition of religion is not an easy thing to do. Indeed, I consider that giving a completely non-arbitrary definition to be impossible. As William Cavanaugh writes, "[W]hat is meant by religion is by no means clear."[15]

---

and anthropology, including a mortal soul with no afterlife, which the Sadducees held." Cooper, "Absent from the Body," 321.

12. Yandell and Netland, commenting on an argument against the reality of the "self" from the Buddhist philosopher Nagasena write, "Just as there is no chariot beyond the constituent physical parts associated with what we call a 'chariot,' so too there is no soul or mind or person beyond the constituent parts associated with the idea of a person." Yandell and Netland, *Buddhism*, 123.

13. Yandell and Netland, *Buddhism*, 126.

14. "We are inclined to think that there must be something in common to all games, say, and that this common property is the justification for applying the general term 'game' to the various games; whereas games form a *family* the members of which have family likenesses. Some of them have the same nose, others the same eyebrows and others again the same way of walking; and these likenesses overlap." Wittgenstein, *Blue and Brown Books*, 17. For a discussion of this point, see Monk, *Ludwig Wittgenstein*, 336–46.

15. He continues, "Most scholars who write on religion and violence give no definition of religion. Others will acknowledge the now notorious difficulty of providing a definition of religion . . . " Cavanaugh, *Myth*, 16.

Still, some sort of definition must be attempted. One recent definition of religion is the following: "*[R]eligion is constituted by a set of beliefs, actions, and experiences, both personal and corporate, organized around a concept of an Ultimate Reality which inspires worship or total devotion.*"[16] This is a very broad definition that, I think, will prove useful. I will take this as a starting point, and we will see how it compares to actual examples.

Again, take the Marxism mentioned above. It constitutes a *set of beliefs, actions and experiences*. What is the *ultimate reality* is matter in motion. The *beliefs* include the idea that history is governed by a dialectic which will inevitably bring about the destruction of all class societies, and the final establishment of a classless one, with the triumph of communism. The *actions* include the attempt to overthrow the capitalist order by revolution, and the bringing in of a socialist one. The Marxist *believes* and *acts* as an individual, but more primarily as a member of his class or party. Further, all this belief and its resulting actions are organized around a *concept of ultimate reality*—that the material universe is ultimate reality, and that complete devotion ought to be given to the establishment of communism, which is considered a sort of heaven on earth. If this does not make Marxism a religion, it is at least a very close analog to it.

However, a case may be made that we should limit the term "religion" only to those sets of beliefs, actions and experiences that involve the *supernatural*, and/or *gods* and an *afterlife*. By *supernatural*, what I will simply mean here are things that do not exist in or that cannot be explained in terms of the natural universe, which is composed of physical entities. But then is consciousness therefore supernatural, assuming that dualists[17] are correct about the nature of consciousness? The matter is somewhat controversial. However, given that the consciousness of human beings and other animals is based in, and normally operates in, the physical world, I will not count them as being supernatural. Given some form of mind/body dualism, consciousness is not physical, but is at least in some sense natural. The concept of an *afterlife* is, I think, clear, while the concept of *God* or *gods* will merit its own discussion below. The concept of God or gods is especially important.[18]

On the other hand, limiting the term religion to supernatural belief systems has problems too. I have already noted that Buddhism, at least in

---

16. In Peterson, *Reason*, 7.

17. By dualism, I mean here the view that human beings (and perhaps some animals) are composed of two basic kinds of thing: the physical, which is the body, and the mental, which is immaterial.

18. Rodney Stark agrees with this. He writes, "Indeed, the phrase 'godless' religion is a self-contradictory oxymoron." Stark, *Why God?*, 7.

some variants, is basically godless, in not having a creator God. However, Buddhists do typically believe in other levels of reality, and in the existence of demons, demigods, finite gods, etc. So, probably Buddhism may be a supernatural worldview, and hence a religion. A problem with defining religion may be that there is some difficulty in defining the term "supernatural," but we must begin somewhere.

There is another religion, Mormonism, which may also cause trouble for the given definition. Some important versions of Mormonism are materialistic.[19] That is, they believe that the physical universe is all that exists, that their God or gods (for most Mormons believe in a plurality of gods) are beings who exist within it. Spirits are said to be composed of *spirit matter*, which is held to be material, though also a quite different kind of matter than that of the objects we experience around us. (I have never found a detailed explanation of what "spirit matter" is or what it is supposed to be like). Miracles are held to be the Mormon God's acting through the laws of nature with his superior knowledge and power, not an overriding or temporary suspension of the laws of nature. The Mormon god on this conception is as much bound by the laws of nature as everyone else; he just knows how to operate those laws better than we do.

Is Mormonism, at least in the above-described varieties, a religion defined as including a belief in the supernatural, or not? I think that this kind of Mormonism is a borderline case. Again, I will say that it is a religion, because it does acknowledge the existence of a *superior being* (or beings) who has control of nature (in the sense of being able to perfectly manipulate it) and who is supposed to be worshipped. Also, Mormons strongly affirm the existence of all human beings in an *afterlife*—indeed, they also believe in the pre-existence of persons. In addition, Mormonism involves worship of the beings that they consider to be God, so I think that it can count as being a religion—though one that was influenced by the science and philosophy of its day, and so can be thought to be both naturalistic and materialistic at the same time. Sometimes the lines between what should or should not be considered religious is thin, and perhaps the lines may be drawn somewhat arbitrarily.

Finally, what is the relationship between the concept of religion and that of worldview? This is a question that can be answered in several ways. As the above discussion should show, I doubt that a completely satisfactory definition can be given. As was said, for the purposes of this book, *a religion*

---

19. See for example, Paulson, *Comparative Coherence*. This is Paulson's doctoral dissertation. For a Mormon theology, see Ostler, *Exploring Mormon Thought*. For philosophical critiques of Mormonism, see Beckwith and Parrish, *Mormon Concept of God*; Beckwith, et al, *New Mormon Challenge*; and Parrish, "Tale of Two Theisms," 193–218.

will be a theistic or supernatural worldview. This is to say, a religion will be defined as a worldview in which there are *God* or *gods* or in which there are other *supernatural* entities, or else the concept of an *afterlife*, which consists of an individual's further existence as that individual. There are different concepts of this too, but I shall not discuss them at length.

For now, I will simply postpone the issue of the definition of God or gods to the relevant section below. Mormonism, and any other worldviews like it, will also be included as religions, even though they do not literally contain supernatural elements within them. Nonetheless, they are similar enough to supernatural religions so that that they may be legitimately placed in the religion (or supernatural religion) category.

Political Religions and Ideology

> We are the happy Hitler Youth;
> We have no need of Christian Virtue;
> For Adolf Hitler is our intercessor
> And our redeemer.[20]
>
> HITLER YOUTH SONG

> Ideology is existence in rebellion against God and man.[21]
>
> ERIC VOEGELIN

By "political religion" I mean a system of beliefs and practices which is naturalistic or this worldly, in which some aspect of the natural world is held to be divine in the sense of being ultimate, and political structures are organized around this belief. Some scholars have called some secular worldviews like Marxism as *ersatz* or *political* religions.[22] That is, they are either secular

---

20. Part of a Hitler Youth camp song. The rest of the song is, "No priest, no evil one can keep us from feeling like Hitler's children. Not Christ do we follow, but Horst Wessel! Away with incense and holy water pots. Singing we follow Hitler's banners; only then are we worthy of our ancestors. I am no Christian and no Catholic. I go with the SA through thick and thin. The Church can be stolen from me for all I care. The swastika makes me happy here on earth. Him will I follow in marching step; Baldur von Schirach, take me along." Veith, *Modern Fascism*, 67. Notice the religious language about Hitler. A different translation is given by Evans, *Third Reich in Power*, 250–51. For an examination of the idea that National Socialism was a political religion, see Burleigh, *Third Reich*, esp. 1–23.

21. Voegelin, *Israel and Revelation*. Vol. 1 of Order and History, xiv.

22. On political religions, see "Political Religions," in Voegelin, *Modernity*, 27–73. See also, Franz, *Eric Voegelin*.

ideologies that are substitutes for a real religion, or an attempt to construct religions which are purely this-worldly. In a sense, some of the ancient pagan religions were this-worldly religions, because their gods were finite beings who existed wholly within the natural universe. It seems to me that much of contemporary political and social discourse is an attempt to replace the traditional theistic religion as the foundation for culture with various ideologies—political religions, so to speak. Although political religions are not necessarily atheistic in the sense of denying the existence of a transcendent deity, what they are about is establishing a state, run by principles the ideologues espouse, and being the focal point for the whole culture. All meanings and morality would flow from the state and the people running it.[23]

By ideology I shall mean a worldview which, in the words of Kenneth Minogue, holds that "all evils are caused by an oppressive system."[24] To put things another way, ideologies hold that human beings are perfect, or perfectible, and it is only the evil of an oppressive system that prevents them from achieving a kind of heaven on earth, however conceived. Of course, something may be both a political religion and an ideology. Most ideologies are naturalistic, such as some versions of Jacobinism, fascism and Marxism, but there can be theistic ones too, such as other versions of Jacobinism.[25]

The above discussion should make it clear why the term "religion" is so difficult a thing to define—or to limit to a definition. A case can be made that all worldviews can be called religions, including secular or political ones, like Marxism. Indeed, sociologists sometimes use the word to describe purely secular worldviews.[26]

Worldviews that are secular, or this-worldly, which have no belief in gods or an afterlife I will simply call secular worldviews, which of course can also be political religions or ideologies. Included among them would be such worldviews as Marxism and secular humanism.[27] It should be remembered, though, that the definition here is somewhat arbitrary—no one is obligated to

---

23. On the state attempting to fulfill the place of God, see Wiker, *Worshipping the State*.

24. Minogue, *Alien Powers*, 1. The whole quote is, "[I]ts [Ideologies'] simplest formulation is that all evils are caused by an oppressive system."

25. For more on this, see Gray, *Seven Types of Atheism*, 71–93.

26. See for example, Cavanaugh, *Myth*, 15–56.

27. For works on secular humanism, see the various manifestos that have been issued. These include Kurtz, *Humanist Manifestos*, and *Secular Humanist Declaration*, and *Humanist Manifesto 2000*. They may issue another one in a few years. See also Kurtz, *In Defense*, for an exposition and defense of secular humanism. A brief critique is Hitchcock's, *What is Secular Humanism?*

accept it—and that it is rather "fuzzy" at the edges. There are worldviews that do not clearly fit into either the religion or non-religion categories.[28]

Why limit religions to worldviews that have the concept of gods or the supernatural? For one thing, I have noticed that some atheists become rather unhappy when their beliefs are designated as being a religion. It is *religion* that they are reacting against, frequently forcefully, and what they mean by religion inevitably involves the concepts of God or gods and the supernatural, with such ideas as an afterlife. Besides, there is unquestionably a large difference between purely naturalistic and materialistic belief systems such as Marxism, and supernatural ones such as Christianity. So, it seems useful that we should restrict the term 'religion' to worldviews that include the supernatural.

One more thing should be said. People sometimes make statements such as "religion is harmful," or sometimes the opposite, "religion is helpful." The problem with this is that, even limiting religions to the supernatural or quasi-supernatural kinds, there is no generic religion; rather, what there are, are the various religions, which are often quite different from each other. Some criticism or praise that may be justly made of one religion may be totally inapplicable to another religion.

For example, it is sometimes said that religion causes war, such as with Islamic *jihads*, both past and present.[29] Whatever the case with some religions, it is quite unfair, for example, to tar the pacifistic Amish with violence, since violence is strictly forbidden in their theological teaching. It is wrong to simply lump religions together so that all of them are blamed for the activities of only some of them. Similarly, secular worldviews are often quite different from each other. Ayn Rand's objectivism, though completely and outspokenly atheistic, should not be blamed for the Gulag created by the equally atheistic Marxists.[30]

---

28. A relevant point is that since everyone has a worldview, and religions are worldviews, everyone will have a religion or some godless secular equivalent of a religion. It is sometimes argued that since there are many religions, and that this division of people in a society can cause friction and even violence, then if everyone abandoned religion and became an atheist, these divisions would disappear, and a cause of strife would disappear as well. The problem with this argument is that it is founded on an ambiguity. If one is an atheist, then one does not have a religious position, in the sense that one does not have a belief in a god or the supernatural. However, being an atheist, one would have a position about religion, in that they are all false. Therefore, what an atheist who makes the argument outlined above is doing, is saying that the divisions in society are bad, so everyone should agree with her or him. However, anyone, from any perspective can make that argument.

29. On jihad see, Fregosi, *Jihad in the West*.

30. For a history of the Gulag, see Applebaum, *Gulag*. For an exposition of Ayn Rand's views, see Peikoff, *Objectivism*. For a response to objectivism see Robbins,

What is Science?

> [T]here has grown the feeling that science and religion are inherently incompatible and antagonistic . . . For their part, scientists have demolished a lot of cherished religious beliefs and have come to be regarded by many as faith-wreckers . . . The tremendous power of scientific reasoning is demonstrated daily in the many marvels of modern technology. It seems reasonable then, to have some confidence in the scientist's world-view also.
>
> PAUL DAVIES[31]

> In the dimension of describing and explaining the world, science is the measure of all things, of what is that it is, and of what is not that it is not.
>
> WILFRED SELLARS[32]

> [T]he possibility of an applied mathematics is an expression, in terms of natural science, of the Christian belief that nature is the creation of an omnipotent God.
>
> R. G. COLLINGWOOD[33]

It is also difficult to say what science precisely is. When speaking of science, one usually is speaking of the natural sciences, such as physics, chemistry, geology, and biology. The human disciplines such as anthropology and sociology are also considered to be sciences, but are often put in another category, because their subjects cannot be described according to the laws of nature. Simply put, science is the systematic attempt to understand the natural universe in which we live. This definition seems simple enough, but therein are problems of definition, as we shall see.[34]

Without a Prayer.

31. Davies, *God and the New Physics*, 5–6.
32. Sellars, quoted in Baker, *Naturalism*, 5.
33. "Essay on Metaphysics," quoted in Jaeger, *What the Heavens Declare*, 58.
34. What is science? A dictionary definition is "A branch of knowledge involving the systematized observation of and experiment with phenomena." *Illustrated Oxford Dictionary*, 736. This certainly covers a lot of what science is but is vague. It also does not include the invention of hypotheses, which involve imagination as well as observation. For an investigation into the nature of science from a Christian perspective see Moreland, *Christianity and the Nature*.

History of Science

How long has there been science? In some basic sense of the word, there has been science since the beginnings of humanity. Ancient people had to observe the world around them if they wanted to survive. Of course, this beginning of science was very different from what we call science today. There was then no systematic, continuous activity geared for the understanding of nature. As civilization advanced, so did science, albeit slowly. There began to be people who specialized in scientific or technological matters, sometimes in the interest of the different religions. To varying extents, this happened in all the great civilizations. In this sense, the ancient Greeks, Chinese, Indians, and others had sciences, though the sciences were quite different from what we call science now. The concept of the universe as a system of things whose workings could be understood according to natural law was missing in some of these.[35]

What might be called 'modern science,' the science which in different forms still exists, might be said to begin in the late Middle Ages in Europe.[36] Though originally quite dissimilar from science today, the contemporary systematic ongoing investigation of nature had its roots there. One thing that distinguishes modern science from that of the ancient world is its very strong empirical bent. That is, modern science has an emphasis on experimentation, of looking at how the world is and operates. Ancient and Medieval sciences, although they did not totally ignore experiment and observation, often tended to rely on, to a greater extent, *reasoning* about how nature must be. Aristotle was one of the greatest minds in Western history, but most of his beliefs about physics and astronomy were false. Aristotle's theories about physics and astronomy were more based on reasoning on how things must be than on performing experiments (which admittedly were sometimes very difficult to do in astronomy, given the state of technology at the time). In contrast to his theorizing in physics

---

35. Writes Paul Collins, "The story of Agobard and the sky sailors takes us to the heart of tenth-century cosmology, to the way people viewed the world. Natural events were not natural in the sense that nature was an interacting, self-explanatory, independent system . . . Existing parallel with official church ministry was a vast world of what today we would call 'popular religion,' a realm of miracle-working saints, relics, pilgrimages, angels, devils, charms, spells, magic, a vast amalgam of orthodox Christianity and the still-lively paganism of the vast subclass of peasants and serfs. People believed that all of these forces could be manipulated for good or evil." Collins, *Birth of the West*, 13–14. The churches slowly overcame these beliefs. See also Eire, *War against the Idols*; and Hart, *Atheist Delusions*, 199–215.

36. On the Medieval roots of modern science see Hannam, *God's Philosophers*; Brown, *Abacus and the Cross*; Jaki, *Science and Creation*; Grant, *Foundations*; *God and Reason*; and Pearcey and Thaxton, *Soul of Science*.

and astronomy are his studies in biology, where he empirically examined many different specimens.

Above I stated that modern science is an ongoing, systematic investigation of the natural world. But how can it be investigated, that is, how should scientists go about doing this? Someone who tried to discover how subatomic particles work, for example, would be advised to not rely on counting tea leaves, or examining sheep livers.[37] In a sense, science is pragmatic—it uses what works—that which leads to results and more fruitful investigation.

Science is not a worldview

It should be noted that *science is not in and of itself a worldview*. Sometimes people speak of a "scientific worldview." This is a misnomer. If science is a method for investigating the natural universe, it cannot be a worldview. To say that it is, is to commit a category mistake. A category mistake is when someone applies terms applicable to one part of reality to some other part of reality to which they do not relate. For example, suppose that someone invites a friend to see the college where she attends. If after showing the friend the class rooms, the library, the dorms, etc., the friend says, "This is all very nice, but when will we see the college?" the friend has made a category mistake. A more popular way of putting it is comparing apples to oranges.

Science is not, and cannot be, a worldview, for reasons that will be discussed below. Even for the materialist, science can only be a part, albeit a very large part, of his or her worldview. Science inevitably has limitations and cannot answer certain questions. For example, science can ask and attempt to answer how the natural objects in the universe are constituted, and how they operate, but it cannot answer the question as to why there exists anything at all. The answer to that question may only be supplied by philosophy and, arguably, theology.

Conflict between science and religion?

Since science is not a worldview, it is wrong to say that there is a necessary conflict between science and religion. This is not to say that some scientific theories may not conflict with some religious beliefs; this is obviously true. For an extreme example, some of the ancient Manicheans apparently believed that the light of the moon was caused by souls made of light escaping

---

37. On sheep livers and related matters, see Barfield, *Why the Bible*, 21–22.

28 ATHEISM?

from earth.[38] It should also be noted that it is possible for some naturalistic beliefs to conflict with scientific theories. For example, Jonathan Sperber writes of Friedrich Engels, Karl Marx's collaborator:

> If Engels saw dialectical philosophy, in good positivist fashion, as the expression of the natural sciences, he also could reverse the procedure, rejecting scientific findings when they did not fit his philosophical views. Denouncing the Second Law of Thermodynamics, he wrote to Marx: 'You cannot imagine anything stupider.' The idea of gradual equalization of temperatures, or, as it would later be formulated, increasing entropy, led to a world 'that begins in nonsense and ends in nonsense.' Although the second law was seen as 'the finest and highest perfection of materialism,' it envisaged a progressive cooling of the universe. Such a development implied 'the original hot condition, from which things cooled off, absolutely inexplicable, even absurd, thus presupposes a God.'[39]

For Engels, as for most atheistic naturalists, the universe had to have existed forever, because if it had not, the existence of God was implied. *What basically there is instead of a conflict between science and religion is a conflict between theism and naturalism.*

Scientism

There is a theory, sometimes known as *scientism*, which has held a lot of sway in modern academia. In its strongest formulation, it is the thesis that the sciences are the only way to understand reality. A weaker version of scientism holds that science is the best way to understand things, though not the only way.[40] To evaluate scientism, it is necessary to dig deeper into what the essence of natural science truly is.

---

38. "By this mechanism or arrangement the Light that is separated out is conveyed to the Moon, whereby it waxes for fifteen days, and then when full discharges its load of Light for another fifteen days into the Sun." Burkitt, "Religion of the Manichees," 273. Manicheans apparently believed that souls are made of light.

39. "Since, for Engels, philosophy included atheism and materialism, and that philosophy was based on the natural sciences, a science that led to a questioning of atheism and materialism could not be science." Sperber, *Karl Marx*, 417.

40. For a critique of Scientism see Sorell, *Scientism*; Williams and Robinson, *Scientism*; Loke, *God and Ultimate Origins*, 2–22; Feser, *Scholastic Metaphysics*, 9–31, and Moreland, *Scientism*. One may also consider Husserl's book, *Crisis of European Sciences*.

Scientific Method

Philosophers and others sometimes refer to the *scientific method*. So, what is the scientific method? Generally speaking, it seems to be a way of learning about things by looking at evidence, formulating hypotheses, testing these hypotheses against the evidence, and so on. For example, a scientist might be investigating a problem. One well known historical example of this is the discovery of the planet Neptune. The problem was that the planet Uranus wasn't orbiting where it should according to what was known at the time. This was the problem. A hypothesis was formed that the reason that Uranus wasn't going where it was supposed to was that there was another planet beyond it, whose gravity was pulling on Uranus.[41]

Calculations were done, the position of the suspected planet was hypothesized, and an astronomer looked where it should have been. Neptune was quickly sighted, and the theory regarding the reason for the difference in Uranus's orbit was vindicated. There was a situation in the physical universe that was not understood, theorizing was done to determine what was causing the situation, there was thought out a means of testing the theory, and then there was empirical research done to see if the theory correctly predicted what was seen.

A question then arises: "Why call this the scientific method?" After all, it is not just applicable to the natural sciences. One can use the basic method of identifying problems, forming hypotheses, and doing experiments in many disciplines other than the natural sciences: the social sciences, history (why did modern science begin in Europe rather than in China, or India, or the Muslim world?), literature (why did Mary Shelley write *Frankenstein*?), and religion (is there historical evidence for the resurrection of Jesus?). For that matter, one could use the scientific method in cooking. For example, why are the cakes that are now being cooked not as tasty as the ones that were cooked last week?

The point of the above is that it seems something of a misnomer to call this kind of method "the scientific method," as its use is not restricted to the natural sciences. It seems better to simply use the term *reason*, rather than the *scientific method*, when one is using logic and evidence to evaluate and attempt to understand some problem.

Be that as it may, science in general, and, in particular natural science, cannot be a worldview by itself. It cannot exist on its own apart from philosophical commitments. The reason for this is simple, and helps to show why philosophy, instead, is the most fundamental of all disciplines.

---

41. For a brief history of the discovery of Neptune, see Couper and Henbest, *History of Astronomy*, 189–92.

Strong Scientism

Take for example, a definition of *strong scientism*, which states that the natural sciences are the only way to discover truth, and therefore, that all true statements are scientific statements. A problem with this formulation is that the statement itself is not a scientific statement. It is a philosophical statement, since it is about what science and knowledge are. Thus, the advocate of *strong scientism* contradicts himself, for this theory depends upon a definition that lies outside of what he considers to be the limits of allowable statements.[42]

Weak Scientism

Proponents of a weaker form of scientism are not so immediately refuted, as they do not deny that there can be true non-scientific statements. However, since given *weak scientism*, science is held to be the best way of knowing things, and since the means that the definition of what science is, is thus important, it means that there is one nonscientific statement that is important (the definition of science). And since there is one, there may be others. In which case, there is no reason to think that only scientific statements are important, or necessarily superior to other kinds of statements. The natural sciences are of course an important part of our understanding of reality. However, this is not to say that they are the only things that matter, or the only disciplines that give us information about the nature of that reality.

Reason

Of course, as I said in the discussion of reason and the sciences, if defenders of *scientism* are merely giving first place to that which can be known by reason, as opposed to the natural sciences alone, this puts things in a different light. However, there seems to be no basis why *reason* cannot be used in such areas as philosophy, religion, history, art, and so on—so, the natural sciences again are not necessarily better than the other disciplines.

Discovering Truth

There is one more point to be made here. Sometimes science is held to be the only or best method of discovering truth because it depends upon repeatable

---

42. See especially Feser, *Scholastic Metaphysics*, 9–31.

experiments. If one does an experiment under some set of conditions, and gets a certain result, and one can duplicate the experiment any number of times, then the conclusion is strongly supported. Since philosophy and other disciplines cannot do this, they are held to be substandard.

The problem with this is that every scholarly discipline must be approached in terms of its own nature. History is certainly a rational discipline of scholarship, yet one cannot run repeatable experiments to prove that, say, Napoleon lost the battle of Waterloo. Indeed, the same can be said of much of science. One cannot have repeatable experiments that show that birds evolved from reptiles, or why Mars has a lot of craters on it. This is, of course, not to say that science cannot be done, but that it must be done in accordance with the nature of what is being investigated.

Science cannot be a worldview

To be complete, all worldviews should contain science as part of their description of reality. There are worldviews in which science is more important than in others—philosophical naturalism is one where science is held to be very important, while in ancient Gnosticism it was not very important at all. But a worldview is necessarily more than the natural sciences. Worldviews are, by their very nature, philosophical. *Science is therefore a component of the different worldviews, not a worldview in and of itself.*

Implications

This point has important implications. For example, take the question of miracles. A miracle, let us say, is an act of God where the laws of nature are suspended. Suppose a person is suddenly cured of multiple sclerosis by God. This is something that would not have happened in the normal course of natural events, so, a miracle has occurred.[43] Does science rule out the possibility of miracles like this one?

I maintain that it does not. The natural sciences investigate the natural world. They try to explain how it works, and what has happened in it. They cannot, by their very nature, rule out such things as miracles, as they only investigate what happened, or what happens if the laws of nature are not suspended.[44]

---

43. Which happened to a friend of my wife.

44. For a major work on miracles, both from a philosophical and an evidentiary viewpoint see Keener, *Miracles*.

It is *philosophic naturalism* that rules out the existence of miracles and does so *a priori—before investigating* them. This is because, among other factors, there is in naturalism no transcendent God who can work miracles. The problem is that sometimes *science* is used as a surrogate for *naturalism*. The reason for this should be clear. One sounds like one is making a much stronger argument when one says that "*science* demands there are no miracles," than when one says that "*naturalism* and *materialism* demand there are no miracles," or even more so that "*atheism* demands that there are no miracles." *The prestige of science is illicitly used to give support to philosophical views.*

Science is not identical with materialism

Materialism is a *philosophy*; science may be best thought of as a *methodology* for investigating the natural world. Materialism is an important part of much of philosophical naturalism. Science, a *methodology*, is therefore neither identical with, nor dependent upon, materialism or philosophical naturalism. This brings out a distinction. *One can practice science without believing in materialism.*

Materialism does *not* own science

There is one other point to be made here: calling all rational investigation the "scientific method," in effect discriminates against theism. What most people think of as science are the natural sciences: chemistry, biology, geology, astronomy, and so on. Methods used to investigate these are not the same ones that one can use to investigate God. Thus, science, as most people understand it, cannot be used to understand the existence and nature of God. Even if there is evidence from the sciences for design in the universe, one would still have to use philosophical reasoning to move from the evidence to God. By identifying rational inquiry with science alone, one begs the question against theism, for it assumes that reason (held to be basically the same thing as the methods of the natural sciences) is irrelevant to study God.

In response, by holding that reasoning includes, but is not limited to, the natural sciences, one can see that one *can* investigate God rationally by philosophy.

Often, as noted, materialists present an assumption of their "owning science." Perhaps the basic thought behind this is that the natural sciences study only physical things. Naturalism combined with materialism is the philosophy that all that exists are physical things. Therefore, it is thought, science and naturalism/materialism are the same thing. This reasoning is fallacious, and obviously so. To say that the natural sciences study only natural things does not imply that only natural, physical things exist anymore than the fact that organic chemists study chemicals with carbon in them means that only chemicals with carbon exist.

Atheistic naturalists and materialists have gotten a lot of mileage over the years by conflating their philosophy with science, but it is an illegitimate thing to do.

What is Reason?

> Reason is the greatest, the inestimable, gift of God.
>
> Martin Luther[45]

> How did reason come into the world? As is only proper, in an irrational manner; by accident. We shall have to guess at this accident as a riddle.
>
> Friedrich Nietzsche[46]

> They [philosophers] pose as having discovered and attained their real opinions through the self-evolution of a cold, pure, divinely unperturbed dialectic . . . while what happens at bottom is that a prejudice, a notion, an 'inspiration,' generally a desire of the heart sifted and made abstract, is defended by them with reasons sought after the event . . .
>
> Friedrich Nietzsche[47]

Reason as I will define it, is a capacity or ability. It is the ability to think about things, drawing conclusions based on evidence. So, when one thinks about something—whether something as mundane as what fast food restaurant to go to, or as deep and profound as to what worldview is the correct one—and one is using evidence and logic to try to arrive at a conclusion, one is using one's reason. I say this to make clear what reason essentially is. *Reason* is a fundamental ability of human beings, and therefore, to a certain extent, may be used by everyone. This is not the only definition of reason that there is.

---

45. Cited in Gerrish, *Grace and Reason*, 17. Luther also wrote, "[I]t is certainly true that reason is the most important and the highest in rank among all things and, in comparison with other things of this life, the best and something divine." Luther, *Luther's Works*, vol. 34, 137.

46. Nietzsche, *Dawn*, aphorism 123, 66.

47. Nietzsche, *Beyond Good*, 36.

Some people seem to use the words *reason* or *rational* to mean that it agrees with them. I am using the words in a more objective way.

Reason is thus a part of almost everything that we do as conscious beings, as we constantly think and evaluate the situation in which we are. Being able to use language is an important part of being rational. Indeed, in a sense, reason is the essence of what human beings are. The Aristotelian definition of a human being was that of being a rational animal. We cannot understand anything without the use of reason.

Other animals may use reason in some sense, but not in the full sense of the word as it is being used here. They may be able to figure out what is the best way to get to be fed[48] or where to sleep, but though they think, they do not use language, they think non-verbally. Further, it seems that they do not think about thinking. Human beings do.

Rationality is therefore part of the essence of being a human being. This does not mean that a person must be reasoning at every moment to be counted as a human being. Babies, people asleep or in a coma, who are not currently reasoning, are still human. It is, thus, not the case that a person is not a human being if he or she is not currently being rational or using reason, or even attempting to reason but doing it badly. Rather, to be a human being is, in part, to be a kind of being which is, in the normal development, or will at some time have an adult human's rational faculties. Babies, including preborn babies, are therefore fully human, even though not all their faculties have developed. So, too, are people who are severely retarded, for though they may not become beings who will sometime be rational, they are still members of a species whose normal development includes being able to use reason.

One must be careful here. Reason, like many words, has more than one meaning. Sometimes atheists write to the effect that they rely on reason, while Christians and other theists rely on faith. The explanation given is this: atheists use their own minds to reason to conclusions, while theists rely on purported divine revelations rather than on thinking things through themselves.

The Argument and the Ambiguity

This argument depends upon an ambiguity. The ambiguity lies in the difference between reasonable or rational as a mental activity that one does, and "reason" denoting what conclusions that logic and evidence lead to describing. That is, just because one uses one's mind does not automatically mean

---

48. In the case of my cat, by meowing at me until I give in and feed her.

that one is being rational; one may be thinking very illogically. Further, just because one depends on a purported revelation to understand reality does not automatically mean that one is being irrational. Besides the fact that one must use reason to understand and apply any alleged revelation, it may be the case that one has good reason for thinking that it is a genuine revelation.

Logic and the senses

Two large parts of *being rational* are 1) the use of logic, and 2) using evidence obtained through the senses in thinking. Using logical thought is obviously an important part of being rational. So, too, is using evidence about the external world that we get through the senses, including both external and internal senses. External senses include sight, hearing, and touch. Internal senses include feeling hot and cold, pain and pleasure, emotion, and even, in a way, intuition and our own status as thinking beings.

Plausibility Structure

However, there is another factor that we use when evaluating thinking and acting rationally. This factor is what may be called a person's "plausibility structure." A *plausibility structure* is part of one's worldview. What a particular plausibility structure does is give, for each person who has it, a *standard of judgment* about which things are probably true or false, based on the nature of the worldview for that person.

For example, discussing views of astronomer Fred Hoyle, Heather Couper and Nigel Henbest write, "As an atheist, Hoyle felt that the explanation [about the properties of carbon] had to be rational, rather than theological."[49] Why cannot a theological explanation be rational? For Hoyle, an atheist and naturalist, as well as for other naturalists, rational explanations cannot include God. For naturalists, giving a *rational* explanation, by their definition, can only include *natural* features.

Different worldviews contain different plausibility structures. The plausibility structures arise from the structure of the worldview of which they are components. Which is to say, that because a worldview contains certain beliefs as to how reality is formed, what is ultimate, what we can know, and what is valuable, each worldview will have its own plausibility structure. Different worldviews will give rise to different plausibility structures.[50]

---

49. Couper and Henbest, *History of Astronomy*.

50. For an examination of how basic intellectual commitments have vast

To give an example, think of an alleged miracle such as the resurrection of Jesus. That Jesus rose physically from the dead is a major part of traditional Christian beliefs. Indeed, it is an essential part of orthodox Christianity. As the apostle Paul wrote, "[I]f Christ is not risen, then our preaching is empty and your faith is in vain."[51] Therefore, a person who believes and is committed to Christianity will necessarily believe that Jesus rose from the dead. On his plausibility structure, therefore, the plausibility that Jesus was raised from the dead is 100 percent. To be sure, a person might not be personally 100 percent committed to this—they may have doubts. Or, they may think that the historical evidence for the resurrection gives a lower estimate of probability.[52] But insofar as the person is judging from a Christian perspective, it will be the case that they will judge the plausibility of Jesus's rising from the dead to be 100 percent, because that is part of his or her worldview, and the plausibility structure is an essential part of his worldview.

Take another person, one who is a naturalist atheist. He will have as part of his worldview the concept that all that exists is nature—there are no gods for him, and especially no transcendent God. This being the case, there is, as part of what he believes, no one who can cause a miracle like the resurrection of Jesus. Therefore, if he is a consistent naturalist, he will judge that miracles *as such* cannot happen. This is because of the nature of his worldview, which itself contains a plausibility structure. However, though the naturalists will reject the possibility of miracles before looking at the evidence (or *a priori*, a word that means a thought that is held before examining evidence that comes through the senses), if they want to remain consistent naturalists, they would perhaps be open to the possibility of a non-miraculous resurrection. I will explain.

It is open to the naturalist to say that the possibility of Jesus's rising from the dead is either zero, or else astronomically low. They would give the

---

consequences, see Sowell, *Conflict*.

51. 1 Corinthians, 15:14, *New King James Version*.

52. For scholarly works on the resurrection, see Licona, *Resurrection of Jesus*, and Wright, *Resurrection of the Son*. For a more popular approach, see Habermas and Licona, *Case for the Resurrection*. See also Pitre, *Case for Jesus*. Debates on the historicity of the resurrection include Miethe, *Did Jesus Rise?*; Copan and Tacelli, *Jesus' Resurrection*; and Copan, *Will the Real Jesus?* It is undeniable that the Christian church and the New Testament existed in the first century. How can they be explained? One way to explain them is to take the New Testament at face value; that it basically tells the story of the rise of Christianity. For example, why then did the early church believe that Jesus rose from the dead? Because he really did. The main problem with this is that if one accepts this view, then orthodox Christianity is true. The rejection in my opinion is not based on evidence, at least not primarily so, but on the *a priori* rejection of orthodox Christianity.

possibility of such a miracle's happening a zero, because if he is a philosophical naturalist, he must believe that miracles—different events that could not happen according to natural law, being caused by the action of God—cannot happen, because in naturalism there is no God who could work the miracle. They would have to say that in the extremely unlikely event that a resurrection happened, it was some sort of freak natural event.

It is possible, though vastly more than astronomically unlikely, that the arm of a marble statue could wave its arm on its own, or do the Macarena for that matter, simply because it could happen that all the atoms of which the arm is composed could, by chance, all move in the same direction at the same time. Similarly, one might be able to believe that someone could come back from the dead if all the atoms in the body came back into the correct organization and energy. This is particularly true if the naturalist is also a materialist and thinks that all that there is to human beings is matter and energy. One might judge that the odds of this happening are so remote that practically speaking, it would never happen. At any rate, for the naturalist, events like the resurrection are either impossible or extraordinarily unlikely, as has been argued by many different naturalists.[53] At the same time, the naturalist may agree that his worldview is possibly wrong, and on that basis, concede miracles are possible.

It is not just naturalism that denies *a priori*—before looking at the historical evidences—the possibility of Jesus's rising from the dead, however. Islam does the same thing, though for quite another reason. Muslims believe in the existence of a God who can and has worked miracles, so there is no problem there. However, in the Qur'an it states that Jesus was not crucified, did not die in that manner, and so could not have risen from the dead.[54] Although the denial of the resurrection is not as foundational in Islam as is the commitment to the resurrection in Christianity, it is difficult to see how Muslims can ignore it, given their beliefs about the nature of the Qur'an as being directly given by Allah. Therefore, on the Islamic plausibility structure, as with the naturalist one, the plausibility of Jesus's rising from the dead is effectively 0 percent. Again, the Muslim may concede that his or

---

53. See for example, the section by Antony Flew in Habermas, *Did Jesus Rise?*; and Lüdemann in Copan and Tacelli, *Jesus' Resurrection*.

54. Muslims believe that the Qur'an was dictated by Allah and therefore is his very words. Surah IV, verse 157 states, "And because of their saying: We slew the Messiah Jesus son of Mary, Allah's messenger—They slew him not nor crucified, but it appeared so unto them; and lo! those who disagree concerning it are in doubt thereof; they have no knowledge thereof save pursuit of a conjecture; they slew him not for certain . . . " *Meaning of the Glorious Koran*, tr. Pickthall.

her religion may be wrong, but while thinking as a Muslim, will think that the resurrection certainly did not happen.

The point of the discussion above is this. When investigating, for example, the historicity of the resurrection of Jesus, a Christian, a naturalist, and a Muslim will bring to the investigation radically different ideas of what is possible. *When people investigate something, they will ordinarily bring to the investigation their ideas of what is possible and impossible, plausible and implausible.* When a Christian looks at the evidence, he or she will judge that the resurrection was a historical event and have no problem with the idea that historical evidence supports it.

When a naturalist or a Muslim looks at the evidence, on the other hand, they will bring with them, before looking at the historical evidence, the concept that the resurrection did not happen, because it could not happen in their worldview, and thus they will try to show how the evidence fails to support its historicity. If they became convinced of the resurrection by the evidence, then they must change their worldview, or else be guilty of believing contradictory things. And logical contradictions are fatal to any system.

Using Reason to Judge Worldviews

So, when *using reason to judge the truth of different worldviews*, several things must be kept in mind. First, one must use *logic*. Second one must use *evidence* gathered through perception, both internal and external. Though questioned by some, I do not see how one can avoid these in thinking.[55] There is, however, another important factor, which is the *worldview* of the person doing the investigating, and the *plausibility structure* which is embedded in that worldview. It is something that is brought to the investigation.

When people are told to think about more abstract issues rationally, they do so in terms of the rationality of the worldview to which they hold. For example, a philosophical naturalist will try to think about some issue—say the existence of miracles—using reason. Since, on the naturalist's plausibility structure, miracles are impossible, he will judge them to be impossible and hence that it is irrational to believe in their existence. However, the irrationality will not be in the concept per se (such as the irrationality of believing that $2 + 2 = 5$, the equation is necessarily false because

---

55. There are and always have been skeptics in philosophy. Skepticism is the view that there is no knowledge. For an examination and refutation of skepticism, see Huemer, *Skepticism*; and Butchvarov, *Skepticism*. On a related topic, the idea that knowledge is merely socially constructed, see Boghossian, *Fear of Knowledge*. See also Augustine, *Contra Academicos*.

the equation is contradictory), but only relative to one's worldview. With theism, it is quite possible that miracles could occur, and hence, belief in their existence need not be irrational.[56]

Worldviews and Plausibility Structures

So why do we have worldviews and their accompanying *plausibility structures*? It's because we cannot do without them. All normal adult human beings necessarily have these, simply because we all have beliefs about the nature of reality (worldviews), and plausibility structures are embedded therein. All that can be done is to recognize one's own biases, and to honestly compare what one already believes against the evidence of reason, which is given to us by logic and perception.

Neutrality in Worldviews?

There is one last matter that must be discussed concerning the nature of worldviews. This is the matter of *neutrality*. Simply put, *there is no neutral worldview*, no worldview that serves as the default position. Sometimes, in the debate between naturalism and theism, it is asserted, or at least seems to be assumed, that unless the theist can demonstrate the truth of theism or otherwise show it to be probable, then one must simply assume the truth of naturalism. I believe that this is false, and is, indeed, an instance of the fallacy known as "begging the question."

I have seen people argue that they are not biased; that they go purely by logic and empirical evidence alone. This claim should be rejected, not because it is possible yet just very hard to do, but because it is impossible to do.

It seems that when ruling out the possibility of such things as miracles because they are deemed to be irrational, naturalists are giving a sort of autobiographical statement. What I mean by this is that they are naturalists, they are committed to the naturalist worldview, and it would take a great deal of evidence to move them to the acceptance of another worldview. In other words, they are projecting what it would take for them to accept a different

---

56. Writes Herman Dooyeweerd on this point, "If all philosophical currents that pretend to choose their starting-point in theoretical reason alone, had, indeed, no deeper presuppositions, it should be possible to settle every philosophical argument between them in a purely theoretical way. But the factual situation is quite different. A debate between philosophical trends which are fundamentally opposed to each other usually results in a reasoning at cross-purposes, because they are not able to find a way to penetrate to each other's true starting-points. The latter seem to be masked by the dogma concerning the autonomy of philosophical thought." Dooyeweerd, *Twilight*, 3.

worldview onto everybody; they presuppose that everyone should begin with naturalism and only accept theism say, based on overwhelming evidence. Naturalism, it often seems to be assumed, doesn't require evidence; it is the unquestioned starting point, the "default," position so to speak.

Naturalism is not neutral

However, naturalism is not a neutral worldview—*there are and can be none*—and one cannot simply assert it as "truth" just because the theist does not make the case for his worldview to the naturalist's satisfaction. The naturalist will need arguments to support his or her position just as the theist will. When the naturalist appeals to *reason*, what is often being appealed to is *reason* used in the service of a naturalist world-view and plausibility structure—not *reason* purely in the sense of using logic and looking at evidence.

Why then is there the widespread belief, at least among intellectuals and pseudo intellectuals, that naturalism is the necessary starting point for worldview investigation? One answer is that there is the belief, also widespread, that *science* implies philosophical naturalism. Science has a very high reputation, and understandably so, given the many wonders that it has discovered or produced. As noted above, naturalists have worked hard at linking science with philosophical naturalism, and in many minds the idea has sunk in, so that the two are *mistakenly* identified as being one.

Another reason may simply be this: in a sense, we all see the same universe. Few people think that the world that we experience around us is an illusion. So, a naturalist may argue the following: everyone sees the same objects in the universe. We all see the earth, moon, sun, stars, and the sky itself. We see rocks and trees, animals, and plants. Further, almost everyone accepts most of what modern science reveals. That is, we accept that there are black holes, galaxies, radiation, and atoms made of subatomic particles. However, we don't see God, or angels, or an afterlife (at least not usually!). Also, it is argued, we don't see miracles today, though that can be, and is, disputed.[57]

So, the argument may go, we all perceive that the natural world around us exists, while we do not, except in disputable cases such as various religious experiences, perceive that a supernatural world exists. So, "since the natural world is all that exists" is a fundamental tenet of naturalism, the implication is that all should accept this limitation of reality, and anyone who thinks that

---

57. For the latter viewpoint, see Keener, *Miracles*.

there is more to reality than the natural world has the burden of proof. This line of thought seems to be persuasive to many people.[58]

However, I believe that it is mistaken. For, although we all do, in a way, perceive the same universe, in another respect we do not. At a sensory level, we perceive the same things, but at an intellectual level we do not. The naturalist sees the universe and thinks that it is *ontologically independent*.[59] That is, it exists on its own, uncaused by something else. The theist perceives the same universe and thinks that it is *ontologically dependent*. That is, that it is caused to exist by something else, namely God.

The dependence or independence of the universe is not discoverable by perception. Indeed, many naturalists seem to think it obvious and unproblematic that the universe can be independent—can exist on its own. However, it is rather an *interpretation* that we put on the objects revealed to us by perception. After all, we do not literally "see" via perception the universe existing without any support; we simply see the universe and the objects which compose it. *Naturalism* is just as much a philosophical interpretation of the world as *theism*.

Naturalism is not the "default" position

To sum up this point, in my personal experience, many atheists just assume the truth of philosophical naturalism, thinking that it is the "default" or necessary beginning position, and that it needs no proof. The *burden of proof* is assumed to rest on the theist. Thus, theists are sometimes accused of believing in God on "blind faith," while the naturalist can just presuppose the truth of naturalism without evidence and be thought to be entirely rational. However, this position is quite mistaken; *there is no default worldview*. A worldview is not an object of perception; it is an abstraction and needs to be defended, rather than assumed.

---

58. If the theist has what he or she thinks to be good reasons or grounds for believing in God, why is there some burden to convince the atheist? The same reasoning applies to the atheist or naturalist. The main reason that someone has a burden of proof, it seems to me, is when one is trying to convince someone else of the truth of what they believe. For example, if a theist tries to convince an atheist that God exists, the theist then assumes a burden of proof. The opposite is also true; if an atheist is trying to convince a theist either that God does not exist, or that there are no good reasons to think that God exists, then the atheist assumes a burden of proof.

59. By ontological I mean regarding existence. To be ontologically independent means to be uncaused by anything else, to be ontologically dependent for something means to be dependent on some other being.

Naturalism's "God of the gaps" argument

The final reason for believing in philosophical (or *metaphysical*) "naturalism" is what may be called the "God of the gaps" argument.

Let me clarify here that to this point our conversation about "naturalism" has been about *Metaphysical Naturalism*. The term *metaphysical* refers to "what kinds of things exist." So, *Metaphysical Naturalism* literally means "All kinds of things that exist are Natural"; all that exists is the natural universe and the stuff of which it is made. There is nothing else, save possibly for abstract objects. In the "God of the gaps" argument, we encounter *Methodological Naturalism (MN)*. This is the notion that to do the natural sciences (using scientific *methods*), one must use concepts only from nature, even if one might also believe in supernatural beings.

So, the term *"God of the gaps"* refers to the concept of using God (or perhaps some other supernatural entity, like "Q" in Star Trek) to explain how things work in the natural world. Isaac Newton is often held to have used a "God of the gaps" argument to explain order in the solar system. Supposedly, he thought the planetary system got out of sync occasionally, and God was then required to put it back in its proper order. However, some recent scholarship denies that this was the case.[60] If so, then Newton was innocent of proposing a "God of the gaps" theory. Indeed, scientists who think that God must intervene to keep the universe in order are hard to find.

In scholarly circles, arguments are often made against "The God of the gaps." These arguments are usually based on the idea that to do science one must take the stance of "methodological naturalism." In other words, anything supernatural is ruled out from the beginning. This includes not only keeping the universe orderly, but also from any sort of divine creation.

Methodological naturalism

Methodological naturalism is thus contrasted with *metaphysical naturalism*. In short, it is often held that one can be a theist—believe in some sort of supernatural God or other reality—and still practice a natural science, if any supernatural entities are excluded. Or, to put things simply, one can believe in God if God is excluded from science.

Of course, if *philosophical (metaphysical) naturalism* were true, then God and other supernatural entities would not exist and therefore could not ever interfere in the course of natural events. But *methodological naturalism*

---

60. For a telling that Newton believed in a God of the gaps, see Davis, "Did Newton's God Vanish?" For a refutation, see Meyer, *Return of the God Hypothesis*, 426-33.

only assumes that nothing non-natural has any effect on nature. This is an assumption upon which most of contemporary science is based. If that assumption were false, and God actually *did* miraculously intervene and create the first life forms, for example, then methodological naturalism would prevent one from ever discovering this, because therein a supernatural cause can never be considered.

The general point of methodological naturalism is that it is wrong to use God to explain things. However, if there is something unexplained, like the origin of life on earth, and God is used to explain it, there are bad implications. First, we may find a purely natural explanation, in which case God is chased out, and appears increasingly unnecessary. Second, using God to explain something is said to impede scientific progress, because one will not look for a natural cause if one simply assumes that God did it, which of course could lead to the lack of discovery of the real cause. In other words, using "God of the gaps" is said to be a "science stopper."

It should not be thought that "the God of the gaps" argument is only put forth by naturalists. Some theists use it too.[61] The general idea is that one should never look within nature itself for evidence of God. My own thought here is this: what if God (or some other designer) doesn't cooperate? That is, what if God ignores our strictures on what is allowed in science, and creates things directly anyway? The question reminds me of a joke going around when I was a child. "Where does the 800-pound Gorilla sleep? Anywhere he wants to." The same answer may be given to how did God create? "Any way he wanted to."

The problem that I have with using methodological naturalism's God of the gaps argument in this fashion is that *science aims at discovering truth*.[62]

Discovering or Dismissing the Truth

If it is possible that there is a supernatural god who causes something in nature to exist, then *methodological naturalism* would lead *away* from truth. For,

---

61. Holder gives one of the best popular defenses of the Fine-Tuning argument for God that I have read but rules out *a priori* the idea that life was designed. Describing a conversation that he had, he writes, "Susskind may not be aware of the important distinction between Intelligent Design, the flawed idea of seeing God as filling gaps in the processes of biological evolution, and the more general and robust design argument based on the question as to why laws of nature take the particular form they do." Holder, *Big Bang*. 122.

62. There do exist anti-realist theories of what science is, which argue that science doesn't aim for truth but rather for usefulness, but I think that most people, including most scientists, think science is an attempt to discover the truth about the natural world.

given this assumption, one could *never consider the possibility that God or some other supernatural entity was the cause of anything*. In short, methodological naturalism rules out *a priori* (from the start) the possibility of a non-natural cause.[63] In fact, methodological naturalism is sometimes used more broadly than just to rule out arguments from science for God. For example, it is used to rule out arguments for the existence of miracles, religious experience, and even philosophical arguments for God. David Hume's famous argument against our ever knowing that a miracle could occur is an example of this.[64]

If one accepts that supernatural explanations can never be allowed, one should not be surprised that no supernatural explanations ever succeed. It is a sort of a "heads I win, tails you lose" game. The game is often played, because, for many naturalists, it seems to be the case that they think that *Reason = Science = Naturalism*, and that therefore, by definition, to give a rational explanation of something is to give a naturalistic explanation of it. It is for this reason that *atheists often claim the title of being rational, while denying rationality to everyone else*.[65] However, this would be true only if naturalism were true. Below, I argue against this.

It might be argued that science only tries to discover certain kinds of truth: truth that can have no reference to any supernatural entities. This is arguably true, and science as science may not be able to directly argue to God. For that, one needs philosophy. However, it seems to me that a scientist could decide that there is not a natural explanation for some phenomenon, and that none seems likely to be forthcoming.

What is Faith?

> Faith may be defined as an illogical belief in the
> occurrence of the improbable.
>
> H. L. MENCKEN[66]

---

63. For a critique of methodological naturalism, see Bartlett and Holloway, *Naturalism*.

64. Hume's argument against miracles is in Geivett and Habermas, *Defense of Miracles*, 29–44. The rest of the book is a response to Hume. See also Parrish, *God and Necessity*, 145–73, for a response to Humean type objections to the knowledge of miracles.

65. This factor seems to be why naturalist atheists are holding a "Reason Rally" the past few years instead of "Atheism Rally." They think that they alone are rational. But what "reason" do we have for thinking that atheists are rational, besides the fact that they are constantly saying how rational they are? It mainly is, I think, the identification of atheist naturalism with science, and of science with reason. But they do not have a monopoly on science *or* reason.

66. Quoted in *Daily Dose of Knowledge*, 336.

> Faith is not belief without proof, but trust without reservation.
>
> D. Elton Trueblood[67]

Faith is often held to be the opposite of reason. Frequently in class, when I ask students what faith is, the immediate response that many give is that faith is believing something without any evidence.[68] Especially among atheists, faith is often held to be the belief in something based on no evidence, or even *against* the evidence, or even believing something that you know isn't true. These are, however, not the only or even the primary definitions of faith. Indeed, I will argue below that this kind of *"blind" faith* is rare, though not non-existent. A much more common definition of faith is simply *confidence or trust in some person, idea, institution, or entity*. This confidence is normally because one has reasons for the *trust* or commitment. This point may be illustrated by examples from everyday life.

If one has faith in one's automobile mechanic, for example, one usually does not obtain that faith without some reason. Normally, one does not think, "I have never been to this auto mechanic shop before, and know nothing about it, but I have complete and utter confidence in his ability to cure my car from whatever ails it at a fair price." Even less likely is the thought something like the following: "I have been to this automobile repair shop several times, and every time they have failed to fix my car and badly overcharged me. Nonetheless, I have complete confidence that they will fix my car perfectly this time and charge me a fair price, even though nothing has changed in the shop." Indeed, were one to think this way, there would be some serious mental health issues involved, and the person would need a psychiatrist more than a mechanic.

Reason to Have Faith

Normally, one has faith in something because one has a good reason to. If faith is defined as trust or confidence, this makes perfect sense. *We trust things that we have a reason to trust.* In the case of the auto repair shop, normally one would have confidence in the mechanic's ability to repair one's car correctly because of such things as: they are recommended by people you know; you have been to that shop before and they always fixed

---

67. Unfortunately, I cannot find the original source for this quote. It is on the internet in various places, such as https://answers.yahoo.com/question/index?qid=20070619072059AAc2o1V. It does sound like something that Trueblood would write.

68. A paper showing what is a false definition of faith in an unpublished paper by Jahdiel N. Perez, "Three Popular Bad Arguments."

your car so that you have no complaints; and they are recommended by other mechanics.

Indeed, rather than being opposite, reason and faith are *complementary*. This can be checked simply by looking at a dictionary. For example, one meaning of faith is this simple one, "Complete trust or confidence."[69] This is not the only definition, but I think that it is the basic one. One has faith in someone or something when one has complete or great trust in it.

Not only is this the common definition, it is also the biblical definition, which is relevant because we are investigating religious matters. The Zondervan *NIV Exhaustive Concordance* lists three Hebrew words that are translated into English as 'faith.' The lexical definitions are:

- *'aman*: to confirm, support, uphold (Qal); to be established, be faithful (Niphal); to be certain, i.e., to believe in (Hiphil).
- *'emun*: faithful, trusting.
- *'emuna*: firmness, fidelity, steadiness.

One main verbal stem in New Testament Greek is translated into English as 'faith.'

- *pistis*: faith; faith and confidence, fidelity, and faithfulness; conviction of the truth of anything, with the predominant idea of trust (or confidence); firm persuasion, a conviction based upon hearing, trustworthiness, a ground for faith, an assurance, in contrast to belief in its purely natural exercise, which consists of an opinion held in good faith without necessary reference to its proof.[70]

Reason vs. Faith?

This being the case, why are faith and reason so often set in opposition to each other? Why are religious people so often accused of having "blind faith?" This concept of "blind faith" is a definition of faith that differs from the one given above. With blind faith, someone will believe something because of

---

69. *DK Illustrated Oxford Dictionary*, 287. An ordinary dictionary will give the different definitions of faith. The English word itself comes from the Latin "*fidere*, to trust . . ." A longer definition is "1a: allegiance to duty or a person: Loyalty b(1): fidelity to one's promises (2): sincerity of intentions 2a(1): belief and trust in and loyalty to God (2): belief in the traditional doctrines of a religion b(1): firm belief in something for which there is no proof (2): complete trust 3: something that is believed esp. with strong convictions; *esp*: a system of religious beliefs." *Merriam-Webster's Collegiate Dictionary*.

70. Cited in Ross, *Matter of Days*, 265.

no evidence or reason at all; or even against the evidence. The concept of believing something for no reason is sometimes known as *fideism*.

If one reads much atheistic writing, one quickly sees that many atheists believe, even strongly believe, that all religious belief is based on blind faith. Religious belief for these atheists is always understood as blind faith, whereas atheists, on the other hand, it is strongly affirmed, believe what they believe based on *reason* and *evidence*. Indeed, this picture is obviously very important to many an atheist's self-image. However, this assumption or assertion itself seems to me somewhat blind, for one does not have to look very far to see that there is a vast literature of Christian apologetics, which is often giving reasons and evidence to believe in Christianity. That some Christians and other religious people (and some non-religious people) have embraced blind faith is true. That this is the historic or majority view of Christians is false.[71]

Belief Without Reason?

The question I will now ask is the following: does anyone—or at least any normal person—ever believe something for no reason at all? In answer, it seems to me that it is dubious that human beings, at least psychologically normal human beings, do this. While it is certainly true that people often believe things for bad reasons, at least they usually have reasons that they falsely believe are good reasons. In the case of *rationalization*, people somehow convince themselves their reasons are good, while deep down they know they are not. This process of rationalization not only does happen but, in fact, happens quite often. However, it still shows that people at least *think* that they should have good reasons to believe something.

Rationalization vs. Evidence

And, of course, it is not just pure rationalization. Some of the reasons for why people believe what they do are reasons that are based on emotion or prejudice, rather than logic or evidence. People believe things because they have motives for believing them, because they want them to be true, and not just because they have evidence for their truth.[72] This may not be pure ratio-

---

71. See for example, Dulles, *History of Apologetics*. Some may argue that Christian apologetics fails, and that therefore Christians are fideists. There is however, a large difference between, "Xists believe in Xism for reasons I find unconvincing," and, "Xists believe in Xism for no reason at all."

72. Remember the quote from Thomas Nagel in the Preface about how he hopes

nalization, because desire may be mixed with genuine evidence and logic. Indeed, I think that this is rather normal. For one thing, we have built into us a sort of epistemic conservatism; we initially continue to believe what we already believe. Overall, this must be considered a good thing. Chaos would prevail if people changed their minds instantly on important issues just based on some new evidence. But like everything else, this can be taken too far. Shutting one's mind to new evidence is also a bad thing.

Belief

The fact is, belief is not, or at least usually is not, volitional. We do not just decide to believe something. When I see a tree in front of me, I do not, at least under ordinary circumstances, decide whether I will believe that there is a tree in front of me. I simply and automatically believe that there is a tree there. The only times that we would doubt something like the existence of the tree would be when, for example, I think that a mad scientist has put a tree inducing hallucinatory drug in the tea I drank earlier in the day. But absent such very unusual circumstances, we come to believe that there is a tree, and indeed cannot be easily convinced otherwise. This is true for most sense perception, for basic necessary truths such as those of simple arithmetic (2 + 2 = 4), and for many of our memories. We ordinarily cannot *choose not* to believe these things, nor do we *choose to* believe them.[73] We just believe them automatically.

There may be more latitude when it comes to theoretical matters, such as in deciding what worldview to believe. Still, whether or not that is so, it is true that *one can influence what one will believe*. For example, if one wants to believe in the truth or falsity of some religion, but does not at present do so, a way of obtaining belief would be to read books only favorable (or unfavorable) to that religion, and none of the opposite. Although we cannot just decide what to believe, we can influence to some extent what we come to believe. These choices can skew our "truth" and persuade us to a stronger belief.

---

that there is no God.

73. On this, Plantinga writes, "My beliefs are not for the most part directly within my control. If you order me now, for example, to cease believing that the earth is very old, there is no way I can comply with your order." Plantinga, *Faith and Rationality*, 34. For our ability to alter our beliefs, see the following discussion in the above.

Deciding for Faith?

The question now is, "Can one just decide to have faith in something?" If one does not and cannot just decide to believe something and one normally comes to believe based on evidence, then how can one believe something, anything, without any evidence? It seems that no person whose cognitive system is operating normally comes to believe things without having some reason to think that these things are true.

When I say *reasons* or *evidence*, I am being very broad. They can include things like empirical evidence (e.g., seeing something), logical evidence (e.g., if either A is true or B is true but not both, and we know that A is not true, then therefore B must be true), a good authority—both professional (e.g., all or almost all physicists believe in the theory of special relativity is true, so it probably is) or personal (Sarah says that her car is blue, so it is)—, and even intuitions (it just 'feels wrong' to get drunk, so it is), or memory (I remember eating Cheerios for breakfast this morning, so I did). Some may use other evidences, like mystical or religious experiences, or divine revelation, such as in a book held to be divinely inspired. The point is that as it is the case that people use many different things as reasons or evidences for what they believe, we therefore have a very broad conception of what reason or evidence could be.

On Authority?

By believing something on authority, we believe something because someone else tells us that it is true. Some people on the internet apparently hold that believing anything on authority is wrong, that one should be able to test the truth of everything oneself. Frankly, this is ridiculous. As David Marshall writes, "How do I know that electrons circle the nuclei of atoms? That Earth contains an outer core of molten iron and nickel? Or even that I have two lungs?"[74] It takes a good deal of time and energy to learn how to answer any one of these questions; to be able to answer all of them is far beyond any human capacity. The fact is that a very large part of what we know we know on authority. We cannot do without authorities—it is impossible. The fundamental question is thus not *if* we should believe everything on authority, but rather *which authorities* are trustworthy?

---

74. David Marshall, *How Jesus Passes*, 26.

Based on Worldviews?

Why then do people espouse the worldviews that they do? For many different reasons, depending on the individual person's background, personality, history, what he or she has read or experienced, intuitions, and so on. To a large extent, most people accept the worldview that they do because of the *environment* into which they were born and raised. When it comes to *justifying the beliefs* that they have, in the final analysis, people believe things because, overall, the things that they believe make more sense to them than the alternatives. For example, why do so many people believe in God? According to Justin L. Barrett, it is because belief in God is a belief that naturally arises from the way that our minds are made.[75] There may, of course, be other reasons, but if he is right, then many people are sort of pre-programmed to believe in God.

For No Reason? On Blind Faith?

Thus, I doubt that any normal person believes things, at least anything important, purely as a matter of blind faith. Since what makes most sense to people, especially those untrained in philosophy, is often difficult for them to articulate, they may have a difficult time explaining why. And thus, it sometimes ends up sounding like they believe the things that they do simply on blind faith, when they may in fact have what seems to them compelling reasons for what they believe.

Nonetheless, the idea that religious belief is all *fideistic*, all based on *blind faith*, is a very popular one. Some Christians (and others) do, in fact, embrace this view, though it is not now, and never has been, the only or even the most popular view.[76] Many atheists, especially on the internet, seem to have a dogma that Christians all embrace fideism. That this understanding is false can be seen simply by the large number of books of Christian apologetics that have been published.[77] However, for some atheists, it seems to be an important part of their self-image that they are seen as the defenders

---

75. Barrett, *Why Would Anyone Believe?*.

76. On this, see for example, Marshall and McGrew, "Faith and Reason." For Martin Luther's view of faith and reason, see Andersen, *Martin Luther*. Luther has often been falsely accused of being a fideist, because Luther called reason the devil's whore. However, according to Andersen, what Luther was referring to was not reason—the ability to think rationally—but rationalism, by which he meant taking some position based on one's own thinking and remaking Christian doctrine to fit in with one's own preconceived ideas.

77. Which probably is in the thousands.

of science and rationality, and that they are opposed by "anti-rational" religious people.

Fodder for the Atheists

This stance does serve a practical purpose for atheists. Simply put, by identifying a position as one for which there is no reason or evidence, which one must accept only on blind faith, one has thereby made that position irrelevant. If one says that there is no reason to accept the position that one holds, that it is totally unverifiable, then there is no good reason to pay any attention to that position. It can simply be dismissed. This is, I think, one motive for such an emphasis from many atheists on the notion that one must be a *fideist* to be religious and a theist. *By delegitimizing the concept of faith, atheists can rule any version of theism out of bounds at the beginning.* Ironically, many atheists seem to me to be "fideists," because they hold that naturalism is the default position or worldview. They are presupposing the truth of naturalism rather than demonstrating it. They are therefore taking naturalism on "blind faith."

Faith Commitment and the Work of the Holy Spirit

There are two more points that need to be made here. *First*, since faith is a commitment to something, then one may accurately be said to have faith in many things. Thus, various forms of naturalism and atheism may be considered to be faiths, and those people who believe in these systems may truly be said to have a faith commitment.

The *second* point is specifically about Christian faith. No knowledgeable Christian would say that they have faith entirely because of their own reason. There is necessarily also the work of the Holy Spirit, who gives people saving faith.[78]

Faith in which Worldview?

There is a significant problem here that must be examined. People hold to the worldviews that they do, as I have argued, to the extent that they are the worldviews which, on reflection, make the most sense to them. But *what makes the most sense to people to a large degree depends upon what*

---

78. See for example Plantinga, *Knowledge and Christian Belief*. For a more scholarly statement of Plantinga's argument, see *Warranted Christian Belief*.

worldview they hold to. That is, one will believe in worldview A because that is the worldview (of which they are aware) that makes the most sense to them. However, one reason that worldview A makes the most sense to them is because they already believe in worldview A, and they judge things according to how plausible things are according to the *plausibility structure* that is inherent in worldview A. Thus, there is inevitably a certain amount of circularity involved, which complicates the issue.

Circularity

This is a problem for everyone and for every worldview, as it is inherent in the way we come to believe anything. *Reasoning does not take place in a vacuum.*[79] Rather, when we reason about things, we are depending on background information, and assumptions of which we might not even be consciously aware. Even in simple matters, like going to work, we depend upon notions such as: the external world exists; it is like the way that we perceive it; our minds can understand reality; and so on. I am not saying that these are unreasonable assumptions, but they are there as part of our background knowledge.

For example, let us take two people, John and Mary. John is an atheist materialist. When it comes to judging the plausibility of the existence of God, he deems it extremely unlikely or impossible that such a being exists. Part of the reason for this judgment is that, being a materialist, he thinks the existence of non-material entities is impossible or even meaningless. With most conceptions of God, God is immaterial. So, while thinking of things *as a materialist*, he must think that the existence of God is impossible.

He may step back for a moment, so to speak, and question the truth of his materialist worldview, and the judgments made on the plausibility structure it contains. To think that non-material entities may exist would be to question the truth of his whole worldview, which, he thinks, is very unlikely. Thus, based on principles derived from naturalism and materialism, he thinks that naturalism and materialism are true, which is, of course, circular reasoning.

To be sure, it isn't only materialists who have this problem—everyone has it. For example, Mary is a theist—she believes that God, an immaterial personal being, exists. Since she thinks that God exists, immaterial persons can exist. Therefore, she thinks that because an immaterial person can, and in fact does, exist, materialism, which denies this possibility, is therefore false. Since she thinks that it is very unlikely that either God

---

79. For an extended argument to this point, see Clouser, *Myth*.

doesn't exist or that if he does, he is a material being, she judges that materialism is very improbable.

Again, standards taken from a worldview are used to determine the truth of that same worldview, as well as other worldviews. Like John, Mary could "step back" from thinking in terms of her worldview and judge the worldview itself. But again, she would probably be using criteria that are inherent in the worldview she holds to judge the truth of that very worldview. And again, this involves some circular reasoning.

Getting around circularity

Is it possible we get around this problem? I will argue that it is, but I must first make some distinctions, and to do so I must expand on points made above. Above I argued in detail in the section on "reason" that there are *three major elements in how we come to think about matters*. They are:

1. *Perception*. We see, hear, smell, taste, and touch things existing in the world. We also feel cold and pain, and we have emotions. This is the usual way in which we learn things about the world—we experience them, or else we accept on authority what someone else who has experienced them says about them. For an extreme example, as Helen Keller depended upon Annie Sullivan. Without perception, even were it possible for someone to exist without having any, we would be almost devoid of concepts. Nothing that comes through seeing, hearing, touching, etc., would be available to us, and hence we would be cut off from all reality.

2. *Logic*. Even those who deny logic must use it. The fundamental laws of logic are the law of identity, the law of non-contradiction, and the law of the excluded middle. The *law of identity* is that everything is what it is—existing as a particular thing with particular properties. Without the law of identity, nothing could exist as something definite. The *law of non-contradiction* is that there can be no real contradictions in reality. Without the law of non-contradiction, things could exist with contradictory attributes, which again denies that things exist as a certain thing and in a certain manner. The *law of excluded middles* states that every statement is either true or false.

3. *Plausibility structure*. This is an essential component of a great deal of our thinking. A plausibility structure determines how plausible something is for the individual who has it. Plausibility structures are not reducible to perception, as we do not actually perceive them via

the senses. Nor are they matters of strict logic, though they too must follow the laws of logic. Rather, a plausibility structure is inherent in the nature of the worldview that an individual believes.

Perception and Plausibility Structures

All people with normally functioning senses have the same basic perceptions of the world, at least insofar as their perceptual equipment is functioning correctly. Similarly, everyone must use the same laws of logic if they are thinking correctly. Since we all live in the same reality, and human beings are the same species of creatures, then if our eyes, ears, etc., are working correctly, and we are using logic correctly, we should be able to examine different questions with a great deal of objectivity, since we are using the same tools to examine them. This may be more difficult to prove than it may first seem; though, it is hard to take the opposite view seriously.[80]

However, a real problem arises from the notion of the *plausibility structure*. The obvious fact is that there are many different plausibility structures in the world, and many of them are radically at variance with others. For example, a Marxist is not going to look at questions, such as the existence of God, the objectivity or subjectivity of morality, or the nature of human beings, in the same way that a Catholic, or a Buddhist will, etc.

This leads to the problem of how we know which is the correct plausibility structure? To have the correct plausibility structure, we must have the correct worldview. If a Marxist examines the plausibility of Marxism using the Marxist plausibility structure, there will inevitably be a bias in its favor. On the other hand, if a Catholic or a Buddhist examines Marxism in terms of the plausibility structure of Catholicism or Buddhism, there will inevitably be, of necessity, a bias against it. Of course, the opposite is also true.

The problem is thus one of *question begging* or circular reasoning. However, I will argue that the situation, though more complicated, is not hopeless. There are still the objective factors from perception and logic. If a particular worldview has a plausibility structure that for some weird reason holds that the moon must be shaped like a taco, then there is a problem, for we can all see that is not. Similarly, if a worldview necessarily contains the belief that circles all have four corners, or that $2 + 2 = 83$, one can immediately reject it, for the worldview contains contradictions.

---

80. For a discussion, somewhat skeptical, that nonetheless concludes that we should accept our basic beliefs gained through sensation, see Alston, *Reliability of Sense*.

Testing Worldviews

Despite the natural tendency of human beings to judge relevant matters based on the worldview that they hold, including the plausibility of that worldview, it is still possible to come up with *tests to apply to the different worldviews*.

Consistency. One of these is the test for *consistency*. A worldview, or any other belief, that contains contradictions that cannot be eliminated, must, therefore, necessarily be false.

Correspondence with Facts and Justifiability. Other tests include *correspondence with empirical facts* and the ability to give an account of why things in the universe are the way that they are, *the ability to justify knowledge, simplicity*, and the ability for the worldview in question to be *livable* in some sense.

Transcendental Test. There is one more test that I will mention here, that will become apparent in the following chapters. This may be called the *transcendental test*. The transcendental question is, "Can the worldview in question justify there being knowledge of itself and any other matters?" That is, if someone holding to the worldview cannot have justified knowledge, because of the nature of that worldview, then it is self-refuting—because belief in the worldview itself would be unjustified. Beliefs, even if they are true, if obtained by some non-justified means, do not count as knowledge. Therefore, a test for a worldview is that *justified true belief must be possible in that worldview*—if it is not possible, then the worldview is self-refuting and false.

Verification or Falsification of Ideas

It should also be noted that the whole problem of verification and/or falsification of ideas is a large and much discussed topic in philosophy.[81] I have pointed out some tests that move us in the direction of answers. Even though there is an infinite number of worldviews that are possible to hold, they all (or almost all) ultimately break down into three fundamental kinds: *naturalism, theism*, and *pantheism* (or an attempt to combine two or all three of these positions). The first two of these worldviews are the primary focus of this book, though I will also argue a few things about pantheism, as well as about panentheism, which is a sort of hybrid system with elements

---

81. For an introduction to various issues in epistemology, see Steup and Sosa, *Contemporary Debates*.

of theism, naturalism, and pantheism. Most atheists today are naturalists. However, pantheists, insofar as they deny the existence of a personal god, are also atheists.

The Questions To Be Answered

To sum up, *the question of which worldview is the correct one is of the highest importance*, as it impacts so many other questions—such as ethics, free will, politics, the status of human beings, and many other things. There is no direct test that will give a direct answer to the question of which worldview is correct. Still, there are tests that one can use to judge them. Most of the rest of the book will be an exposition of the different worldviews, and the testing of them. The ones that prove to be flimsy will topple like a house of cards.

In the next chapter I will begin an examination of the various issues and questions to which the diverse worldviews give different answers.

The Mystery of Existence

The first group of questions might be called *the mystery of existence* and has these parts.

1A. Why does anything *exist* in the manner that it does? That is, why is there something instead of nothing? Further, why does this particular reality exist? Given that something exists, specifically our universe, why does it exist instead of all the different ways that things seemingly could have been?

1B. Why do things *remain in existence*? I think that this is logically just as compelling a question as to the one above, or perhaps even more so. If something exists, it will remain in existence unless destroyed. We take this for granted (and in these cases, the matter/energy which composed the things also remains in existence). However, there is the question as to why this is the case.

1C. Why is the *universe orderly*? That is, why is it orderly in the sense that the same laws and constants of nature seem to be in place everywhere and at all times? There are other kinds of order, but this is the most fundamental. All worldviews need to answer this important question.

The Mystery of Consciousness

The second group of questions might be called *the mystery of consciousness* and has five parts.

2A. Why does *consciousness* exist at all? Why do conscious beings exist? How did consciousness come into existence in a purely non-conscious universe?

2B. Indeed, why do *minds* exist? Why do beings that can have such attributes as reason, knowledge, will, and emotions at the center of a subjective awareness exist? How does subjectivity, that of being an "I," exist in a universe of impersonal things?

2C. Why does *rationality* exist? It is not just the case that consciousness exists, but that it exists in specific forms. One of these forms is rationality, which is closely related to the ability to use language.

2D. Why does *intentionality* exist? Intentionality is another aspect of consciousness. Rational conscious beings have thoughts that intend toward things; that is, when one thinks, one necessarily thinks of *something*. How can this be the case?

2E. Why is there *free will*? The existence of free will is controversial, especially as compared to the others listed above. However, most people believe in free will, and there are good reasons for thinking that some form of it must exist.

The Mystery of Values and Evil

The next two questions might be called *the problem of the existence of values*, especially objective values. These values include *moral* and *aesthetic* values, but I will also examine *the problem of evil*.

3A. Why is there *morality*? Most human beings feel the pull of morality. Those that do not feel this pull seem to be defective, or more precisely, evil psychopaths. Why is this situation the case? Do objective moral truths exist? If so, then how and why do they exist?

3B. Why is there *beauty*? Why is the universe, or most of it anyway, so beautiful? Why do we have the categories of beauty and of art?

3C. Why is there *evil and suffering* in the world, especially the amount that there is?

Answering the Questions

In giving *answers to these questions*, I intend to compare and contrast the positions that theism and naturalism give. This next chapter will be concerned with *the mystery of existence* and the way that the opposing worldviews answer the question. This will involve giving some further definitions, but for the most part, I will draw out the *implications* of each general worldview and compare them. Chapter 3 will address the *existence and order of the universe* (question set number 1). The *mystery of consciousness* and the *existence of persons* is expounded in chapter 4 (question set number 2). Similarly, chapters 5 and 6 investigate *moral and aesthetic values* and *the problem of evil* (question set number 3).

The arguments given here are philosophic ones, rather than scientific. The major reason for this is that *both theism and naturalism are philosophical theories, not scientific ones*. For example, even if it could be proven that the physical universe had existed forever and that every event that had ever happened in it happened according to natural law (which actually would be pretty tough things to prove), this by itself would do nothing to prove that naturalism is true.

Indeed, I have found that a confusion of science and philosophy, of physics and metaphysics, is one of the problems in understanding the issues. That the universe has existed forever, and that every event that has ever happened has happened according to natural law are both compatible not only with naturalism, but also with theism (if an infinite series of time is possible, which has been questioned),[82] though not compatible with every religious teaching about God and the universe.[83]

The Big Question

The real issue that differentiates theism and naturalist atheism is: "Does the physical universe exist independent of anything else, or does it depend on some other being, namely God?" This is the primary question that will be explored in this book.

---

82. See for example, Craig, *Kalam*. For a more recent defense of what is called the Kalam Cosmological Argument, see Craig and Sinclair, "*Kalam* Cosmological Argument."

83. There is a position which might be called *Theistic Naturalism*. With it, God exists and created and sustains the existence of the universe, but never works miracles. Rather, God works through the laws of nature. See Cooper, "Whose Interpretation?" 240.

Chapter 2

The Competing Theories of Existence

> Why is there something rather than nothing?
> The question encapsulates the puzzle of existence.
>
> Tyron Goldschmidt[1]

What is the Mystery of Existence?[2]

Basically, it is the question as to why the universe that we live in exists instead of some other world, or even nothing at all. It is perhaps the most fundamental question that there is. Closely related to it are the questions as to why the universe *remains* in existence, and why the universe is *orderly* in the sense that the laws and constants in it seem to be the same at all places and at all times. To answer this, the question of what *ultimate reality* is must be answered.

What is Ultimate Reality?

To define the term, *Ultimate Reality is that upon which everything else depends for its existence, but which does not itself depend upon anything else for*

---

1. Goldschmidt, *Puzzle of Existence*, 1. Actually, the problem is broader than this as Goldschmidt goes on to recognize. For there are also questions such as why does this particular universe exist rather than some other, and why does it, and the things that exist in it, remain in existence over time? One famous philosopher who dealt with this issue at length is Heidegger, *Introduction to Metaphysics*. Unfortunately, though he asks over and over why does anything exist in a text of 247 pages, he never gives any sort of clear answer.

2. Three recent books that discuss the "mystery of existence," are Leslie and Kuhn, *Mystery of Existence*; Goldschmidt, *Puzzle of Existence*, and at a more popular level, Holt, *Why Does the World Exist?*

its existence.[3] In theism, or at least in classical or perfect being theism, *God* is the ultimate reality. In naturalist theory, the *universe* itself is ultimate reality, or else, at a different level of being, matter/energy is, or else, spacetime itself. For the different worldviews, these are as far as concrete entities can get to rock bottom reality—there is no concrete reality in existence that causes them to exist.

One major answer to the question of why anything exists, and exists in the manner that it does, is the theist's answer, namely God—who necessarily exists, and is the cause of the existence of everything else. However, to examine this response, we must understand what is meant by the term "God," to which I must turn.

Defining the Concept of God

> The source of all contrasts between paganism and Christianity is the difference in their concepts of God. In any system, the ultimate principle determines the form of the whole and shows its implications in the details for ethics, physics, and epistemology.
>
> GORDON H. CLARK[4]

In this section, I will attempt to define the concept of *God*, that is, what is required for some being to count as a god. By the end of the discussion, I think that it will be clear that to get an unambiguous definition of what it is to be a god is very difficult. There are many different concepts of "God," and they have different philosophical implications.

Throughout history there have been countless gods that have been believed in. The problem is, what counts as being a *god*? Where does one draw the line as to what constitutes a god? (I will reserve the word "God" with a capital G for the God of perfect being theism, which will be explained below).

Concepts of God

Unfortunately, the word "god" is about as vague as the word "religion," and is subject to multiple interpretations. The fact is that there are many things that have been called god throughout history, and into the present time. Some of these concepts are,

---

3. I got this basic idea from Clouser, *Myth*, 9–41.
4. Clark, *Thales to Dewey*, 183.

1. Theism: The *God of classical theism* or *perfect being theology* is defined as being all powerful, all knowing, all good, etc. This God is *transcendent* to the universe, having created it out of nothing. Very importantly, the God of classical theism is *personal*, that is, has the attributes a person.[5]

2. Panentheism: The *panentheistic* god is *personal*, but also has a body, which is *the universe itself*. Neither god's mind nor its body can exist without the other, as they are usually conceived in some manner to be identical with each other.[6]

3. Pantheism: The god of *pantheism* is considered to be identical in some way with the physical universe, or else to somehow *permeate* the physical universe. In pantheism, ultimate reality is usually considered to be *impersonal*, which means that in the final analysis ultimate reality is not an agent—not someone who makes decisions and acts on them.[7]

4. Polytheism: gods are conceived of as *finite beings* who exist *within* the physical universe. Gods who fit this description include the gods of ancient Greece and Rome, or of the Scandinavians. Examples are Zeus and Hera, and Thor. A modern version of this would be the god of some versions of Mormonism.[8]

5. In some sense, *lesser beings* than these can be called gods. One may be so attached to some person, or even something, that one holds it as one's ultimate value. In this sense a person may be said to have money as his god, as is the case with Scrooge in Charles Dickens's story, *A Christmas Carol*. Indeed, it could be said that whatever is the highest value for some person could be named, in some sense, as that person's god. The problem with this definition is that it includes things that most people, for good reason, would want to exclude from the category of gods. Were that to be the case, one might possibly say that not only could money or fame be a god, but also things like a set of golf clubs, a retirement account, or the star of some soap opera—when these are held as one's highest value.

---

5. See Parrish, *God and Necessity*. Here I will also state that classical theism and perfect being theism are not necessarily always in agreement.

6. For a history and exposition of panentheism, along with a critique, see Cooper, *Panentheism*.

7. For a philosophic exposition and defense of pantheism, see Levine, *Pantheism*.

8. Few people these days believe in old pagan gods. However, the largest Mormon Church still holds to the concept of a finite god—though sometimes Mormon scholars deny that the Mormon god is finite.

Criteria for a "god"

In one university class I asked my students about what could be legitimately called a "god." What about Justin Bieber? If someone worshipped him, could he be called a god? The answer I received was, "Yes—his worshipper would be an idiot, but the fact that Bieber was worshipped promotes him to god status." I then asked about a partly used pencil eraser that was lying on the table. If someone worshipped it, would it be a god? The answer was, again, "Yes."

Though I can understand why the students were saying this, I find these answers quite unsatisfactory. Just because someone worships something, no matter what it is, does not rightfully entitle it to be called a god. To put things another way, if someone worships something, then for that person, the object of worship is a god. However, to be a god objectively, the god, whatever it is, must have a minimum of certain attributes or properties. The question is, what properties allow something to legitimately be included in the class of gods?

Therefore, without denying that there are other legitimate ways of using the word, I will assume, for the sake of the book, that for some being to qualify as a god, it must be a *personal* being. *A god must be a person in some sense of the word.*

Person

What is it to be a person? That is another important question. Simply put, a person is a being who, at some point in a normal development, will have characteristics that include *rationality, will, feeling,* and the ability to use *language* in some form or another. These characteristics include, as a part of their nature, the property of being *conscious*—that of having *sentient* awareness, including an awareness of their own being. Human beings are therefore obviously persons, as are angels. Such things as Klingons and Hobbits would be persons, if they existed. The Mormon god would also be a person, as were the Greek gods and the other gods of the different ancient polytheisms. On the other hand, such beings as Plotinus's One,[9] Spinoza's God or Nature,[10] and the Hindu being Brahman (as defined by the Indian

---

9. Plotinus's philosophy is developed in his work, *Six Enneads*. For an introduction to the philosophy of Plotinus, see Hadot, *Plotinus*.

10. See Spinoza, *On Improvement*. *The Ethics* is the most important work when it comes to the fundamentals of Spinoza's philosophy. For an introduction to that philosophy see Scruton, *Spinoza*.

philosopher Sankara) would not be called gods by this definition, as they are not personal agents.[11]

In some philosophical and religious theories, such as pantheism (described above), ultimate reality is conceived to be a spiritual but impersonal being, which has many important consequences.[12] In the philosophy of Plotinus for example, the "One," which is the highest reality, is not conceived in personal terms. Rather, the One is thought to be beyond being, beyond thought. Thus, were the One to exist, even though it would be ultimate reality, it would not be a "god" in the sense that I am using.

At a more popular level, a similar example is that contained in the Star Wars movie series. In those movies, there is the concept of the "Force." The Force is supposedly an energy field that permeates the galaxy where the movies take place. Both the heroes and villains draw their super powers from it. The Force is sometimes spoken of in the movies in religious terms. Yet it is (or would be, if it existed) not a personal being who knows things, desires things, wills things, etc. Therefore, on my definition, it does not count as being a god.

Having made this distinction, it must be admitted that it is in some sense arbitrary, and certainly no one is obligated to accept it. Yet I think that this definition is not without good reason or plausibility. Most of the gods believed in throughout history have been considered personal in some respect, and *only a personal god could be rationally prayed to or worshipped.*

Another point that should be noted is that, unfortunately, not every conception of god will neatly fit into this description. For example, one problem with this definition is Allah, the God of Islam. Although many consider Allah to be equivalent to the God of Christianity, minus some features such as the Trinity, this is arguably not so. On some versions of Islam, Allah is above any knowing, and is utterly unlike human beings. This is different from the Christian concept of God, where human beings are made in the image and likeness of God. All that we know of Allah is his will, and that he is omnipotent.[13]

---

11. For a brief exposition of Sankara's thought, see Harrison, *Eastern Philosophy*, 56–60.

12. Writes Thomas Molnar, "A transcendent and personal God excludes the possession by man of divine insight into things and excludes also man's absorption in Being. God reminds us that man is not the creator of nature, nor is nature the creator of man; both were created distinct and limited." Molnar, *God and the Knowledge of Reality*, 226–27.

13. For an examination of Islamic thought regarding God, see Reilly, *Closing*, especially 41–90. For a history of Islamic philosophy, see Adamson, *Philosophy in the Islamic World*. For an examination of the effect of Islamic theology on science, see Jaki, *Science and Creation*, 192–218.

On this basis, some have said that Allah is impersonal, like the concept of the One or Absolute of pantheism. On the other hand, Allah is alleged to have communicated with prophets, in which case he is capable of rational thought and speech. The Qur'an, the book that Muslims consider to be not only divinely inspired, but was supposedly actually dictated by Allah, is mainly composed of statements, which only a personal being could make. In addition, Allah is supposed to have given commands or laws by which he wants human beings to live. These facts seemingly imply that Allah is a person, or at least has personal traits (whatever that means).

Given this, it may be easier to say that Allah can be defined as a god, but that the descriptions of him are inconsistent, or that there are rival interpretations as to what Allah is like. This may be a problem for Muslims, but it does not rule out considering Allah a god by the standards that I am using here. However, other concepts, such as pantheistic ones like the Brahman postulated by the Hindu philosopher Sankara, and those that are considered to ultimately be impersonal, do not. Obviously, just because a person exists does not automatically mean that person is a god. Some other attributes are needed. These would include having great power, knowledge, and goodness, for example.

Other characteristics

The God of classical or perfect being theism, which is the god in which Christians have historically believed, is *omnipotent* (all powerful), *omniscient* (all knowing), and *omnibenevolent* (all good). However, it seems that other concepts of god may be legitimately considered to be gods even though, in contrast to the God of classical theism, their attributes are not infinite.

For example, the gods of the ancient Greeks seem to be legitimately considered to be gods, even though they were not omnipotent, omniscient, or even the ultimate beings. (According to the mythology, the gods of Olympus had risen to their place by defeating an older race of gods. Further, the gods of the ancient Greeks existed in the spatio-temporal universe and were themselves subject to fate, which was thus superior to them). What is the cut off line?

Power over the laws of nature

One suggestion might be that to be a god one must be able to override the laws of nature. That is, one must be able to alter the laws of physics.

Certainly, the God of classical theism can do that, as he is omnipotent, and established the laws in the first place. Some of the gods of ancient polytheism could apparently work magic, which over-ruled the laws of nature. This may seem to be a plausible place to draw the line.

There is, however, a problem with one of the Mormon concepts of god regarding this definition. There are different Mormon theories of god, but one of them is that there is an infinite number of gods, all finite beings, living in an infinite material universe. Our God, the one that Mormons consider to be the one in the Bible and the Book of Mormon, is the one who oversees our world. According to some Mormons, their god did not create the laws of physics, nor can he alter or suspend them. Rather, his powers come from being able to master and use the laws of physics with a far greater ability than we can. Miracles, then, are the Mormon god's manipulations of the universe and the laws by which the universe is governed, rather than the suspension of those laws.[14]

Given this, does the Mormon god count as being a god as I have defined it? I will say, "Yes," as he is a personal being with powers far exceeding our own. The main reason that I can think to deny the Mormon god the title of being a god, is that, according to some descriptions, he cannot alter the laws of nature. It might be argued, then, that he is not a god, but rather merely an extremely powerful or advanced alien. However, since, according to Mormon theology, his natural powers far exceed ours, and he is an immortal being who has control over our lives and what happens to us after death, I will accept that the Mormons have a legitimate god concept, though perhaps one on the edge—a much different edge than that of the Muslims.

What about Hitler's God?

Another god concept to be considered here is the one held by Hitler and National Socialism, or Nazism. Hitler and the Nazis are toxic, and understandably so. Nobody wants to be associated with them.[15] Therefore, atheists sometimes claim that Hitler was a Christian, or at least a theist. Christians and other theists on the other hand often argued that he was an atheist. In a recent book, Richard Weikart has argued that Hitler is probably best thought of as a pantheist.[16]

---

14. See for example, Paulson, *Comparative Coherence*.

15. I am going into greater detail about this, because there is so much discussion and disagreement on the internet.

16. Weikart, *Hitler's Religion*. The laws of nature are of course impersonal. Weikart has published other works on Hitler's philosophy. See his *Hitler's Ethics*.

The truth is not easy to ascertain, for a couple of reasons. Hitler was born into the Roman Catholic Church and never officially left it. He was, however, not a believing or practicing Catholic as an adult. Also, Hitler was a politician (not to mention the fact that he was a consummate liar) and would say things to gain people's support, whether he believed them or not. In his early years, before he attained power, he sometimes told people that he was a Christian, and a supporter of what is called "Positive Christianity." Indeed, the term "Positive Christianity" is in the National Socialist Party manifesto.

What was exactly meant by the term "Positive Christianity" is not entirely clear, nor does the Nazi manifesto describe it. There was a movement of liberal theology in Germany that attempted to alter Christianity to fit in better with some contemporary intellectual movements. This form held to at least three points. First, the whole Old Testament and parts of the New were deleted—in short, anything that smacked of Judaism. Second, Jesus was declared to be a non-Jew, that he had been an Aryan who had been persecuted by the Jews. Third, there was almost a total disinterest in theological doctrine. All the doctrines that Christians have been so concerned about through the ages—the Trinity, the Incarnation, the Atonement, etc.—were ignored. Indeed, even an atheist could still be a "Positive Christian" in this sense.[17] Reading about Hitler's own beliefs, one can see that they matched the above fairly closely.[18]

Later, after Hitler had achieved power, he became more non-Christian or even anti-Christian, at least in his actions. I do not know of any historians who believe that Hitler was a practicing or believing Christian anywhere close to an orthodox definition of Christianity, at the very least in his last years. This is clearly spelled out in Hitler's *Table Talk*, and in many other places. Though some questions about the accuracy or legitimacy of the English translation of the *Table Talk* have been raised, historians who write on the matter take the German versions as being accurate.[19] Further, the same viewpoint can be found in other works, such as Goebbels's diaries. Goebbels, the Nazi propaganda minister, cites Hitler's putting forth his hatred and contempt for Christianity in no uncertain terms. Indeed, there is evidence that Hitler wanted to destroy Christianity in Germany after winning the war.[20]

17. For more on the "Positive Christianity" of the Nazis, see Conway, *Nazi Persecution*. For a study of the paganism in Nazism and the relation of Nazism and Christianity, see Poewe, *New Religions*; and Terrell, *Christ, Faith*.

18. See Weikart, *Hitler's Religion*, esp. 67–105.

19. Weikart, *Hitler's Religion*, 281–82.

20. See for example, Colimore, "Papers Reveal Nazi Aim." For a detailed examination

However, even though Hitler was not a Christian in any meaningful sense, was he a theist? He is not as clear here as he is regarding Christianity. He often appealed to God in public, and sometimes in private. Again, however, one should be careful. In one place, Hitler, ridiculing the Christian concept of God as similar to human beings, is cited as saying "[T]hen the ant would have to conceive of God as an ant, just as every animal would conceive of God, i.e., Providence, the laws of nature, in its own form."[21] Here he seemingly identifies God with the laws of nature—which is a form of naturalism rather than theism, given a choice between the two. Basically, the same thing is said by Martin Bormann, Hitler's closest aide in the last few years of his life,[22] and by his private secretary Traudl Junge, in her memoirs.[23]

What, then, can be said about Hitler's god? As Weikart himself states, the evidence we have is not completely clear, and it may be the case that Hitler's beliefs were not entirely consistent. People may change their minds over time, or even in different moods. Still, from the evidence, it seems that Hitler did not believe in a personal god, a god who is conscious and wills various things rather than their opposite. Certainly, he rejected the traditional Christian concept of God in which he had been raised. However, in another sense, he did seem to accept that there is some "god" who was in control of the universe. He also attacked the explicit atheism of the communists. For these reasons, Weikart argues at length, and I agree, that it is best to think of Hitler as a pantheist; that is, as someone who identified the Deity with the universe itself, or else with the basic laws of nature that undergird the universe.

This pantheism can easily go along with a religious sentiment, wherein the universe itself is an object of worship or reverence; and, indeed, Hitler himself seemed to have such a reverence towards the universe. On the other

---

of the question see Weikart, *Hitler's Religion*, 107–46.

21. Adolf Hitler, "Monologue on July 11–12, 1941."

22. Martin Bormann, Hitler's right-hand man for the final few years of the Nazi regime, wrote, "When we National Socialists speak of a belief in God, we do not understand by God, like naive Christians and their spiritual opportunists, a human-type being, who sits around somewhere in space . . . [Christians don't believe this, though Mormons do.] The force of natural law, with which all these innumerable planets move in the universe, we call the Almighty or God." Bormann, "Circular."

23. Junge, Hitler's private secretary for the final few years wrote, "He [Hitler] was not a member of any church, and thought the Christian religions were outdated, hypocritical institutions that lured people into them. The laws of nature were his religion." Junge, *Until the Final Hour*, 108. According to Weikart, the remarks in Traudl's book are almost identical to ones made in another book by another of Hitler's secretaries, Christa Schroeder. *Hitler's Religion*, 284.

hand, Hitler did not believe in life after death, or apparently, any kind of supernatural reality, and did not want to establish any rites of nature worship. So, with the definition of religion given above, it was not a religion per se.[24] This shows, once again, how complicated, confused, and difficult to define is the whole notion of *religion*.[25] Nazism was a "Political Religion" because it was a totalitarian system.

In an earlier work, I called Hitler an atheist.[26] Above, I stated that the best term for Hitler's beliefs was pantheism. However, since Hitler's "god" was merely either nature itself or else the impersonal laws of nature, and since I have defined the term "god" as denoting a personal being, then in the sense that I am defining the terms, Hitler may quite legitimately be thought of as an atheist.[27] This is because his pantheism seems basically to be a form of naturalism combined with a religious feeling of reverence toward the universe itself. This form of pantheism included trying to follow the "will" of this pantheistic deity, by obeying the laws of nature, which Hitler primarily thought of in terms of the survival of the fittest. However, because he used the terms "god," and "religion," Hitler's "atheism," was much different from the militant atheism of the Marxists.[28]

The "One" or Absolute

This basic concept of an impersonal, immanent "god," or the One or Absolute as I have called it, was popular in Germany in intellectual circles in the century or so before Hitler. In various forms, it was the concept held by

---

24. Weikart, *Hitler's Religion*. 1–37. Alan Bullock writes "Stalin and Hitler were materialists not only in their dismissal of religion but in their insensitivity to humanity as well." Bullock, *Hitler and Stalin*, 382. If one is a pantheist and believes that God *is* the material universe, and that the universe is all that exists, one can be a pantheist, a materialist, and an atheist.

25. See for example Burleigh, *Third Reich*, 1–23.

26. Beckwith and Parrish, *See the gods Fall*, 139. Others have said the same thing.

27. Payne writes, "They [fascist ideas] represented a specific attempt to achieve a modern, normally atheistic form of transcendence." Payne, *Fascism*, 11. Nolte offers more on the roots of fascism and argues that "[F]ascism was termed 'resistance to transcendence.'" Nolte, *Three Faces*, 537. This definition could be derived from fascism's oldest as well as its more recent forms. A rejection of transcendence entails the rejection of a transcendent God. However, fascists sought an entirely different transcendence; something that would transcend their contemporary society. Payne, *History of Fascism*, 9.

28. "The Fuhrer is deeply religious, though completely anti-Christian. He views Christianity as a symptom of decay. Rightly so. It is a branch of the Jewish race." (April 8, 1941). *Goebbel's Diaries*, 77.

the German thinkers Fichte,[29] Schelling,[30] Hegel,[31] Haeckel,[32] and others, even including, in a way, Schopenhauer.[33] The English Hegelians such as F. H. Bradley,[34] also developed a form of pantheism, in which the universe is the expression or appearance of an impersonal being, called the Absolute. Indeed, such a concept of God goes back to the pre-Christian world, where ancient philosophers such as the Stoics put forth the notion that God is a material being whose substance fills the universe.[35]

How much of these thinkers Hitler had read I do not know, but the ideas were floating around, and could easily have been picked up by an intellectual dilettante such as Hitler. So, Hitler did not believe in a personal god, certainly not the classical or biblical God, but he did seem to believe in the universe, and the laws by which it operates, as a sort of deity. However, by the standard I have established above, he was not a theist.

What about Spinoza's "God"?

Now, compare this concept to one held by someone who was completely opposed to Hitler and what he stood for—Albert Einstein. He also seemed to conceive of God as one who is responsible for the rationality that expresses itself in the orderliness of nature. By his own admission, Einstein believed in the God of Spinoza.[36] Spinoza was a seventeenth century Jewish philoso-

---

29. For a good, short introduction to Fichte, see Copleston, *History of Philosophy*, Vol. 7, Part I, 32–93. See also Pinkard, *German Philosophy*, 105–30.

30. On Schelling, see Copleston, *History of Philosophy*, Vol. 7, Part I, 94–158; and Pinkard, *German Philosophy*, 172–98, and 317–32.

31. On Hegel, see Copleston, *History of Philosophy*, Vol. 7, Part I, 159–247; and Pinkard, *German Philosophy*, 217–304.

32. On Haeckel, see Gasman, *Scientific Origins*; Weikart, *From Darwin*; and Noll, *Jung Cult*, 47–54. To show how variegated the ideas that went into making National Socialism were, see also Goodrick-Clarke, *Occult Roots*.

33. On Schopenhauer see Copleston, *History of Philosophy*, Vol. 7, Part II, 25–59; Jaquette, *Philosophy of Schopenhauer*; and Pinkard, *German Philosophy*, 333–45. Schopenhauer is admittedly a rather odd case. He rejected both pantheism and the idealism of Hegel but thought that what was ultimately real was "Will." Schopenhauer's main work is *World as Will and Representation*, 3 Vols. According to Weikart, Hitler claimed that "he carried a five-volume set of Schopenhauer's work with him during World War I and learned a great deal from reading them." Weikart, *Hitler's Religion*, 16.

34. On Bradley, see Copleston, *History of Philosophy*, Vol 8, Part I, 214–47. Bradley's most important work is *Appearance and Reality*.

35. On the Stoics, see Copleston, *History of Philosophy*, Vol. 1, Part II, 120–44 and 165–81. For longer works on the Stoics, see Introduction, note 6.

36. Einstein stated, "I believe in Spinoza's God who reveals Himself in the orderly harmony of what exists, not in a God who concerns Himself with fates and actions of

pher, who lived in Holland, and was excommunicated by his fellow Jews because of his unorthodox views.[37]

Spinoza's "God," which he sometimes called "God or Nature," was everything. That is, Spinoza thought that everything that existed was a part of God. Spinoza's views have been labeled by different people as theistic, atheistic, and pantheistic. My own opinion is that he is best described as a pantheist, for he thought that everything that exists is part of God, and that God is not to be thought of as being personal, though conscious in some sense. Spinoza theorized that because we human beings and other creatures are conscious, and since we are part of "God," then this "God" is conscious.

Even though in some sense Spinoza's "God" is conscious, it is doubtful that such a being should be described as a god—since I have defined a god as necessarily something that is a personal being. For this reason, to make things clearer, I will call the "God" of the pantheists the "Absolute." However, can the gods ascribed by Spinoza and Einstein be coherently described as being *impersonal*? The problem can be expressed, for example, in Einstein's statement that his god expresses himself in the rationality of the universe. How can an impersonal being express itself in rationality? The answer to this inconsistency is not clear. We can perhaps conceive of God as being some sort of super computer, and the universe is the product of its programming. But the computer would not be conscious. So, it would not be considered a god by the account given here.

But, by the description given by Einstein and others, it seems to be implied that their God is conscious. And if so, and if their God is rational and able to create the universe in all its complexity, then it must be a conscious, purposive, personal being. If this would be the case, then it would also seem that their God would be able to speak in some way. Thereby, it could hear prayers and respond to them, and so forth. Of course, their God might not actually do this, but it is at least conceivable that it could. In short, this impersonal god, to exist as described, must be thought of in personal terms. This is the same basic problem that I mentioned above with the Islamic concept of god—that he is conceived as being non-personal but has at the same time characteristics that entail existence of a personal being.

So, we should ask *what is meant by a personal god*. Perhaps what Einstein and some others meant by this term is simply that their God was not interested in individual human beings—listening to and answering prayers, working miracles, and so on. Instead, this God thinks constantly about eternal necessary truths. Aristotle's God seemed to be like this, as

---

human beings." Jaeger, *Einstein*, 86.

37. Scruton, *Spinoza*, 38–55.

his God eternally considered eternal truths that were in his mind but knew nothing about the concrete universe. This may be personal in one sense, but not in another sense.

Panentheism.

To make things even more confusing, there are attempts to combine theism and pantheism. This theory is known as "*Panentheism*." As was explained above, in panentheism, the universe is God's body, as in pantheism. However, panentheists also think that God is *personal*, that in effect, God has a mind as well as a body.[38]

By these criteria, panentheists must be theists, as they believe that their God is personal. But at the same time, God is also impersonal in some respects, as the physical universe is considered his body. Indeed, panentheists typically think that their God's mind and body are, in some sense, identical with each other. There are many other aspects to panentheism, but I will address only a few relevant points about it here.

Panentheism may, therefore, be "half way" between theism and pantheism. Perhaps panentheism's strongest following is in some of the more liberal religious denominations in North America. The idea behind *panentheism* is to keep the notion of a personal God, but to limit him in various ways—to avoid the problems of evil and the existence of free will and divine foreknowledge. The concept of a limited God, they argue, cannot be legitimately attacked for having created a universe with so much evil in it, as he does not have the power to stop it.[39] Further, since on the panentheistic model of God, God doesn't know the future in exhaustive detail, the problems of how human beings can have free will in the face of God's having an exhaustive knowledge of the future—which many have thought to be contradictory to each other—are thus avoided.

Summary of Concepts of God

It can be seen from the above discussion that there are many different concepts of God, and that the very concept of God is vague around the edges, in

---

38. On panentheism or process theism, see Whitehead, *Process and Reality*; Hartshorne, *Creative Synthesis*; *Omnipotence*; and *Logic of Perfection*; and Dombrowski, *Analytic Theism*. For critiques of panentheism, see Gruenler, *Inexhaustible God*; and Nash, *Process Theology*. See also Richards, *Untamed God*, 152–94.

39. This may clear God from allowing evil, as he cannot prevent its existence. But it comes with the considerable price that there is no hope for a final triumph over evil.

the sense that in some cases it is difficult to say whether the being in question should legitimately be called a god or not. On one end, we have various versions of pantheism or panentheism, in some views of which God is the Absolute but at the same time is either considered to be personal, or else have properties that imply that the being is personal. On the other side, we have concepts like those of ancient paganism, or with the modern religion of Mormonism, with unquestionably personal but finite gods.

The problem here is: *how finite, how limited can a being be, and still be considered a god?* There is, I think, no completely clear answer to this question. At some point, a being which is alleged to be a god, but which is finite, becomes so weak that it is not worthy of worship. I would say that the god in question must be able at least to supersede the laws of nature, or, as in the case of Mormonism, must have powers that are the equivalent to being able to have a complete knowledge of nature's laws, and act in accordance to them.

The God of Classical or Perfect Being Theism

We have seen that there exists a cluster of concepts that are necessarily included in the concept of *deity*. They include a great deal of power, knowledge, and immortality. To be a god, a being must be personal, as only a personal being can have knowledge. One version of it is called *classical theism,* or the classical concept of God. A closely related concept is called *perfect being theology,* because in it, God is a perfect being. These terms are not identical, as will be discussed below, but for the most part they agree with each other. This is the *fundamental concept of God* that has been held by most western theistic thinkers for the last two thousand years and has been considered *orthodox* in many different Christian denominations. It is to this concept of God that I will now turn.

> And indeed, we believe that thou art a being than
> which nothing greater can be conceived.
>
> Anselm[40]

---

40. Anselm, *Basic Writings,* 7. For some recent defenses of theism, see for example Craig and Moreland, *Blackwell Companion to Natural Theology*; Feser, *Last Superstition* and *Five Proofs*; Foster, *Divine Lawmaker*; Parrish, *God and Necessity*; Pruss and Rasmussen, *Necessary Existence*; Spitzer, *New Proofs*; Swinburne, *Existence of God*; Loke, *God and Ultimate Origins*; Bussey, *Signposts to God*; and Walls and Dougherty, *Two Dozen.*

I put these two concepts of *classical* and *perfect being* theism together, though they are not necessarily the same. However, the two terms will be used as synonyms unless I indicate otherwise, because they are quite close in meaning—both conceive of God as the "Greatest Possible Being." The major reason that they may be different is that classical theism has a doctrine of absolute *divine simplicity*, which perfect being theism need not necessarily have, or at least not the same doctrine of simplicity. This difference will be discussed on the section of simplicity below.

The perfect being concept of God sees God as omniscient, omnipotent, omnipresent, necessarily existent, omnibenevolent, incomprehensible, transcendent, immanent, simple (in some sense), and infinite.[41] I will explain these one at a time. It should be noted that theologians and philosophers, even those who consider themselves to be classical theists, are not in complete agreement on exactly what God's attributes are. Nonetheless, there is a common core that is essential to perfect being theism. These attributes are all derivable from the concept of God as the Greatest Possible Being. That is, God is the greatest being, not only that exists, but also that could ever possibly exist. In other worlds, necessarily nothing can ever be greater than he is, or be equal to him.

Omniscient

This means that God knows everything, or, to be more specific, God knows the truth of every statement or proposition. God knows all that exists or could exist. He not only knows how many hairs there are on your head, he knows how many electrons there were in Argentina on February seventh, 1953, at 6:02 in the evening, Eastern Standard Time. He knows if there is any place in the decimal expansion of pi where there are seven 7s in a row. In short, God's knowledge is identical with both all actual, existing things and all possibilities. Anything that is coherently thinkable is thought of, in some manner, by God.

What I mean by this is that all the truths that there are, or could be, are contained in God's mind. In a sense, they are identical with God's mind. Another way of saying this is, all propositions are thoughts in the mind of God. God has all possible calculations forever in his thoughts. Indeed, on the theistic view being propounded here, this is what numbers are—truths about math thought by God. In my view, all these "abstract entities" (to be

---

41. Or at least the maximal combination of these. See Nagasawa, *Maximal God*.

discussed later) are therefore ideas in the mind of God, rather than independent objects as in Platonism.[42]

This does not settle all the disputes about the concept of *omniscience*. There is the problem of *indexicals*, for example. How can God know the truth of statements like, "It is raining now," if in some sense, he exists at all places and times?[43] Or how can God know the statement, "I, Paul am the poorest poker player in Plymouth," if, in fact, he is not Paul? There is also the problem of God's knowledge of the future. How does God know things that haven't happened yet, and if he knows the future in exhaustive detail, how is free will possible?[44] However, whatever one thinks of these issues, the basic idea is that *God knows everything*.[45]

Omnipotent

Omnipotence means that *God has maximal power*. Anything that can be done, can be done by God. The only limitations to God's power are the laws of logic. Even God cannot make $2 + 2 = 5$, or make a triangle have fourteen sides (while remaining a triangle), or make married bachelors, or anything of that nature, because doing so would entail a contradiction. God is purely rational and in him there is no darkness at all.[46]

However, it must not be thought that logic is something foreign to, or prior to God, over which he has no control. God cannot "break" the laws of logic because he cannot deny himself.[47] In the theistic view being propounded here, in a very real sense, logic is God-thinking. Our thoughts are logical when they match God's.

In short, God has total power over all things, *in accordance with his nature as the Greatest Possible Being*. He has the power to do anything that does not break the law of non-contradiction. The law of non-contradiction is itself a part of God—it is the way that God thinks. Can God therefore create a rock that he cannot lift? No, he cannot, but the reason is *not* that there

---

42. For a presentation and discussion of the different theories on this matter, see Gould, *Beyond the Control of God?* The essay in this that I endorse is that of Welty, "Theistic Conceptual Realism."

43. On the problem of indexicals and God's knowledge, see Kvanvig, *Possibility*.

44. Books about different positions of free will, and how they relate to God's foreknowledge, see Basinger, *Predestination*.

45. Although holding that God is omniscient, some philosophers think that God does not always entertain or think about everything that he knows. See Craig, *God Over All*, 88–89.

46. 1 John 1:5.

47. 2 Timothy, 2:13.

is any limitation to his power. He can create a rock of any size (or weight, or slipperiness, or whatever) and can lift a rock of any size. The only rocks that God cannot create are ones that cannot exist.

Omnipresent

By omnipresent, what is meant is that *God is everywhere*, in some non-spatial and non-temporal sense. Fundamentally, God is present everywhere and is causally active at all places and times. There is nothing that is independent of God. Indeed, it is not possible that anything exists independently of God. All possibility resides in him, and thus anything that exists or could exist is subject to him. There is nowhere that could possibly be, that is outside of God.

Necessarily Existent

God is a necessarily existing being.[48] This has been interpreted in a couple of ways. One way has been to define him as *factually* necessary. Simply put, if God exists, then he has always existed and cannot cease to exist. However, on this definition, God might not have existed at all.[49]

The other interpretation, and the interpretation that I defend, is that *God exists in all possible worlds*. This concept is probably unknown by many readers of this book, so I shall briefly clarify it.[50]

Possible Worlds

The term "world" being used here is not understood in the usual sense of a planet like Earth. Rather, a possible world is *a totality of what could have been*. The actual world, the one in which we live, consists of everything that exists, everything that was, and everything that will be. The actual world is therefore one of an infinite number of possible (or at least imaginable)

---

48. Parrish, *God and Necessity*.

49. Philosophers who take this view include Swinburne, *Coherence of Theism*; Yandell, *Christianity and Philosophy*; and Geisler and Watkins, *Perspectives*. There are philosophers and others who hold that God does in fact exist, and is omnipotent, omniscient, and so on, but that he might have failed to exist or have existed and not have been omnipotent, etc. Since God cannot be caused to exist, and on this theory does not either exist nor have his attributes by his own nature, then he must exist in the manner that he does by chance. See Parrish, *God and Necessity*, 23–48.

50. On this see Plantinga, *Nature of Necessity*.

worlds, but the one that is—that has been actualized—that is *real*. Anything is possible in this sense if its denial does not entail a contradiction.

Other possible worlds are ways that things could have been otherwise. For example, there are possible worlds where the North did not win the Civil War, or where the Roman Empire never fell, or where the Detroit Lions win a Super Bowl.

There are worlds where each of us human beings, individually or collectively, does not exist. There are worlds where not only human history is different, but so is geology—where the earth or whole the universe is formed differently than it is. There are possible worlds where the laws of nature are different than they are. This is because no contradiction is entailed by thinking that the laws of nature could be other than they are.[51]

There are, however, no possible worlds where, for example, 2 + 2 = 5, or where people can be taller than themselves, or where red is a number rather than a color. By this I do not mean that we might not have different names for things. For instance, we could have called the number three "red" instead of three. Rather, red, the actual color, is necessarily a color, instead of a number or anything else. This kind of thing is precluded by what these entities are essentially—what their basic nature is.[52]

In some sense, if we delve deeper, however, we see that the existence of God changes what is possible. There are worlds that could have been, in the sense that God could have created them if he had wanted to, but that he never *would* have. Worlds where evil is finally and forever triumphant in a universe would be worlds that God has the *power* to create but not the *will* to do so. Such a world would contradict God's fundamental goodness, and therefore he would never want to create it, even though he had the sheer power to do so. So, such a world as the one where evil is triumphant is not, in the final analysis, a possible world at all, given theism.

God, a Necessary Being

By saying that God is a necessarily existing being, I am not just saying that in every world where God exists, he exists as God instead of as a meter maid working in Ypsilanti, Michigan. Rather, just like the statement 2 + 2 = 4 is true

---

51. This is denied by Oppy, among others. See his essay "Ultimate Naturalistic Causal Explanation," 46–63. For a critique of Oppy, see Parrish, "Against a Naturalistic Causal Account of Reality," 415–26. For more on this matter, see Parrish and Wartick, "Coming into Existence," 71–89. See also Parrish, "Rundle," 471–77, and "Theism," 433–50.

52. On this see Plantinga, *Nature of Necessity*, 1–13.

in every possible world, so too, given classical or perfect being theism, the statement that God exists, and exists as God, the greatest conceivable being, is true in every possible world. God is, therefore, a necessary being.[53]

Of course, not everyone agrees that the existence of such a being is, in fact, possible. These reasons given by the detractors of God's absolutely necessary existence seem to me to be *question begging*.[54] Here I will just mention one objection that has been influential. Jim Holt writes in response to the concept of a necessarily existing God, "There is nothing inherently self-contradictory . . . in the supposition that a maximally great being does *not* exist . . . The God it [the Ontological Argument] purports to deliver is a necessary being. His existence is a truth of pure logic, a tautology.[55] But tautologies are empty propositions. Since they are true regardless of how reality is, they are devoid of explanatory content."[56] This has been a common objection to the idea of God's necessary existence; that we can conceive of his non-existing. Since it is supposed that anything that we can conceive of without contradiction is possible, then God's non-existence is possible, and God cannot *necessarily* exist.

There are several things in the above quotation that need explaining. First, Holt is speaking here in the context of the Ontological Argument, which argues from the concept of God to the necessary existence of God. I am not using this argument here, though I have defended a version of it elsewhere.[57] He seems to think that the concept of the necessary being depends upon the validity of the Ontological Argument. If that is what he means, I disagree. God can be thought of as necessarily existing whether the Ontological Argument is a good argument or not.

Second, Holt's point that we can think of God's non-existence without self-contradiction, and that therefore he cannot necessarily exist, is misguided. There are statements that we can immediately see to be either necessarily true or false. For example, $2 + 2 = 4$ is obviously necessarily true, while $2 + 2 = 137\frac{1}{2}$ is obviously necessarily false. Other truths are

---

53. Sometimes it is called *metaphysical necessity*. In an earlier work (Parrish, *God and Necessity*) I called this kind of necessity, a *broadly logical necessity*, or sometimes just *logically necessary*—though this last phrase is sometimes reserved for concepts in formal logic. Though I still think that this is a good name for it, the concept of necessarily existing in all possible worlds has another name, which is *absolutely necessary*—see Bob Hale, *Necessary Beings*. In this work, these titles will be used as synonyms.

54. For a response to these objections, see Parrish, *God and Necessity*, 49–80.

55. A tautology is something that is true by definition, like all bachelors are unmarried.

56. Holt, *Why Does the World Exist?*, 117–18.

57. Parrish, *God and Necessity*, 81–119.

beyond our ability to see. For example, there is Goldbach's conjecture, that every even number greater than two is the sum of two primes.[58] The conjecture is either necessarily true or necessarily false, but it is not intuitively obvious to us, and at present, it cannot be proven by mathematicians to be either true or false. So, that God's non-existence seems conceivable to us shows little, because God, being the Greatest Possible Being, entails that he is beyond our capacity to fully comprehend. Just as the falsity of Goldbach's conjecture may seem conceivable to us, but in fact may be necessarily true, so God's non-existence may be conceivable, but God would still necessarily exist. Indeed, this is what I maintain. *God's necessary existence is obvious to God, because he fully comprehends himself, but not to us, because we cannot fully comprehend him.*

Finally, the main reason that I am here putting forth the concept of a necessary God is not because his existence seems intuitively possible (though to many people it does). Rather, as will become apparent in the next chapter, *God's necessarily existing can explain better than any other concept why reality is the way that it is.* Indeed, I will argue that it is the only concept that can explain why the universe exists in the manner that it does.

Omnibenevolent

God is *all good*. It is not just the case that God is pretty good, or very good, or good most of the time, but he is completely, always, and necessarily good. He could not possibly be other than completely good. Further, he is the source and sanction of all other goodness.

With the view of God that I am putting forth, what moral truths are—truths like one ought not torture innocent people for fun—are ultimately ideas in the mind of God that God endorses. They are necessarily existing truths. The opposite statement, that one ought to torture innocent people for fun, is a necessarily existing falsehood, for though God understands the statement, he does not endorse it, and instead, absolutely rejects it.

Incomprehensible

Incomprehensible is a word that has more than one meaning. Taken literally, it means that nothing can be understood of that particular thing. Taken in a more moderate sense, it means that something of said thing cannot be

---

58. Rucker, *Infinity*, 99.

fully or completely comprehended, that there are aspects about it that we do not understand, and perhaps never can understand.

Literally vs Moderately Incomprehensible

The position that I will take here is the latter, moderate sense of the word. The main reason for taking the moderate view is that the former, literal meaning, with its idea of a totally incomprehensible being, is incoherent; it is self-contradictory. In the proposing of some being that we cannot know anything about, we are saying that we do, in fact, know something about it, hence the contradiction. To say the thing is incomprehensible (in the strong, former sense of the word) is to say that there is something, about which we know that we don't know anything—which is a contradictory statement. To say anything about a thing is to imply that we know something about it. Surprisingly, there have been many thinkers who have believed the idea that we can know absolutely nothing about God, though they could not consistently hold to this.[59]

Another reason to take the moderate view of "incomprehensible" is that a being about which we know nothing is totally useless. To say of God that he is completely unknowable is to say that he is irrelevant to anything. For these reasons, and more, I will defend the position that God is, in part, knowable. In other words, we can, and do, know something about him, though because he is the greatest of all possible beings, he is also far beyond our capacity (or the capacity of any finite being) to ever completely understand. Only God can completely understand God.[60]

Analogical vs Univocal Knowledge of God

There is a related matter which needs to be discussed here. This is, whether our knowledge of God is entirely *analogical* or also partly *univocal*.[61] To say that two different things are *analogical* is to say that they are similar, but not the same thing. For example, we can call both a person and a cat good. But what a good person is, is quite different from what a good cat is. There is a similarity, but the concept of good is not the same in the two cases. *Univocal*

---

59. Clouser, *Myth*, 167–95. For a response to Clouser on this issue, see Parrish, *God and Necessity*, 75–80.

60. See Plantinga, *Does God have a Nature?*

61. For a sophisticated Thomistic defense of analogical knowledge of God that does admit of univocal concepts, see Geisler and Corduan, *Philosophy of Religion*, 252–71. For a critique of this viewpoint, see Henry, *God, Revelation*, 363–66.

simply means the same. For example, two women may be good in the same way. Both are honest, kind, hard-working, and so forth, while a good cat is merely friendly and doesn't harm things.

It may well be the majority view in the history of theology that we have only analogical knowledge of God. Not only is there a long tradition, but also many theologians today defend this view. It is understandable why people hold to this view, as human beings are so different from God that it may seem that the only knowledge of God that we can have is analogical.

Nonetheless, I will argue that we must also have some univocal knowledge of God. This subject could fill a whole book by itself, but I must be brief here. I will give two arguments.

First, a purely analogical knowledge of God would not give any real knowledge. For example, let us suppose that someone tells you that there is such a thing as a good "Broxable." You have no idea what a broxable is. All you know is that your friend says that it is a good one. In this case, how much would you know about the broxable? You would know nothing. For not only do you know nothing apart from the fact that it is in some sense "good," you would not know how to apply the term "good." We can call a cat a good cat and have some idea of what we are talking about, even though the goodness of a cat is different from the goodness of a human being, because we know what cats are. We have some univocal knowledge of what it is to be a cat: they are mammals, small, are domesticated, fuzzy (except for a very strange hairless breed), sleep a lot, etc. Because we have this univocal knowledge of cats, we can then legitimately use analogical knowledge of them.

But if we have no univocal knowledge of a broxable—no clue as to what it is or what it is like—then it follows necessarily that we have no, and can have no, idea how to apply the concept of goodness to it. Similarly, with God, we can say that God is good and have some idea of what that means because we know some of what God is like—that God is the greatest possible or conceivable being, rather than a human being or an animal.

The second argument for univocal knowledge is simply that, in fact, we do have some univocal knowledge of God. Both God and some human beings know that two plus two equals four, and that Cleveland, the home of the Indians and the Browns, is in Ohio. It is, of course, true that our knowledge is temporal—there is a time when we learned it—fallible, and not exhaustive. God's knowledge, on the other hand, is eternal—he always knows everything—infallible, and exhaustive—he knows everything about every subject. Nonetheless, the kernel of the knowledge that two plus two equals four and that Cleveland is in Ohio, is the same, though grasped by quite different modes of access—human versus divine. Though the modes of access are different for God and a human being, the proposition or statement known is the same.

For some reason, many theistic thinkers have been attracted to the idea of an unknowable God.[62] Perhaps it is because it can be made to sound quite pious—as in, "God is so much greater than we are that we can't know anything about him." Besides being self-contradictory, it seems to me that this position contradicts the Bible in many places. For example, in Romans 1:20, Paul states, "For since the creation of the world His invisible attributes are clearly understood by the things that are made, even His eternal power and Godhead . . . " Having an unknowable God also makes "God" a useless concept (remember the Broxable?) because, were God completely unknowable, one could not relate to him.

Transcendent

The concept of God's transcendence is that he is not an object in the spatio-temporal universe. Unlike atoms, rocks, the Eiffel Tower, the planet Jupiter, the Andromeda Galaxy, and we humans, God does not exist as an object in space and time. The concept of transcendence also implies that God *is not* space and time, unlike the pantheistic and panentheistic theories that have been discussed above, where space and time are purported to be part of God. Further, the universe is not an emanation of God, but rather a free creation.[63] God does not emanate the universe like the sun emanates sunlight; rather, God freely chose to create this universe and this possible world, instead of the infinite number of other universes and worlds that he could have created (or not have created anything at all).

It should be noted that the traditional view of transcendence includes God's being outside of time. Many theologians and philosophers today consider God to be inside time, in some manner. I will not investigate this matter in this book.[64]

---

62. See for example, Holmes, *Quest*, 200. To which I reply that the concept of a completely unknowable God (or anything else for that matter) is a totally useless idea, and if it were true that we couldn't know anything about God, theologians would be out of a job. If God were literally unknowable, then we could not say or even think about God at all. The concept of God would be meaningless. For a history of the concept, see Smith, *Indescribable God*. Unfortunately, Smith endorses the concept of an unknowable God.

63. See Jaki, *Science and Creation*. See also his *God and The Cosmologists*; *Origin of Science*; *Purpose of It All*; *Road of Science*; and *Savior of Science*. Jaki holds that the doctrine of God as a free creator rather than as the necessary emanator of the universe allowed for the rise of modern science.

64. One defense of God's being in time in some sense is found in Padgett, *God,*

Immanent

This is the opposite, but not contradictory to, transcendence. What it means is that all of space and time are the present to God, and he is causally active in all parts of space and time. It must be remembered that God's "being everywhere" is not like being spread out throughout space and time like some sort of cosmic gas. Rather, no place or time is a place or time where God is not active. Perhaps the best way of thinking about this is the following: when thinking about something, and understanding it completely, one is close to it in some non-spatial respect. Similarly, because God knows everything perfectly, including everything that he has created, everything is present to his knowledge, as well as his power, because it is only by God's continual exercising of his power that everything else that exists (besides God) continues to exist.

Infinite

God is described as being infinite. One meaning of this is that it is shorthand for his omni-properties: omniscience, omnipotence, omnipresence, etc. That is, his knowledge, power, and presence are infinite in extent. For example, there is an infinite number of true propositions or statements. There is even an infinite number of propositions in mathematics alone. That is, it is true that one plus one equals two, one plus two equals three, and so on for all the infinite "number" of numbers. There is also an infinite number of tasks that God could perform, and since God is omnipotent, all tasks that he would try to perform would be successful, whether he actually does perform them or not.

Sovereign

God is sovereign. God is in *complete control* of everything. He knows everything and has power over everything. Anything that exists only does so because God created it and sustains it in existence. Nothing could possibly exist that is outside of God's control. What this means is that without God's sustaining power over any other thing, it would simply cease to exist, or cease to exist as the kind of thing that it is. To the extent that any creature goes against God, it is only because he lets it do so. God chooses which of the infinite number of different worlds to be actualized.

Eternity. For a defense of the notion that God is timeless, see Sansbury, *Beyond Time*.

Trinity

This is one additional attribute that is accepted by orthodox Christians, but no one else. Put simply, the doctrine is that God is one being who is composed of three persons. This is a doctrine that is difficult to understand, but which is rich in implications. Not all who claim to be Christians hold to this, for there are theologians who are Unitarians, and also some who claim to be Trinitarians and yet hold to a trinity that does not have three persons in one God, but three something else.[65] I will not enter into a long discussion of this here, but I believe that the trinity is best thought of as three persons—three centers of consciousness in the one God.[66]

The concept of the trinity also helps provide a solution to the philosophical problem of the One and the Many. Put simply, the problem of the one and the many is how both the unity and diversity of reality can be explained. If ultimate reality is sheer oneness, then where does the diversity come from? If, on the other hand, diversity is ultimately real, what explains its unity? In the trinity, both are equally ultimate.[67]

One additional point about the doctrine of the trinity should be made. The doctrine that God is three persons in one being ensures (or should ensure) that God is truly thought of as a personal being—that he is conscious, knows, wills, and feels.[68]

Simplicity

> How then do all things come from the One, which is simple and has in it no diverse variety, or any kind of duality? It is because there is nothing in it that all things come from it: in order that being may exist, the One is not being, but the generator of being.
>
> PLOTINUS[69]

The above idea has always seemed to me to make no sense. How can something that has nothing be the cause of everything? Yet this view has had a long history in Western thought.

One of my books is entitled *God and Necessity: A Defense of Classical Theism*. In the book, I briefly criticized the doctrine of divine simplicity,

---

65. See for example Ward, *Christ and the Cosmos*. For a more orthodox doctrine of the trinity, see McCall, *Which Trinity?*

66. See Clark, *Trinity*.

67. On the One and the Many and the doctrine of the trinity, see Frame, *Apologetics*, 44–47, 80–83, 126, 267–70.

68. Van Til, *Defense*, 47.

69. Plotinus, Enneads, V.2.1.3–8. Quoted in Shaw, "Platonic Siddhas," 282.

specifically the notion that all of God's attributes are identical with each other. It was pointed out to me that this judgment is a denial of simplicity as it has been classically understood, so, for me to subtitle the book as a defense of classical theism is something of a misnomer.

In retrospect, I should have subtitled the book a Defense of Perfect Being Theology, which would have avoided the problem. I also should have been clearer in the brief discussion that I gave in the book about simplicity, for there my emphasis is mostly negative, without much about the doctrine of simplicity that I do accept.

However, I will note several caveats. First, not all writers in the Christian tradition have held to what I call the *strong version of divine simplicity*; in the last century, the doctrine has come under heavy attack. Second, what is meant by simplicity by the different writers may not be the same concept. Though the words may be the same, they might not always mean exactly the same thing. Third, I do accept a doctrine of divine simplicity. What I reject is the strong or absolute[70] version of simplicity wherein all of God's attributes are identical with each other, because it seems incoherent to me. I think that my concept of God may be considered a legitimate form of classical theism. But people do not always agree on what a word should mean, so there is room for a difference of opinion here.

As stated, this doctrine holds that God is *simple*. However, what is meant by this? First, God is a unity, and cannot be divided. Second, it has usually been the case that God is conceived of as not being spread out in space and time—which is another way of saying that God is aspatial and atemporal. Unlike us, God does not experience a series of moments of time in his consciousness, nor does he think of himself as existing as a certain point of space.

Another meaning of simplicity is that God's *essence* is identical with his *existence*. Which is to say that God *is* his properties; God is identical with being omniscient, omnipotent, omnibenevolent, etc. This is unlike us human beings, who are not identical with what we know, what power we have, our moral status, etc. For example, I could have existed and known different things than I know, have different powers, and have a different moral status. We are not identical with our properties, at least not most of them. It may be true that, for example, I am identical with having the property of being human—I could not exist and have not been a human being. God is identical with his properties; it is not possible that God could exist other than he is, though this can be interpreted in more than one way. It could mean that God could not be different from what he is in any possible world, or it could mean that God is somewhat different from world to world, because what he knows is different.

---

70. See Feser, *Five Proofs*, 189–96.

One other way in which God has been considered *simple* is that not only is he identical with his properties, but he is *absolutely simple*, which entails that all his properties are absolutely identical with each other. This would mean, for example, that God's omniscience is identical with his omnipotence. Or more specifically, that his knowing that Cleveland is in Ohio is *absolutely identical* with—is the exact same thing as—his ability to create kangaroos, or his knowledge that two plus two equals four, or the fact that he is loving. I think this is problematic.

Though this very strong kind of simplicity seems to have often been held by Christian and other thinkers throughout history (probably the majority), as stated, it seems contradictory, and thus should be rejected. The reason I say this is because many concepts involved are irreducible to each other. That is, if the concepts involved in the notion of two plus two equals four are reduced or equated in some manner with the concept of the creation of kangaroos, then they describe neither. If they are eliminated, then they no longer exist, and hence are not part of God's essence.[71]

One reason given to hold to "strong" simplicity is that if God is composed of parts, then it is possible that the parts separate, and hence God would not necessarily exist, and if he did, would not necessarily exist as God. The problem with this argument seems apparent to me. Take for example the number seven. The number seven has the properties of being odd, of being a prime, and being one larger than the number six, for example. None of these properties is conceptually reducible to one of the others. Yet it is also true to say that the number seven cannot lose any of these properties, and hence cease to exist, or turn into another number. In a sense, the number seven is simple (although in another it is not, being composed of seven ones), yet its properties are not reducible to each other, and seven cannot be other than it is. Likewise, I argue that God's properties are not identical, yet God cannot lose them, for they are all contained in the concept of God as the Greatest Possible Being. God's attributes or properties are not things that are simply added onto him, but in a real sense, *are* him. God's being omnipotent entails

---

71. For a defense of a strong definition of simplicity, see Dolezal, *God Without Parts*. For a critique of Dolezal, see Parrish and Wartick, "Dilemma of Divine Simplicity," 13–24, and 71–84. For a more philosophical defense of divine simplicity see Miller, *Most unlikely God*. He writes, "Moreover, even though the likeness is not of any univocal kind—no matter how attenuated—it cannot be dismissed as inconsequential, for a slight knowledge of God is to be more esteemed than a profound knowledge of lesser beings." Miller, *Most unlikely God*, 162. For all of Miller's insightful work, I think that it must be rejected. What this leads to is an unknowable, and impersonal god, which is a similar problem to the one that Muslims have in some theologies. For more of this critique, see Hinlicky, *Divine Simplicity*.

that he is omniscient, and vice versa. *God is simple in that all of his properties are analytically included in the concept of God.*

The problem with the argument *for* strong simplicity is that it is thinking of parts in God in the same sense that a material object is made of parts. A chair for example is made of the legs, seat, and back. These parts may be removed, and hence the chair is dependent for its existence upon the parts. However, God is not like this. His "parts" are necessarily included in his being and cannot possibly be removed. To be God is just to necessarily have the attributes that he has.

There is something seriously wrong here, for if God is, as the classical theists have always maintained, the source of all other things, then they must exist in God as their own concepts. In other words, if everything that exists or could exist has its source in God, it follows that everything exists as a distinct concept in God. This naturally means that since God knows every possibility, everything that exists or could exist does so initially as a concept in the mind of God. But for this to be the case, the concepts must be distinct, and hence not identical with each other. This seems to me to be inconsistent with absolute simplicity, where there are no distinctions on God at all.

Another problem for strong simplicity comes with the doctrine of the trinity. In strong simplicity as we have seen, there are no "parts" of God. But if that were true, then there should be only one person in the Godhead. The members of the Trinity would be numerically identical with each other. *Numerical identity* means that they are exact same thing—Clark Kent is numerically identical with Superman, as they are the same person. The Father would be numerically identical with the Son, and both would be numerically identical with the Spirit. Strong simplicity is, thus, a denial of the Trinity.

So, instead of a doctrine of absolute simplicity, I would put forth the following: God is the Greatest Possible Being, and all his attributes are necessarily contained in that concept. That is, to be the Greatest Possible Being, one must be omnipotent and omniscient, and therefore God has both attributes, and thus what he is, is contained in a simple statement. Hence, all of God's properties are contained in his definition as the Greatest Possible Being. In a sense, God, simply *is* his properties, as he necessarily exists and necessarily has them.[72] He could not exist without having them, but because he exists necessarily, they necessarily exist too.

---

72. For more critiques of the concept of divine simplicity, see Hughes, *On a Complex Theory*; and Smith, *Oneness*.

Atheism[73]

> Philosophy makes no secret of it. The confession of Prometheus: [I hate the pack of gods (Gr. Transl.)] is its own confession, its own aphorism against all heavenly and earthly gods who do not acknowledge human self-consciousness as the highest divinity. It will have none other beside.
>
> KARL MARX[74]

> But to reveal my heart entirely to you, friends: if there were gods, how could I endure not to be a god! Therefore, there are no gods.
>
> FRIEDRICH NIETZSCHE[75]

> Thus the best way to conceive of the fundamental project of human reality is to say that man is the being whose project is to be God.
>
> JEAN-PAUL SARTRE[76]

---

73. For some recent defenses of atheism, see for example Everitt, *Non-Existence of God*; Martin, *Atheism*; Martin, *Cambridge Companion*; Martin and Monnier, *Impossibility*; and *Improbability*; Mackie, *Miracle of Theism*; Oppy, *Arguing About Gods*; Philipse, *God in an Age of Science*; and Sobel, *Logic and Theism*. For an older view see Nielsen, *Philosophy and Atheism*. For a response to some of the attacks on the coherence of theism, see Stone, *Atheism is False*. For a history of ancient atheism, see Whitmarsh, *Battling the Gods*.

74. Marx, "Forward to Thesis," 14–15. Similarly, Ayn Rand thought, "[T]he concept of God is insulting and degrading to man—it implies that the highest possible is not to be reached by man, that he is an inferior being who can only worship an ideal he will never achieve. By her view, there could be no breach between conceiving of the best possible and deciding to attain it. She rejected the concept of God as morally evil." Nathaniel and Brandon, *Who is Ayn Rand?*, 129. Rand's logic here is rather bizarre—it amounts to saying that if I cannot be the greatest being, then a greater being than I cannot exist. Regarding the attitudes expressed here, Shafaravich writes, "It would be more correct to speak here not of 'atheists' but of 'God-haters,' not of 'atheism': but of 'theophobia.'" Shafaravich, *Socialist Phenomena*, 235. The attitude of many of the "new atheists" would fit right into this category. See also, Jaki, *Paradox of Olbers' Paradox*, which shows the reluctance many scientists had to admitting the existence of a universe finitely old, for fear of theism.

75. Nietzsche, *Thus Spoke Zarathustra*, 110. Writes Lesley Chamberlain about Nietzsche, "The *Ubermensch* had no *ressentiment*, but Nietzsche the man was full of it." *Nietzsche in Turin*, 142.

76. Sartre, *Being and Nothingness*, 694.

> I deny God's existence and name myself his successor; or I transcend God and aim at a super-god; or I absorb God in my soul and proclaim my own divinity; or I identify God with some collective event or project; or I hold that God is the future and as such he becomes in proportion as I (or we) carry him into the dawn of a new existence. Yet, if we look closely at this list of possible atheisms, . . . we find that they present no great variety, that they are reducible, indeed, to one: putting man in the place of God.
>
> THOMAS MOLNAR[77]

Having defined theism, it should be much simpler to define *atheism*, and the kindred term, which is *agnosticism*. *Atheism* may be simply defined as the *belief* that there are no gods. *Agnosticism* on the other hand, may be thought of as the belief that one does not know if any gods exist, or, in a stronger form, the belief that one cannot know if there are any gods or not. Simple though these two definitions may seem to be, there are at least two problems attached to them that have caused confusion and that need to be explored.

Distinction between Atheism and Agnosticism

The first point is that the distinction between atheism and agnosticism may be debated. In effect, the difference between the two is based on how strongly the person disbelieves in the existence of gods. People who are thoroughly convinced that God does not exist are atheists, while those who are uncertain about the existence of God are agnostics. However, this distinction has been challenged with another definition.[78]

Some have said that these are both forms of atheism, as they both eschew any belief in the existence of God. Since theism means godism, and in Greek (the origin of the word) an "*a*" before a word means "no," then *a*theism means "no godism." And as we have seen, both atheism and

---

77. Before this, Molnar writes, "God is not god, it says, because I, man, would then be nothing, my being would be a borrowed one, I would not be *causa mei*; my freedom would be curtailed; my choice would be narrowed between good and evil; the creativity I feel surge in me would be a mere copy of the Creator's act; the feeling of elation over my exceptional gifts or deeds would be embittered by the reminder to be humble; the times in which I live and which are happiest and the most advanced, would be just one among the limited many in the economy of God; the maturity that I sense in me and in mankind would subject to errors and exaggerations like any age preceding ours." Molnar, *Theists and Atheists*, 179–80.

78. For a defense of the "atheism is simply a lack of belief in God" viewpoint, see Smith, *Atheism: The Case against God*. For a response, see Morey, *New Atheism*, 38–50.

THE COMPETING THEORIES OF EXISTENCE   89

agnosticism are "agodisms," or "no godisms." So, in both there is no belief in the existence of any gods. The first version might be named hard atheism, while the second might be named soft atheism.

The Burden of Proof

The major advantage for some people of this latter approach, and probably the main reason it is popular, is that some believe that it shifts the *burden of proof* onto the theist. The reasoning behind this is the following. If atheism is defined as merely lack of belief in God, then the atheist is not making any positive claims in saying that he or she fails to believe that God exists. All that it may mean is that there is a lack of a positive belief in the existence of God. The theist, on the other hand, is claimed to be making a positive claim that God does exist. People who make a positive claim are generally held to have the burden of proof, that is, they are supposed to be able to demonstrate or give evidence for their claim. Therefore, it is alleged, the theist bears the *burden of proof* when making the statement that God exists, while the atheist does not.

There are a couple of things that may be said in response to this. First, and obvious, if one makes the essence of atheism to merely a lack of belief in God, then it seems that rocks and blades of grass are atheists. To be made into a sensible position, one would have to specify that atheists are beings who can have a belief in the existence of God but fail to have one. This rules out things like rocks and grass, but does include adult human beings, and any other rational creatures that might exist.

The other and more important point is this: even if we accept the idea that to be an atheist is to merely have a lack of belief in God, it is still true that the vast majority of atheists do, in fact, have other relevant beliefs. Indeed, if they are adult, rational, functional human beings, they will *necessarily* have certain fundamental beliefs about the nature of reality. The clear majority of atheists today are philosophical naturalists—they believe that all that exists concretely is nature. They therefore must believe that nature's existence is independent and self-sustaining. They will also almost certainly believe that human beings and all other creatures exist because they are the end products of an unguided process of evolution. They will usually believe that human beings are purely material creatures, that all that exist are physical entities (though some are property dualists),[79] and that there is no life after

---

79. Property dualism is the theory that although the person is the brain, it has not only material properties such as size and shape, but also immaterial ones like beliefs and feelings.

death. They may believe these points with differing degrees of certainty, but most atheists will believe something similar.

People who might also be called agnostics will probably believe something of the sort, but with the proviso that they will allow that there may be more to reality, such as God, than is allowable in philosophical naturalism. They are not, if they are truly agnostics, so certain about the truth in these matters. If the atheist thinks that there is no God, then he *does*, in fact, bear some burden of proof, for he believes a statement about the nature of reality. *If the atheist thinks that there is no evidence for the existence of God, that none of the many arguments that attempt to show that God exists succeed, that too requires work. To be totally honest, he needs to answer the evidences for theism which have been put forward.*[80][81]

So, if the atheist is also a naturalist, then the atheist *does* have positive beliefs, and hence also bears some burden of proof—to be fair—if the theist does. (One can be an atheist and not be a naturalist. For example, one could be an absolute idealist, though absolute idealists are rare these days).[82]

Another point to be made is that just as with the atheist, there is, indeed, a burden of proof on the agnostic (or "soft atheist"), also. This can be put simply. To *justify theism* via evidence and argument, the theist must show that the weight of evidence is on the side of theism. Likewise, for

---

80. It is not always the case that if we have no evidence for something, then that gives us a reason to think that it does not exist. We may simply not be able to evaluate any possible evidence.

81. For a history of theistic arguments, see Levering, *Proofs of God*. See also Schneider, *God in Proof*, for an entertaining story of the history of the arguments for and against God's existence and their contemporary status.

82. Non-naturalist atheism also has debilitating problems, though since they are much less popular in modern times, I will not examine them in detail. Molnar writes, "[W]hen . . . the personalness of God is denied, only something mechanical can take its place, whether this mechanical is spiritual or material. In this case, however, the reality of the world of human experience, its wide range from mysticism to science, must be either denied and declared to be an illusion, or, if it is accepted as reality, it must be explained *why* the Supreme Mechanism—Nature, One, or Weltgeist—produced it. Now if the Supreme Mechanism produced reality by an act of will or out of a need, or again out of a benevolent or malevolent whim, then it is no longer a mechanism, it possesses a personality, a soul, an intelligence, an aspiration—all of them attributes that the pantheist philosopher rejects nevertheless as anthropomorphic! If it is not produced by any personal or intelligent ingredient in the mechanism, then the mechanism cannot be the single substance in the universe; some other substance, force, or will outside the universe compelled or influenced it to produce 'otherness', that is the things which we find in the world and in ourselves. In my view, pantheism cannot escape the horns of this dilemma." Molnar, *Theists and Atheists*, 19. See especially 137–78, for critiques of non-naturalist or spiritualized atheism.

someone *to justify atheism*, I will argue that in the same manner the atheist must show that the weight of evidence shows that God doesn't exist.

Similarly, for the *agnostic to justify that position*, he must show that the evidence for theism or atheism is roughly equal, or else show that there is no way that we can know (at least at present) whether God does or does not exist. The agnostic is therefore not off the hook, if agnosticism as an intellectual position is to be rationally justified.[83]

If an agnostic merely claims that he or she doesn't know, then it is still the case that this takes a lot of intellectual work. If one takes the stance that one must have evidential justification for one's beliefs, then the agnostic also has this burden. That is, the theist should try to establish the truth of theism—that the given evidence shows that God exists. The atheist (understood here as a hard atheist) should try and show the opposite. The agnostic to be justified, should try and show either that the cases for theism and atheism are roughly of the same strength, so that one cannot decide, or try to show that one cannot possibly decide the question.

The only way that agnostics could plausibly claim that they have no idea about whether or not God exists is if they are totally uninformed on the issue. (I would argue that not even then, for I think that at least everyone has an intuitive knowledge of God to some degree).[84]

An argument is then sometimes made that theists do not believe in every god that has ever been thought of, so why do they believe in the one that they do? An obvious response to this is that theists may think that there is good reason to believe in their God, but no good reasons to believe in other ones. The atheist may not agree, but then one may rationally believe something even though others disagree.

Is Everyone an Atheist Of Sorts?

A related argument is sometimes made that everyone is an atheist. The reason given for this is that there are countless gods which have been believed in throughout history, and no one believes in all of them. Indeed, given that the law of non-contradiction holds to religion the same as it does for everything else, no one could consistently do this. For example, if one believes that Yahweh is held to be the only God in existence, as Jews and Christians do, one cannot simultaneously believe that the gods of ancient Greek and Norse mythology exist.

---

83. On this, see Dore, *Theism*, 104–10.
84. Barrett, *Why Would Anyone Believe?*

I make this point because some atheists (frequently posted on the internet) have made the argument that Christians and other monotheists are not very different from atheists. They say something like, "You believe in one God, we believe in none. We both disbelieve in all the other gods. So, you are not that different from us. We just believe in one less god than you." There is the implication that monotheists ought to be consistent and abandon belief in all gods.

This may be put another way. Suppose that John believes in 10,000,000,001 gods (not even noticing the contradictions in doing so). However, Mary only believes in 10,000,000,000 gods, omitting only the one in charge of grass on my yard. Since she disbelieves in the one additional god that John believes in, does this make her an atheist even though she believes in the existence of 10,000,000,000 gods? That seems to be a rather strange thing to say.

To say that everyone is necessarily an atheist because they do not believe in every god that they have ever heard of or could conceive of also seems rather silly. In that case, some atheists would believe that all that exists are physical entities, while other atheists would believe that everything is caused by a personal transcendent God, who is the ultimate being in existence. To call this latter position atheism is frankly ridiculous.

There still exists a vast gap between atheism and perfect being monotheism. The Christian theist, for example, believes that ultimate reality is a personal God; that he is the creator and sustainer of all else that exists; that human beings are made in his image; that ethical truths are necessarily existing apart from human beings, coming ultimately from God; and that human beings will survive death. The average atheist on the other hand believes that ultimate reality is composed of impersonal physical entities; that the universe exists on its own; that human beings are the products of an unguided process of evolution; that either there is no objective morality or that there is morality which doesn't depend on God; and that this life is all there is.

Why is this argument made at all? Perhaps atheists who take this line of reasoning think of God in terms of being a finite, contingent being, like the gods of ancient polytheism. In this case, the atheist is thinking that there is the universe, and that the theist believes that there is a god in it. This god is just one of countless gods who have been believed in throughout history. The theist doesn't believe in any of them except for one. Therefore, says the atheist, get rid of that one final god and be consistent. We got rid of Odin and Athena; why not just get rid of Yahweh too?

The problem with this argument was shown above. Christians and other perfect being monotheists don't believe that god is just one being living in the natural universe. Rather, God is ultimate reality, upon which everything else depends.

Therefore, one should only be called an atheist if one disbelieves in any and all gods. No people who believe in some God or gods, are simultaneously atheists because they disbelieve in the existence of other gods. Theism means that one believes in the existence of some gods or God, not that one believes in all of them.

Finally, if atheists want to call everyone who does not have a positive belief in personal gods or God an atheist but does claim to believe in some sort of god, they need to be prepared to claim some disreputable characters—like Hitler—as being one of them.

Now let us turn to a discussion of *philosophical naturalism*, the belief system held by most contemporary self-proclaimed "atheists."

Naturalism

> [N]aturalism seeks to apply the methods of empirical sciences to explain natural events without reference to supernatural causes; and it derives ethical values from human experience, not theological grounds.
>
> JOHN R. SHOOK AND PAUL KURTZ[85]

> The tendency to personify nature and deify 'her', for instance, is found in many of the freethinking philosophers of the Enlightenment . . . 'Nature'—now with a capital N—came to epitomize truth, reason, and justice . . .
>
> ALLAN CHAPMAN[86]

Naturalism is a philosophical theory that holds that nature—the material universe—is all that exists. This is to say, the material universe in which we live is, in effect, rock bottom reality; there is nothing concrete that is deeper or more fundamental upon which the physical universe depends. An additional part of naturalism that is held by many is that the only (or at least by far the best) way of thinking about things and discovering truths about everything is by the natural sciences. More specifically, by natural sciences like physics, astronomy, and biology.

---

85. Shook, *Future of Naturalism*, 7.
86. Chapman, *Gods in the Sky.* 19.

The Universe(s)

In contemporary naturalism, the universe is usually thought of as being purely physical. That is, all that exists is the universe, and what the universe consists of, is matter and energy, which can be converted into each other. Besides these, there is also space and time, which are often thought of as being different attributes of the same thing.[87] Indeed, sometimes material objects and energy are themselves held to be attributes of the space and time universe. Physics is therefore considered to be the most fundamental of all the natural sciences.

When the term "universe" is used, it usually refers to our universe—the physical universe that is filled with atoms, molecules, cats, rocks, planets, stars, and galaxies, among many other things. It is the universe which has a common history, and which is apparently governed by the same natural laws everywhere and at every time. However, it is sometimes thought that there might be physical universes other than the one in which we live.

These universes might be much like ours in many ways, but have different histories, and perhaps a different set of natural laws which govern them. In some concepts of other universes, we cannot travel to them, even if, contrary to the laws of physics, we could go faster than light. In thought, though not in reality, we can conceive of ourselves traveling through space to go anywhere in our universe. For example, we can imagine ourselves traveling on the Starship Enterprise to the Andromeda galaxy, or to places vastly farther away than that. However, when it comes to other universes, we could never get to them by traveling through space and time—no matter how far we went. These places and times are not physically connected to ours. This concept is common in science fiction and fantasy.

One can imagine other universes in other ways, also. They might be, in some sense, connected to our universe, or even part of our universe, but be so far away that we cannot see them. Different sections of the universe might conceivably behave according to different laws than the ones that describe our section of the universe. Or, it can be conceived that our universe goes through cycles of expansion and collapse, and each time the universe recovers from a collapse and expands, the laws of nature might be different. In some sense of the word, these other sectors or time periods might be described as other universes.

Whether or not there are other universes is controversial, but at least it seems possible that they could exist. Indeed, there seems to be no contradiction in the existence of both God and multiple universes. However, to

---

87. On this, see Sklar, *Space*. For a more recent view of the nature of space, time, and the things that exist within them, see Wilczek, *Lightness of Being*.

be a thorough-going naturalist, one would have to believe that these other universes, if they exist, are themselves independent; they are not dependent upon anything deeper or more fundamental. Most specifically, they are not dependent upon God.

Materialism/Physicalism

Most, though not all, *naturalists* hold to *materialism*, or what is sometimes called *physicalism*. This is the theory that all that exists are material or physical entities, of the space-time continuum in which matter and energy exist. Matter and material objects themselves are things that basically take up space, and move around in space, interacting with each other. Even mind and consciousness are reduced to physical things.

Dualism

However, just to complicate issues, there are some naturalists who hold to the idea that there are also non-physical things in existence—such as *conscious thought*—like the colors that we see, the thoughts that we think, and so on. With this view, these latter items cannot be reduced to purely physical ones. To further explain this, I must detail the difference between *objects* and *properties*. Anyone who holds to the view that there are physical things in existence, but also non-physical things like thoughts, is a *dualist*. Dualism, as was noted in chapter 1, is the view that there are two different kinds of entities in existence in our universe—*physical things and conscious things*.

Objects and Properties

Objects are things that can exist by themselves, at least as far as the universe is concerned. (According to many versions of theism, all things that are not God are dependent upon God for their existence, but we will ignore this for the moment). They *have* properties, but themselves cannot *be* properties. A cat may have the properties of being fuzzy and gray, but a cat cannot be a characteristic of something else.

A *property*, on the other hand, is something that is had by an object—an attribute or characteristic. A shirt may be colored green. The shirt is the object or substance, while the green color is a property. Properties may themselves have properties—the green of the shirt will be in a certain shape, have certain hue and brightness, and so on.[88]

Most of the naturalists who hold to non-physical aspects of reality are *property dualists*. By this I mean that human beings are material objects, but that we have properties, like thoughts, for example. A few may hold that there are also non-material substances in the universe—souls for example. However, most people who believe in things like immaterial souls are theists rather than naturalists. The main reason for this is that theists usually conceive of God as being a mind—a being who is essentially one who thinks and is not material or physical at all. If one believes this, it is easier to think that other immaterial conscious things exist.

Naturalism and Atheism

Most contemporary naturalists are atheists. They do not believe in any god whatsoever. However, one can be a naturalist and still believe is some sort of god(s). The ancient pagans were naturalists, in a sense, because they believed that their gods—Zeus, Hera, Aphrodite, and so on—were immortal and powerful beings that nonetheless existed *in* the physical universe. Some versions of the modern religion of Mormonism hold that there are gods who are themselves material beings who live in the greater material universe. However, these are very much minority views among naturalists today.

Naturalism vs Theism

A fundamental difference between theism and naturalism is that theism holds to a two-level view of concrete reality, whereas naturalism holds to only one. Theists believe that God is the ultimate reality, necessarily existing, and that the physical universe is created and sustained by God. Naturalists believe that the physical universe is all that there is—that it exists on its own. However, there is another purported category of being—that of abstract entities.

Concrete vs Abstract Objects

One matter that will doubtlessly seem obscure and strange to those who have not had much exposure to philosophy (even at times seeming rather obscure and strange to experts in philosophy), is the difference between *concrete and*

---

88. For an exposition of these points, see Moreland, *Universals*.

abstract objects. Things such as molecules, cats, grass, mountains, etc., are instances of *concrete entities*. Concrete entities are almost always things that exist at a certain time and place, and which can cause other things to be, and can be acted upon. If there are also such things as immaterial minds or souls or angels, they also would be concrete entities, as is God.

Abstracta, on the other hand, are (if they exist, for their existence is controversial) things like numbers, universals (such as colors and shapes), propositions, etc. Take, for example, the number four. What is it? Does it exist in Plato's heaven (is it something that exists necessarily and eternally on its own), or is it just a concept we invented to aid in our understanding and interaction in the world? Or perhaps it is something else, such as an idea in the mind of God?[89]

The point here is that there are long-standing disputes among philosophers about the nature of abstract objects like the number four. This dispute may sound like the most obscure philosophical subject that one could imagine, but, in fact, it has important ramifications. Every philosophical issue is in some way connected with every other one. *Ideas have implications, often far beyond what they originally seem to, and of which the believer may be unaware.*[90]

Abstract entities do not exist at a certain place and time, do not change, and are not the cause of anything. That is, most philosophers think that they do not enter causal relations. Again, let's ponder the number four. While there may be many combinations of four changing things, the number four by itself does not change. The number four and other abstract entities, such as the color green, by themselves do not cause anything. They do enter a sort of strange and mysterious relationship, however. For example, if greenness exists, it can somehow be exemplified in the green concrete things that do exist, such as a chair.

It should also be noted that some alleged abstract entities have a contingent existence. For example, the equator may be considered abstract, but would not exist if the earth itself did not. However, these kinds of things are different from the kinds of abstract objects that philosophers usually consider.[91]

---

89. For an exposition of these points, and a defense of the existence of abstracta such as universals, see Moreland, *Universals*. For a discussion of abstracta from a philosopher who denies their existence as such, see Craig, *God Over All*.

90. Again, see Weaver, *Ideas*. This is quite appropriate, for part of Weaver's thesis is that the decline in Western Civilization is due to the rejection of realism and the triumph of nominalism about abstract entities.

91. Craig, *God Over All*, 4–5.

A naturalist and materialist may also accept the existence of abstract entities, though to me it seems more consistent that a naturalist and materialist should deny their existence. Be that as it may, there is, for the naturalist, only one level of existence of concrete entities—entities which can cause things and be acted upon by other physical entities.

Putting it all together

To sum up then, both theists and naturalists agree that the physical universe exists.[92] They may also agree that there are, or that at least it is possible that there are, other physical universes in existence. Indeed, at least one theistic philosopher has argued that God would necessarily create many universes.[93] What they do not agree on is if there is anything else concrete existing that is more fundamental than the universe.

This issue shall be discussed at greater length in the chapter on the nature of *physical reality*. For now, let me just conclude by saying that although both theists and naturalists agree that the universe exists, and may agree about how virtually everything in the universe exists, they most emphatically disagree with *why* the universe exists. For theists, the universe is a creation of God, while for naturalists, nature is just there, by itself. The material universe is therefore, for the naturalists, the ultimate being, and everything that exists is part of it, or at least is dependent upon it. Everything that exists is to be explained in terms of these foundational beliefs.

Faith Commitment

One final point should be made. Naturalism can be a *faith commitment* just as much as theism can be. Since naturalism is a worldview, or a collection of similar worldviews, it is, in a sense, for one who *believes in and is committed*

---

92. This is true by definition of naturalists. Almost all theists also believe in the existence of the universe. A possible exception to this is George Berkeley, who was an eighteenth-century idealist philosopher who may have thought that the world was just an idea in our minds. However, as Herman Philipse writes, "Husserl denies that he is a Berkeleian idealist, because he does not deny the existence of the world. But this attempt to disassociate himself from the unpopular bishop fails, being based on a misunderstanding of Berkeleian immaterialism. Like Husserl, Berkeley claims merely to remove an absurd interpretation of the existence of the world; he does not deny its existence." Philipse, "Transcendental Idealism," 286.

93. O'Connor, *Theism*. O'Connor argues that God will want to express in creating universes the different qualities that he possesses, and that one universe would be inadequate to do so.

to naturalism, the ultimate faith commitment for that person. Because of this, reason for the naturalist is reason in the light of the commitment to naturalism. Thus, *reasoning is done within the constraints of the naturalistic worldview*. Of course, it is possible to consider things hypothetically, from a different point of view than the one that is held.

Thus, for the committed naturalist, to give a *rational* explanation of something is to give a *naturalist* explanation. Anything that does not fit into the naturalist's framework is rejected as being irrational. Therefore, explanations that depend on the existence of the supernatural are often rejected out of hand as being irrational. Of course, the same can be said about theists, and indeed the holders of any worldview whatever. In one sense, *reason necessarily serves a worldview commitment*, the question is, what commitment is being served?

Ultimate Reality

> A religious belief is a belief in something as divine per se no matter how that is further described, where "divine per se" means having unconditionally non-dependent reality.
>
> ROY CLOUSER[94]

There is a final area that I will define before going into the main part of the book. This is the question of *ultimate reality*. This is an important question, for whatever is ultimate in a system will largely determine what the rest of the system is like.

Ultimate reality is that reality (howsoever conceived) that in any worldview does not depend upon anything else for its existence, but upon which everything else depends. It is ultimate in the sense, therefore, that everything that exists is derived from that being or beings.

For example, as we have seen, in classical theism, God is the Ultimate Being. God is also considered to be the reason and cause of everything else that exists.[95] In naturalism, things are different. The physical universe, or else the things out of which it is composed, are held to be ultimate reality.

---

94. Clouser, *Myth*, 23. Clouser argues that for any system, the ultimate reality in that system is held to be divine.

95. "The Christian worldview thus splits reality in half: a sacred God and a wholly profane universe; a necessary God and a contingent universe. This is a universe in which things happen in certain ways according to divine providence but could also, under the same divine providence, happen otherwise, in a completely different way." Molnar, *Pagan Temptation*, 99.

There is, however, a question here for naturalism. Naturalism cannot explain in terms of itself why the physical universe exists and continues to exist (even though in some versions of naturalist materialism, matter/energy is considered the Ultimate Concrete Existent). The reason being, why physical entities exist and are in the form that they are *cannot be explained by the physical entities themselves.* Given naturalism, the question remains, "*Why* does the physical universe exist?"

In classical theism, as I have described above, God is defined as the Greatest Possible Being (GPB) and thus has *the reason for his existence internal* to himself. Being the GPB he could not possibly be other than he is, that is, being infinite in his capacities, because to exist in any other way would mean he could be less than he is, and thus not the GPB.

To show what I mean, consider God's attribute of being omniscient. This means, as was explained above, that he knows the truth of all propositions. Were he to be other than this, for example, knowing the truth of only half of all propositions, then he would not be the Greatest Possible Being. So, if God exists as the GPB, he cannot be other than he is. Thus, there is no further explanation of why he exists outside of himself.

However, this is not the case with the physical universe. The universe seems to be logically contingent; which is to say, that it might have *not* existed.[96] The reason why this is the case should be obvious. *For something to exist necessarily, it must be the case that to deny its existence entails a contradiction.* The denial of a necessary truth entails a contradiction. Let me give a simple example to illustrate.

$2 + 2 = 4$ and necessarily so. It isn't the case that $2 + 2 = 4$ just happens to be true, but could have just as well, been 137½, instead of 4. Rather, it is impossible that $2 + 2$ equal anything other than 4. The reason should be clear. 2 is the same as $1 + 1$. So, $2 + 2 = 4$ breaks down to $1 + 1 + 1 + 1 = 1 + 1 + 1 + 1$. In other words, $2 + 2$ equals 4 necessarily, because the terms $2 + 2$ and 4 are in some sense or way identical to each other.

But if the universe does not exist out of its own inner necessity, and if it is not caused by God to exist (as in theism), why then does it exist? To make this clear, I will describe all the options that might be conceived *to explain the existence of the universe* as it is. Ultimately, the choices come down to the following. *Either*:

1. The universe exists ultimately *for no reason* at all,

    or,

---

96. Parrish, *God and Necessity*, 185–250.

2. The universe exists *for a reason*. This position can be divided into two different possibilities:

   2A. The universe exists for a reason *internal* to the universe.

   2B. The universe exists for a reason *external* to the universe.

These are the only possible options; it is a matter of simple *logic*. Either there is a reason or there is not. And if there is a reason, either the reason lies within the universe itself, or it lies outside of the universe. Logically, there are no other options. I will argue in the chapter below that naturalism fails to give a logical account of why the universe exists in the manner that it does with any of these imaginable possibilities.

One other point must be noted. The same analysis could be applied to any individual object in the universe, and not just the universe in its entirety. One may ask the same question about why an electron exists, or a rock, or a tree or animal, or planet or star, etc. Why do these exist in the manner that they do, and why do they remain in existence? Why does the matter or energy, of which the entity at hand is formed, continue in existence? Why, for example, should not an electron simply disappear, leaving the matter of the universe with one electron less? Though not frequently asked, these are also important questions.

Chapter 3

The Universe: Its Existence and Order

> When two doctrines meet, opposed in spirit, and logically irreconcilable in their principles, what would you have them do, oh sensible Philonous, save seek to devour each other? One must consume the other, not for the pleasure of destroying it, but for its own nourishment and the maintenance of its own life.
>
> JACQUES MARITAIN[1]

> [W]hat are philosophers for but to fight with each other?
>
> WILLIAM JAMES[2]

> The World exists either through blind chance, or through inner necessity, or through an external cause.
>
> IMMANUEL KANT[3]

IN THIS CHAPTER, I will outline the course of the book. In comparing and contrasting theism and naturalism, I will mainly concentrate on *cosmological questions*. These include questions such as the following: Why does the physical universe exist at all? Why are the laws of nature orderly and constant? Why does the universe remain in existence?[4]

It should be seen from the above list that these are mainly philosophical questions, rather than scientific ones. Science may try to describe *what* the

---

1. Maritain, "System of Philosophic Harmonies," 236–37.
2. Quoted in Brent, *Charles Sanders Peirce*, 219.
3. Kant, *Critique of Pure Reason*, 109.
4. All of these questions are examined in detail in my book *God and Necessity*, albeit at a much more technical level.

laws of nature are—it does not and cannot tell us *why* there are any laws at all.[5] Questions like this are *philosophical* rather than *scientific*—that is, they are questions about concepts that science assumes to be true in its investigations, not questions that science itself tries to answer, for by its very nature it cannot. It is not that there is anything wrong with the natural sciences; it is simply that the questions are not ones that science addresses.

Foundational Questions

Recall the outline of the foundational questions at hand, as outlined in the previous chapter. A simple way of putting these questions is, "Why does the universe exist, and why does it remain in existence, and why is it orderly?" However, as noted in chapter 1, an even more fundamental question as to why the universe exists is, "Why does *anything* at all exist?" For some philosophers, the mere fact that something—that anything at all—exists, is a mystery. This sense of mystery may be heightened by the fact that all the things in the universe in which we live seem to be contingent; things do not have the reason for their existence as part of their natures.

On the other hand, some have denied that there is a need to ask these questions. "Why," they ask, "is nothingness assumed to be the default position?" "Why should we assume that it is somehow more fundamental for things *not* to exist than for something to exist?" This is a good question. In fact, it is true that *if one makes nothingness as the default position, then one makes certain assumptions*.

Possible Worlds—What Could Have Been

In chapter 2 we saw what was meant by the term "possible world."[6] Put simply, a possible world is the way that reality *could* have been. The actual world, the one in which we live, is the possible world that is actual—unlike all the other possible worlds, it is the one that exists. It should be noted that when I say that other possible worlds exist, what I mean is that they existed as possibilities, as the way that things *could* have been, not that they exist in the way that our world does.[7]

---

5. Philosophical studies from different positions on the laws of nature include Armstrong, *What is a Law of Nature?*; Lange, *Laws & Lawmakers*; Van Fraassen, *Laws and Symmetry*; Jaeger, *What the Heavens Declare*; and *Einstein*.
6. It is in the section on the necessary existence of God.
7. On this see Lewis, *On the Plurality of Worlds*.

Other possible worlds may differ from the actual one in many ways. For some, the difference may be trivial. Take, for an example, a possible world which is just like the actual world save that in the Andromeda galaxy there is one electron that swerves to the left one nanometer for one nanosecond, whereas in the actual world the same electron swerves to the right for that same nanosecond.

There are, however, possible worlds which are greatly different from our own. Take another example—a world in which all that exist are two steel spheres orbiting each other. Or imagine worlds in which the laws of nature are radically different from our own. Or a world in which Barack Obama, instead of becoming president of the United States, becomes a professional golfer.

If God does not exist, it seems that there is either only one possible world, or else that there is an infinite number of possible worlds. Either this is the only way that things could have been, or else there is an infinite number of ways that things could have been otherwise. Most philosophers think the latter—that this world is not the only way that things could have been, that there is an infinite number of other possibilities. With naturalism, where there is no necessarily existing God who chooses to actualize one world, it seems that there is an infinite number of ways in which reality could have existed, and, of course, a possible world where nothing concrete exists.

It may be argued that there is only one possible world in which nothing exists, or at least in which no concrete objects exist. After all, how would two different worlds in which nothing concrete existed differ from each other? It seems that they wouldn't. In contrast, there is an infinite number of possibilities with worlds which have objects in them, like stars and atoms, cats, and cars. Why then should we assume that the world in which there is nothing is the favored one?[8] If there is an infinite number of possible worlds, and only one where there was nothing, it seems that the odds are infinitesimal for a world wherein nothing concrete exists.

On the other hand, some have argued that there is a question as to why things exist at all—that absent some sort of cause or reason, the natural world would be one in which nothing concrete exists. In this case, the world would be empty, void of anything.

However, note that both these arguments presuppose the falsity of theism, as they both assume that things exist or fail to exist apart from God. In an earlier paper, I thought that in the absence of God, nothing would exist.[9] However, I now think that the question is unanswerable, because I think

---

8. For discussion of this controversy, see Goldschmidt, *Puzzle*.
9. Parrish, "Theism, Naturalism," 433–50.

that God exists necessarily, which means that the question as to what would happen if God did not exist is impossible to answer.

Chance or Necessity?

This brings us to another consideration. Although I have said that in naturalism the physical universe is the ultimate being, in a different sense, either *chance* or *necessity* is the Ultimate. Either whatever exists, exists by chance, or else exists of absolute necessity.

So, the question comes down to the following: "What is ultimate reality: God, chance, or the necessary existence of this world on its own?" Perhaps the best way to begin is to consider, of all the infinite number of possible worlds that may be conceived, why is our world the one that has been actualized? Why not one wherein there is a ten-million-dollar Swiss bank account in my name, instead of the actual world, where, sadly, no such account exists.

As was argued at the end of the last chapter, there are very few possible responses. In fact, I will argue that ultimately there are only three. These three can be called Brute Fact theory, Necessary World theory, and Necessary Deity theory. These three options correspond to the three given in the last chapter. They are simple. To begin the discussion, for clarity's sake, I will call our world, the actual world, Sue.[10] *Brute Fact Theory* holds that Sue exists for no reason. That Sue exists for a reason internal to herself, is the *Necessary World Theory*, and that Sue exists for a reason external to herself, which means she exists because God caused her to be, is the *Necessary Deity Theory*.

Brute Fact Theory

Brute Fact Theory holds that our world, the world named Sue, is the one that exists rather than some other one because of *brute fact*—a matter of *chance*. That is, why world Sue exists rather than worlds Joe, Sally, Fred, etc. is that one world had to exist (including the world in which there are no concrete objects), and Sue was just the lucky one whose number was drawn. As the philosopher, Bertrand Russell once stated in a famous debate with Frederick Copleston, a Jesuit priest and historian of philosophy, "The universe is just there, that's all."[11]

---

10. I was going to call it something philosophical like *Wa*, but my wife suggested going with something a non-philosopher could relate to. So, it's Sue.

11. See "A Debate on the Existence of God," between Russell and Copleston, in Hick, *Existence of God*, 175. More debates on the existence of God in print include

Necessary World Theory

In contrast to Brute Fact Theory, there stands *Necessary World theory*. In a way, Necessary World theory is the exact opposite of Brute Fact Theory. Here, it is alleged that our world Sue is the only one that could have existed, ever. Sue's existence is held to be necessary in the strong sense of the word, in that it is impossible that some other world could have existed instead of ours, just as it is impossible that 2 + 2 could have equaled a number other than 4. The question then arises as to *why* specifically Sue had to exist. I will look at this in detail below.

Necessary Deity Theory

The third and final theory is what I call *Necessary Deity theory*. In this theory, there exists a necessary being "God" (who exists necessarily) and who is the cause of the existence of the rest of reality. This God, I have argued at length in chapter 2, can only be the God considered as the Greatest Possible Being. In this theory, God exists necessarily as part of any world that could have existed and is the one who chooses to create Sue rather than Fred or Joe or some other possible world, for reasons best known to himself. It should be noted that with Necessary Deity theory some worlds are not possible which would be possible in Brute Fact theory, such as worlds where evil finally and forever triumphs over good. Such a world would never be created by a perfectly good and all-powerful God.[12] God would have the power to create such worlds but would never have the desire to create them.

It is unknown how many possible worlds there are with Necessary Deity theory. If there is a best of all possible worlds, then God might never have chosen to create another. If there are several best of all possible worlds, better than all others, but equal among themselves, then God just picked one. Similarly, if there is no best of all possible worlds, then God would, it seems, in some sense, arbitrarily pick one. This is a difficult subject, but in any case, God is the being who decides which world is created.[13]

Miethe and Flew, *Does God Exist?*; Moreland and Nielsen, *Does God Exist?*; Wallace, *Does God Exist?*; Craig and Simon-Armstrong, *GOD?*; Craig and Smith, *Theism, Atheism*; Peterson and Ruse, *Science, Evolution*; Plantinga and Tooley, *Knowledge of God*; and Smart and Haldane, *Atheism and Theism*.

12. The problem of evil can be said to be that the actual world, Sue, is a world that a perfect God would never create.

13. For discussion of this topic, see for example Rowe, *Can God Be Free?*; Almeida, *Metaphysics*; and *Freedom, God*.

So, these are, as a simple matter of logic, the only three possibilities. Of course, there are still some questions that need to be answered, such as, if the universe has a cause of its existence, then must that cause be a deity instead of something else? In response, it must be a necessary deity instead of some other concept because the God of perfect being theism is the only coherent concept of a concrete necessary being, as shall be argued below.[14]

Atheists' Challenges. Let's look at an argument that atheists frequently make. They may challenge that if the cause of the universe is God, this only pushes the question back a step, for now one can ask the question, "Why does *God* exist?" The answer to this challenge is one that I have already given. God is a necessary being and the reason that God exists is God's nature. This is hardly original with me; many prominent thinkers over the centuries have said the same thing. Nor is God's necessary existence unique in one sense.[15] If there are any abstract entities like numbers thought of in a Platonic sense, that is, existing independently of anything else, they too exist necessarily. Either they exist on their own, or they are ideas necessarily existing in the mind of God (which is the position that I maintain).[16]

An atheist's response may be that the very concept of God is meaningless, and therefore God cannot be the cause of anything. A weaker but related argument is that the concept of God is meaningful (i.e., is understandable), but self-contradictory. That is, we can understand it, but there are irremovable contradictions in the concept of God, so they say. Again, if true, this would mean that God's existence is impossible, and that he could not be the explanation for anything.

This argument would, if fully spelled out, take a whole book to respond to. Briefly, just let me say here that I do not think that the arguments that purport to show that God is either meaningless or impossible are successful.[17] However, my main response to the challenge shall be that the existence of the God of classical theism is required to account for the existence of everything else, and hence, God must exist, and therefore he cannot be either meaningless or impossible. If it is necessary that something exist, then obviously, it must be possible for it to exist.[18]

---

14. Which I argue for in detail in *God and Necessity*, 23–119, and 217–79.

15. Parrish, *God and Necessity*.

16. There is another position, sometimes known as Absolute Creationism, wherein abstract objects exist outside the mind of God, but are created by God. In this case, they might not have existed at all, if God had created some other universe than the actual one.

17. See Parrish, *God and Necessity*, chapter 10.

18. Parrish, *God and Necessity*, chapter 10.

It should be noted that asking why the universe as a whole exists is not the only way that one could go about this. One may enquire about the entities of the universe individually. The universe is composed of many different objects, from subatomic particles to whole galaxies. One may also ask why any one of these objects exists, and/or continues to exist. For example, one can ask why my car exists, or why each one of the atoms of which it is composed exists.

Necessary Deity Theory Examined

> [T]he concept of God is explicated in the Anselmian way as that of a greatest possible, or maximally perfect, being ... [A] maximally perfect being must have as an essential property that of existing in every possible world, or of being a necessarily existent entity.
>
> Thomas V. Morris[19]

Let us examine the possibilities one by one. Let us take Necessary Deity Theory first. In this view, God exists necessarily, and then for reasons best known to God himself, he chooses to actualize—that is, make real—the world and universe in which we live. To further explain this, a couple of questions need to be answered.

Why Must the Necessary Cause be a Deity?

First, why must the necessary cause be a deity, rather than something else, like Plotinus's One, Bradley's Absolute, or even a physical object? There are good reasons for thinking this. To begin with, there is the issue of God's necessity. Atheists will sometimes pose the question (mainly on the internet and private conversations, though occasionally professional philosophers may ask related questions) in response to any argument that the universe needs a cause, "If everything needs a cause, doesn't God need a cause too?"

No theist who knows what he or she is talking about, and is speaking carefully, will start with the premise that "everything needs a cause." The appeal to causation is part of what is often called *the cosmological argument for the existence of God*. There are three basic forms of this argument: the Thomist, the Leibnizian, and the Kalam.[20] The *Thomist* version appeals to

---

19. Morris, *Anselmian Explorations*, 179.

20. For an investigation in the different kinds of the cosmological argument, see Craig, *Cosmological Argument*.

the principle of existential causality, which asserts that all beings that are composed of essence and existence (i.e., they do not have existence that is identical with, or a necessary property of the essence of that being) need a cause. Only God, for the Thomist, has his essence and existence identical with each other; they are the same thing.[21] The *Leibnizian* version of the argument states that everything needs a reason, but not necessarily a cause, to exist. The Leibnizian God has the *reason* for his existence within himself and thus exists necessarily but does not *cause* his own existence; he does not bring himself into existence. The *Kalam* version holds that everything that *comes into existence* needs a cause of its coming to be. God never came to be, and hence by this argument, does not need a cause. None of these versions have the premise that "everything needs a cause to exist."

Does Everything in the Universe Need a Cause?

Does everything in the universe need a cause to come into existence and remain in existence? I think so. As J. L. Mackie wrote, causation is the cement of the universe.[22] Why do things have causes? Because God made a rational, orderly universe. On Brute Fact Theory there is no reason why this world exists rather than another, so there is with this theory no reason why things cannot exist without a cause.

Doesn't God Need a Cause?

Second, the best answer to the question "Doesn't God need a cause?" is: "No, God is a necessary being, and exists out of reasons internal to himself as the Greatest Possible Being." Given perfect being theism, he absolutely *must* exist, in the strong sense that 7 + 5 must = 12, or any other necessary truth. To deny God's necessary existence is to entail a contradiction.[23]

What would the contradiction be? As was stated above, God is defined as the Greatest Possible Being. He is greater than any other conceivable being. He is, among many other things, sovereign. This means that he has total

---

21. I find this a difficult concept to understand. See the section on divine simplicity in chapter two.
22. For example, see Mackie, *Cement*.
23. Of course, the contradiction may not be easily apparent. Another response that is sometimes given is that God is eternal, and thus doesn't need a cause of his existence. To me, this answer is insufficient. For one can still ask the question as to why did God exist at all? One can conceive of a being that always existed but was caused to exist by some other being.

control over everything. He decides which of the infinite number of possible worlds is actualized. A being who was not the greatest possible or conceivable being would not be sovereign, which is to say, would not be in control of everything. Such a being would be limited by other things, and thus also could not be the ultimate reality, upon which everything else depends for its existence and nature. If God were not sovereign, then brute fact or chance, or some other purportedly necessary thing, rather than God, would be ultimate, because whatever existed would not be totally in God's control.[24]

Why Does God Exist?

Why then does he exist? He exists because necessary existence is in his essence. God, as I have defined him, is rock bottom reality—the source of everything else. Not only is he the cause of the existence of concrete entities, all possibilities exist as ideas in his mind—that is their ultimate nature. As was said above, numbers, propositions, universals, possible worlds, and other purportedly abstract entities exist as ideas in the mind of God.

Think of things another way. How could it be that God fails to exist? He cannot fail to exist by chance, as again he is a necessary being. For any purportedly necessary being, only necessary existence or the impossibility of existence is conceivable. Since God is defined as the Greatest Possible Being, he cannot be destroyed or fail to come into existence. Indeed, he cannot *come into* existence at all. Nothing is or possibly could be as powerful as God, and thus nothing can destroy, damage, or control him. Unlike us, he could not fail to exist because his parents never met, for he has no parents or any other cause.

How then could such a being as God fail to exist? He can fail to exist if and *only if* there are irresolvable contradictions in the concept of God. In other words, if the concept of God is incoherent, he does not and cannot exist. But if there is no such incoherence, if there is no contradiction in the concept of God, then God exists and necessarily exists.[25] Strange though it may sound, in a way, it is as simple as that—though figuring out all the details would be extremely complex, and indeed, only fully comprehensible to God.

It should immediately be pointed out that because we are not God, the totality of God's being is not open to us. Therefore, we cannot necessarily see whether there is or is not some contradiction in the concept of

---

24. Parrish, *God and Necessity*.

25. Yujin Nagasawa has recently given an argument that undercuts any attempt to show God's existence is contradictory. See his *Maximal God*.

God. Only by knowing God exhaustively could one do that, and only God can know God exhaustively. However, I have argued in another work that if one examines the concept of God and does not see any contradiction in the concept of God, this gives one some reason to think that God's being contains no contradiction, and that therefore God exists.[26] This is a form of what is called *the ontological argument.*

Although God may be simple in some senses of the word, in another sense God is the most complex thing that exists or ever could exist, *for everything else that exists or could exist is contained in him*. Everything possibly thinkable is being thought of by God—even, for example, all the infinite numbers that there are. Nevertheless, God's existence and properties are analytically included in him—that is to say, that they are all necessarily included in the concept of God as the Greatest Possible Being. They are thus *necessarily contained* in the concept of God, just as being "even" is analytically included in the concept of the number four or having eight vertices is included in the concept of a cube.

Brute Fact Theory Examined

> [T]he metaphysics to which it must resort is nothing other than a version of an ancient pagan narrative of being as sheer brute event . . .
>
> DAVID BENTLEY HART[27]

> The universe is just there, that's all.
>
> BERTRAND RUSSELL[28]

> Why is it that there is being? . . . Being is without reason, without cause, and without necessity; the very definition of being releases to us its original contingency.
>
> JEAN-PAUL SARTRE[29]

---

26. Parrish, *God and Necessity*, 81–119.

27. Hart, *Beauty of the Infinite*, 36. Hart here is discussing John Milibank's critique of postmodernism, but I think that the basic appeal to brute fact as ultimate explanation is intrinsic to most non-theistic versions of reality.

28. "Debate on the Existence of God," between Russell and Copleston, in Hick, *Existence of God*, 175.

29. Sartre, *Being and Nothingness*, 758.

> In truth at first Chaos came to be ... From Chaos came forth ... black Night.
>
> HESIOD[30]

Standing in opposition to Necessary Deity theory is what I have called *Brute Fact theory*. Here, all concrete beings and the universe in which they all exist, exist in the manner that they do ultimately *for no reason*. To show why the above is purported to be the case, and to show the implications of this supposition will take some explanation.

First, according to this *Brute Fact theory*, the universe (broadly defined) is all that exists, and its existence is a brute fact—there is no reason why it exists. As Bertrand Russell stated, it just does. It is not simply that we don't know of the reason for its existence, rather, it has no reason, and in fact could have none. Seemingly, there is an infinite number of possible worlds—worlds that could have been actual. One of them had to be, and ours was the lucky one.[31] However, these concepts need some exposition and explanation.

Possible Worlds

There are different conceptions of possible worlds. These worlds each represent every possible way that reality could have existed. One prominent conception of these worlds is that possible worlds are analogous to books full of statements and propositions. That is, every possible world (or in the analogy, book), is describable by a set of statements, or what are often called *propositions*. The actual world, the one that exists, can be described by a system of propositions. These propositions would include descriptions of everything in our universe—that Cleveland is in Ohio; that 2 + 2 = 4; that Pluto was exactly so many inches from the Sun at 2:13 in the afternoon, United States Eastern time on July 14th, 1913; that there are N number of electrons in Madagascar now, and so on. *All of reality is ideally describable by propositions.*

The descriptions in each possible world will be the same in some respects, and different in others. In every possible world two plus two equals four, triangles will have three sides, and all other necessary truths will hold sway. In other respects, each possible world will be different from every other one, even if only by a tiny amount. A description of the actual world

---

30. Hesiod, *Complete Hesiod Collection*, "Theogony," lines 115–24.

31. This point can be contested. Some have said that there is only one possible world.

would include a description of my sitting at my computer desk typing this out. A description of another possible world, where I am an Antarctic explorer instead of a philosopher, might have included a description of my examining penguins, and shivering in my boots.

Indeed, it seems that there is an infinite number of propositions about our world, and every one of the propositions must be either true or false. The same may be said about every possible world, even one inhabited entirely (and perhaps impossibly) by one rubber ball. For here there would be a description of that world that would include propositions such as: "Mount Rushmore doesn't exist, the planet Mars doesn't exist, there are fewer than 9,000,000,000 objects in existence," and so on.[32]

The same can be said for all other possible worlds. Each one is describable by a set of propositions, and the propositions that are true for each possible world are different from the numerous sets that describe every other possible world. In our world Sue, the proposition that says that the North won the American civil war is true, whereas in some other possible world, say Frank, one where the South won, the proposition is false. Alvin Plantinga calls the set of propositions a *world book*. Every possible world has its own world book, different from every other one. Since there is an infinite number of possible worlds (or at least imaginable worlds, even if some of them are not really possible), there is an infinite number of world books.

In Brute Fact theory, the concrete entities of the universe, and the way that these entities are arranged, are ultimately here for no reason, simply by chance. Another way of putting it is, out of the infinite number of possible *world books*, one was pulled off the shelf at random. It is simply a matter of chance—our world's number came up. Even though there may be an infinite number of possible worlds, one of them had to be actual (even if it were the world where no concrete objects exist), and ours just happens to be that one.[33]

Now, assuming Brute Fact theory, among the worlds that are possible, there is an infinite number that are chaotic. They are not governed by any natural laws, or at least by any consistent set of natural laws over space and time. There is also an infinite number of worlds where part of the physical universe, at different places and times, is law-like (as in the sense that its

---

32. On this matter, see Plantinga's essay, "Actualism and possible worlds," 7. To put things more simply, there is an infinite number of possible worlds, or at least imaginable worlds. Each world is describable by a set of propositions or statements. The set of all the statements that describes each possible world is called the book for that world. On this, see Pruss, *Actuality, Possibility*.

33. Again, see Goldschmidt, *Puzzle*, for the debate on this issue.

behavior can be described by laws of nature) and also partly chaotic, either at different regions in space, or at different times, or both.

Possible Worlds Cannot Contain Contradictions

Why is the above the case? It is because possible worlds are possible in the following sense: they are logically or absolutely possible.[34] To reiterate, because this point is so important: this means that there are no logical contradictions in them. *A world which has genuine contradictions cannot exist.* There cannot be a world where geometric figures have three angles but fourteen sides, where 2 + 2 = 63.57, or where red is a number rather than a color.

So, if an imaginable world does not contain any contradictions, it is a possible world. There is, therefore, seemingly an infinite number of possible worlds, because at first glance, at least, there is an infinite number of ways in which reality could have been.[35] For illustration, it seems that there are worlds where all that exists besides God is one ball.[36] Then there are possible worlds where there are two balls, and so on. Of course, it may not be easy, or it even may not be plausible, for us to see whether these purportedly possible worlds contain contradictions or not.[37]

As was stated above, there may be more than one universe within a possible world, where a universe is described as a set of causally, spatially, and temporally interconnected entities and events. Indeed, there are contemporary cosmological theories that hold that there are many different universes in existence, of which ours is only one. I will call such a multitude of universes existing in one world a *multiverse*.[38]

Now, of all the possible worlds (or world books, as in our analogy above), by the very nature of things, only one of them *could* be actualized (or pulled off the shelf). We cannot have both world Sue and world Frank. The question therefore becomes, why this one rather than another? Why is our world Sue, rather than Fred, Joe, or Sally? Why, of all the infinite

---

34. See Hale, *Necessary Beings*, for a discussion on what these different kinds of necessity mean.

35. Again, this point can be contested.

36. Actually, they might not be possible because God would never create such a world. However, they are imaginable, and God has the power to create them, so they are possible in that sense.

37. I am naming these possible worlds, as they are imaginable. Of course, it probably is the case that God would never want to create a world with just one rubber ball, etc.

38. For an interesting discussion of this, see Barr, *Believing Scientist*, 123–55.

number of worlds which could have been actualized, is this one, the one in which we exist, the one that is real?

By Chance

As stated above, given Brute Fact theory, the answer can only be *"by chance,"* which is to say, *"for no reason at all."* By necessity, one of the various possible worlds must be actual. And, since with Brute Fact theory there is nothing more fundamental than the universe, and since one of the worlds of necessity must be actual, then whichever one is indeed actualized is actualized for no reason.

Our universe is law abiding. Things in the universe happen according to laws that are constant. The speed of light seems to be the same at all places and times. The strength of gravity and the other forces of nature (like the strong and weak nuclear forces) seem to be the same everywhere and at every moment in time. The same may be said for the various constants in nature, such as the mass and charge of the different subatomic particles.

The problem may then be put thusly: for every possible world, where, like ours, the laws of nature are regular and constant, *there seems to be an incredibly vast, perhaps infinite number of worlds wherein things are chaotic*. That is, where there are no regular constants and laws. For everything that happens in a consistent and orderly fashion, there are many ways in which things could be inconsistent and disorderly. A ball that did not fall to the ground after being let go of any support would be violating the laws of nature, but it would not be violating the laws of logic. The laws of nature are contingent; they could have been other than they are without contradiction.[39] That things have a cause is also (*if one ignores God*), a contingent fact. There is no logical contradiction in conceiving something arising without a cause.[40]

In short, it seems that if the world that is actualized is done so by chance (instead of any of the other possible world scenarios which could have existed), then it is extremely, perhaps *infinitely more likely that a chaotic world would have been the one, rather than an orderly, law-governed one* like our own. Thus, given Brute Fact theory, there is an infinite number of possible worlds that could have been actual, the vast majority of them are chaotic. That our ordered one is the one that is actual is strictly a matter of chance. Thus,

---

39. For a list of the fundamental laws of nature, see Gairdner, *Book of Absolutes*, 311. None of the numbers associated with the laws seem to be logically or absolutely necessary.

40. God is needed as the explanation of why causation is seemingly universal in the universe: this is part of the argument against Brute Fact Theory.

given Brute Fact theory, the "odds" that by chance we have an orderly universe are extremely remote, even infinitely remote. Yet we have one.

The Odds

A response to this has been made. Supporting Brute Fact theory, it alleged that the number of orderly universes is infinite, while the number of chaotic universes is also infinite. All infinites are equal, and therefore the chance of getting an orderly universe is 50 percent.[41] We got lucky, and the actual universe is orderly.[42] But this response fails. To illustrate why, consider a library with an infinite number of books. Suppose that in the stacks there are 1 trillion black books, then 1 red book, then 1 trillion more black books, then another red book, and so on forever in the same pattern. Since there is an infinite number of black books, and an infinite number of red books, their numbers are in some sense equal. However, if one were to randomly grab a book off the shelf, the odds that it would be black rather than red are still a trillion to one. The same argument may be made with orderly and chaotic universes.[43]

Another response may be that it is not necessary that the whole world be completely orderly—only enough orderliness for us to come into existence and live in it. This may be true. A small amount of chaos could possibly exist without upsetting the universe too much. However, again, for a universe to be inhabitable, there still needs to be a great deal of orderliness. It needs to exist over enough of the universe for us to live in, and over a long enough period of time for us to come into existence and thrive. This requires a great deal of orderliness. Besides, from an empirical point of view, everywhere we look in both space and time, the laws and constants of nature seem to be consistent.

Further, it is not just chaotic universes that would be uninhabitable. Universes where the laws of nature changed every five minutes, or five

---

41. This is not literally true. Without going into the difficult nature of trans-finite math, what can be said is that all infinites at the same level are equal.

42. For an argument like this, see Johnson, *Atheist Debater's Handbook*. See also Lewis, *On the Plurality of Worlds*, 16.

43. An argument against this may be called "The shuffling response." Since infinites are equal, one could reshuffle the library so that now there are 1 trillion red books, then 1 black book, and so on. So, it might be thought, my argument here fails. In response, it can be said that possible worlds cannot be "shuffled." They are abstract objects and cannot be moved in any sense. What really counts is comparing the number of chaotic or law structure changeable worlds with consistently lawful ones. This comparison never changes. For the objection, see Lewis and Barnes, *Fortunate Universe*, 308–10.

seconds, or where there were one set of laws in one section of the universe, and quite a different set in the next section probably would also be unlivable. If the law of gravity doubled suddenly, life as we know it would become difficult, if not impossible. If the law of gravity changed every five minutes, or at random intervals, doubling, tripling, halving, or ceasing to exist entirely, any sort of orderly existence would be impossible.

A counter argument from the Brute Fact theory espousers might be this: If it be granted that the existence of our world is a brute fact, then it may also be granted that the laws that govern our universe are also just brute facts. At the moment when the universe came into being, it is thought, the laws of nature came into being too, and once set, these laws have remained. Thus, it is argued that the laws of nature are merely brute facts, but that they are nonetheless orderly.

However, this response doesn't work in rescuing Brute Fact theory. In fact, it fails spectacularly. It is not that there is only one brute fact that holds forevermore, rather, every object and event in the universe throughout time and at every time is itself a brute fact. Just because at the beginning of time the laws of the universe were one way by chance, does nothing to establish the same laws throughout time. At every moment, an object exists as it does only by a fluke. The same is also true for the same object the next moment, and the next, as long as it exists. There is no logical connection between a brute fact object or event at one moment, and the same object or event at the next moment, as will be argued below. Given Brute Fact theory, the universe is simply a vast collection of logically unrelated entities and events, which have only a brute fact or *chance* relationship to one another.

This issue can be looked at from another angle—from the existence of the different objects of which the universe is composed. The universe is full of many kinds of physical objects. The behavior of these objects at the most basic level—the level that physics studies—is describable by a set of invariable laws and constants. In other words, the laws of nature, and the kinds of fundamental particles that exist, seem to be uniform across space and time. Electrons from the Andromeda Galaxy are apparently the same as the ones in our Milky Way Galaxy and are the same at any point in the history of the universe. Further, the laws of nature seem to be invariable. Even were any of them to change tomorrow, it still would have been the case that there was a long period of uniformity spread out over a vast area of the observable universe.

The problem with *naturalism* here is that there is no deeper explanation to which to make an appeal. Naturalism is like a show on a television that has not been sent from anywhere—which has never been aired. Granting that the television may have been turned on and that there may be some random activity of electrons lighting up on the screen, it is extremely far-fetched to expect that any sort of coherent picture would be generated by this, let alone a whole program for an hour, or a day—and would be even more unlikely if the picture persisted for many years. Yet this scenario is analogous to what naturalists must believe about the universe. For them the universe and everything in it exist brutely, for no reason. And yet over the whole of the universe, over vast amounts of time, the same laws and constants keep coming up with a consistent history of the objects existing therein.

The question then becomes, how can a Brute Fact theory account for this uniformity? I will now argue that it can't. Let me start with an analogy. Suppose that there were one trillion fair (unloaded) dice, each with six sides. Imagine rolling the dice one trillion times. If this actually were done, what would the likelihood of all the dice's coming up with a "six" all one trillion times? The odds of rolling one die and getting a six on this unloaded die is one sixth. The odds of two such dice getting sixes is one sixth times one sixth, or one over thirty-six. The odds go down rapidly, exponentially, with each roll of the die. The odds of all one trillion dice coming up sixes on one roll are 1/6 x 1/6 x 1/6 . . . for a trillion rolls of the dice. I won't bother calculating it out, since the exact number is not what is important here, but it amounts to $6^{1,000,000,000,000}$, or 6 to the trillionth power. Try that one on your calculator!

If one then adds the supposition that each of the trillion dice does these one trillion times, one will quickly see that the odds of this complete set of trillion 6s are remote in the extreme. To call the odds astronomically low is a tremendous understatement.

The salient point here is that the odds of the above unlikely dice rolls' happening are infinitely better than the odds of the universe and all its basic particles' acting in uniformity throughout the whole history of the universe. The reasons why are as follows.

There are considerably more than one trillion subatomic particles in the universe. According to a common estimate, there are 1×10^{80} baryons in the observable universe. (Baryons are subatomic particles made up of three quarks).[44] The most common baryons are protons and neutrons. The scientific consensus at present is that the physical universe has existed for a very long time.[45] Also, per contemporary mainstream science, the laws

---

44. http://www.merriam-webster.com/dictionary/baryon. "Quark."

45. The standard view is that the universe is about fourteen billion years old. Given even a much shorter period, such as a year, the fact that the universe and the objects of which it is composed have remained constant given brute fact, is extremely unlikely.

THE UNIVERSE: ITS EXISTENCE AND ORDER 119

and constants of nature have been the same everywhere almost from the moment that the universe came into existence

If we compare 1×10^{80} for fundamental particles to 1×10^{12} for the trillion die rolls it is obvious that a trillion dice are insignificant to the number of baryons in the observable universe. If we arbitrarily say that one second of existence for a baryon is equivalent to one roll of a die, then it is also obvious that the number of seconds that the universe has existed so far is astronomically greater than 1 trillion rolls of a single die.

For simplicity's sake let us say that every baryon is a proton (which is not true—neutrons are also baryons). All the protons have different properties, such as the strong nuclear force. Let us say for simplicity's sake that each proton's strong nuclear force is a strength of 1.0. However, it certainly seems possible that the protons could have a different strong nuclear force than the one that they actually have. For example, why couldn't a proton have a strong nuclear force of 0.9, or 1.1 or some other number than 1?

One possible answer to this is the following. Any proton is a kind of entity that has certain properties. To be a proton rather than an electron or a neutron or any other kind of thing, it must have the properties that protons have. Since protons have a strong nuclear force of 1, then all protons must, because of their nature as protons, have a strong nuclear force of 1. If it didn't then it wouldn't be a proton.

However, this response fails. The reason is as follows: Let us take a proton, which for obscure historical reasons I will call Bob. If Bob the proton's strong nuclear force changes from 1 to 1.1 say, then Bob may no longer be a proton (though this might be argued, if the change is small enough), but this does not mean that Bob as an individual cannot still exist as something, even if it no longer exists as a proton.

To illustrate, all dice have six faces. Let us imagine a large die made of clay. If one takes this die, and crushes it, remolding it into the shape of a ball, so that it no longer has six distinct faces, it will no longer be a die. However, in another sense it will still be the same object it was before. Before being crushed, the object was in the form of a die, now it is in another form, so it is no longer a die. But it is in a real sense the same object that it was before, because it is composed of all the same material that it was previously. Going back to Bob the proton, we can now see that if Bob changed its strong nuclear force from 1 to 1.1, it might now no longer be a proton, but it would still be the same object. This being the case, there seems to be no reason from this angle why a proton like Bob could not change its strong nuclear force, or any of its other forces, to some other strength.

Much the same point can be made about the sheer existence of things. Take Bob the proton again. Suppose that Bob exists for a year. During every second of the year, the possibility that it will cease to exist is always there, yet Bob remains in existence. Why is this?

What About the Laws of Physics?

In response, it may be argued that once things are in existence, they stay in existence, unless something destroys them. This is merely a common observation of how the universe is, and as pointed out above, it is the situation described by the law of the conservation of energy. A fundamental law of nature ensures that things will remain in existence, or at least the matter/energy of which they are composed will. The question is, *why* is this so? Why is the law of the conservation of energy true?

To reiterate, the problem is that things (or the physical material out of which they are made) remain in existence. I would be highly surprised if something just disappeared into complete nothingness. *The problem is why is this the case*? Everything contingent may or may not exist. There was a time when every one of us did not exist. Further, contemporary science seems to show that the physical universe itself came into existence a finite time ago.[46] Also, there is apparently no contradiction in imagining the non-existence of any one thing in the universe, or even the universe itself. The universe, or Sue, or Bob, could, possibly, NOT exist. So why do they remain in existence?

There have been attempts to respond to these kinds of reasonings. For example, Adolf Grünbaum writes,

> [T]he eighteenth-century French chemist Lavoisier showed there is, indeed, matter conservation (or matter-energy conservation) in a closed finite system on the medium-sized macroscopic scale *qua spontaneous, natural, unperturbed behavior of the system*. And, if so, Descartes was *empirically* wrong to have assumed that such conservation requires the intervention of an external cause. Therefore, if he was thus wrong, his claim that external divine intervention in particular is needed to keep an object from disappearing into nothingness was based on a false presupposition.[47]

This quote from Grünbaum shows that he is relying on a scientific law to explain something metaphysical, and thereby commits a category mistake. Grünbaum does not even attempt to answer the question as to *why* that

46. See, for example, Singh, *Big Bang*.
47. Grünbaum, "No Explanation Needed," 59.

scientific law or principle is true, given a universe that is ultimately reducible to brute fact. *Why* are there any natural laws at all? *Why* do they apply across the whole of space and time? What Grünbaum is saying is that things remain in existence because they remain in existence, which is frankly no answer at all. More is said about the laws of nature below.

Why Do Things Remain in Existence?

This brings us to the next question. Since it is possible for contingent beings to *not* exist, why then is it the case that the universe and everything in it remain in existence? Just to clarify, if an object is "destroyed" in the sense of breaking or being crushed, or shape shifts, the physical stuff (matter) of which it is composed remains. In this case, why does the matter or energy of which the universe, or Sue, or Bob, is composed remain in existence? As Tyron Goldschmidt asks, "What grounds their existential inertia?"[48]

Let's look at Bob the proton again. Bob exists at a time t_1 and also a different time t_2, which is a second later. Why is this situation the case? This query applies not just to protons, but also to any contingent concrete thing whatsoever.

Two Possibilities for Contingent Beings

Consider it this way: there are *two possibilities*. Since contingent beings do not have the reason for their existence internal to themselves, *they either exist for no reason at all, or they exist for a reason external to themselves.* Let us first look at the possibility that they exist for no reason at all.

For No Reason At All. If it were the case that Bob exists for no reason at all, then for every moment at which it exists, it has both the possibility of existing or not-existing. That Bob exists at time t_1 is a matter of chance, as there is no particular reason that it exists at t_1. That it also exists at time t_2 is also a matter of chance. The same must be said about any other time that it exists. That Bob exists at time t_1 is logically unconnected to his existence at any moment after t_1. That he exists at t_1 does not at all require that he continues to exist at t_2—the two times are not logically necessitated by each other.

Let us assume that for anytime that Bob might exist, there would be, in fact, a 50/50 chance of his existing. Although the real "odds" would be incalculable, I think that the possibility that any particular object's existing

---

48. Goldschmidt, *Puzzle*, 6. I can say that the term "existence inertia" was earlier used by me in *God and Necessity*, 210.

by chance, out of the infinite number that could exist, one time after another, is in fact infinitesimally remote. So, making the odds 50/50 is, in fact, being extremely generous.[49] Be that as it may, the assumption here is made that, for any contingent being such as Bob, for any moment it exists, there is a 50/50 chance that it exists the following moment. The same holds for the next moment, and the next moment, and so on. Since for a contingent being, non-existence is just as good as existence, there is no reason why the mere fact that it exists at t_1 will mean that it will continue to exist at t_2. Given the huge number of entities in existence and the long times that they have existed, it becomes impossible to hold that all this orderliness happens for no reason at all.

The basic problem here for the Brute Fact theorist is that there is *no logical relation* between different beings and between the same beings at different times. There is no logical contradiction that a proton will have a different strong nuclear force than other protons, or that if a proton like Bob exists at one moment, it will still exist at the next.

An appeal may at this point again be made to the laws of nature. Surely, it might be argued, the laws of nature are such that if a proton has a strong nuclear force of some strength (or any other property of any other physical object), then it will keep it. Further, there must be some sort of law, wherein things that exist at one moment will continue to exist at the next moment. Of course, it may be argued, whatever laws there are may be a matter of brute fact, determined when the universe came into existence but once they are here, these laws don't change.

These considerations may have a good deal of intuitive support. But this tendency is simply because the universe we see is orderly and consistent, at least as far as the laws and constants of nature are concerned. But though the universe does act in this way, these suppositions do not give us a reason *why* it does so. The laws of nature are descriptive, not prescriptive. They describe how the universe and the things of which it is composed act. The laws are not things themselves that stand over the universe, forcing it to act in a certain way. The laws are statements of *observed consistencies*, not celestial legislative decrees.

In effect, given Brute Fact theory, *there can be no laws of nature*.[50] All that there can be is descriptions of how things are and how they act at

---

49. I think that the odds are strictly speaking incalculable. This does not however mean that we cannot know that they are very small. For example, we cannot with exactitude calculate the odds that the next forty-three presidents of the United States will all have the name Fred, but we do know that they are very small.

50. Writes Van Til on this, "Suppose we think of a man made of water in an infinitely extended and bottomless ocean of water. Desiring to get out of the water, he

different times, ultimately for no reason at all. Such are the logical implications of Brute Fact theory.

It is ironic that philosophic naturalist philosophers and scientists often hold to the unbreakability of the laws of nature, while at the same time holding that these laws exist in the manner that they do, ultimately for no reason at all. The universe for them is thus quite *rational* in the sense of being orderly, and yet clearly is *irrational* in the sense that everything happens by chance,[51] or brutely, without reason. This is fundamentally contradictory.

It should be noted that I am not begging the question as to whether everything needs a reason for its existence. Although I think this is true, that everything does need a reason for its existence, I am not assuming this to be true.[52] That is, I will admit for the sake of argument that things may exist without a reason. I am simply showing the implications of doing so. *It is here that the absurdity of the Brute Fact theory really comes to light, for it tries to derive universal lawfulness and orderliness out of pure randomness and chance.*[53]

It is not only theists who have noted this problem. Writes Quentin Smith, an atheist, about this,

> At each moment the world could either *happen* or *not happen*, and I marvel that the world happens, and continues to happen, and avoids the possibility of not happening. At each moment, the world-whole stands before the abyss of nothingness, but it does not vanish into this abyss; it continues, and in so continuing it overcomes again and again the possibility of nonexisting. It is miraculous that the other possibility, the possibility of plunging into nothingness, is not realized, for this is *equally as possible* as the possibility that it is realized.[54]

---

makes a ladder of water. He sets this ladder upon the water and against the water and then attempts to climb out of the water. So, hopeless and senseless a picture must be drawn of the natural man's methodology based as it is upon the assumption that time or chance is ultimate." Van Til, *Defense*, 124.

51. As Van Til writes, "About chance no manner of assertion can be made. In its very idea it is the irrational. And how are rational assertions to be made about the irrational? . . . [I]f the natural man is to make any intelligible assertions about the world of 'reality' or 'fact' which, according to him, is what it is for no rational reason at all, then he must make the virtual claim or rationalizing the irrational." Van Til, *Defense*, 148.

52. Since I think that God exists necessarily, this question is a "per impossible" one.

53. Parrish, *God and Necessity*, 185–215.

54. Smith, *Felt Meanings*, 181–82. I believe that Smith no longer holds to this position, and instead thinks of the universe as somehow self-caused. I think this position also is absurd. For how can a being that has no reason for its own existence be the cause of itself? See his, https://infidels.org/library/modern/quentin_smith/self-caused.html, Note 1.

I would argue that given philosophical naturalism, Smith's thought that the likelihood of the universe's vanishing into nothingness is basically correct, but that instead of the universe as a whole vanishing into nothingness, it is much more likely that individual objects would vanish into nothingness. In other words, there would be chaos.

Another response to the argument that I have been giving is by Herman Philipse. In a recent book he states, "[W]hy should we assume that an abyss of nothingness threatens each entity at every moment of its existence, and endorse the PNCN [Principle of the Natural Collapse into Nothingness]? If no convincing arguments for this devilish assumption are put forward, we should reject it out of hand."[55] Well, how about this argument that I have given above: no contingent being has the reason for its existence internal to itself, contained in its existence, and so unless it is caused by something else, there is no reason for it to exist. Why then does it continue to exist, moment after moment, for no reason? These are not novel thoughts. Philipse ignores, for example, the whole of Thomism and scholastic metaphysics. It is also interesting that he calls it an *assumption* that things need a reason for their continuing in existence. It is not an assumption; this is an argument. Interestingly, Philipse labels this "assumption" as "devilish." But calling the position a name does nothing to refute it.

Even if we lived in a universe which by sheer luck has been orderly up until now, the odds are vast, perhaps infinite, that at the next moment it will become chaotic. Or, even if our portion of the universe remained orderly for a time, other observable portions of it would be chaotic. Indeed, this is much more likely than the whole universe's remaining orderly. It is much more likely that there would be a temporary island of order in a sea of chaos, than that the whole of the universe would be orderly. But this is not what we observe.

Further, since with Brute Fact theory the universe is much more likely at every moment to become chaotic than that it remains orderly, we cannot rationally believe anything about what the future will be like. Indeed, it seems that on Brute Fact theory we cannot trust any of our thoughts, for they would be thoughts just caused by random occurrences in the brain and the mind, rather than be the result of rationality. If this were the case, there would be no reason to trust our reasoning. But we do and must do so. So, to act as rational beings, Brute Fact theory must be false. Taken seriously, it destroys order, being, and knowledge.

One last point: it might be thought that given Brute Fact theory, things should really be so chaotic, that it is a misnomer to talk about a universe,

---

55. Philipse, *God in the Age of Science?*, 238.

something that by its nature would have some set of consistent laws. I agree with this and have been giving the Brute Fact theorist more than what I think he is really entitled to. And the theory still fails.

To sum up, with Brute Fact theory, what is ultimate is *chance* or pure possibility. Whatever contingent things exist, do so for no reason. They are merely the random products of nothing.[56] This brings us to the next theory.

Due to a Reason External to Itself. If Bob does *not* exist only by chance, then Bob's existence must be due to a *reason external to himself.* This has been discussed above in this chapter in the section on necessary deity theory. If contingent beings exist for a reason other than themselves, then ultimately one must arrive at a being that exists for a reason internal to itself, a necessary being. I have argued that only God can be this necessary being. Contingent beings may exist, but they do not have a reason for their existence within themselves, and therefore cannot give a reason to something else. One can only give what one has.

Necessary Universe Theory Examined

> Nothing in the universe is contingent, but all things are conditioned to exist and operate in a particular manner by the necessity of the divine nature.
>
> BENEDICT SPINOZA[57]

This brings us to the second non-theistic view of the nature of the universe—that the universe exists in the manner that it does necessarily, rather than by chance. By *necessary*, I mean in the strong sense of the word—that it is logically or absolutely impossible for things to be other than they are. As was stated above, most philosophers agree that either there is an infinite number of possible worlds, or there is only one world. With necessary universe or world theory, there is only one possible world, and this is it.

As outlined in the last paragraphs of chapter 2, this position can be held in two basic ways. The first is that the physical universe itself is necessary in the sense that it has within itself its own necessity. The second way is that there is some entity or entities other than God that necessarily emanate the universe.

---

56. In short, the elimination of God brings us back to the "chaos and old night" of ancient Greek cosmogony. Van Til, *Defense*, 265.

57. Spinoza, *Ethics*, Part I, 68. It should be noted that Spinzoa's "God" included the universe as part of its being. It was not a personal being. See chapter 3, note 62.

Option 1—The Universe Itself is Necessary

As for the *first* idea, that the universe itself is *necessary*, an initial objection to this view of natural law is that it seems strongly counter intuitive. Holding that the universe is *necessary*, means that it could not possibly be other than it is. At this moment in time there could not be any more or less crooked politicians in Washington than there are right now, and there could not be any fewer atoms in my desk than there actually are. If the universe is *necessary*, then there is no chance of other possibilities.

In response to this, it seems counter-intuitive to think that this world is the only one that could exist. However, it has been pointed out that there are limits to our ability to conceive of things. This is especially true regarding more abstract or complex matters. For example, both the existence and non-existence of God seem to be conceivable—we can imagine either case.

I agree that intuition by itself is of only limited value in these matters, but it does not derail this project. My view is that we do not so much rely on our *intuitions* of what is possible or impossible, but rather on the *law of non-contradiction*. In other words, *if we can show that there is a contradiction in some conceivable state of affairs, then it must be impossible*. If on the other hand, we cannot show a contradiction, then this gives us proof, or at least a reason for thinking, that there is no contradiction, and that the state of affairs is possible.

Getting back to the universe and the *laws* that describe its behavior, how likely is it that they are all necessary—in the sense of absolutely or logically necessary? Not very. That is, one may easily conceive of something in the universe as being different than it is without a logical contradiction being generated. For example, there does not seem to be a logical contradiction entailed if I were to think of the pen on my desk as being two centimeters to the right of where it is, or if my cat Bobbin has one less hair on her body than she does.

This being the case, the burden of proof is on the Necessary Universe theorist to show that real contradictions are generated by any change, no matter how trivial, in the universe. I do not see how this can possibly be done. Take any fact in the universe, describe even a small change, and see if you can derive a contradiction. Say that the pen on my computer desk was two centimeters to the right of where it is. Is there a logical contradiction involved in thinking this? It is very difficult to see where. It is not just the fact that we cannot derive a contradiction by making this assumption; it is that it seems impossible to see, even in theory, how one *could* derive a logical contradiction.

A weaker version of this view is that the laws of nature are logically necessary, even though the existence and position of the objects in the universe are contingent. For example, the laws of nature such as the speed of light or the strong nuclear force must have the strengths that they do have, but the entities to which they apply are different from the ones that actually exist. Let's say, for example, that there might be a world where there is one less electron than the number that exist in the actual world.

Again, the problem with this watered-down view is that there does not seem to be any reason to think that the laws of nature could not be other than they are. For example, as was argued above, one cannot derive a contradiction from saying that the speed of light be 186,283 miles per second instead of 186,282 miles per second, which it is. Indeed, it again seems difficult to imagine how there could even be a contradiction in this.

Consider the following argument. Take any kind of finite measurement—size, shape, weight, mass, speed, etc.—of some object. Give the measurement some particular value. Say, 2 inches, 3 pounds, 40 miles per hour, etc. Now change the value to twice what it was: e.g., 4 inches, 6 pounds, 80 miles per hour. Does changing the value generate a logical contradiction in the object itself? There may be a contradiction in the way that the object behaves; obviously, if the object is twice as heavy, then it will exert twice as much force on anything that it is set upon. But no contradiction can be derived.

If the laws of nature are merely descriptive of how things do in fact behave, then they explain nothing. They just *describe how* things act, without answering the question of *why* they do. On the other hand, if they are coercive, then they somehow cause natural objects to act in a certain manner. Laws are perhaps most plausibly thought of as abstract entities. However, abstract objects are held by almost everyone to not cause things. If so, then how could they possibly cause the relevant objects to act in the prescribed manner?[58]

The most plausible way of saying that the laws of nature cause objects to act in a certain manner is to hold that what the real situation is, is that the objects themselves have certain natures, and these natures are what make them act in that certain manner.[59] The problem with this is the same as that which was described in the section above. There is no reason that the nature of objects would remain the same, or even that the objects would remain in existence over time.

---

58. See Jaeger, *What the Heavens Declare*.
59. For an exposition and defense of essentialism, see Oderberg, *Real Essentialism*.

If one asserted that the universe and the laws that govern the actions of objects in it were necessary, there is still a major problem. This is that none of the laws of nature are necessary and universal. The fact is, there is an infinite number of laws that exist abstractly, and which could apply to the objects. Why, then, do only some of them affect the objects in the universe? Take the nature of objects themselves, for example, Bob the proton. That Bob has a certain nature at some time does nothing by itself show why it has the same nature at other times, or even why it continues to exist. In short, there is still no plausible account for the necessity of natural law, and hence no account of why the universe is not chaotic.

Option 2—Something Emanates the Universe

The *second* way of holding to the Necessary Universe theory seems more plausible, at least initially. This holds that there is some necessary thing (or things) which in some manner emanates the universe. Take the Plotinian One (which is a kind of the Absolute), which supposedly emanates the universe necessarily out of itself, as the sun emanates sunlight. The sun does not choose to emanate sunlight, but does so because of its nature, and so does the One.[60]

The Plotinian One

The One may be thought of, in some ways, as being like God, but the One is in other ways radically different. It is like God in that it exists necessarily transcendent to the universe and is the supreme and most fundamental part of reality. The main difference is that while God is a personal being, the One is thought of as being impersonal. Indeed, it is thought of as being beyond thought, as even beyond being or existence (whatever that means). Some describe it as so totally other, that it cannot be described, or even coherently thought about.

Of course, there is a problem for this kind of thinking. First, as was argued above, if we say that there is something about which we can know nothing, we have contradicted ourselves, for we are saying that we know something (that the something is unknowable), and that we know nothing about it. Second, if something is truly unknowable, then it is completely useless as an explanation. To explain something means to give a *reason why* it is the way that it is. This view fails to do so. For some Entity *A* to

---

60. See chapter 2, note 9.

explain another Entity *B*, is to show how *A*'s existence causes *B* to exist in the manner that it does. For example, a football (Entity *B*) is soaring in a Hail Mary because Tom Brady (Entity *A*) threw it to his tight end. But with the Plotinian One we can derive no explanation, for we do not know how the unknowable thing exists in such a manner that it can explain the thing to be explained.[61]

The God of Spinoza

Another option for the emanating cause of the universe is the "god" of Spinoza. Spinoza has been subjected to different interpretations, but basically his idea is that everything is a part of "god," or the One. Not God as described by classical theists, but a pantheistic god which either is the universe or else includes the universe as part of it—which is why Spinoza calls it "god or nature." It exists in an infinite number of "modes." The ones of which we are aware are the modes of thought and extension. This "god or nature" is a necessary and infinite being that includes everything that exists, and everything could not exist in any other manner.

Among its infinite number of properties Spinoza's god includes thoughts. Some of these are the thoughts of finite creatures such as we are. But even if Spinoza's "god or nature" itself has thoughts, it is not an agent. It is not itself personal. In a sense, it is just everything considered as being one big substance or thing.[62]

What can be said about this? As is the case with Plotinus, discussing Spinoza's philosophy in the depth that it deserves would take a discussion a lot longer than this book. However, we can address this issue briefly here, as there is a criticism that I think is deadly to Spinoza's theory. Remember that Spinoza thought that everything happens of necessity. So, for example, the fact that my cat is sitting exactly ten feet away from me at this moment is a necessary truth. But how could this be the case necessarily? What is it about my cat that sitting ten feet away from me at this moment makes it a necessary truth? There seems to be nothing in the situation that makes it necessarily so.

Whence comes then the necessity? It cannot come from any particular part of Spinoza's god's being, because one may coherently ask why it is ten

---

61. Another criticism is that by bringing in an entity such as Plotinus's One, it is more a form of pantheism, than it is naturalism. But some forms of pantheism are not that different from naturalism.

62. Spinoza wrote, "[N]either intellect nor will pertain to the nature of God." Cited in Lawhead, *Voyage*, 271.

feet and not nine feet. What then entails the existence of the universe as it is, rather than in some other manner? Where in Spinoza's "god or nature" is the necessity located; what part of it entails the existence of my cat's sitting?

Further, this reasoning can be applied to all of Spinoza's god. Every individual part seems contingent. One cannot have a necessary being entirely composed of contingent parts. Saying this does not commit the fallacy of composition, for if a being is composed of contingent parts, then by definition the parts could have been different. If all the parts are contingent, then where is the necessity?

Spinoza's god cannot be omniscient, for it is not an agent or a personal being. It cannot choose between the infinite number of possible worlds (and indeed, for Spinoza there is only one possible world), for it does not know them. Its being in the manner that it exists is derived from its nature. But where is the nature that entails the existence of cats, atoms, continents, stars, etc? If god just *is* the universe, then there is no nature apart from the universe that can explain why the nature is the way that it is. Therefore, it seems that Spinoza's theory isn't able to get off the ground.

To comprehend all the things in existence, and to have a necessary reason for why they are as they are, rather than the infinite number of other ways that they could conceivably be, would require an infinite mind. As we have seen the concept of God in perfect being theism holds that he has an infinite mind.

However, this is classical or perfect being theism, not Spinoza's impersonal god, which in a very real sense doesn't know anything. In short, Spinoza has no answer as to *why* things must be the way that they are, nor does it seem possible that his "god" has one. His form of pantheism seems impotent, and as it seems that all forms of pantheism necessarily share the same defects, then pantheism cannot account for the existence of the universe in the manner that it does exist. Rather than choosing to create a universe out of the infinite number of universes that are conceivable, it must just mindlessly produce or emanate one, or else just be one, and hence the contingency and complexity of the universe are inexplicable.

Oppy's Explanation

A more recent attempt to account for the necessity of the universe comes from philosopher Graham Oppy. He argues that the universe may have had an initial state, and that this initial state was necessary, and that the universe flowed from this initial state, whether in a necessary or contingent manner.[63] Oppy holds (or at least theorizes) that the way that the universe was at its beginning was necessary (in the strongest sense of the word). It was absolutely necessary. Everything else in the universe, either necessary or contingent, came from this necessary initial state.

But does the existence of a necessary physical entity make sense? The criticism that I will make here should sound familiar by now, as it applies to all versions of the Necessary Universe theory. *For something to be absolutely necessary, to deny it must entail a contradiction.* And from the denial of the existence of a physical initial state of the universe, no contradiction arises. Any physical entity must have properties such as size, mass, various forces, etc. Each of these properties must have some value; i.e., a certain size, a certain mass, a certain amount of entropy, a certain strong nuclear force, etc. It seems clearly impossible that any value would be absolutely necessary.

Again, even were it granted that there could be a necessary physical state of the universe, and that this suffices to account for the creation of the universe, it does not account for the continued existence of the universe. That is, suppose the universe is at one thousand years after its creation. Why do the physical things of which the universe is composed continue to exist at that point? That a necessary initial state caused them to come into existence (if that were possible) still does not explain their continued existence.

So, it seems that Oppy fails—no physical entity can be absolutely necessary. It appears that a contingent being cannot explain the coming into existence of the universe, for its coming into existence would have to be explained, and the continued existence of the universe would be unexplained. Further, the concept of a necessarily existing physical entity is incoherent. So, all other alternatives to God's creating and maintaining the universe fail.

Modal Realism

Naturalists may make another attempt to explain why the universe exists as it does. This is the theory that everything exists! In other words, every possible world exists. This seems like a contradiction in terms, because as I have defined it, a possible world is reality as it could have been (or, in the case of the actual world, how it is).

---

63. Graham Oppy, "Shape," 281–87. See also his "Ultimate," 46–63. Another naturalistic theory of a necessary universe is held by Ayn Rand and the objectivists. For example, See Rand, *Philosophy*, 23–34. In response to this line of thinking, see Parrish, *God and Necessity*, 217–28; "God and Objectivism," 169–210; and "What's Good for the Goose," 395–415.

However, according to this theory, there is only one possible world with everything possible in it. Every conceivable, logically consistent world, including the one we live in, is just a separate universe among an infinite number of such universes. Necessarily, everything logically possible must exist in one universe of the multiverse. So, there are universes where there are dragons and talking donkeys, and so on. As Stephen Barr says, "If all possible universes exist, then there is a universe where the *Wizard of Oz* is a true story, and another where Kermit the Frog is a real person."[64] Although each universe exists, only ours is considered actual in the sense that we live in it. This theory is known as *modal realism*, or sometimes as *extreme modal realism*.[65] Barr concludes, "It is not surprising that very few people have ever adopted modal realism."[66]

Other universes, say one where you ran away and joined the circus instead of holding the position you do, would exist. But the person who was you in that universe would not literally be you, but a counterpart of you—someone exactly like you except with changes that the alternative universe would make on your counterpart.

What can be said against this rather strange theory? Why would reality be such that everything exists? The only answer that I can think of is that in this theory to be possible is to necessarily exist. In other words, the infinity of "everything that could possibly exist, exists somewhere." This seems strange enough by itself, for it clearly seems impossible for something to exist without actually existing. It seems clear that I might have taken a different route to work today than the one that I did take; not that there is another universe where a counterpart of me took a different route. However, a defender of extreme modal realism could rightly respond that my reply is question begging, so I do not think that it refutes the theory.

I think that a fatal objection to the theory is this: according the extreme modal realism every universe that can possibly exist, does exist. Therefore, anything that does not entail a contradiction exists. So, this means that there are universes where there are no consistent laws of nature, or where the laws are temporary, after which time the universe becomes chaotic, or where part of the universe is lawful but other parts are chaotic, etc. Indeed, though it is impossible to calculate the odds precisely, there is an infinite number of universes where things are or become chaotic compared to one where they remain lawful. This being the case, the odds of our universe's having been

---

64. Barr, *Modern Physics*, 155–56.

65. See Lewis, *On the Plurality of Worlds* for an exposition and defense of this theory, and Pruss, *Principle*, 300–14, for a brief refutation.

66. Barr, *Modern Physics*, 156.

lawful as long as it has been are exceedingly remote. Ironically, extreme modal realism theory has some of the same problems as brute fact theory.

This being the case, extreme modal realism should be rejected because despite its appeal to necessity, it too depends upon brute fact. Neither pure necessity nor pure chance can explain the universe. *Necessity cannot account for any of the contingencies of reality, while chance cannot account for any of the order therein.*

Caused by Abstract Entities?

There is one more theory of a necessarily existing universe that I will examine here. This states that the universe is caused by abstract entities. As we have already seen, by the very nature of abstract entities, this view seems impossible. However, there are philosophers who have defended it at length. One example of this that will be used as being representative of them all, is that propounded by John Leslie.[67]

Leslie's view holds that the existence of the universe is *ethically required*. This is to say that the universe exists because there are certain abstract entities, which in Leslie's view are ethical, that require that our universe exists. According to Leslie, there may be a god or gods, but if there are, they are not ultimate, for they exist because their existence is "ethically required," or to use different words, that they exist because moral principles bring them into being. Indeed, in one book Leslie argues that there is an infinite number of infinite minds and everything else concrete that exists (including us) is a thought in one of these minds.

Presumably, if the universe is ethically required, it must in some sense be the best universe, or one of the best possible universes, because given the ethical requiredness of the theory, it would seem that given different possibilities, it would be ethically imperative that the best possible situation be mandatory. Leslie is not the only philosopher to defend this kind of thinking. In his book *Hating Perfection*, John F. Williams argues to the same basic notion—the world in which we live is the best possible world, and it was abstract entities that caused it to exist.[68] Going back to ancient times, the Pythagoreans apparently believed in something similar.[69]

---

67. Leslie, *Value and Existence*. See also Leslie, *Universes*, and *Infinite Minds*. Perhaps Thomas Nagel could be placed somewhere around here. He seems to envision a scenario wherein abstract entities are causally active, though not the cause of the whole universe. See Nagel, *Mind and Cosmos*.

68. Williams, *Hating Perfection*.

69. The Pythagoreans not only seemed to believe that abstract entities—in this case

What may be said about this rather unique theory? Although Leslie himself argues that the probability of its being true exceeds 50 percent,[70] I will argue that the theory fails to do what it is supposed to do in several respects.

First, it is very difficult to see how mere abstractions can cause the existence of concrete spatio-temporal objects. For philosophers, it has often been part of the very definition of an abstract entity; that abstract entities cannot cause the existence of concrete things.

Second, I find it hard to understand how there could be such a thing as "ethical requiredness" apart from persons. The only kinds of beings that are interested in ethics are persons. By person I have in mind a broader category than human beings. God, angels, Klingons, and Hobbits (if the latter two categories of beings existed) are personal beings. Other kinds of things are amoral. Rocks don't care if they hit you on the head. Cars feel no guilt if they run you over or if they break down and cost you a lot of money to repair them. Germs feel no shame at all if they make you sick. If there are any animals that do comprehend ethics, and to the extent that they do have ethical concerns, they only do so because they share some of the characteristics of persons.

Third, even if we overlook the first two responses, I think that this third argument is decisive. This world is an extremely complicated place, with countless things and properties existing over a vast amount of time. Ethical or moral principles, on the other hand, are not complex. They are quite simple, even apart from the fact that they are mindless. So, to put things "user-friendly," how would abstract entities cause the existence of this incredibly elaborate and intricate universe in which we live?

Further, how do abstract principles make decisions when it is not clear what would be the most ethical thing to create? After all, to create what is ethically obligated would take knowledge of what is ethically required. For example, which situations are good or the best? How does an abstract principle distinguish between different good situations and discern which one is better? Also, it is imperative that the abstract objects can put these

---

numbers— caused reality, but worshipped and prayed to numbers. Here is a prayer to the number ten: "Bless us, divine number, thou who generatest gods and men! O holy, holy tetraktys, thou that containest the root and source of eternally flowing creation! For divine number begins with the profound, the pure unity until it comes to the holy four; then it begets the mother of all, the all-encompassing, the all-bounding, the first born, the never swerving, the never tiring holy ten, the keyholder of all." Quoted in Clouser, *Myth*, 21.

70. Leslie states, "I'd say my confidence in it [His Axiarchic theory of the universe's existence] is just a little over 50 percent. A lot of the time, I feel that the universe just happens to exist and that's it." Leslie, "Ethical Requiredness," 209.

"good" or "best" situations together in a coherent universe. Since there is an infinite number of conceivable worlds, the abstract entities would have to understand them completely, and compare each world to every other one. Are we really supposed to believe that some mindless abstract ethical principles can do all of this? Is the fact that there are N amount of hairs on my head (at this moment—earlier in time there were a lot more), determined by simple, unchanging, mindless abstract entities? This is asking an awful lot of abstract entities.

It might be argued that the abstract entity simply moves, by its intrinsic nature, to choose the "right" world. I do not see how this could possibly work. What about the best possible world is such that the abstract principle or entity can select it? Do the various possible worlds emit some sort of goodness radiation, and that ethical requiredness has a goodness detector? What about them would cause these possible worlds to have a goodness radiation? This sounds ridiculous on the face of it, and indeed seems wildly implausible at best. But with ethical requiredness's lacking knowledge and judgment, *something* like this would have to be the case.

The God of perfect being theism can do this because, by definition, he is omniscient, and thus contains all knowledge as part of his essence. *All things are included in him in the sense that he understands them all in their fullness*, including all their relationships with each other. But abstract entities do not know or understand anything and are incapable of making decisions. Indeed, only a personal being could contain all things, at least as objects of knowledge, within him. Therefore, only a personal God can be the foundation of other things' existing.

As with the explanation of the existence of the universe by abstract ethical principles, it seems that all creation by abstractions must fail to account for the existence of the universe in the manner that it exists. There are other proposals, but I think that none of them are any more successful than the one from ethical requiredness or extreme modal realism or the different versions of pantheism that I have described.

Summary

So, it seems that *there is no justification for the concept that the universe in itself is necessarily existent*. We have also seen that Brute Fact theory cannot account for the existence of the universe in the manner that it does. So, to reiterate, since this universe could not have come into existence by pure chance (Brute Fact), and since it cannot of itself be necessarily existent, *the universe must have been caused to come into existence*. Of the possible causation scenarios there are only two rivals to Necessary Deity theory. The rivals have been deflated, proven empty, through our discussion above. Therefore, it follows that *the only viable theory is that the universe is caused to exist by a necessary God*. Theism can explain the existence of the universe, while neither philosophical naturalism nor pantheism can. Naturalism in particular, interpreted in terms of either Brute Fact theory or Necessary Universe theory, only has whatever plausibility that it has by absolutizing some aspect of contingent reality, and founding everything else that is supposed to exist upon it. So, they essentially assign the "God role" to something else. However, each aspect of the universe is only a contingent entity, property, or event, which can neither explain its own existence nor the existence of the universe as a whole.

Indeed, in either Brute Fact or Necessary Universe theory, nature is not the ultimate "thing." Either *pure possibility* or *pure necessity* are. Seeing as both are abstractions, it seems that ironically naturalism leads to its own undermining, for what is ultimate is not nature itself, but some sort of abstract principle instead! Brute Fact Theory attempts to base the universe, to base reality, on something that has no explanation for its own existence. On the other hand, Necessary Universe Theory, if not founded upon a necessarily existing God, must appeal to abstract entities, which are by themselves incapable of accounting for the existence of any contingent or physical thing. Both thus fail utterly to account for the existence of reality as we find it.

As Cornelius Van Til wrote, in *Brute Fact Theory*, what the universe is like is a vast number of beads without a string, and even with no holes in the beads for the string to go through. With *Necessary Universe theory*, what one has is a superhighway with no exit ramps.[71] In neither case is it possible to give an account for the universe as it is. On neither theory can we have knowledge of how things are. Therefore, given the impossibility of the alternatives, theism must be true, and indeed, all our thinking, whether we know it or not, presupposes the truth of perfect being theism. Because the universe is created by God's infinite rational mind, human beings, who are created in the image of God and therefore have finite rational minds, can understand the universe and the things that exist in it, at least to an extent. Brute Fact cannot account for order or rationality; Necessary Universe cannot account for contingency. Hence, in order to justify that we can understand an ordered but contingent universe, *we must conclude that theism is true*.

---

71. These examples from Van Til were given to me by Richard Ostella.

Chapter 4

The Existence of the Mind

> In a proper theory of consciousness, the Emperor [the conscious self] is not just deposed, but exposed, shown to be nothing other than a cunning conspiracy of lesser operatives whose activities jointly account for the "miraculous" powers of the Emperor. Banished along with the Emperor are what might be called the Imperial Properties: the two most mysterious varieties being the Qualia Enjoyed by the Emperor and the Imperial Edicts of Conscious Will.
>
> DANIEL DENNETT[1]

> [J]ust as it turned out that there was no such thing as impetus, there may be no such thing as awareness.
>
> PATRICIA CHURCHLAND[2]

> After decades of concerted effort on the part of neuroscientists, psychologists, and philosophers, only one proposition about how the brain makes us conscious—how it gives rise to sensation, feeling, subjectivity—has emerged unchallenged: we don't have a clue.
>
> ALVA NOË[3]

> Do they profess to have delighted us by telling us that they hold our soul to be only a little wind and smoke, especially by telling us this in a haughty and self-satisfied tone of voice? Is this a thing to say gaily? Is it not, on the contrary, a thing to say sadly, as the saddest thing in the world?
>
> BLAISE PASCAL[4]

1. Dennett, *Sweet Dreams*, 71.
2. Patricia Smith Churchland, *Neurophilosophy*, 309.
3. Noë, *Out of Our Heads*, xi.
4. Pascal, *Pascal's Pensées*, number 194, 57.

The Nature of "Persons"

IN THE NATURE OF "persons" there are two major viewpoints generally held. The first perspective we will discuss is called *materialism* or *physicalism* (I will use the terms interchangeably). The second view is called *dualism*—the belief that matter and consciousness are different kinds of things. Traditionally, both among Christians and others, the answer to the question of what persons are has been *dualism*, the view that human beings are both material and non-material "parts," i.e., *body* and *soul*. However, more recently, *materialism* has been more dominant in the realms of science and philosophy; indeed, in many academic circles it is largely taken for granted that materialism is true, and even foundational. This almost unquestioning acceptance of materialism is sometimes the standard even in some sectors of contemporary theology. As Uwe Meixner writes, many philosophers, "[W]ould rather bite off their tongues than profess dualism in any form."[5] We will examine the issue to see which has the stronger case.[6]

Physical Objects

Physical objects have properties such as weighing a certain amount, or having mass, or taking up space (which is called being *extended*) and moving through space (and time). They are usually affected by such things as gravity, electromagnetism, and other physical forces. They exist in space and time (or else *are* space and time). Most fundamentally, physical things are things that have propensities to act in certain manners when they have an effect on, or are affected by, other physical things. The whole physical world is governed by a set of laws that describe how the various physical entities will act in different situations, though the majority view in physics seems to be that there is some genuine indeterminism involved in the actions of subatomic particles.[7]

What about the "Conscious"?

However, there is a part of reality that does not immediately fit into this scheme of things. Though it is highly controversial, it seems, at least at

---

5. Meixner, "Against Physicalism."
6. For a detailed examination of this issue, see Parrish, *Knower*.
7. What is meant by genuine indeterminism is that things could have gone differently given the same prior situation. For example, with indeterminism, one cannot predict how things will turn out just based on how things were to start with.

first glance, that there may be two fundamental kinds of concrete things; the physical, and the conscious. Physical things can be weighed and measured and can be studied by the natural sciences—indeed according to some philosophers, this is everything except for consciousness. Aspects of consciousness, like *qualia* (such as the colors we see and sounds we hear), beliefs, desires, and the like do not fit readily into the list of physical properties listed above.

The Physicalist (Materialist) View

The majority view at this time is that thoughts (and the minds that think them) *can* in some manner be reduced to the physical. They believe that minds and their conscious thoughts *just are* the brain and body existing and behaving in some manner, and that ultimately consciousness can be explained by purely physical factors. Philosophers and scientists who think this are called materialists or physicalists. There are, in fact, many different varieties of *materialism*, but ultimately, they all break down into the proposition that *all the concrete objects that exist are in some way physical*.[8]

The Dualist View

Other philosophers hold that conscious things, like thoughts or minds themselves, cannot be reduced to the physical. Though theses *dualists* are a minority of philosophers in these days, I believe that they may well constitute most of the total number of philosophers who have lived throughout history. Put simply, these philosophers believe that *conscious entities cannot be reduced*—be purely explained in terms of—*the physical*. They are, instead, another *category* of being.

Dualists

There are two groups of dualists. The first group is the *property dualists*, who think that there are conscious properties, such as specific thoughts, that cannot be reduced to the physical. However, for the property dualists, the self

---

8. For some defenses of materialism regarding the mind, see for example: Armstrong, *Materialist Theory*; Patricia Smith Churchland, *Neurophilosophy*; Paul Churchland, *Matter and Consciousness*; Hill, *Sensations*; McGinn, *Mysterious Flame*; Dennett, *Consciousness Explained*; and Melnyk, *Physicalist Manifesto*. For books containing debates on the issue, see Crisp, *Neuroscience*; and Loose, *Blackwell Companion to Substance Dualism*. See also, Beilby, *Naturalism Defeated*?

that thinks these thoughts is the physical brain. The other position is called *substance dualism*, wherein the self, the thing that is conscious, is non-physical. It is also called a "soul" or "spirit" in theology. So, with substance dualism, thoughts are immaterial, as is the self that thinks them.[9] This position is sometimes called *Cartesian dualism*, after the philosopher Rene Descartes, but is in fact broader than just Descartes's own theory.

It should be noted that neither property nor substance dualism denies the importance of the brain and body. One may be an ardent substance dualist and still think that the self and its thoughts are strongly dependent on the brain. Indeed, one may even believe that without the physical brain, the mind could not exist, and still be a dualist in good standing. The chief difference between dualism and materialism is that with dualism, consciousness and the brain are correlated, and almost always are considered to interact with one another, but, in contrast to materialism, *consciousness is not the same thing as the brain*.

Materialists

Materialists believe that in some manner or other, the brain or body is the same exact thing as the mind or consciousness. Given materialism, consciousness is just the brain and nervous system and body existing and acting in a certain manner. What that manner of existence and activity is, is a matter of dispute among materialists. There are many different physicalist theories: identity, functionalism, supervenience, realization, mysterianism, and eliminativism, with these having sub-varieties.

Another way of putting it is this: dualists think that there are two (or at least two) fundamentally different kinds of concrete things in existence—conscious ones and physical ones. Materialists, on the other hand, think that there is only one, or at least only one that we know about and which is relevant to us in the universe we live in. This one thing is the physical. However, there may, of course, be many different types of physical objects, and indeed very different varieties of objects. For example, space and time are different from objects like atoms, cars, and planets.

---

9. For some defenses of substance dualism, see for example: Menuge, *Agents Under Fire*; Foster, *Immaterial Self*; Hasker, *Emergent Self*; Loftin and Farris, *Christian Physicalism?*; Robinson, *From the Knowledge Argument*; Lund, *Perception, Mind*; Meixner, *Two Sides of Being*; Slagle, *Epistemological Skyhook*; Swinburne, *Mind, Brain*; Varghese, *Missing Link*; Fumerton, *Knowledge, Thought*; Moreland, *Soul*; as well as my *Knower*. A classic statement of this position is in Lewis, *Miracles*. For an interesting study of consciousness, see Gelernter, *Tides of Mind*.

Consciousness

The question that I will investigate here is this: *what is the theory of the mind which is most likely to be true?* What is the mind like? In contrast to matter, consciousness is seemingly a radically other kind of thing. Indeed, sometimes the two concepts are defined by the fact that one is not the other. Consciousness as such is seemingly not governed by or describable by the laws of physics. It is something that is not directly affected by gravity or electromagnetism, nor has it a particular shape, mass, color, or motion.[10]

Rather, consciousness is describable by other factors. Four of these factors that seem especially important are *phenomenality, rationality, subjectivity,* and *intentionality*. *Phenomenality* means sheer *awareness*—that one is conscious of things like colors, sounds, and feels; but also, other things like the content of one's thought, or oneself as a thinking thing. By *rationality* what is meant is that consciousness can reason about concepts, using logic and evidence, and come to an understanding of them. By *subjectivity* what is basically meant is that consciousness is *subjective*, that it necessarily has an "I" involved in it. Consciousness is *private*. Every thought is thought by someone, and no one else can share that consciousness. It is also *self-presenting*, in that one is directly aware of one's own conscious thoughts, while only indirectly aware of anyone else's. Outside of one's own thoughts, one is only indirectly aware of material objects. *Intentionality* means that all thought "intends" an object. That is, every thought is *about something*, whether the thing that is the object of thought is material or immaterial.

None of these above characteristics are shared by material objects *as such*. Indeed, it seems at first glance that not only are *consciousness* and *matter* different things, but they are different *kinds* or *categories* of things. Nonetheless, materialists think that they are in some real sense identical with each other. The question then becomes, "How can matter and consciousness be identical, be exactly the same thing, and yet seem to be so different?"

Types of Materialism

There are several materialist theories about how this is supposed to work. I mentioned them above and will now explain the different theories one by one including: *mysterianism, eliminativism, identity, supervenience, realization,* and *functionalism*. These theories in different ways hold that

---

10. Of course, it may be indirectly affected by external physical things, as people who have drunk too much alcohol can testify.

consciousness and the brain or body is the same thing.[11] In reality though, the differences between the various materialist views are small—more variations on a theme than distinct ways of looking at the issue.[12]

Mysterianism

Mysterianism is the view that the mind (which is what I shall generally call the *conscious* aspects of our experience from now on) and the brain or body (which I will henceforth simply describe as the *brain*) is the same thing in some way, but because of the way that our brains evolved and are constructed, we can never understand how.[13] It is simply a mystery. Just as a cat cannot understand calculus[14] because its brain is too small and differently designed, neither can we understand how consciousness and matter are really the same.

Eliminativism

This is the theory that consciousness as such does *not* exist. I have a hard time believing that this is what they think, but that is what they seem to write. Eliminativism holds that the fact that we think that we have beliefs is just a false theory. What is going on is that the brain exists and acts in certain ways, and that as far as thought goes, there is nothing else. That we have phenomenal consciousness is in some sense an *illusion*.[15] Or, to put it bluntly, on eliminativism there are no conscious aspects of the mind; e.g., beliefs do not exist. We only think that we think.

Identity Theory

On this view, the mind and the brain are *identical*—the same thing, only "looked at" from different perspectives.[16] This is to say, that on one reading of this theory, my thought about the funniness of some joke is identical with—the exact same thing as—the neurons in my brain firing in a particular pattern. The brain is what it looks like from the "outside," from a third

---

11. One version of supervenience theory is a form of dualism.
12. Parrish, *Knower*, 117–20.
13. Parrish, *Knower*, 120–33.
14. I had a pretty tough time with it too. Mathematics is not my strong point.
15. Parrish, *Knower*, 133–50.
16. Parrish, *Knower*, 150–64.

person perspective, while the conscious part, my thinking about the funniness of the joke, is what it looks like from the "inside," from a first-person perspective. So, if someone else's brain looks on the "inside" the exact same as my brain, it would have the exact same thought in response to the joke.

Supervenience Theory

This theory purports that the mind *supervenes* on the brain.[17] What does it mean to supervene? Simply, just as wetness supervenes on water, so does the mind supervene on the brain. Wetness is not something over and above water; rather, it is simply a property of water when there are enough H2O molecules at a certain pressure and temperature. No isolated, single H2O atom is wet. It is only when a large enough group of them are put together that wetness appears. It is therefore a property of H2O atoms when they are in a large enough group under the right conditions. Similarly, consciousness arises when enough neurons exist together in the right pattern, but the thought is nothing more than the brain in that pattern.

Functionalist Materialism

This view states that the mind is just the brain's acting or functioning in a certain way.[18] That is, the brain receives input from the environment, processes it in certain ways, and then gives an output. Consciousness is thus held to be the *functioning* of the brain and the relevant inputs and outputs that it receives and gives. It is therefore an activity rather than a certain state of the brain.

Realization Materialism

Here, the mind is realized in the brain when the brain is in a *certain state* or performing in a certain way.[19] Consciousness is therefore just the brain's and its constituents' existing and acting in a certain mode, just as being salt is sodium and chloride atoms' existing bonded together and acting in a certain way. Admittedly, this appears very similar to supervenience theory.

---

17. Parrish, *Knower*, 165–66.
18. Parrish, *Knower*, 171–77.
19. Parrish, *Knower*, 167–71.

Two Major Groupings

These views can be boiled down into two major groupings—non-reductive and reductive theories. Recall that "reduction" is *reducing* consciousness to the purely physical or material with nothing left over. With non-reductionist views, one cannot directly reduce consciousness to the physical, just as in the case with wetness's being a property of a group of H2O atoms. In the final analysis, however, in non-reductionist theories, everything is also physical.

Reductive Materialism

This group of theories views that all consciousness can be reduced to material objects, specifically to the brain and the body.[20] Reductionism is where one thing can be reduced to another in the sense that the former can be completely explained in terms of the latter. As in the example given above, water in its various states is reducible to H2O molecules' acting in various ways. Similarly, a diamond can cut glass, because of the nature of the carbon atoms of which the diamond is made, and the nature of the sodium silicate, calcium silicate, and silicon dioxide molecules out of which the glass is composed.

So, while *eliminativism* claims that consciousness in its various aspects *does not exist* (is eliminated), *reductionism* claims that consciousness does not exist *as such*. That is, if one examines a particular aspect of consciousness such as a particular thought closely enough, one will "see" (that is, come to understand) that the thought is actually a part of the brain's acting in a certain manner—neurons' firing in a certain pattern, for example. The conscious aspect that one encounters therefore is in some sense an *illusion*.

Non-reductive Materialism

This also holds that all that there is to human beings and their conscious minds is matter.[21] Where it differs from reductive materialism is that in non-reductive materialism, one cannot simply reduce a thought to a part of the brain as it is acting in a certain manner. In contrast to reductionism and eliminativism, the conscious aspects of the mind *do exist* as such. Rather, though the thought supervenes on the brain, thought is not straightforwardly reducible to matter. However, ontologically (in the sense of being) it

---

20. Parrish, *Knower*, 46–57.
21. Parrish, *Knower*, 47–53.

must be reducible to the material brain, because if it couldn't be, it wouldn't be materialism—rather, it would be a form of dualism. So even with non-reductionist theories, consciousness must ultimately be material, but for some reason we cannot straightforwardly reduce it to the brain's activity, which in the final analysis means that we cannot understand why or how a material brain is in some way numerically identical with the thoughts that we have. Indeed, I will argue that this fatal flaw holds for every physicalist theory of the mind and the brain.[22]

First, in the final analysis, as was mentioned above, the different materialist theories don't differ from each other that much. There is a difference between non-reductive theories and others, in the sense that in non-reductive materialism consciousness does exist even though, in the end, it too is ultimately material or physical. This is explained in detail below. Materialism has severe problems, as I will now attempt to show. To do so, I will give another, simpler analysis of materialist positions. There are four ultimate positions: mysterianism, eliminativism, and reductive and non-reductive materialism.

Problems with Materialism

Despite the current popularity of materialist theories, I will now show that all of these theories fail to explain consciousness on multiple grounds. This section will outline some of the major problems that materialism faces.

Problem One: The *Existence* of Consciousness

First, given standard philosophical naturalism and materialism, *why does consciousness exist at all?* This problem comes from the following considerations. According to standard naturalism, the universe has either existed in some form forever, or else came into existence at a certain time in the past. Up until the point at which consciousness evolved, all that existed was unconscious material objects in motion. Then somehow, by

---

22. One kind of non-reductionism is *Constitutional materialism*. This view holds that although human beings are purely material objects, they are not identical with their bodies. This is to say that though a person could be composed of a certain matter, they could have instead been made of quite different matter, in perhaps quite varied shapes. Even granting this, it is difficult to see how this helps materialism, for it is still subject to all the problems associated with physicalism. For a presentation and defense of this view, see Baker, *Persons and Bodies*.

chance (that is to say, unplanned), consciousness, a new kind or category of being, came into existence.

To appreciate the strangeness of this whole concept, think of it in this way. As was stated above, material entities are the kinds of things that occupy space, move around in space and time, and interact with other material entities according to natural law. According to the standard cosmological theory, these material entities were the only things that existed for a long time. Then at one point in the evolution of life on the earth (and possibly elsewhere in the universe), consciousness came into existence. Or, to put things bluntly, at one moment in the past there was no consciousness in the universe, then the next moment there was.

This by itself is hard to explain. What caused consciousness to come into existence suddenly when it had never existed before? Presumably, consciousness came into existence when a brain achieved a certain level of complexity. In other words, when a physical object—a brain—was formed in, and acted on in a certain way, consciousness then appeared. It was a genuine novelty in the universe. Let us call the first brain to have phenomenal consciousness "B," and the consciousness that "arose" in some sense or other from it "C."

The problem is that the relation between B and C seems to be entirely contingent, and indeed quite arbitrary. That is, why should a brain of the form B somehow cause or realize in some sense consciousness C? One can examine this brain B until one is blue in the face and not see any reason why consciousness C would arise from it. They seem to have nothing to do with each other—as I wrote earlier, they seem to be different *categories* of being.

Relationship Between the Brain and Consciousness

This is different from most relationships in the physical world. One can understand why the heart pumps blood from the way that the atoms and molecules of the heart and the body are structured. One can understand why water is a liquid when its molecules are at a certain temperature and pressure. One can understand why an object rolls when one knows about the law of gravity and one sees that all the atoms in this object are arranged in the shape of a wheel or a ball. The macro properties that they have, from being a heart, water, or a ball, flow naturally from the micro properties—the nature and position of the atoms out of which these objects are composed. All of this follows from the fundamental laws and constants of nature; given these laws and the relevant situation, the rest is inevitable. Truths like this may not always be easy to find out. In some cases, as in the behavior of subatomic particles, it may be virtually impossible to find out. Nevertheless, there seems to be no difficulty *in principle* in there being a truth about matters like this.

However, the same does not apply to the relationship of the physical brain and the conscious mind. The property of being a mind is not entailed (required)—or at least one cannot see any entailment—by the nature of the brain to which it is associated. Or to put things another way, thinking about how a brain is gives one no clue about what is being thought by the person who has the brain. This applies to any brain and to any consciousness. The relationship between them seems utterly arbitrary and ad hoc. This is not to say that, given a brain and the conscious associated with it, we could not work out some sort of method of correlation between what the brain is doing and what is being consciously thought. Indeed, to a certain extent today we can work out some of the correlations between the different brain states and the different conscious states.[23]

It just means that any correlation between a brain and the consciousness associated does not logically follow from the nature of the brain or the consciousness. The relationship is quite contingent—nothing that we know about matter or the brain would *predict* that when a material object takes a certain shape, consciousness of any kind will then pop into existence. This does not make materialism impossible, but it makes it impossible ever to give a satisfactory explanation of *how* and *why* consciousness exists.

Consciousness an Illusion?

The problem is different for *eliminative materialism*. For with this theory, there simply is no such thing as consciousness. Rather, it is an illusion of some kind. What is going on is that the brain is existing and acting in some manner. The thought that consciousness is an illusion is itself rather a strange one. Isn't it so that one must be conscious to have illusions? Further, if one has the illusion of being conscious, isn't one necessarily actually conscious? If you think there is no such thing as thinking, your action contradicts your belief.

There is a further problem with eliminativism, which it shares with reductive theories. This is that they are both theories of how the mind and the brain *work*. Theories can only be described and understood in terms of propositional attitudes. Put in plain English, propositional attitudes are such things as beliefs, understandings, doubts, and hopes. So, to understand any theories, one needs things like language and concepts to understand

23. Though there are limitations even here. See Satel and Lilienfeld, *Brainwashed*.

them. With eliminativism, all that exist mentally are brain states. And brain states cannot, by their very nature, be used to describe a theory. So, with eliminativism, theories could never be described or understood, because the concepts would not exist to do so. Strictly speaking with eliminative materialism there are no such things as concepts. The same is true for reductionism, which doesn't deny that conscious aspects like beliefs exist, but holds that they are misdescribed, being the brain and its activities.

Intentionality

Further, physical objects have no *intentionality*. They are not "about" things. If all that existed were the physical aspects of the mind, then nothing could be known—for knowing or understanding something is not a part of the physical description of a brain. One could never think about even something as simple as the chair on which one is sitting. A complete understanding of one's brain's physical aspects gives no information about the chair. At most there could be an "as-if" kind of intentionality. For example, a missile might be programmed to go after an airplane. Whenever its radar detected the plane it would fly towards it. But the missile would not be "about" the plane. The missile would just be programmed to act in a certain way with certain stimuli. There is no knowledge about the plane in the missile, and the missile does not know what it is doing when it pursues the plane.

Similarly, writing marks on a paper or on the computer screen is meaningless. Only a conscious mind can impart to or read off with any meaning in them. *Intentionality* is only in the mind, not in the brain as such. Given all of this, with eliminative materialism, no one could ever know that it is true, for no one could know anything.[24]

The Fundamental Problem

The fundamental point here is, besides the general weirdness of denying that either consciousness exists at all or that it exists *as* consciousness instead of something physical, is that when the concepts associated with consciousness are removed, there is nothing left to describe theories like eliminativism or reductionism. In short, they are self-refuting.

---

24. As Dinesh D'Souza writes about Paul and Patricia Churchland, two leading eliminativist materialist philosophers, "My conclusion is that, without being aware of it, the Churchlands have lost their minds. This, however, should not disturb them very much since they don't believe that they have minds in the first place." D'Souza, *Life After Death*, 116.

Overlooking the fact that without consciousness, there is no description of anything, there is the following problem. With eliminativism and reductionism, the only things that are describable about the "mind" are really about the brain. That is, one could describe its size, weight, shape, motion, etc. But there would be no resources to describe thought. How could one describe wittiness or profundity, for example, if all the terms that one had to use were physical ones? It seems that, taken literally, eliminativism and reductionism are hopeless. *They depend for their very existence upon factors that they deny exist.*

Problem Two: Are Consciousness and the Brain Identical?

The second problem for physicalism is simply that it seems to assert things that are obviously false. To put things plainly, *on any form of materialism, conscious thought is identical with the brain*, part of the brain, or is the brain acting in some manner. If consciousness and the mind are not so identical, then materialism is false.

The problem with this seems obvious. As I already stated, conscious thoughts and the brain seem to be radically different things. The brain is a material thing. It is a very complex piece of fat, with billions of neurons embedded in it.[25] Like all other material objects, it has a size, shape, mass, location, force, movement, and other properties. Consciousness on the other hand, has a quite different set of properties. Properties of consciousness include, as I wrote above, phenomenality, rationality, subjectivity, and intentionality. Thought has other secondary properties too, such as clarity, dullness, humor, feeling, willing, the ability to understand and grasp truth, and the desire to accomplish things, among countless others.

In other words, we seem to be thinking about two exceedingly different kinds of things. This point should not be overstated. The brain and the conscious mind do have several properties in common. These include logical properties (such as being self-identical); existing at a certain place and time (I think that minds do exist in space); and being, in some sense or other, part of the person to whom they belong. So, there is an overlap. Nonetheless, the difference between the brain and its activities on one hand and the conscious mind on the other are great and systematic. Yet, it is confidently asserted by many, perhaps most, philosophers and cognitive scientists that they are really,

---

25. For an amusing short story about brains being made of meat, see Schwartz and Begley, *Mind and the Brain*, 21–23. The story is by the science fiction writer Terry Bisson and was published in Omni magazine in 1991.

in some manner, the same identical thing. The same thing in the sense of not just being alike, but of being numerically identical.

How can this be understood? It is easy to comprehend how the Morning Star can be identical with, be the same thing as, the Evening Star, as they both are the planet Venus. It is also easy to understand how Mark Twain could be the same as Samuel Clemens, for these are simply two different names for the same person. It is even easy to see how Bruce Wayne can be Batman.

The above examples are easily understandable as being the same things because they are the same kind of things seen as or understood from a different viewpoint or by different aspects. Venus is the morning star when seen in the morning and the evening star when seen in the evening—it is the same thing seen under different circumstances. Mark Twain and Samuel Clemens are simply different names for the same individual. In the case of Bruce Wayne and Batman, they are the same person just wearing different clothes and acting in different manners. If Batman is battling with the Joker it is still the case that so is Bruce Wayne (even though he is not dressed as Bruce Wayne usually is, and not acting the same as Wayne usually acts).

But as we have seen, the brain and the conscious mind do not seem to be the same thing at all. How can, for example, my thought that Shakespeare is more profound than Dr. Seuss be identical to—exactly the same thing as—a certain number of neurons in a certain part of my brain firing in a certain pattern? Or how can being a particular input from the environment cause a specific output from my brain with some conscious thought that I have? It is not just that we cannot see how this is the case, it is that we cannot even imagine how it could be the case. How can a thought such as that be numerically the same, which includes having exactly the same properties, as n number of neurons acting in m manner? To even ask the question is to show the depth of the problem here.

A human brain has certain properties, a certain size, color, shape, hardness, as well as possessing neurons which have a certain electrical charge, etc. If the person is thinking of something, such as the profundity of Shakespeare, the thought will have properties of understanding, clarity, wittiness, intensity. None of these properties can be found in the brain itself.

Every object has properties, and these properties can usually be had by more than one object. For example, a ball has the property of being spherical, green, a certain size, and with a certain amount of elasticity. Another ball could have the same properties of being spherical, green. etc. But in comparing the brain with consciousness, the properties are quite different. Even in the case where the person is thinking about something physical—say the green ball mentioned above—the properties are different. The brain is not green, nor spherical, and doubtless has a different elasticity than the ball. Even were it the case that the brain was round, green, and with the same elasticity when it was perceiving or thinking about the ball, it is hard to see how this would enable it to know the object of intention, which is the ball. Physicalism cannot explain intentionality, nor understanding.[26]

The problem may be put another way. One manner of thinking about objects is to consider them as being *concrete universals*. For example, any green object somehow has the universal of greenness in it. What this means, and how this works, are matters of dispute, so we will just say that it is obviously true that, in some sense, green objects have greenness in them.[27]

The brain is an object with many different universals in it: color, size, shape, electrical charges, etc. It does not contain universals of consciousness, such as profundity, stupidity, wittiness, or dullness. None of the universals in the physical brain are these, or include these, nor is there any conceptual link from the physical universals to the conscious ones. For that matter, even such things as colors and certain shapes do not belong in the brain. If I see something green, my brain does not turn green, or have greenness anywhere in it. The same may be said for some shapes, such as being perfectly square. The brain is not perfectly square, nor are any parts of it. If these cannot be found in the brain itself when one is thinking them, then they cannot exist if one is a materialist. Therefore, it seems that the universals associated with consciousness cannot be in the brain itself. At most, there is only a correlation between the brain and the thoughts that we think.

Problem Three: The Causal Closure of the Physical

The third problem is as serious as the first two. This is the problem that arises from what is called *the causal closure of the physical*.[28] According to a widely accepted materialist principle, only physical or material things cause other physical or material things. Here, the universe is causally closed to anything that cannot be described according to the laws of physics, combined with the prior arrangement of the physical objects in the universe.

If this principle is true, then there cannot be any non-physical things that are causally active in the physical universe. This principle does not by itself necessarily show that non-physical things do not exist. There is a position known as *epiphenomenalism* that holds to this view, but this also

26. Parrish, *Knower*, 292–303.
27. There is a complex debate on the nature of universals, which I shall not go into here.
28. Parrish, *Knower*, 99–100.

results in some serious problems for the defender of physicalism who opts for this theory.

Consciousness Becomes Useless

The first major problem with epiphenomenalism, is that *consciousness as such becomes a completely useless thing.* For example, we ordinarily ascribe much of people's behavior to their having certain beliefs. A man gets in his car and drives to work. Why does he do this? We think that it is largely because, for instance, he believes that he has a job where he makes money in order to live and that if he drives a car in a certain manner that it will take him to work. But given the causal closure of the physical, this cannot be true. He may have those beliefs, but the only reason that he gets in his car and drives to work is because his brain and body are programmed, so to speak, to do so in certain circumstances. Theoretically, if one knew the man's body and brain, and understood his situation perfectly, one could tell exactly why he did what he did without reference to his beliefs or any other aspect of his consciousness.

In short, given the principle of the causal closure of the physical, and that only those things that are studied by scientists can act as causes, entities like beliefs become irrelevant to actual behavior. In theory, if one knew everything about the person's brain and body, and the environment in which they were situated, then from the physical facts alone one could with perfect, or at least great, accuracy predict what the person would do without any reference to conscious factors such as beliefs and desires. This leads to at least two problems.

Belief Becomes Irrelevant? First, *it is strongly counter-intuitive to say that our beliefs have no effect on our actions.* For example, given the Causal Closure of the Physical the fact that I wanted to type this sentence has nothing to do with its actually being typed. My beliefs become irrelevant to the operation of typing. In the final analysis, the only thing that causes my typing this paragraph is the fact that the laws of physics exist in the manner that they do; that the computer and my brain and body are constituted in a certain way; that my brain is programmed so that it will cause the muscles in my fingers to behave in a certain way; and so on. In short, assuming this theory of the causal closure of the physical, my typing of this treatise is caused by purely material factors and has nothing to do with my thoughts *as such.* All of this seems to be self-evidently absurd. With epiphenomenalists, thoughts are just along for the ride, but do nothing.

THE EXISTENCE OF THE MIND 153

Even if one were to adopt a *non-reductionist physicalist theory of the mind*, the problem does not go away. Non-reductionist physicalists think that the mind is purely material, and that when the atoms are arranged in a certain manner, the brain acts differently from what it does when the neurons of which the brain is composed act on their own. For example, H2O molecules, when together in mass at the right temperature and pressure, will act differently than when alone. Similarly, with non-reductive physicalism, the constituents of the brain, such as neurons and the molecules of which they are composed, will act differently when combined in a brain than they would alone, or in some other manner.

However, even given this situation, all the constituents of the brain are still material, and are governed by the laws of physics applied to that situation. How the laws of physics apply may well be different, but not the fact that everything is still governed by these laws. So even here, it is hard to see how beliefs as such could have any impact on our behavior, according to non-reductive physicalism.

Indeed, this view has always struck me as a position that tries to have its cake and eat it too. Consciousness is held to be, in the final analysis, physical, because otherwise dualism would be true. But on the other hand, consciousness is considered to be irreducible to the physical in the sense that the concepts involved in consciousness cannot be reduced to physical ones. So, it is simultaneously physical and non-physical. The most favorable thing that I can say about this theory is that it is utterly mysterious, and there is no way the mystery can be resolved.

Beliefs Have Nothing To Do With Reality? The second argument against the Causal Closure of the Physical is that if it were true that our beliefs had nothing to do with the way that we act, there would be no reason to think that they had anything to do with reality. Because, no matter what our thoughts might be, our physical brains and bodies would act in the same way, making our thoughts irrelevant.

According to Darwinian evolutionary theory, living creatures have the traits that they do because of mutation and natural selection. Creatures obtain new traits because of mutations. The creatures with these mutations are then subject to natural selection. Those new traits that impede the creatures' survival and reproduction are winnowed out, while those new traits that aid the creatures in survival and reproduction flourish and are transmitted to the descendants, hence, becoming a part of the species' future biology.

The problem with the notion that our conscious thoughts, such as beliefs, have nothing to do with how the creatures act is that there would be no winnowing process like the one described above. Given this epiphenomenalism, true beliefs would not help the creature in any way, while false beliefs would not impede the creature in any way. Because the beliefs as such are non-causal—do not cause anything—they have no effect on the creatures that have them. In other words, as beliefs are irrelevant to anything that the creature does, there would be no reason why any of the beliefs would have anything to do with reality at all.

Given this, if a cave man with epiphenomenal consciousness were trying to escape from a saber toothed tiger, there would be no advantage to his thinking about the tiger and possible ways to escape in contrast to thinking about how pretty the flowers were, or that one plus one equals sixteen and three quarters, or anything else that might be thought.

The Upshot. The upshot of all this is that if epiphenomenalism were true, then we would have no reason to trust anything that we reason about or believe. In this case, we have no reason to believe in epiphenomenalism. Thus, the theory that our beliefs are not the cause of anything ends up being self-referentially defeating or self-refuting.[29] Further, given that God in some way created us, it scarcely seems likely that he would do so in such a manner that our thoughts are irrelevant to our actions.

It does no good to reply that our thoughts are identical with the brain events which are involved in making decisions and causing the body to act in relevant ways. Even if that were the case, though the brain events are the causes, and our thoughts are in some sense identical with these brain events, it is still the case that it is the brain events as *physical objects* that do the work—the brain events as *conscious thoughts as such* do no work. In effect, were the above scenario to be the case, the physical aspects of the brain do the work, while the conscious aspects are just along for the ride, so to speak, being causally ineffective.

Problem Four: The Relationship Between the Mental and the Physical

The above are all serious problems for physicalism. However, there are still others—problems which have to do with the supposed relationship between the brain and the conscious mind. Given that in materialism the brain and the body as material objects are supposed to be the final explanation of why we think whatever we do, I will argue that there is a serious problem here.

Natural events are explainable in terms of natural laws and the nature of the situation to which they apply. For example, take two objects that exist

---

29. Parrish, *Knower*, 190–200.

close to each other in space. Ignoring all other factors, the two objects, both physical entities that have mass, will be attracted to each other in a way describable by the law of gravity. The strength of the law of gravity is a constant; it seems to be the same everywhere in space and time.

However, the situations in which gravity will apply are different. In the case of the situation outlined above, given the mass of the two objects and the distance by which they are separated, the effect of gravity will lead them to draw together at a certain rate. However, if the masses were doubled, or halved, and if also the distance separating the two of them were doubled or halved, the rate at which they drew together would be different. So, we have here two factors, the law of gravity and the nature of the situation to which the gravity applies. The situation may be quite complex, but the law of gravity is fairly simple.

Of course, in physical reality the clear majority of situations are much more complicated. There are more laws than gravity, and there are a lot of things in existence besides these two objects. But the basic principles apply—the laws of nature involved and the nature of the situation to which the laws are relevant.

The Brain

At this point, we run into a problem. A human brain is an extraordinary thing, with about 100 billion neurons, each with thousands of dendrites connecting the neurons.[30] In spite of the complexity however, in essence a brain is a piece of tissue, weighing several pounds, and being constrained by the laws of physics and the body in which it exists.

Nonetheless, in some respects the brain is simple. This is because it is a physical object, and as I have noted, the laws governing the behavior of physical objects are relatively simple, being reducible to a small number of equations. Also, even though the net of the system of neurons and dendrites is inconceivably complex, it is still just a system of neurons and dendrites embedded in the slab of fatty tissue which composes the human brain.

The Mental World

In contrast, the mental world of consciousness is not only vast, but also extremely varied. There are what philosophers call *qualia* (quale in the singular), which are things like redness, the sound of a trumpet, the smell

---

30. See Dembski and Wells, *Design of Life*, 10.

of roses, the taste of chocolate, and the feel of sandpaper.[31] These are the bases of our sense perception. Besides these there are what may be called internal qualia, such as the feelings of fear, anger, happiness, pain and pleasure, and many others.

Additionally, there are *propositional thoughts*, which are sentences that may be true or false. We may think, rightly or wrongly, that it is cold outside, that nine times six equals fifty-four, that a certain politician is corrupt, or that the Detroit Lions will not win the Super Bowl next year. The number of thoughts that are possible to think is literally infinite. Just taking arithmetic, for instance, one can think that one plus one equals two, one plus two equals three, one plus three equals four, and so on to infinity.

The Relationship Between Brain and Thought

This being the case, the question now arises as to the relationship between the states of the brain and the thoughts that are being thought. If one is a materialist, of whatever variety, then necessarily one holds that the thoughts that one is thinking are in some way realized in or reducible to the brain. In other words, *it is the brain that determines what is being thought.*

Given this, it seems to follow necessarily that for Justin to have a particular thought, his brain must be in a particular state for that thought—his neurons in a specific part of the brain in a particular arrangement with dendrites firing in an exact pattern sending impulses to distinct neurons in a peculiar and precise order. If Justin's thoughts are determined by his brain states, then if a brain state B_1 will have a conscious thought C_1 about roller derby, for example, then it follows that if Hilda's and Katherine's brains attain that exact brain state B_1, they will also have the same roller derby thought, C_1.[32]

Now here is where the problem arises. We have already seen that there seems to be no essential or necessary link between a brain state and the thought that it supposedly causes or realizes, but let us ignore that for now. The problem that I am getting at here is that for there to be a specific thought and a brain state, there must be a relationship between them, and that relationship must be rational. That is to say, if the person is dealing with

31. It should be noted that the existence of qualia as such is controversial. For a collection of essays defending their existence, see Wright, *Case for Qualia*.

32. There is a tricky philosophical complication here in the debate about Internalism versus Externalism, involving the nature of the things being thought about, but this does not change the basic point that I am making. For an introduction to the debate between Internalism and Externalism, see Audi, *Epistemology*, 238–45. For a work that takes the internalist side of the debate, see McGrew, *Internalism*.

(and is therefore thinking about) some issue, then the brain must act in such a way so that whatever is being thought must be about the issue.

The problem now is, why does a brain state become the cause of a thought? As we have seen, the relationship between the pattern of neurons in the brain and any thought seems arbitrary. So why does a brain state B cause a conscious thought C? If our thoughts are to have any rationality, then there must be some lawful reason why. There must be a law that if a brain is in state B, then thought C will be produced.

One problem with this is that, as we have seen, there is an infinite number of thoughts that are possible to think. Can we think that there is an infinite number of laws that link the different brain states and the thoughts that they somehow cause?

The problem grows worse when we realize that brains change over time (one's brain is quite a bit different when one is five years old compared to when one is fifty). Furthermore, everyone's brains are different from everyone else's. Is there a set of laws that necessarily results in the existence of every thought when a brain is in a certain shape, especially considering the vast number of brains that there could be? The situation is made even more difficult when one realizes that there could probably be countless more brains than ours. Might there not be brains made of silicon? No one at present can give a definite answer to this, but it seems possible, and therefore there would have to be linking or bridge laws that would make each individual thought actual.

This argument seems especially compelling when combined with the notion that consciousness as such is epiphenomenal, and therefore cannot accomplish anything (as we have seen). If these laws existed, why would these laws linking brain states and conscious states exist if the whole pattern of consciousness is useless? To make physicalism work, all sorts of bizarre things must be assumed. Indeed, all of them are Mysterian in the sense that there is forever a mystery as to why a material brain will produce, in some manner or other, consciousness.

The reason for this is that neither the brain, nor any parts of it, can plausibly be thought of as being a self. Consider the following: we can be aware of many different things at once. For example, if one is looking at a full bookshelf, one is aware of many different books. Simultaneously, one may be aware of having a headache, and of being hungry, and of wishing that the person that you are talking to would speak more clearly, etc. Given materialism, these thoughts must be located in different though possibly very close sections of the brain. The reason for this is that for something to be a thought in materialism, a part of the brain must be such that it holds the information about the thought. Being physical, the brain must store different information at different sites.

To put things another way, that there is no one part of the brain that holds all the information simultaneously, and thus there is no self that could have all the thoughts simultaneously.[33] This problem seems to be inherent in the nature of material things. They are essentially located in space and time, and necessarily exist in some certain manner in space and time, though the manner may change over time. This being the case, it seems that each material thing, in this case neurons firing in the brain, can only store a certain amount of information. Other information would have to be stored in other neurons. Of necessity, no neuron or group of neurons, no material thing in general, could have all the information in one place and time. Since, by its nature no material thing or group of things can do this, only an immaterial thing, a self, could do this.[34]

Further, the brain is a physical object. Physical objects are made up of atoms. However, the atoms are separated from each other by a relatively large distance. Physical objects are mainly space. Atoms themselves are made of smaller things, such as quarks. So, if a human being is purely material, and listening to music, what part of the brain is doing so? Does each quark do so on its own, or do they combine somehow, despite being physically separated?[35]

In contrast, in *substance dualism*, what mind is, ultimately, is a soul, or spirit, or self. It is simple in the sense of not being composed of parts, and thus grounds the unity of consciousness. All the thoughts can be bound in the one single consciousness. Its nature is to be conscious, because it is a finite copy of God, who is intrinsically conscious. A mind is a unified thing.

Problem Five: Free Will

> I conclude that there is no position one can take concerning free will that does not confront its adherents with mystery.
>
> Peter van Inwagen[36]

There is another problem here for physicalism. This is the problem of free will.[37] Most people intuitively think that they have free will. Indeed, the denial

---

33. On this see Parrish, *Knower*, 286–89.

34. On this point, see Parrish, *Knower*, 286–91. See also Moreland, "Substance Dualism," 43–73.

35. On this argument, see Hasker, "Do My Quarks Enjoy Beethoven?" 13–40.

36. van Inwagen, "Essay on Free Will," 427.

37. For a philosophical discussion of the existence and nature of free will from

of the existence of free will leads to some serious problems, as we shall see. What I will argue here is that materialism is incompatible with the existence of free will, and that this gives us another reason to reject materialism.

Libertarian Free Will

There are, in fact, two different definitions of free will. One of these is often called *libertarian* free will. What is meant by it may be illustrated by the following. Given a situation where a person has a choice between two different options and both are roughly equal in their attractiveness, the person may make an undetermined choice of one, but could have just as well picked the other.

For example, suppose that Alice must make a choice between marrying Harry or Carl. Both are roughly equally attractive in different ways. Alice chooses Harry. Now suppose that the universe is a giant video and that God has a VCR (something that is already becoming an antique). For some reason, he wants to replay that section of time where Alice made her choice. So, he rewinds the universe, and then replays it. On the supposition that Alice has libertarian or indeterminate free will, this time she might choose Carl, even though the situation is identical to the situation wherein she chose Harry. This is because her choice is genuinely indeterminate—it was not set which way to go.

Compatibilism

The other definition is called *compatibilism* or *soft determinism*. Herein, the essence of free will is being able to make one's own choice, uncontrolled by external factors. In the case of Alice's choosing whom to marry, if she were to choose Harry, then under the same identical condition, no matter how many times she made the choice, she would always choose Harry. Her freedom consists in her being able to choose based on her own beliefs, values, and desires; Alice is not being caused to act in a certain way or choose a certain option by external factors.

Free Will is Incompatible with Materialism

I will argue that either version of free will is incompatible with materialism. The reason is as follows: with materialism, human beings are completely composed of matter. There is no spiritual "stuff," such as an immaterial mind

---

different viewpoints, see Fischer, *Four Views*. For an extended version of my critique here, see Parrish, *Knower*, 351–59.

or a soul or even thoughts. Matter acts in accordance with the laws of nature. Matter is affected by gravity, electromagnetism, etc. Therefore, any person's behavior will be governed by the laws of nature and the situation in which an individual finds himself. Just as a computer or a transmission in a car is governed by the way that it is made and its environment, having no free will, so also would human beings be governed. Given materialism, we are just machines made of meat and bone instead of metal and plastic.

Suppose that Alice is completely made of only matter, with the mind merely being the brain's acting in a certain way. Why then would she choose Harry rather than Carl? It would have to be because that choice is inherent in the way that she is built and programmed, and the nature of the environment in which she lives. She could not have chosen differently any more than a computer could choose to run a different program than the ones that are installed in it. The algorithms are established and invariable

To this one might object that there is some indeterminism in nature, such as in quantum physics. Most physicists seem to think that there is genuine indeterminist randomness at the subatomic level. However, even if true, this does not change the nature of the problem for materialism here. *Free will should not be thought of as mere randomness.*

One may think that materialism may be compatible with *soft determinism*, because with both, choices are determined. But this stance appears false. Given the soft determinist version of free will, Alice chooses to do what she does because of her beliefs, values, and desires. But with materialism, the reason that she has beliefs, values, and desires is because her brain is formed and situated in a certain manner. She has these beliefs and desires only because she was programmed to have them. The conscious states she has are mere "epiphenomena," which means that they are things that are just emitted by the stuff that is really doing the work, which is physical.

Given materialism, consciousness as such doesn't cause things. Therefore, with materialism it is not the person herself—which is the conscious self with beliefs, values, and desires—who makes the choice, for these values are mere shadows of what is doing the real work—which is the brain and body operating according to natural law.

Nor does it help to say that while the smallest parts of the brain may be determined, the system as a whole can rise above this.[38] Different rules are in place for systems as a whole as opposed to the constituent parts. The argument goes that a molecule of H2O may act quite differently when alone as opposed to when it is part of a large number of such molecules—when it

---

38. As is argued, for example, in Murphy and Brown, *Did My Neurons Make Me Do It?*

Agent Causation

The above discussion brings out a closely related problem with materialism, that of *agent causation*. There are generally thought to be two different kinds of causation. One of these is simply causation per natural law. That is to say, if one pool ball hits another pool ball and the second one moves because it was hit, this causation is according to natural law. All through the universe, we see causation in play.

The other kind of causation, whose existence is controversial in some philosophical corners, is *agent causation*. When a person chooses to do something, as in the example given above where Alice chooses to marry Harry rather than Carl, she chooses to do so because of her conscious self which believes and desires things. Agent causation is *personal* causation. The problem is that it is very difficult to see how there could be personal causation given materialism. For with materialism, there is no self apart from the brain's and body's existing and acting in a certain manner. Given materialism, there are no agents, and hence no agent causation, as such.[39]

Examining all of the problems above, it appears that there is no satisfactory materialist theory. The quest continues to discover one. Therefore, in my opinion, it is better to attempt other approaches. The one that I have in mind is *theistic dualism*.

Theistic Dualism

To put things simply, God is a mind. Being a mind, God is personal in that he has definite attributes such as rationality, subjectivity, and intentionality. Being conscious, God also has phenomenality. In other words, God is analogous to a human mind, although infinitely greater. Persons, specifically human beings' minds, are made in the image of God's mind, and hence can, to a limited degree, do the same things that God can do. In short, because human beings are finite copies or analogs of God, and since God created the universe, human beings are at home in it. The world is thus a *mind-world*, in that it is created by a mind for minds.

---

39. There is another position that I am not covering here: Panpsychism. For a definition see the "Editorial Introduction," in Freeman, *Consciousness*, 1. For a critique, see Parrish, *Knower*, 360–66.

Objections to Dualism

There are, of course, problems with dualism, some fairly difficult. There is scarcely a major philosophic or scientific theory that does not have problems. *Perhaps the major conundrum is this: if mind and matter are such different things, then how can they interact?*

Objection One: How Do Mind and Matter Interact?

It should be noted that this puzzle/question is not limited to dualism. Materialist theories, if they accept the reality of the mental as such, also have the problem of explaining how matter can be expressed as mind, which seems to be quite a different kind of thing. How and why does matter cause (in one way or another) the phenomenal (experienced/perceived) aspects of reality? Even if the materialist thinks that consciousness is an illusion of some sort, there is still the problem of *why* there is the illusion, and *why* does it take the form that it does?

Various answers have been given to this question. The one that I favor is that matter and mind have the *same Source* and are meant to work together. Some versions of quantum mechanics hold that consciousness does, in fact, affect quantum wave collapse. Which is to say, that thought and matter at its most fundamental level are tied together in a lawful manner.[40]

Objection Two: The Pairing Problem

Another objection may be called the *pairing problem*. This points out that it is difficult to see how the mind and brain could be tied together, being such different things. This is especially the case where the mind is thought to be outside of space.[41]

In response, I would say that the mind is *in* space, being located within the brain. It is admittedly a mystery how the mind and the brain are connected. But *a mystery is less of a problem than a contradiction*, which one gets when it is claimed that the mind and the brain are exactly the same thing.

---

40. See for example, Barr, *Modern Physics*; Rosenblum and Kuttner, *Quantum Enigma*; and Stapp, *Mindful Universe*.

41. On this, see Kim, "Against Cartesian Dualism," 152–67.

Objection Three: "Ectoplasm"

This issue is described by Paul Churchland. He writes,

> Suppose we possess a detailed scientific theory of the nature and operations of a marvelous nonphysical substance called ectoplasm, a substance that constitutes the mind of any conscious creature, humans and bats included... This ectoplasmic science may tell us how the bat's sensory system and ectoplasmic cognitive activity actually succeed... but even complete knowledge of the ectoplasmic details will fail to tell you what it is like, phenomenologically, for the bat.[42]

The problem here is thinking that the mind is made up of some stuff, that though not "physical," is nonetheless like physicalism. But substance dualists profess that the mind is not *like* the brain. The mind is a simple thing, not divisible, whose essence includes consciousness.

Other Objections: Based on Presuppositions and Assumptions

Other objections seem simply to *presuppose* the truth of physicalism; such as assuming that human beings evolved by purely natural means and that God had nothing to do with it. Another objection is that if dualism is true, and the mind and the brain interact with each other, then the law of the conservation of energy would be broken. In response to this latter argument, there are ways that one can deny that the law of the conservation of energy would be broken, and that, in fact, the law is not universally true anyway.[43] It seems that matter and mind, though quite different from each other, are such that they naturally work together.

A Better Answer

This by itself shows that *theism has greater explanatory value than naturalism*. Since in theism, reality is ultimately personal, with all the accompanying characteristics, it is easier to understand how personal beings with the same basic characteristics could exist. In contrast, in philosophical naturalism, what is ultimate is impersonal, non-rational, unconscious, non-subjective, and non-intentional. How then can it produce the personal, rational,

---

42. Paul Churchland, *Matter and Consciousness*, 54.

43. Robin Collins addresses and refutes this issue in Collins, "Energy of the Soul," 123–33. See also Parrish, *Knower*, 304–45.

conscious, subjective, and intentional? By their very nature, physical things do not have the ability to explain the existence of consciousness and all of the aspects that consciousness has, as there are no bridge terms between the two realms, no concepts that both have.

In contrast, theism *can* explain the physical. In theism knowledge of the universe is contained in God's mind, because knowledge of everything that is or could be is contained in his mind. In naturalism, however, what are ultimately real are the physical things that exist, and from them one can never derive the concepts, or even the existence, of the conscious aspects of reality. Given philosophical naturalism, the existence of consciousness is not only unexplained, but will be forever inexplicable.

Further, theism can explain why reality is knowable to the human mind. Since the universe is created from thoughts in the mind of God, and since human minds are made in the image of God, one can see why the universe is comprehensible to us. Ultimately, the universe is a mind thing; that is, it was not only created by a mind, but consists of actualized thought, in a sense. For example, God thinks about spheres; he both has the concept of a sphere and knows what spheres there are in the possible world which he has actualized.

Our minds are finite analogs of God's mind, and therefore it is understandable how we can comprehend concepts, including the ones that are physically instantiated (brought into being) in the universe. Although we have seen that the concepts of consciousness are not included in the physical concepts of the brain, the opposite is the case. That is, we can understand physical properties. Thus, in some sense, the physical can be included in the conscious, while the opposite is not the case.

Oppy's Objection

The naturalist philosopher Graham Oppy writes against this. His basic argument is that naturalism is simpler than theism, and thus has the advantage.[44] He thinks that the existence of souls would support the form of the mind body problem that is most favorable to dualism, and then argues that in fact theism does not have any advantage over this version of naturalism here, as both postulate primitive properties that are unexplainable.

---

44. Oppy, *Best Argument Against God*, 55. Naturalism here means for Oppy a form of dualistic naturalism, wherein immaterial souls exist. Peter Unger offers a similar argument to Oppy in his book *All the Power in the World*, and suffers from the same defects as Oppy's work does.

But Oppy is wrong. In the perfect being theism that I have been defending, God is the Greatest Possible Being, and being omniscient (among other attributes) is a necessary part of being just that. In other words, that God is omniscient and hence conscious is analytically contained in the concept of God. Consciousness and rationality are therefore a necessary part of reality, since, with theism, God is the ultimate reality.

Given naturalism, on the other hand, including Oppy's naturalism, the same analysis cannot be made. Assume that consciousness is a latecomer into the universe—that throughout most of history there was no consciousness. Then, when a certain level of brain evolved, souls emerged, unplanned. This story may be conceivable, but it seems extremely improbable. For this holds that souls just sort of "popped" into existence brutely (by chance), unplanned. Yet, though completely by chance and unplanned, these souls have the properties of rationality and intentionality, among many others, allowing us to understand the nature of reality. So, consciousness is not a necessary part of reality, as it is with theism, but merely a weird kind of freak accident.

Furthermore, that human beings are made in the image of God explains why we have within us the mental capacities that we do. For example, we see colors, sounds, and other aspects of perception. We can immediately and intuitively grasp some necessary truths—like two plus two equals four, or geometrical patters. All of these things we can, at least at a basic level, do immediately and intuitively, without training. Again, all of this makes sense if human beings are in some way copies of God's infinite mind, wherein these mental or ideal objects—colors, sounds, mathematical and geometrical concepts—exist.[45]

This does not mean that there are no mysteries with theism and dualism. For example, given that there are souls, how does the individual soul come into existence? There are several different theories. God directly creates them; they are caused by the souls of the parents; or, God has arranged brains and the laws of the universe so that souls emerge whenever a brain of a certain size comes into being.[46] Further, granted that our minds are finite analogs of God's mind, we still do not know how the human mind can understand all the things that it does, nor how it seems to automatically

---

45. For a detailed exposition of this argument, see especially McGinn, *Inborn Knowledge*. McGinn argues at length, and persuasively to me, that our basic mental capacities must be inborn, rather than gained through experience. However, being a non-theist, he has no way to account for these abilities, and resorts to mystery. Again, even though theism can provide the overall theory to explain these facts, understanding the details is another matter.

46. On this, see for example, Hasker, *Emergent Self*.

understand perceptual items and basic necessary truths. So, at present there is much we do not know, and perhaps will never know.

What then are human minds like? As was said above, they are finite images or copies of God. They are the immaterial center of subjective states.[47] They are unified, simple in the sense of being indivisible, and they have the capacities of rationality, subjectivity, phenomenality, and intentionality. Minds are made to exist and be active in this world.

Summary of the Mind-Body Problem

> The human race is just a chemical scum on a moderate-sized planet.
>
> STEPHEN HAWKING[48]

The most striking feature is how much of mainstream philosophy of mind of the past fifty years seems obviously false. I believe there is no other area of contemporary analytic philosophy where so much is said that is so implausible ... [I]n the philosophy of mind, obvious facts about the mental, such as that we all really do have subjective conscious mental states and that these are not eliminable in favor of anything else, are routinely denied by many, perhaps most, of the advanced thinkers of the subject.

> JOHN R. SEARLE[49]

> So God created man in His own image; in the image of God He created him; male and female He created them.
>
> GENESIS 1:27

Another way of saying this is that in theism, there exist all the characteristics that human minds possess, as a necessary foundation of reality. Reality is knowable because it is the creation of a rational, personal God, in whose image we are made. In naturalism and physicalism, these same characteristics of understandability to minds like ours do not flow naturally from the concepts that are basic to naturalism and physicalism, and, instead, suddenly appear without a proper explanation. So, as in the section on the nature of

---

47. On this see Lund, *Conscious Self*.
48. Davies, *Cosmic Jackpot*, 222. Stephen Hawking may have been a brilliant scientist, but in philosophy, he didn't know what he was talking about. See Lennox, *God and Stephen Hawking*.
49. Searle, *Rediscovery*, 3.

the universe itself, including its lawfulness and stability, theism is the better explanation than naturalism.

At the beginning of this chapter I outlined several theories about the nature of the brain and mind relationship. Some of these seem quite odd. Indeed, I will say that the fact that there are strange theories like eliminative materialism and mysterianism, itself shows the intractability of the problem of having a satisfactory materialist theory of the mind.

After all, one does not usually see scholars saying that the reason that they cannot understand a problem is that our minds are not capable of understanding it, as the mysterians say. Still less does one see scholars say that their subject area does not exist, which is what the eliminativists believe to be the case, even though they don't believe in beliefs. In my opinion, the problems are caused not so much by the subject area itself (though admittedly some of it is), but rather with the philosophical *presuppositions* that are brought to the problem. These presuppositions are *naturalism* and *physicalism* themselves. These *are often used as "givens." They are taken to be the unquestionable assumptions that are used as the basis upon which other theories are judged, but which themselves are never questioned.*[50]

---

50. People, including academics, make assumptions in the foundations for their theories, thereby dismissing out of hand other viable theories.

Chapter 5

Value Part 1: Ethics

> They have got rid of the Christian God, and now feel obliged to cling all the more firmly to Christian morality . . . In England, in response to every little emancipation from theology one has to reassert one's position in a fear-inspiring manner as a moral fanatic . . . With us it is different. When one gives up Christian belief one thereby deprives oneself of the right to Christian morality. For the latter is absolutely not self-evident . . . Christianity is a system, a consistently thought out and complete view of things. If one breaks out of it a fundamental idea, the belief in God, one thereby breaks the whole thing to pieces: one has nothing of any consequence left in one's hands.
>
> FRIEDRICH NIETZSCHE[1]

LET'S SUM UP THE contrast between theism and naturalism again. In theism, ultimate reality is a perfectly good God. God is ultimate reality and is a personal being. Personal beings (and conscious but sub-personal beings such as many animals) value some things and do not value others. With the presupposition that not only does God exist, and exist necessarily, but that he also has the nature that he has necessarily, objective values can be based on God, for he necessarily values certain things and disvalues others. Thus, on *perfect being theism*, ethics and values exist eternally as ideal objects in the mind of God.

In contrast, in naturalism, reality is ultimately impersonal and even unconscious in most interpretations of naturalism. Being impersonal and unconscious, values of any kind, including ethical ones, are foreign to it. According to naturalists, only when conscious beings evolve—come into existence by mere chance and natural law—do ethical and aesthetic values come into existence. This does not automatically mean that all naturalists are anti-realists regarding value, but to embrace strong realism, a naturalist

---

1. Nietzsche, *Twilight*, 80–81.

must accept the existence of abstract entities in some form, which is quite problematic for them, as I will argue in detail below.

Metaethics[2]

> It has gradually become clear to me what every great philosophy has been: a confession on the part of its author and a kind of involuntary and unconscious memoir . . . To explain how a philosopher's most remote metaphysical assertions have actually been arrived at, it is well (and wise) to ask oneself first: what morality does this (does he) aim at?
>
> FRIEDRICH NIETZSCHE[3]

Metaethics is a discipline that studies ethics at its most basic. Andrew Fisher says that metaethics is about moral language, moral psychology, and moral ontology.[4] Here I will mainly discuss whether or not there are ethical truths that are true no matter what human beings think. That is, what ethics *is*, in and of itself.

What Are Ethical Truths Like (if they exist)?

I will argue that if one is a *realist* about ethical truths, believing that they exist apart from the existence of any finite minds, then one should believe that they have at least *three characteristics—necessity, universal application,* and *necessary person relatedness*. There certainly are other characteristics, but I will emphasize these three, and see how the different perspectives deal with them.

The point of this chapter will be to discuss *which system is true*, not to attack the individuals who hold the systems. Good people can believe in wrong ethical systems, though having the wrong system can cause them to do bad things.[5]

---

2. For a good introduction to metaethics, see van Roojen, *Metaethics*.
3. Nietzsche, *Beyond Good and Evil*, 37.
4. Fisher, *Metaethics*, 3.
5. Having said that, I think that all human beings are innately sinners. Good is a relative term.

Ethical Truths' Characteristics

Necessity—Necessarily True

First, there is necessity. By this, what I mean is that ethical truths are necessarily true—they could not have been false. They could not have been false in the same sense that two plus two equals four could not have been false. They are necessary truths in the sense that I have used before—*absolutely necessary truths*. For example, take some statement that almost all would agree to. In other words, if there are any ethical truths, this is going to be one of them. Let's say, "It is ethically wrong to torture innocent people for fun."[6] Let us call this statement P. I shall argue that if P is true then it is necessarily true. It must always be true, in all possible worlds.

If P is not necessarily true but is still thought to be true, then we would *think* that P in fact happens to be true (just as in fact Toledo is in Ohio), but that it could easily have been false (as Toledo might have been placed in Michigan).[7] However, does this even make sense? P is not a statement about how one must do something to obtain some goal. P is not like that. It is not about obtaining anything. It stands on its own. If P is true, *necessarily true*, then *nothing could make it false*.

Universal

The second attribute is that of being universal—of being *true everywhere and at all times*. If P is true, then it seems that it must be true *for everyone*. It cannot be true for people in San Francisco but false for people in Altoona; true on weekdays, but false on weekends; true for women but false for men, or vice versa. Indeed, if there are any rational beings other than human beings, it seems that if P is true, then it is also true for them. Angels are bound by them. Even Klingons, Wookies, or Ents[8] would be bound by ethics. More surprisingly, Orcs and Hitler would also be subject to ethics, though they would simply disregard them.

---

6. Torturing anyone for fun, including animals, seems obviously wrong. Even to torture criminals guilty of extremely heinous crimes *for fun* seems wrong.

7. For a basic history of the Toledo War between Michigan and Ohio as to which would have Toledo, see http://en.wikipedia.org/wiki/Toledo_War

8. The examples are taken from *Star Trek*, *Star Wars*, and *Lord of the Rings*, of course, respectively.

Person Related

The final attribute is that of being necessarily person related. Which is to say, ethical truths are *applicable only to personal beings*. By this I do not mean that animals should not be treated in an ethical manner, but rather that they are not bound by the laws of ethics. Ethics are binding on human beings because human beings can understand them. And, if there were animals that could (say some gorillas or dolphins), it is only because they share in having personal properties.

A dog is not acting unethically when it bites you. A car's transmission cannot be legitimately called immoral when it breaks down on the freeway costing you an arm and a leg to fix (even though you may feel that it is). Beings without understanding cannot sin, for they cannot understand what ethical truths are. Animals, not having language, cannot understand abstract propositions like *P*. They may be trained in such a manner to put certain inhibitions in their minds, or they may have some instincts that guide their behavior that resemble ethics, but it is not the same thing.

There is one more feature about ethical truths like *P* that must be explained. This is the fact that if they are necessarily true, then they are not necessary for the same reason that many mathematical necessary truths are true. The reason for this is that to deny necessary mathematical truths will make a contradiction, whereas with ethical truths this is not directly the case.

Therefore, any ethical theory must either explain the existence of ethical truths, or else hold that they do not exist. Some contemporary philosophers deny that propositions like *P* are in fact true. Although I do not think that anti-realist views of ethics can be directly shown to be self-contradictory, I think that I can show that they entail costs to the anti-realist that are very high, too high to be accepted.

Ethical Theory Categories

I will divide ethical theories into three basic categories, depending upon what they hold about the nature of ethical values. I will call them *strong* or robust *realism*,[9] *weak realism*,[10] and *anti-realism*. As the discussion below will show, in strong realism, ethics is *discovered*; in weak realism, ethics is *derived* from some contingent fact of reality; in anti-realism, ethics is *invented*.

---

9. For a defense of what he calls robust realism, see Enoch, *Taking Morality Seriously*.

10. I think that perhaps a better word than weak realism would be "quasi realism," but this term has already been taken. Quasi-realism is an accepted name for the works of Blackburn and Gibbard.

Strong Realism (ethics discovered)

In *strong realism*, there are ethical truths that are independent of the existence or nature of human beings. These ethical propositions are true whether or not human beings believe in them, or even know about them, or even whether or not human beings exist. They are true in the same sense that the truths of mathematics are true—everywhere, at every time, and for everyone. Included in realism are ethical theories such as *Platonism, Intuitionism*,[11] *Axiarchism*, and *theistic ethical theories* such as Natural Law and Divine Command.[12] At least some versions of these theories can be legitimately called realist theories of ethics.[13] The non-theistic realist theories basically hold that moral truths are abstract entities that exist independently and necessarily. Theistic theories hold that they ultimately exist in the mind of God.

Weak Realism (ethics derived)

The second view of ethical theories will be called *weak realism*.[14] The basic idea is that there are some aspects of the world and human nature, or the nature of rational beings, that may be developed into an objective theory of ethics. Various examples of these are such classical ethical theories as

---

11. Some forms of Intuitionism at least. *Intuitionism* is an ethical theory wherein there may be many axioms, rather than one. For an exposition, see Audi, *Good in the Right*.

12. Some versions of Divine Command theories are anti-realist in the sense that in them God could command different ethics. However, the version I will investigate states that God bases commands on his nature, and that therefore he would always command the same ethical system, or at least ethical commands that are consistent with each other. For some recent introductions and works on metaethics see Drier, *Contemporary Debates*; and Brady, *New Waves in Metaethics*. A classic defense of a theistic ethics may be found in Lewis, *Mere Christianity*. For some recent defenses of strong realist theories, see for example, Huemer, *Ethical Intuitionism*; Cuneo, *Normative Web*; Evans, *God and Moral Obligation*; Kulp, *Knowing Moral Truth*; and Ritchie, *From Morality*. For a debate on the relationship of God to Metaethics, see Loftin, *God and Morality*. For a theistic defense of realism, see Baggett, *Good God*.

13. Another division among realist theories is the one between naturalistic and non-naturalistic versions of realism, though I think that all naturalist versions ultimately are forms of weak realist theories. By naturalist I mean ethical theories that ultimately reduce to statements about things in nature, such as how human beings can exist and flourish. For one example of a naturalist theory, see Bloomfield, *Moral Reality*.

14. For some books on weak realist theories, see Blackburn, *Essays in Quasi-Realism*; Brandt, *Theory of the Good*; Gibbard, *Thinking How to Live*; Foot, *Natural Goodness*; and Korsgaard, *Sources of Normativity*. For a work defending an atheist realist theory, see Martin, *Atheism, Morality*.

utilitarianism, Kantianism, virtue ethics, egoism, and the like, as well as more recent ones developed by some contemporary philosophers. These latter include such theories as *constructivism, contractualism,* and *Cornell realism,* and various naturalist theories.[15] They all take some aspect of human existence, or the nature of rationality itself, and out of these construct a theory that, while not external to human beings or any other rational creatures, nonetheless may be considered objective in the sense that they are based on human nature or the nature of rational beings and are therefore allegedly universal. In other words, they take something like human nature, and attempt to build a theory of ethics that is necessarily binding on human beings.

Anti-Realism (ethics invented)

The last category may be called anti-realism. Often, especially at a popular level, anti-realism is referred to as *relativism*. Relativism is the theory that what is moral differs from society to society, with no society's moral code being any better or truer than any other's in an objective sense. Americans have one set of morals, Iranians another, and Japanese yet another, for example. None of these is any truer or "better" than any other. Further, societies change over time. So, two hundred and fifty years ago slavery was accepted by most people; now it is not. However, given relativism, there is simply change, without any moral judgment assigned to the change. Such changes are not an improvement or a deterioration. Relativism is thus a version of anti-realism.

With anti-realist ethical theories, the existence of any timeless ethical truths is denied. It is here alleged that ethics is a false category. We just invented morality. It doesn't really exist. Listed with anti-realism may be such theories as *emotivism, prescriptivism, subjectivism, fictionalism, nihilism,* and *moral error* theory.[16] What these all have in common is the denial that "ethics" are normative moral truths that either exist independently or can be constructed by rational beings. *Emotivism* is the view that ethical statements are simply expressions of emotions. *Prescriptivism* is the view that ethical statements are really imperatives. *Nihilism* is the theory that there are no ethical truths at all; nothing is morally right or wrong—the whole category

---

15. For more on what I have called weak realism, though he just calls it realism see van Roojen, *Metaethics*, 201–52.

16. For several defenses of anti-realism in ethics see Mackie, *Ethics*; Joyce, *Myth of Morality*; and Olson, *Moral Error*. For more on anti-realist theories, see van Roojen, *Metaethics*, 75–200.

is simply empty. *Fictionalism* merely holds that although nihilism is true, we would all be better off if we sort of pretended that there is such a thing as right and wrong. *Moral error* theories hold that we may *think* that moral values truly exist, but we are mistaken in doing so—and although ethical statements are meaningful and often useful, they are also false.

A question arises. Can weak realism consistently and accurately be counted as a form of realism? Perhaps the answer is both yes and no. Yes, in the sense that there are held to be ethical norms or truths that are objective in some sense; no, in the sense that these ethical truths depend for their existence upon the thought of finite creatures like human beings, and hence would not exist if these creatures also were not to exist. I will examine weak realism in more detail below.

Axioms

One additional point that I wish to make is that the different ethical systems may be thought of as being based on axioms. Anyone who has studied geometry will have seen that it is based on different axioms. An axiom is . . .

1. a self-evident truth that requires no proof
2. a universally accepted principle or rule
3. in logic and mathematics, a proposition that is assumed without proof for the sake of studying the consequences that follow from it.[17]

As may be seen from the above, a major use of axioms is in mathematics and logic. However, it seems that they may have use in other areas. One of these is in ethics. Looking at the many different proposals, one can see that the various fundamental statements of the different metaethical systems may be considered axioms, upon which the rest of the system is derived.

It should first be noted that the three principles listed above do not apply easily to ethics. No metaethical statements are universally accepted, or considered to be self-evident to everyone, and they are not principles of logic or mathematics.

There are many different normative ethical systems (systems that attempt to tell what the correct theory of ethics is) but they all have *foundational principles* that may be considered axioms in their systems. However, the axioms of the different normative ethical systems are all radically different from each other. For example, Bentham's and Mill's utilitarianism is based on the axiom that morality is founded on promoting the greatest

---

17. http://www.dictionary.com/browse/axiom

amount of pleasure or happiness in the world—the greatest happiness for the greatest number.[18] Kant's deontological system of ethics is founded on the axiom of the categorical imperative: that one should only will those things that one could consistently will to be a universal law.[19] Another axiom that Kant might employ is that one should never merely use a person as a means, but also should respect one as an end in themselves. In other words, people should be treated with respect, as having intrinsic value, and not just because they serve a purpose.

One could go on and on with this, but the point is that ethical systems are based on some sort of axiom, which is a foundational statement from which all of the specific ethical rules are derived. Why this axiom is accepted is an important matter. It may be considered to be self-evident, but it is only self-evident in a different way than are the geometrical axioms.

The main problem here is that though different ethical axioms may appear to be self-evident to different people, they do not, unlike most of Euclid's geometrical axioms, seem self-evident to *every* qualified individual. Indeed, axioms can appear to be self-evidently true to some people and self-evidently false to others. Further, there seems to be no way that denying them entails a contradiction.

The Law of Non-Contradiction

The *law of non-contradiction* is the basis of necessary truths. Something that is impossible in an absolute sense is so because it either is a contradiction or entails one. The contradiction may not be easy to see. Indeed, many people may have no clear idea how to demonstrate a contradiction. That cubes have eight vertices is a necessary truth, but most of us have no idea how to demonstrate that necessity. It does, however, seem self-evidently true that this is the case.

The same cannot be said about *ethical intuitions*. Again, this is not to deny that certain ethical truths seem self-evident to certain people. However, the denial of these ethical axioms, does not immediately lead to a contradiction, and this is also something that the normal human being will intuitively see.

For example, take the utilitarian axiom that says, "What is morally correct is that which promotes the most happiness in the world." To deny it, one merely has to assert that what is morally correct is not that which promotes the most happiness in the world. The two propositions

18. Mill, *Utilitarianism*.
19. Kant, *Foundations*.

contradict each other, but there is no other apparent contradiction. It is not logically absurd to say that what is morally correct is not promoting the greatest amount of happiness in the world, but something else, or else that there really is nothing ethical at all.

Because of this, the claims of self-evidence in geometry and mathematics on one hand, and metaethics on the other, are different from each other. The scope of mathematical and geometrical axioms seems to be that of logical or absolute necessity. Our knowledge of them seems therefore to be based on an intuitive reason, wherein human beings have the ability, at least in some limited situations, to grasp the necessity of some situation.[20]

The fact that ethical axioms do not seem necessary in the same way that geometrical ones are is important and will be discussed below, for it is a key to understanding the nature of the different ethical theories and seeing how many of them are unsupported.

The Case for Strong Ethical Realism

> That to which all bear testimony is the fact that a man who genuinely says "I ought" means "I ought, though the heavens fall." The command is not conditional, but categorical.
>
> Elton Trueblood[21]

At this point I will make the case for the truth of strong realism.

The Awful Consequences Argument

The first argument might be called *the awful consequences argument*. This is, if there are no ethical truths, then there is nothing that is right or wrong. This leads to the disturbing conclusion that statements like *P*—that is it wrong to torture innocent people for fun—are false, and that there is nothing wrong with carrying this out. In fact, there is nothing that is ethically wrong with literally *anything*. The Holocaust, aggressive wars, slavery, the Gulag, the Killing Fields, torture, rape, mass murder, etc., would then be things that most of us might find repulsive—but would not be considered wrong in an objective sense. An analogy to this scenario might help one understand the implications of it.

---

20. For a defense of this, see for example BonJour, *In Defense*; and McGrew, *Internalism*.

21. Trueblood, *Philosophy of Religion*, 108–9.

Suppose that it were the case that most human beings disliked broccoli and that they found the very thought of eating broccoli repulsive, and strongly wished that no one would eat it. The reason that they thought this was either that there was some part of their nature, say some mutation, that gave an instinctive dislike of broccoli, or that for some reason there had developed culturally among them a strong aversion to broccoli. However, there was actually nothing wrong with broccoli. It was not poisonous, it tasted good, and it was even nutritious. In this case, the fact that most people hated broccoli would be subjective.

There is, however, another sense in which a dislike may be considered subjective, yet also could be objective. Suppose that broccoli really did taste awful, or else was poisonous. In that case, there would be objective reasons in a sense, but subjective justifications in another sense. That is, there could be beings who loved the taste of broccoli, or for whom it was not poisonous. Therefore, the reasons for dislike are in some sense still subjective.

Similarly, if there are no ethical truths, then people's dislike of things like mass murder and rape would be subjective in the second sense of the word. In that case, murder and rape would be things to dislike, rather than things that are true or false in themselves. Based on their nature, people have very good reasons for disliking them, but they are still based on a contingent nature rather than being necessarily true.

An immediate objection to this line of reasoning is that it is no big deal if people like or dislike broccoli,[22] but it *is* a big deal if people were to feel the same ambivalence about murder. The reason being, that if people didn't hate murder and other anti-social acts, then society would not function well. Society would be chaotic, and most people would be either unhappy or dead.

This shows that there are good and pragmatic reasons for people to act in a moral manner, as opposed to worrying about the issue of eating broccoli. The fact is, the vast majority of human beings want to live in a society that permits them and others to flourish. Most people want to be secure in their lives, liberty, and property, and to have the same for their neighbors. Granting the truth of all this, it follows that even just from purely pragmatic reasons, most people will want to live in a world where everyone at least pretended that there are ethically real right and wrong truths.

So, yes, there are unquestionably practical reasons for people to be moral. Indeed, even fictionalists often think that we ought to at least *pretend* that there are such things as moral truths.[23] If we live in a world where

---

22. Though, of course, broccoli farmers would disagree.
23. For example, see Joyce, *Myth of Morality*.

people try to be ethical, then life will be better overall for almost everyone, since most people desire an orderly existence where one can trust people, and therefore can thrive.

There is no question that one can invent all sorts of useful reasons for ethics. However, there are still two problems here. First, even in an anti-realist world where people still acted in what is generally considered to be a moral manner, it would still be true that there is nothing *ethically* wrong with torturing innocent people for fun, or other heinous acts such as genocide, even though they are very impractical with the way that most people want the world to be like. Many people would agree that this is so strongly counter-intuitive that we simply cannot take it seriously.

The second problem is a socially pragmatic one. A society where people believe there truly is right or wrong would have more people acting morally than in a society where they do so just because they generally find it helpful and useful to be "moral." There would be too much of a temptation to cut corners when it was in one's self-interest to do so, and when there was little chance of being caught, or if being caught didn't hold much in the way of consequences. Though this does not disprove anti-realism, I think that it should at least make one leery about adopting it.

Wired to Believe in Morality

The next argument for realism is what might be called the "we are all wired to believe in morality argument." Simply stated, human beings act in such a manner that it seems to be built into us that there is such a thing as morality. This argument can be closely tied with the one above, as it also appeals to our intuitive knowledge of ethical "right and wrong." Further, moral assumptions seem to be built into our very nature, and in the way that we do and must act.[24]

It seems to be true that human beings are wired to believe in certain things or ways. Which is to say, we are built to understand what reality is like. We understand that there are material objects, and that other people are conscious. We understand mathematical and logical truths. So too, we should take the case of fundamental intuitions as to what exists very seriously.

For example, we are all built to see phenomenal colors. We therefore think that they are objective features of the external world. However, most scientists and philosophers seem to think that phenomenal colors

---

24. Terrence Cuneo shows how deeply morality is embedded in the human activity of speech in Cuneo, *Speech and Morality*.

are in our minds—that they do not exist in the external world. What is objective is the reflectance that light rays have as they bounce off objects and into our eyes. So, just because something seems natural to us, doesn't automatically mean that it is really that way. However, even if phenomenal colors are in the mind rather than in the external world, they nonetheless represent some objective aspect of the external world or are an objective way of apprehending that world.

The phenomenal aspects of our consciousness are matched through stimuli to the external world in a regular and objective way. If we take our phenomenal aspects such as color not as things in the external world themselves but as our way of accessing the external world, the intuition that they are an objective part of reality is not in error. So, if our minds are made in such a manner so that they reflect that reality, then it seems that we should think that the fact that we perceive moral truths should be taken as evidence of their reality. Some things are just obviously wrong to any person whose mind is working normally—such as the wrongness of selling one's two-year-old daughter to a pedophile so that one may have the money to get a new tattoo.[25]

Given that we are built to believe in morality—and not just believe in it but feel its call upon us—then the small minority of people who don't feel this way are called sociopaths. Therefore, it seems that there is good reason to believe in the existence of ethical truths. After all, sociopaths are defective or mentally ill. I do not consider this argument to be conclusive, but it does again show that the natural, intuitive belief (or default intuition, if you will) is that there *are* objective ethical truths.

Mode of Being

This brings us to the next reason that I will give for believing in the existence of ethical truths. This is the fact that *ethics* seems to be a genuine, understandable mode of being. In other words, human beings understand the concept of ethical truths. Ethics is something that cannot be conceptually reduced to anything else. As this is a bit more abstruse than the first two reasons, it may take some exposition to clarify.

A main difference between ethics and other areas of human concern is that ethics involves what Kant called the *categorical imperative*, while other areas involve only what he called *hypothetical imperatives*. A hypothetical

---

25. Sadly, this is a real case, as shared by a friend of my wife's who works with a ministry that rescues sex slaves. The two-year old girl died as a result of the traumatic sexual assault.

imperative can be simply described as, "If you want to have some *y*, then you ought to do *x*." If you want to do well on the test, then you ought to study for it. If you want to avoid getting into an automobile accident, then you ought not drink and drive. Hypothetical imperatives are all like these examples; they depend on someone's desire.

A *categorical imperative* is a different kind of thing. Given the existence of a categorical imperative, it is irrelevant what one wants to do. It is not like, for example, "If one wants to be honest and law abiding, one ought not to rob banks or cheat on one's taxes." It is irrelevant whether one *wants* to be honest—there is an obligation laid on rational creatures that they *ought* to be honest, regardless of their feelings on the matter, or how it benefits or harms them or anyone else. It is an obligation that one does not choose. It is, as I explained above, a necessary truth, which is something that is binding on rational beings whether they acknowledge it or not, or whether they even know about it or not. *This obligation is true no matter what.* Just as the laws that govern basic logic or arithmetic exist apart from the existence of any individual human being or humanity itself.

We can all *understand* the concept of a categorical imperative, whether we believe that there are any or not. Further, there are factors that differentiate ethics from other possible examples of categorical imperatives. For example, take beauty. It can be plausibly argued that there is a form of categorical imperative that is attached to beautiful things. That is, if one sees something beautiful one ought to be able to appreciate its beauty. If one is faced with a beautiful object under the right circumstances, and does not appreciate its beauty, then there is something wrong with that person, just as there is also something wrong with someone who does not see the rightness of *P*, for example. However, the two kinds of wrongness—ethical and aesthetic—are different from each other. They are part of different *categories* of truths.

Though there is a wrongness attached to both the lack of appreciation of beauty, and the lack of moral feeling, they are still quite different from each other. Human beings have an ability to *distinguish aesthetics from ethics*—understanding what both different kinds of things are. Neither can be reduced to the other, though it may be said that there is a kind of beauty to things ethical. It is true that being ethical may in some sense be beautiful, and the desire to create beauty may be ethical. Further, evil is ugly, and the desire to cause things to be ugly may be evil. Nonetheless, beauty and goodness are distinct, yet a normal human being in the right circumstances understands both and feels the obligation of both in different circumstances.[26]

---

26. Beauty and morality are two different modes of being. For a detailed examination

For these reasons, we do understand the category of goodness, of being strongly ethical. This being the case, *ethics* does exist as a real category. Just as the fact that we can understand mathematics and its difference from other things means that in some sense there is a legitimate mathematical part of reality, so also does the fact that we sense and understand morality means that ethics is a true part of reality.[27] If we can trust our mathematical intuitions, why cannot we trust our ethical ones?

With the above arguments, we can see that there are such things as strong ethical truths. Before moving on, however, *the arguments against ethical realism* ought to be considered. I will turn to the arguments against realism in the ethical sphere and point out the weakness or implausibility of each.

Arguments Against Ethical Realism

> To talk of intrinsic right and intrinsic wrong
> is absolutely nonsensical.
>
> FRIEDREICH NIETZSCHE[28]

> [C]ould I believe that, say the wrongness of a lie was any more intrinsic to an . . . utterance than beauty was to a sunset or wonderfulness to the universe? Does it not make far more sense to suppose that all of these phenomena arise in my breast, that they are the responses of a particular sensibility to otherwise valueless events and entities?
>
> JOEL MARKS[29]

Ethical Anti-Realism is the view that there are no ethical truths. This goes on to hold that *ethics is something we invent*, in some manner or other.

The Argument from Strangeness

This argument *for ethical anti-realism*, articulated by J. L. Mackie and others, states that there are no ethical truths because they would be, if they existed,

---

of what this means, and how reality is composed of different modes or categories that cannot be reduced to one another, see Dooyeweerd, *New Critique*.

27. Though of course what mathematics is, is itself a matter of philosophical debate.

28. Nietzsche, *Genealogy*, 49.

29. Marks's "Confessions of an Ex-Moralist" is quoted in Baggett, et al., *Good God*, 68. The short answer I have to this is: "No, definitely not."

too strange and different from the rest of reality. Physical things and the truths about them are quite different from ethical truths. "How," Mackie asked, "could they exist in a world entirely made of physical things?"[30]

An answer to this can be quite straightforward. Mackie is here *presupposing* the truth of naturalism and physicalism. Yes, it is true that in a world which is basically physical it would be strange that there would exist such entities as ethical truths. Yet one may respond to this by saying that this is, in fact, an argument *against* naturalism and physicalism. On the other hand, in a theistic world, there is more to reality than just the kinds of things that physicists study. There is also God, who is a personal reality and who is concerned about ethics. Indeed, Mackie stated that *if* God existed there *could* be ethical truths in a strong realist sense of the word.[31] One might agree with him about this but take it as *an argument for the truth of theism.*[32]

There is a saying that one philosopher's Modus Ponens is another philosopher's Modus Tollens. Modus Ponens and Modus Tollens are logical rules of inference. Simply put, *Modus Ponens* is the form "If P implies Q, and P is true, then Q is true." *Modus Tollens* is the form "If P implies Q, and Q is false, then P is also false." Philosophers may agree that P implies Q, but disagree about the truth of P showing the truth of Q, or else the falsity of Q showing the falsity of P. In this particular case philosopher *Anthony* may think that physicalism is true, and that therefore there are no ethical truths in the realist sense. Philosopher *Bernadette*, on the other hand, might think that ethical realism is true, and that therefore physicalism is false.[33]

This leads us to the next anti-realist argument, that of ethical relativity, which argues from the great difference in ethical systems among the different cultures of the world, now and further, over the course of history.

---

30. Mackie, *Ethics*, 38–42. Another philosopher who defends one version of the argument from strangeness is Jonas Olson, *Moral Error*.

31. Mackie writes, "[W]hat concerns us more is that if this theistic position were not only coherent but also correct it could make a significant difference to moral philosophy. Morality could still have very largely the functions we have assigned to it, and much the same content, but the good for man might be more determinate, more unitary, than we have allowed in chapter 8, and our task might be less that of making or remaking morality than of finding out, with the help of some reliable revelations, what God's creative will has made appropriate for man and what his prescriptive will requires of us. It therefore matters a lot for moral philosophy whether any such theistic view is correct: the theological frontier of ethics remains open." Mackie, *Ethics*, 231–32. It should be noted that Mackie himself was an atheist who strongly rejected theism. On this point, see Mackie, *Miracle of Theism*, 68 and following.

32. There is a strong feeling among many philosophers that God is not the source of morality. On this, see Rist, *On Inoculating Moral Philosophy*.

33. On the effect that this may have, see Baggett and Walls, *God and Cosmos*.

The Argument from Ethical Relativity

The argument from ethical relativity *holds that because there are different beliefs about ethics, there are no ethical truths for anyone.* In the West, marriage has long been considered such that a man can only have one wife at a time.[34] In Saudi Arabia one can have four wives simultaneously. According to the values of most cultures, treachery—the betraying of a person who trusts you—is considered to be highly immoral. However, in the past, among the Sawi, a tribe in Western New Guinea, treachery under some circumstances was highly esteemed.[35] There are also changes in ethical views within cultures. Not too many years ago, in the West, abortion under most circumstances was held to be a highly immoral act. Now many people hold that there is nothing wrong with it under almost any circumstance.

Different cultures and different individuals have different sets of values, and sometimes they are extremely different. It is argued that this shows that ethical values are merely relative. This is held even though there are some ethical values that are widespread, being believed in by most cultures around the globe—such as the importance of courage and loyalty to one's family. Anti-realists may respond to the widespread acceptance of such values as merely showing the pragmatic importance of such values and argue that the still widespread disagreement about values undercuts realism.

However, I do not think that it does. The defender of strong ethical objectivity can merely respond to this argument that some cultures and individuals are mistaken in what ethical values they believe in. This is especially true regarding matters that are not about objects of sense perception, as moral values are not. There is more agreement among different people about things that can be seen, heard, touched, and so on. Few people disagree that fire is hot, that water runs downhill, that iron is harder than grass, etc., because these can be easily verified through sensation.

We do not apprehend moral values in the same way, via sensation. Since different cultures have different histories and live in different environments, it is not surprising that their ideas of what is right and wrong differ. Additionally, different cultures and increasingly different individuals have different worldviews, and these different worldviews contain different ethical values. For example, the reason why it is considered legally and morally permissible to have four wives at once in Saudi Arabia is that

---

34. See Tucker, *Marriage and Civilization*, for an examination of the virtues of monogamy over polygamy.

35. See Richardson, *Peace Child*. Fortunately, the Sawi abandoned this belief when they were converted to Christianity. When they first heard the Gospel, they thought that Judas was the hero.

it has a very traditional Muslim culture, and Mohammed, the founder of Islam, decreed (as a command from God) that a man could have up to four wives simultaneously.

An argument for realism may be developed here. That is, as stated above, though cultures differ on what is right and wrong (though this can be overstated), there is much that is agreed on.[36] Perhaps more importantly, *all cultures have a concept of ethics*. They all think that there are some things that are ethically right and wrong, though they may disagree on what they are. *The notion of morality is universal.* So, the argument from ethical relativity doesn't have much weight.

But, what about the weak realist theories? Can they give us a coherent and satisfactory account of the existence of ethical truths? It is to this question that I will now turn.

What about Weak Realism?

> [O]ur identity as moral beings—as people who value themselves—stands behind our more particular practical identities.
>
> CHRISTINE KORSGAARD[37]

Weak realism is the name that I have given to those numerous ethical theories where it is held that although there are no ethical truths existing independent of human minds, nonetheless, an objective ethical theory can be constructed based on human nature or the nature of reason and of the creatures who can reason. There are many of these theories and many of them have sub-varieties. Briefly, here is a list of some of them along with a brief explanation.

- *Utilitarianism* holds that what is good is what causes the most pleasure or happiness for the most people—the greatest happiness for the greatest number.[38]

- *Egoism* is the belief that what is good for every person is what causes the most happiness for that person.[39]

---

36. See Lewis, *Abolition*, 95–121.
37. Korsgaard, *Sources of Normativity*, 121.
38. Mill, *Utilitarianism*. For a good introduction to utilitarianism and many other classical theories, see for example, Wilkens, *Beyond Bumper Sticker Ethics*. Actually, any introductory book on Metaethics will cover the different theories.
39. On egoism, see Wilkens, *Beyond Bumper Sticker Ethics*, 43–58.

- **Kantianism** is the theory that the nature of reason gives us the *categorical imperative*, which then tells us what is morally right.[40] (It is debatable whether Kantianism is a form of strong or weak realism. I think that it is weak, because it depends upon human beings as their own moral lawgivers).
- **Virtue theory** holds that what is good is becoming the right kind of human being, and that there are certain foundational virtues necessary for this.[41]
- **Contractualism** is a theory that holds that morality arises out of contracts that people make in society to live together.[42]

However, I believe that these weak realist theories ultimately collapse into *anti-realism*. Angus Ritchie writes, "[N]one of them [secular accounts of morality] manages to avoid the following dilemma: *either* the positions fail to vindicate our pre-philosophical commitment to objectivism *or* they generate an explanatory gap."[43]

The Explanatory Gap

What is the *explanatory gap*? There may be more than one explanatory gap. One gap, the gap that Ritchie mentions, is the question of how human beings, who have evolved in a purely physical universe, can understand ethical truths?

However, I have another, more fundamental gap in mind. There is inevitably *a gap between statements of fact and ethical truths*. What I mean is this: how does one move from statements of fact, to statements of obligation? If there are any such things as ethical truths, which I certainly think is the case, how can we move from merely saying that X is the case, to saying that we ought to *do X*?

In the View of Utilitarianism

To give an example, given *utilitarianism*, how does the fact that doing some act X that will be the cause of the most happiness among the most people,

---

40. On Kantianism, see Wilkens, *Beyond*, 113–28.
41. On virtue ethics, see Wilkens, *Beyond*, 129–46.
42. For an exposition of contractualism, along with much else, see Parfit, *On What Matters*. For critiques of Parfit's view, see Singer, *Does Anything Really Matter?*.
43. Ritchie, *From Morality to Metaphysics*, 6.

mean that I ought to do it? What seems to me to be the case is the following: if I choose as an ethical goal to have the most people experience the most happiness, then one would be obligated to act in such a manner to bring about the desired result. However, the prior choice, to choose that goal as one's own, is not an obligation.

In the View of Kantianism

Another example is that of *Kantianism*. Kant himself rather invented the hypothetical-categorical imperative distinction and thought that his own ethical theory was of the categorical kind. His fundamental ethical rule is, "Act only according to that maxim by which you can at the same time will that it should become a universal law."[44] For example, take the ethical statement, "One should never break promises." If one has a qualifying rule that it is alright to break a promise if keeping it would be too inconvenient, then this would destroy the whole institution of promise making. If people made promises with that proviso, one could never be certain that anyone would keep a promise, which would render making promises useless.

One can see Kant's point here but reject his conclusion. For where is the necessity in accepting Kant's categorical imperative? That some of the consequences might be bad, such as the breakdown of the institution of promise making, may well be true, but there still is no necessity in the acceptance of Kant's basic rule. Really, Kant's appeal here is pragmatic and, ironically, in the final analysis, consequentialist.

In the View of Any Consequentialist Theory

Consequentialism is the view, expressed in egoism and utilitarianism, that what is good or bad depends upon the *results* that are obtained. Kant's view is that breaking promises is bad because it would have the consequence of destroying the institution of promise making. I therefore think that Kant's categorical imperative is only another form of a hypothetical imperative.

The above are thus examples of hypothetical imperatives, not categorical ones. The question would remain, "Why should I accept utilitarianism rather than some other ethical theory, like egoism?" If the theory is dependent upon a free choice, it is not necessary, and hence not binding on anyone. Therefore, it does not answer the question as to why certain ethical

---

44. Kant, *Foundations*, 39.

truths are true, and indeed necessarily so. *If the choice comes before ethics, it cannot be an ethical choice!*

Attempts to Found Ethics on Human Nature

There are attempts to do more than this, to found ethics on facts of human nature, for example. One such attempt is the following argument.

1. We are human beings.
2. It is the nature of human beings to act rationally. That is, we are rational animals.
3. To act rationally is to act in such a manner to enable us to flourish as human beings.
4. Included in flourishing as human beings is treating other people in a manner that respects their status as rational, human beings.
5. To act in this manner is to act in accordance to the following principles—ethics/morals (which may vary from philosopher to philosopher).[45]

Versions of the above argument have been given by Christine Korsgaard and others. These theories are better than the simple argument listed above for utilitarianism, for they do identify a characteristic that human beings have that, when used, does seem to have ethical implications built into it. However, the above argument is flawed in a couple of ways.

Rationality?

First, there is a subtle equivocation in the term "rationality." To be rational in one sense, as is used in statement (2) above, is to be able to think in a rational manner—correctly drawing conclusions from premises and basing our actions on the conclusions that we come to. However, there is another meaning to the term "rationality," being used in number (3) here, which is that it is rational to act in such a manner to enable oneself and others to flourish.

While undoubtedly, we consider someone rational who lives in such a manner as to enable himself and/or other people to flourish, it is not the case that this consideration allows us to conclude that only people who act in this manner are rational.

45. Korsgaard and some of the others listed above, for example.

Consider someone who is so disgusted with his life and with the universe in general that he develops the desire to die, but also to take as many other people with him as possible before dying. So, he buys or steals a gun, takes it to a school or mall, and there kills several innocent people before killing himself. This is, unfortunately, not a merely hypothetical situation; rather, situations like this happen with depressing frequency.

A defender of the ethical theory that I described would have to say that a person who did this is irrational and unethical. But why would this be the case? If the shooter is not literally insane, why would it be irrational for him to start shooting? We assume that he has thought that matter over, and this is what he, after careful consideration, wants to do. He plans what he will do with extreme carefulness, using *reason* to figure out what would have the most impact. What makes his actions intrinsically irrational?

One answer would be that he would be choosing something that is not in his best interest—which would include a long, flourishing life. This is what most people want. In response, why could the shooter not believe that going-out-killing-as-many-people-as-possible is more attractive to him than attempting to live a long, flourishing life? This is not what most people would choose, but there seems to be no basic reason why everyone should choose what most people want. Most people don't want to be Navy Seals, astronauts, or circus clowns (or philosophers). Yet there are people who find these satisfying ways to live. There are many ways to be human, and human nature is variegated enough to encompass a vast number of life decisions. Even the choice to die is a choice that, unfortunately, many people make every year. Why is it necessarily irrational for everyone to think that they would be better off dead? Indeed, the fact that euthanasia is now being strongly pushed is evidence that many people *do* think that some people would be better off dead.[46]

The main point that I am making here is that if ethics is based on a choice to live in a certain way, then the choice to live in that manner is *amoral*, literally because it is prior to ethics, and hence is not itself ethical or unethical. This mode of ethical reasoning is, hence, being a form of the hypothetical imperative. As we have seen, hypothetical imperatives can never, by their very nature, give one a normative ethical theory, because there is no necessity in accepting the theory in the first place. Once one has accepted the theory, one may feel bound by the ethical rules it contains. But there is

---

46. I should note that I do not agree with this. People should not murder others, or kill themselves, or help others to die. There might be some exceptions, such as a man choosing to die to save his family. These are not the kind of cases that I am discussing here.

nothing unethical about not deciding to be ethical in the first place, unless some realist ethical theory is true.

Human Nature

There are a couple more problems with weak realism that should be mentioned. That is, it is based on human nature. As we have seen, one problem with this is that human nature is to a certain extent mutable. It contains kindness and cruelty, love and hate, courage and cowardice, generosity and stinginess, greed and envy, and so on. So, it is not enough just to appeal to human nature. One must appeal to certain aspects of human nature, which means that *one must have a standard of what is morally right and wrong apart from human nature.* If one is judging what part of human nature to accept, then human nature as such cannot be the standard.

There is a certain amount of objectivity in using human nature as the foundation for ethics, *in the sense that human beings have a nature.* But what if human nature changed? Suppose that there was a mutation caused by a virus that, instead of turning everyone into zombies (as on television or the movies), had the following result. With the mutation, people found that they would double their life spans if they cooked and ate children under five years of age. Furthermore, the mutation caused people to have deep cravings for young human flesh. Would this then make cannibalism moral? I do not think so; indeed, I think even few anti-realists would "really" believe that.

If *human nature* is our standard, then since human nature changed, ethics should change with it. But this seems intuitively wrong. Were such a mutation to happen, it seems that we should think that human nature had become horribly perverted, not that it had merely changed, with a corresponding change in what is ethical.

Further, these systems may be objective in the sense that they are all based on some maxim, from which the actions that are considered to be moral and immoral are derived. But even though they are objective in a sense, they are not necessarily true, and hence cannot give us a truly categorical imperative. They are chosen as axioms in an ethical system.

Cultural Influences

It seems to me that most ethical theories that weak realists put forth are based on the culture into which they were born. But why not accept the morals of the Vikings or of Tamerlane? The concept that all human beings should be treated with respect is not one that comes naturally to human beings. Rather, it is the result of a long cultural history, which was influenced by many things.[47] In this case, Christianity had a large part in propagating the notion that all human beings are deserving of respect.[48] Absent this cultural history, what people would believe to be right and wrong could be quite different than what we see today.

Sinnott-Armstrong's Moral System

For example, Walter Sinnott-Armstrong argues that the basis of morality is that people should not harm one another.[49] This has a fair amount of intuitive support, and most people would agree with much of it, though, like all ethical systems, there are problems with it. However, here I just want to focus on one problem. Why should anyone buy into the system in the first place?

The first principle or axiom of Sinnott-Armstrong's moral system is something like, "One should not unnecessarily harm people," and being immoral comes from breaking this principle. Since this is the first principle, the choice to accept it is therefore amoral, because it is logically prior to the moral system based on the principle. Since there is no moral necessity in accepting this principle, then logically one cannot morally condemn anyone for not accepting Sinnott-Armstrong's axiom.

After all, as Sinnott-Armstrong writes, there are many other ethical axioms one could accept. He writes, "I myself disavow subjectivism, relativism, egoism, nihilism, conventionalism, non-cognitivism, and postmodernism."[50] Besides these, there are the other systems—utilitarianism, naturalism, Kantianism, and many others—that one could accept.

---

47. See for example, Weikart, *Death of Humanity*.

48. Regarding the influence of Christianity, see for example, Berman, *Law and Revolution*, and *Law and Revolution II*; Glover, *Biblical Origins*; Hart, *Atheist Delusions*; Schmidt, *How Christianity Changed the World*; Mangalwadi, *Book that Made Your World*; and Robbins, *Christ and Civilization*. On the effect of Christianity on the idea that all individuals are intrinsically valuable, see also Siedentop, *Inventing the Individual*.

49. Sinnott-Armstrong, *Morality*. His theory is based on one of a number of ethical axioms. Julian Baggini presents a similar proposal in *Atheism*.

50. Baggini, *Atheism*. 76.

The Weaknesses of Weak Realism

Non-Moral Choice

In any event, all weak realist theories are based on a *non-moral* choice to accept an ethical system. Since the choice is prior to the ethical system, it cannot *be* ethical—which means that it is, ethically speaking, arbitrary. Suppose that Mary accepts some version of weak realism, and is considering whether to adopt Kantianism, utilitarianism, or egoism. Whatever choice she ultimately makes, it is not an ethical choice, for Mary does not have ethics yet.[51]

Prudence

Another point is that in the end, weak realism seems to reduce to prudence. If some course of action would result in my having a large amount of pain in the future, then this gives me a reason to avoid it.[52] I agree with this. However, while it is irrational and imprudent not to avoid such a course, is it unethical? Am I doing something morally wrong, in addition to being stupid? How does one derive an ethical "ought" from a prudential "should"?

A Matter of the Will

So, any weak realist theory ultimately comes down to a matter of will. Therefore, it cannot be unethical to reject any particular theory, or ethics in general. All law is therefore imposed value. What becomes important is *whose* will is being imposed on everyone else—in other words, who has the power to impose their values on the rest of the people?[53] Weak realist theories are therefore built on sand. Since they are founded on a non-moral choice, they really are versions of nihilism.

---

51. What this means is that ethics would be founded on a non-ethical choice. It would be a choice that is ethically arbitrary.

52. Parfit makes this basic point in his magnus opus trilogy "*On What Matters*."

53. Writes Ludwig von Mises, "Mankind is to be divided into two classes: the almighty dictator, on the one hand, and the underlings who are to be reduced to the status of mere pawns in his plans and cogs in his machinery, on the other." von Mises, *Human Action*, 113. Granted, the form of the government may not be dictatorship, but because the power relations are prior to the ethics, they are thus of necessity nothing more than one group imposing its will on all of the others.

Not a Categorical Imperative

To conclude, weak realist theories may generate ethical systems based on a hypothetical imperative, but not on a categorical one. We need ethical truths wherein one has an obligation to do certain acts no matter whether one wants to do them or not. In short, we need some form of strong realism.

Which is the Best Theory of Strong Ethical Realism?

Let's recall that *ethical realism holds that there are ethical truths that exist apart from the human mind and would exist whether human beings existed or not*. These may be divided into two basic groups—those that are *personally* and those that are *impersonally* based. By *personal* what is meant is that the ethical truths exist because they exist in a mind—which is to say, God's mind. *Impersonal* means that the ethical truths exist by their own intrinsic necessity. They exist as abstract entities that are necessarily independent of the other parts of the structure of reality.

Impersonal

One thing that may be said immediately is that there is a serious problem with impersonally based ethical truths by their very definition. As I wrote earlier in the chapter, ethics seems not only to contain necessary truths, but truths that are necessarily personal. They are about persons, and their relations with other persons. The question arises for the impersonal theory—why are there ethical truths necessarily existing?

Why, for example, is it true that adultery or stealing are ethically wrong in a universe that is ultimately impersonal? If ultimately the existing ethical propositions are abstractions, and a physical universe that exists is undersigned and uncaused by anything more fundamental, then there seems to be no reason as to why ethical truths, such as the noted adultery and stealing, would even *be*, let alone be true. Why, in a reality that is impersonal, and in which persons may be considered a sort of strange accident of evolution, are there necessary truths that necessarily refer to personal beings?

One answer, given by Wielenberg, is that ethical norms exist out of brute necessity.[54] In other words, ethical truths are necessarily true for no reason. To me this position seems self-contradictory. For something to be necessary means that there is no possibility that it could be otherwise. For something

---

54. Wielenberg, *Robust Ethics*, 37–38.

to be brute means that it is the way it is ultimately by chance. For something to be a brute necessity it would have to exist in some manner for no ultimate reason, but at the same time it would have to exist in some manner that it could not possibly be other than it is on pain of logical contradiction. For something to be necessary there must be a *reason* why it is so, which rules out "brute (chance) necessity," as it has no reason.[55]

An answer might be given that ethical truths are analytically true; that is, they are necessarily true by their very nature, just as by their very nature mathematical truths are necessarily true. Two plus two necessarily equals four, by the nature of the numbers and the nature of addition. So, it might be argued, ethical truths are true by their nature. Indeed, for non-theistic realist philosophers, something like this would seem to have to be the case.

However, as I stated above, this is not the case. Mathematical truths are true by their nature because to deny the nature entails a contradiction. Mathematical statements like two plus two necessarily equals four are necessarily true because to deny this entails a contradiction.

This does not seem to be the case with ethics. It is not the same with ethical statements like, "It is wrong to torture innocent people for fun," which we have labeled P. One can deny P without contradiction. To say that it is *not* true that it is wrong to torture innocent people for fun, is morally reprehensible, but it is not self-contradictory. Where, then, does the necessity come from? I shall argue that the necessity of ethical truths is synthetic rather than analytic. That is, that it must come *from* something else rather than being contained in the very nature of the ethical truths themselves. *Necessary ethical truths need* an ontological ground—something that provides the *basis for their existence.*

Therefore, it seems that an atheist can be a weak realist, building ethics on a contingent fact of the universe, but to be a strong realist must be a Platonist. Platonism is the view that abstract objects exist independently of anything else. But Platonism regarding ethical truths seems very implausible, as Platonism is ultimately impersonal, and ethical truths are necessarily personal.

Personal

Theism, on the other hand, provides a powerfully sufficient ontological ground—explanation of the source. God is, by his very definition, a

---

55. Brand Blanshard makes the same argument that I do. He writes, "Now it seems to me that the notion of contingent necessity is a half-way house in which we cannot rest." For his full argument, see Blanshard, *Reason*, 469.

necessary being, who is personal and omniscient—knowing the truth of everything. Indeed, in theism there is a long history of saying that abstract entities like ethical truths, universals, and numbers are ideal objects in the mind of God. Since God is also, by definition, wholly good, he knows all ethical truths and supports them. In other words, ethical truths exist in the mind of God, and since he necessarily exists and has the nature that he has, his will that these truths be followed supplies the necessity.

The Euthyphro Objection

There are, of course, objections to a theistically based ethical system. The most prominent of these is known as the Euthyphro objection.[56] This objection is an attempt to impale the defender of a theistic basis of morality on the horn of a dilemma: Why does God approve of and command certain ethical truths? If he approves of them because they are right in themselves, then they are logically independent of him, and thus God is not the explanation of morality. On the other hand, if they are right simply because God says that they are, it follows that God could have commanded that what we now consider to be evil to be good. So, God could have commanded us to torture and kill innocent people just because we enjoy doing so.

It should be noted that there are theistic ethical theories in which God's decision about what is ethical and what is not seems arbitrary. This theory is known as *voluntarism*. Some of the medieval Christian philosophers seemed to accept this, and a major school of Islamic thought accepts this viewpoint.[57] Were this view to be accepted, it would dissolve the second horn of the dilemma, because if God commanded it, then it would be right, and our intuitions would be wrong. But, this seems to me to be an inadequate response.

However, there is a better response to the Euthyphro dilemma. This is that God's commands do indeed make principles ethical, but that they are not based on a whim. As shown above, God, in the teaching of classical and perfect being theism, not only exists necessarily but has the *nature* that he has necessarily. So, God would not and could not command things like P or other acts of evil because they go against his necessary nature, and he cannot deny himself. So, there are no possible worlds where God commands that people do P, or anything like it. Given perfect being theism, values are all ultimately based on God's nature. God exists and has the nature that he

---

56. The original Euthyphro objection is found in the Socratic Dialogue with the same name. See *Plato: The Collected Dialogues*, 169–85.

57. See Reilly, *Closing*.

has necessarily. On the Christian concept of God at least, one of the things that God necessarily has as part of his nature is love.

Secure Grounding

Given this, theism does give a secure grounding to categorical imperative ethics. *Therefore, given that ethical realism is true, and that theism provides the best explanation for ethical realism, this is an argument in support of theism.* Given theism, it can be understood how personal laws, as of those in strong ethical realism, can be an intrinsic part of reality.

Theism, being personally based, also has another advantage. There are times when what one ought to do is hard to say, because one's ethical duties seem to clash. Should one tell a lie to save an innocent person's life, or steal from an apple orchard to prevent one's family from starving? With naturalist atheist's impersonally based ethical principles, it is hard to see how one could take precedence over the other. All the ethical principles just are, with equal reality. On theism on the other hand, God could "rate" the different duties one has and decide that in certain situations some of the duties outweigh the other ones. Thus, it could, for example, be the case that lying is generally immoral, but lying to save the life of an innocent human being is justified, because one ethical value outranks the other.

Love

There is one more point that needs to be made here. This is the issue of the problem of love that was mentioned above. Love is in itself good (when it has the right objects). Indeed, a large part of ethical value is about love. It should be remembered that love should primarily be considered to be a *volition*, rather than an emotion or feeling. Further, the good person will love the good in the sense of having feelings of attraction toward the good and against the bad. The good person will necessarily love other good persons (and even bad persons, in at least the sense of willing them their good, though it probably isn't what they themselves want). The problem here is, if God is the ultimate being, then how can God be loving, let alone *be love* (or be essentially loving) as the first epistle of John states?[58]

Why this is a problem is the following: God is the ultimate being and is free. According to traditional theology, God was under no compulsion to create the universe. He could have just as well created a different universe or

58. 1 John 4:8.

not created anything at all. But if God had not created anything, and is one person, then how could he be a loving person, and indeed an essentially loving person? There would be no one else for God to love. To say that God just loves himself seems inadequate to the notion of being a loving person. How can God be essentially love or loving without there being anything else to love, without having an object to love? The Christian answer to this problem is that God necessarily exists as a trinity of persons in the One Godhead, and that the members of the trinity love each other. Therefore, God is essentially a loving being, composed of three persons, each of whom loves both the others, and this would be so even if he had not created anything. Thus, Christianity has a personal God, partly because it has a God in whom relations are fundamental and intrinsic to his nature.[59]

This is the Christian answer to the problem of ethics. God exists necessarily and essentially as three persons, who necessarily and essentially love each other. It could scarcely be otherwise, for only if the three persons of the trinity love each other could they eternally exist as one being. This love is good, indeed, the ultimate good, and all other goods are based on it. Since God is three persons, then persons are the ultimate reality. Only a personal God can be the creator, rather than the emanator, of the universe, for only thus can both the contingency and the rational order of the universe be accounted for. Unitarian concepts of God tend toward the impersonal. Yet the fact that God is a personal being is a major reason why theism has explanatory powers that non-theistic systems do not have.

We see this issue in Islam. In Islam, God has sometimes not been thought of as a personal being, and human beings are not made in his image, though at the same time, given other beliefs that Muslims have, their God must be personal in at least some respects.[60] The notion of an impersonal "god" is very difficult to maintain, and at any rate would be useless as a basis for a strong realist form of ethics.

59. This has been questioned by Keith Ward, *Christ and Cosmos*.
60. This problem was discussed in chapter 2. Again, see Reilly, *Closing*.

Chapter 6

Value Part 2: Beauty and Evil

Is the world a work of art?

FRANK WILCZEK[1]

> [B]eauty is a category indispensable to Christian thought; all that theology says of the triune life of God, the gratuity of creation, the incarnation of the Word, and the salvation of the world makes room for—indeed depends upon—a thought, and a narrative, of the beautiful.
>
> DAVID BENTLEY HART[2]

Beauty

THERE IS ANOTHER ASPECT of reality for us to briefly consider. This is the aspect of the *beautiful*. Human beings have as part of their nature the recognition of the existence of beauty, both in the natural world, and in the works of man.

A point that I wish to make about beauty is that it, like ethics, cannot be reduced to anything else without losing its essence.[3] What I mean by that is that if one argues that beauty can be reduced to subjective feelings, then beauty *as such* is lost. To understand it, beauty must be thought of as a real part of the world. To deny this, and to say that beauty is merely our feelings about certain experiences that we have, means that, for example, if someone thought that garbage was beautiful, but that the Alps or Bach's music was not,

---

1. Wilczek, *Beautiful Question*, 1.

2. Hart, *Beauty of the Infinite*, 16. For a couple of classic works on beauty, see Burke, *Philosophical Enquiry*; and Kant, *Critique of Judgment*.

3. Here I am disagreeing with the early Wittgenstein when he wrote, "Ethics and Aesthetics are one and the same." Wittgenstein, *Tractatus Logico-Philosophicus*, 71. For a discussion of the difference between ethics and aesthetics, see Audi, *Moral Perceptions*, 103–20.

that person's view would be just as valid as the opposite. About the kindest thing that I can say about this view is that it is strongly counter-intuitive. Although there is a certain amount of subjectivity in judgments about the beautiful, there is also a large amount of objectivity and agreement. A heap of garbage is not beautiful, while the Taj Mahal is.

There is indeed a great deal of beauty in the world. In fact, I think it can be argued that most things are beautiful. The sky is beautiful, during a sunny day or at night. Cloudy or rainy days are beautiful in a way. Forests are beautiful, mountains are beautiful, meadows, plains, and even deserts are beautiful. Most plants and animals are beautiful, though there are exceptions. The mere fact that almost everything that we see is colored, and that colors are beautiful, gives a hint of the beauty that is ubiquitous among the things that exist in our universe.[4]

The list may even be broadened. Many scientists and mathematicians say that the equations that describe the behavior of the physical things in our universe are beautiful. Though these things may only be appreciated by a select few who can understand them, the fact that even the laws of the universe seem beautiful to them indicates that beauty is built into the very fabric of the universe and the things of which it is composed.[5]

What is the explanation for this? We are in a situation here that, to a certain extent, resembles the situation about ethics. Beauty may only be recognized by sentient, intelligent beings—by persons, in short. A sand dune, a tree, or a cluster of stars may be beautiful, but they do not recognize their own beauty. Neither do plants or animals, apparently. If there are some higher animals that do, to any extent, recognize beauty, then it is because they are like persons to some degree. So, like ethical right and wrong, beauty is for persons.

So why do we perceive beauty? Again, we come down to the choice between a personal and an impersonal reality. In theism, God is personal and appreciates beautiful things. Because of this, he creates both beautiful things and creatures—human beings (and possibly others)—that can recognize and appreciate that beauty.

Given naturalism and an impersonal universe on the other hand, one would have to say that beauty is something totally subjective, and the fact that

---

4. See Wynn, *God and Goodness*, 16–36.

5. "Just as ancient geometers assumed the existence of an elegantly contrived geometric cosmos, so also modern chemists suspected that the elements were ordered in some elegantly contrived and harmonious way. As is almost always the case, the underlying order was far more elegant and harmonious than even the most conspiracy-minded chemists could imagine. They suspected a beautiful melody. They discovered a symphony." Wiker and Witt, *Meaningful World*, 135.

we see beauty and enjoy beautiful things is a product of mindless evolution. In this case, it is something of a quirk. If the mutations of our ancestors had been a little different, we might think that piles of garbage were beautiful, while mountains, the Grand Canyon, and the Mona Lisa are not.

With the naturalist's account, we would see beauty because, for some reason, doing so aids us in the quest to survive and reproduce. This seems to be the approach of evolutionary psychologists. Apparently, the reasoning is that we are attracted to beauty because, among other theories, it helps make certain things special, and thus helps with group cohesion. Or, perhaps, people are attracted to more beautiful members of the other sex, and thus are more likely to mate with them, which means that they will be more likely to reproduce than others. This will mean that there are more beautiful people, and the idea of there being beautiful things is reinforced.[6]

Whatever the truth of these theories, they do not explain the existence and nature of beauty itself. Any of the supposed benefits that beauty gives could be had in other ways, without adding a whole new aspect of being. Instead of beauty, there could have been, for example, specialness or attractiveness that was inculcated by doing physical activities like running or boxing. In some animal species, the males must fight for their mates. Why could not humans do something like that and obtain the benefits without beauty? Why come up with a whole new category of being to attract mates? In animals, like the peacock, apparently, the females find the feathers on the male attractive, in the sense that it draws them to the male peacock who has the feathers. Human beings might agree with this judgment. Yet there is no reason to think that peacocks appreciate the beauty of a sunset or the northern lights, or even that they appreciate the very beauty of peacock feathers. Again, animals do not appreciate beauty as such, yet they seem to have as strong a will to live, just as human beings do.[7]

Further, even if one supposes that human beings ultimately judge other human beings as beautiful to aid in reproduction, this does not explain why human beings also think that things like clouds, desert sand dunes, or symphonies are beautiful.

The simpler theory is that beauty is not an illusion—that it is not just another weird product of evolution, but a true and important part of reality. Since persons are the only ones who can appreciate beauty, this is another indication that matter in motion is not all that exists, nor that everything

---

6. For an attempt to give an evolutionary explanation for art and beauty, see Pinker, *How the Mind Works*, 521–38.

7. See Scruton, *Beauty*, 29–39.

must somehow be reduced to it. Rather, beauty and the beautiful are real things—important parts of the world in which we reside.

The point of this is that there seems to be no naturalistic explanation for beauty that explains the distinctiveness or ubiquity of beauty—nor the fact that it is found in so many areas that apparently have nothing to do with the simple survivability of the individual or the species. Take music for example. Music can be very beautiful. Yet no other creature makes music as such, and music seems to make no direct help to survivability or reproduction. Yet all human cultures seem to have music, and it is often very highly valued.

Thus, given naturalism there seems to be no explanation for the existence of beauty as an objective phenomenon of nature. Given theism, there is. God, who is perfect, loves beauty, and thus would have motive for creating a world where beauty in many different forms was ubiquitous, and fashioning creatures like human beings that can both appreciate beautiful things and fabricate them on their own.

The Problem of Evil

> Is he willing to prevent evil, but not able? then he is impotent. Is he able, but not willing? then he is malevolent. Is he both able and willing? whence then is evil?
>
> DAVID HUME[8]

> "Rebellion? I am sorry you call it that," said Ivan earnestly. "One can hardly live in rebellion, and I want to live. Tell me yourself, I challenge you—answer. Imagine that you are creating a fabric of human destiny with the object of making men happy in the end, giving them peace and rest at last, but that it was essential and inevitable to torture to death only one tiny creature—that baby beating its breast with its fist, for instance—and to found that edifice on its unavenged tears, would you consent to be the architect on those conditions? Tell me, and tell the truth."
>
> "No, I wouldn't consent," said Alyosha softly.
>
> FYODOR DOSTOEVSKY[9]

> And it seemed at last that there were two musics progressing at one time before the seat of Ilúvatar, and they were utterly

8. Hume, *Dialogues*, 108–9.
9. Dostoevsky, *Brothers Karamazov*, 227.

> at variance. The one was deep and wide and beautiful, but
> slow and blended with an immeasurable sorrow, from which
> its beauty chiefly came.
>
> J. R. R. Tolkien[10]

> [E]vil ... [is] as real as stone.
>
> Dean Koontz[11]

There is one more topic to discuss that involves value: the problem of evil. So far, all the issues that have been discussed have, I think, been such that they are much better explained by theism than by naturalism and materialism, though I will wait to summarize the situation in the conclusion. However, the problem of evil is different, as it seems to be difficult for theism to explain, at first glance at least. But not so for naturalism—something that naturalists have not been slow to point out. It is, as the German theologian Hans Kung wrote, "The Rock of Atheism."[12]

Let me lay out the facts simply. The concept of God that has been defended here is of a being who is all knowing, all powerful, and all good. The implications of this are that such a God would know how to abolish evil and suffering, have the power to accomplish it, and would want to accomplish it. *Why* then is there evil?

This problem cannot be dismissed as small or unimportant. There is a vast amount of evil in the world, and much of it is horrendous. One need only think of such things as the Bubonic Plague, which killed off perhaps more than one third of the population of Europe in the fourteenth century; the devastation among the native Americans caused by disease after the coming of Europeans; the Holocaust, which killed about six million Jews and millions of others;[13] the Holodomor where at least five million starved to death;[14] Mao's great famine where up to forty-five million died;[15] the ravages of many conquerors, such as Tamerlane,[16] who may have slaughtered seventeen million people (or about 5 percent of the human race at the time)

---

10. Tolkien, *Silmarillion*, 16–17.
11. Koontz, *Husband*, 191.
12. As quoted in Peterson, *Reason*, 129.
13. Gilbert, *Holocaust*; Snyder, *Black Earth* and *Bloodlands*.
14. Applebaum, *Red Famine*.
15. See Dikötter, *Mao's Great Famine*, and Becker, *Hungry Ghosts*.
16. Marozzi, *Tamerlane*. See also https://en.wikipedia.org/wiki/Timur, for the number of deaths.

back in the fourteenth and fifteenth centuries, eons before modern technology made that relatively easy to do; and, various slave trades.

Besides these major events, there are the tragedies and miseries of everyday life. These include getting cancer, having miscarriages, becoming a quadriplegic, going blind, and countless other misfortunes in life like unrequited love, taxes, and expensive machinery breaking and having to be replaced. The question is, if one were God, would one create and sustain a world in which bad things like these happened?

These challenges are not easily answered by theists. In response to the problem that evil poses for theism, a vast literature has developed, both attacking theism and defending it. Indeed, so vast is the amount of writing about the problem of evil that this collection of literature itself may be considered a minor part of the problem.[17] The discussion has been going on for millennia and shows no sign of stopping.

Moral Evil *vs* Natural Evil

What can be said in response to the problem of evil? First, there is not just one problem, but at least two. There is the *problem of moral evil*, which is "*Why do human beings choose to act in immoral ways?*" And there is the *problem of natural evil*, which is "*Why is there destruction and pain in the natural world?*" Both can be subdivided into different more basic problems. Together, both kinds of evil produce an immense amount of suffering among both human beings and animals. A true solution must attempt to answer *all* of the different parts.

Logical Argument *vs* Evidential Argument

Another important distinction involving the problem of evil is the difference between the *logical* and *evidential* versions. *The* logical *version argues that the existence of evil, of any kind and in any amount, is logically contradictory to the concept of God.* That there exists a God as classically described and that there also exists evil is a contradiction, in this *logical* version. *The* evidential *problem of evil, on the other hand, argues that the existence of so much evil in the world* (and/or the awfulness of some of the evil in the world) *makes it unlikely that a classically described God exists.* The evidential problem of evil

---

17. Various books on the problem of evil include: Little, *God, Why This Evil?*, Feinberg, *Many Faces*; Howard-Snyder, *Evidential Problem*; Johnson, *Calvinism*; van Inwagen, *Christian Faith*; and Welty, *Why is there Evil?* See also, Almeida, *Freedom, God*. A classic work on this subject is Lewis, *Problem of Pain*.

therefore deals with *probabilities*. In other words, it argues that the existence of so much evil in the world makes it *unlikely* that God exists.

The Logical Argument Fails

At the present it seems to be generally (though not universally) agreed that *the* logical *problem of evil fails to show that God does not exist*. It is difficult to show a logical contradiction between the existence of God and the existence of any evil. To refute the argument against God from the logical problem of evil, all one need show is that it is at least possible that God could have a good reason for allowing evil to exist. It is sometimes said that one cannot prove a negative. This is not always true, but in the case of the logical problem of evil, it is very difficult to show that there is no possible good reason that God could have for allowing evil to exist.

The Evidential Argument

The *evidential* problem of evil is both weaker and stronger than the logical problem of evil. Weaker, because at most what is used to establish this is that given evil of a certain sort, it is *unlikely* that God exists, not that it is impossible for him to exist. Stronger in the sense that it is also more difficult to handle and refute. At any rate, most discussions of the problem of evil today are about the evidential version.

Defense *vs* Theodicy. Another point must be made clear. This is the distinction between a *defense* and a *theodicy*. A *defense* simply attempts to *show that the problem of evil does not show that God does not exist*. A *theodicy*, on the other hand, attempts to *give the reason* why *God allows evil to exist in the universe that he has created*. A theodicy is thus more ambitious than a defense. For my purposes here, I will not try to clearly distinguish the two. Any theodicy that is successful is also a defense, and a defense that is successful may also point to a theodicy, for if something is a successful argument that shows that the problem of evil does not disprove God, it may be thought of as a reason or justification as to why God permits evil.

Attempted Solutions

There have been several attempted solutions given to the problem of evil: among them are *Free Will*, *Soul Making*, and *Natural Law*.[18]

Free Will Defense

The *Free Will* defense argues that libertarian free will is an important and good thing for human beings to have,[19] and that with their free will, sometimes people freely do evil things. This defense may have some value for those who accept libertarian free will by explaining human wickedness and the suffering that results from it, but it does not explain natural evil. An exception to this is the argument that natural evil is caused by the free will of demons or other superhuman creatures. This response has been used successfully in my opinion, to answer the logical problem of evil; for, if it is a logically or an absolutely possible scenario (no matter how implausible or counter-intuitive it may seem to be), it refutes the logical problem of evil.

Most philosophers and probably all naturalists consider the suggestion that "supernatural beings are the cause of all natural disasters like earthquakes and tsunamis" to be ridiculous. Of course, this does not prove that it is false; though I, too, consider it wildly implausible. This might be considered an example of the "incredulous stare" refutation of some theory, as David Lewis mentions in another context. However, I think that there are better explanations for natural evil than this.[20] Namely, that the same laws of nature that allow us to survive on a planet like this also necessitate that things like volcanoes and hurricanes happen. However, this belongs to the natural law defense, which is outlined below.

Soul Making Defense

The *Soul Making* defense is basically that evil and suffering are necessary for soul making—that is, for people to develop the character that they need. Only saints can live well in heaven, and suffering is a necessary part of their character

---

18. For example, Plantinga uses the free will defense in *God, Freedom, and Evil* and elsewhere. For the soul making defense see Hick, *Evil*; and for the natural law defense see Dore, *Theism*. There are other defenses, such as in Ross, *Philosophical Theology*. Another valuable work is Howard-Snyder, *Evidential Argument*.

19. See the section on free will in chapter 5 for a brief definition of *libertarian free will*.

20. See for example Ross, *Why the Universe*.

development. One problem with this defense is that much suffering does not seem to be necessary for making people better (e.g., some of the suffering of animals),[21] or it even seems, in some occasions, to make people worse. Great suffering may make some people gentle, but others become bitter. Still, it does seem that the existence of some kinds of evil may be necessary to produce some virtues in human beings. The apostle Paul wrote, for example, "[B]ut we also glory in tribulations, knowing that tribulation produces perseverance; and perseverance, character; and character, hope."[22]

Natural Law Defense

The *Natural Law* defense holds simply that to have a universe in which human beings and other creatures can live and flourish, there needs to be a consistent set of laws of nature. Water is a great good, and life could not exist without it. Our bodies are partly composed of water; we need water to drink, to clean, and to move around on. However, water can at the same time be deadly, as in floods and storms. The laws of nature that ensure that the water is beneficial also, at the same time, ensure that it can be harmful under certain circumstances.

The only way that this could be avoided is if God were constantly working miracles, which would defeat the purpose of having natural laws in the first place. This defense is limited in the sense that it may explain a great deal of natural evil, but it doesn't explain human wickedness. In a way, then, the natural law defense is the opposite of the free will defense in what is explained and what is not explained.

Understanding God's Purpose

Thus, these different defenses have their strong points and weaknesses, though I cannot here give a detailed examination of each of these defenses. Which of them can be adopted depends partly on the theology that one holds. For a couple of decades, however, there has been another approach to handling the problem of evil by theistic philosophers. This may be stated like this: given that God has a good reason for allowing the existence of evil, how likely are we to know what it is? The general idea is that while God is infinite, we are finite, and subject to all sorts of limitations of knowledge.

---

21. Of course, it may be the case that some animals do go to heaven. It is hard to see, even in this case, that suffering makes the animals more fit for heaven.
22. Romans 5:3–4.

However, it is not obvious that we can at all understand God's purpose. This concept has been the cause of much discussion and debate.

Austere Theism

At this point I would like to add another facet to the problem of evil. So far, when using the concept of God, I have been using what Plantinga called "austere theism."[23] *Austere theism* is simply theism considered from a purely philosophical position, apart from the teachings of any specific religion. If we look at the teachings of existing religions, such as Christianity, an interesting fact about evil emerges. This is that *the existence of evil is, in fact, entailed by Christianity*.

Think for a moment about the central symbol of Christianity—a man being tortured to death. Crucifixion is one of the, if not the most, agonizing ways to die. We get the word "excruciating," which means being in extreme pain, from crucifixion. It is a central doctrine of orthodox Christianity that Christ died for a very important purpose. Christ is understood by Christians to be the perfect man. Indeed, more than just that, God incarnate. Therefore, a crucifix is the image of the crucified God, the just suffering for the unjust. The central narrative of the Christian story is about evil and suffering, the reasons for it, and God's solution to it. If, by some bizarre miracle, some person were to wake up and find that there was no evil in the world and never had been, then this fact would refute Christianity.

Why did Christ die, according to orthodox Christian doctrine? Per orthodox Christian theology, whether Catholic, Orthodox, or Protestant, Christ's death was to make propitiation (substitutionary atonement) for the sins of human beings. In short, the existence of evil—of heinous and widespread evil—is an essential part of Christian doctrine, or at least of any orthodox Christian doctrine. How then can the existence of evil in the world be an argument *against* Christian theism? This point of doctrine may be thought to defeat the problem of evil at least from the perspective of Christian theism.

Unfortunately, things are not this simple. Though the existence of evil is predicted by Christianity, and therefore the fact that evil exists does not immediately refute Christianity, consistency of Christian doctrine may be challenged. Christianity holds both to the perfect goodness of God and the existence of great evil. It might be argued that those two Christian doctrines are logically inconsistent with one another.

---

23. For this term, see Plantinga, "Reply to Beilby's Cohorts," 221.

In other words, the opponents to a belief in God may argue that the existence of God as described by Christian doctrine contradicts the doctrine that God created this world—that eventually became full of evil—even though Christianity holds to exactly this. So, the problem of evil is not immediately solved by pointing out that its existence is an essential part of Christian doctrine.

However, this does not mean that an appeal to specific Christian doctrine might not lead to a defense against the problem of evil. For, it is not immediately obvious what a perfect, all good God may be like, or would want to create. That is, what would such a being think is the best world to create? For example, is it better to create a world, W_1, in which there is no evil but also a limited amount of good, or a world, W_2, in which there is some evil but a much greater amount of good? The answer is not obvious. One cannot break down the amount of good and evil into an exact number of points to compare them. One cannot objectively assign points to evil and good events, and then calculate which one comes out with the highest score. (This is not a video game)! In this sense, W_1 and W_2 are what is known as incommensurable—they cannot be exactly measured.

Therefore, the old question about the "best possible world" may not be meaningful. That is, if worlds are, to a certain extent, incommensurable, then it is impossible to say in every case if a world is better than another. I am certainly not saying that it is always impossible to say that one world is better than another. A world which contained nothing but purely evil sentient creatures whose main occupation was inflicting pain on each other is obviously not as good as a world in which there are only good sentient creatures who rarely suffer from any pain whatsoever. However, this ability to compare is not always the case. W_1 and W_2 may be considered examples of this.

Nonetheless, it might be asked, is there a best possible world? Is there a world that is better than any other? Philosophers are divided on this matter, though the majority seem to reject the view that there is one specific best of all possible worlds. My own thoughts are that there is not, but I will look at both options. If there were, actually, a best possible world, then God, being a perfect being, would create it. If *this* is the best possible world, then the problem of evil is dissolved, for even God cannot be fairly blamed for creating better than the best. This may lead to other issues, such as God's lacking freedom, but there is no space to address this issue here. There is also the problem that, given libertarian free will in human beings, God cannot just by himself actualize a particular world, because the human beings in it might not cooperate and instead freely choose to do things contrary to that which would make that world the best.

On the other hand, if there is no best possible world, then God cannot be blamed for creating a world that is not as good as others. Necessarily, God must make actual some possible world. Even if God decided not to create anything, and existed forever all by himself, that is the making of a possible world. Further, if there is no best possible world, then for any world that God creates there could be a better one. As long as he creates a good world, he cannot be blamed. Indeed, given this difficulty, I think that it would be better to say that the best possible world is the one that God creates. In other words, there is no viable standard of judgment apart from what God thinks. These are the alternatives: either this world, the actual world in which we live, is the only one that God would want to create; or, there were several possible worlds whose value is equal in God's eyes, and he arbitrarily chose this one. Both of these options seem hard to understand, but given theism, they are ultimately the only options.[24]

Still, it might be argued that God would create a much better world than this one, even if for any world that he created there were better ones. A world with a lot less suffering, with a lot less moral evil in it, would be a world that *a priori* one would think that God would create. But again, it is difficult, if not impossible, for us to judge such matters as to which world should be instantiated—which world would actually be brought into being. Is there another way to look at things?

There may be. Let me ask a different but related question as to whether or not God would create the best. The question may be put, "Was humanity worth creating?" That is, was our race of beings, with all our capabilities, but also with the moral depravity that is an intrinsic part of us, worth creating, along with the world in which we can, in various ways, flourish? If God were to create humanity, and a world in which it can live, then I think that one is going to get a world something like this one in which we live. Because human beings are morally corrupt, there will necessarily be moral evil, which explains evil's existence. It might also be asked if other creatures that live on earth were worth creating—cats, octopuses, manatees, and kangaroos, for instance? If yes, then their existence is explained also.

Admittedly, it is rather difficult to see that some other creatures, such as mosquitoes and tse tse flies, were worth creating, not to mention some bacteria and viruses.[25] One would have to account for their existence in other ways. Perhaps they are a necessary part of keeping the ecology of the world in balance?

---

24. For a detailed look at these problems, see Almeida, *Metaphysics*.

25. But on the usefulness of viruses, see Roberts, "Why Would a Good God Create Viruses?" 59–67.

Natural Evil

The issue of natural evil is harder to account for. Certainly, it seems that there could exist a world or planet with human beings living in it with much fewer natural evils. This argument is difficult to evaluate. It can be argued that things like earthquakes, volcanoes, and hurricanes are a necessary part of the earth to keep it inhabitable.[26] Other evils, such as diseases, can be partially accounted for by the existence of complex organisms according to natural law. That is, given that the universe must be governed by natural law, and that organisms which live in it must be built according to these laws, inevitably, things will start going wrong. Even the tiniest organisms are extremely complicated, and mutations—which are unavoidable, given to the laws of the universe—will sometimes cause things to go wrong, against their original design, so to speak.[27]

Entropy is a necessary law of nature. Entropy is what the second law of thermodynamics is all about. It can be stated in different ways, but basically, and perhaps too simply put, it is the idea that "things run down."[28] There is, as time goes on, less usable energy in the universe. Another way of stating it is that there is a continual loss of information in the universe.[29] A simple example of entropy is of putting an ice cube in a glass of hot water. It will melt, but the water will also cool off to some degree. Eventually, the water from the ice cube and the water that was originally in the glass will become the same temperature.

Without entropy, life as we know it would be impossible. If entropy didn't exist, the world would be a bizarre and unpredictable place. A newly laid uncracked egg may be turned into a scrambled egg. If entropy wasn't a natural law, scrambled eggs could turn themselves back into an uncracked egg. Although this may sound good, a universe where things like this

---

26. Ross, *Why the Universe*, 147–63.

27. On Plantinga and the concept of the design plan, see his *Warrant and Proper Function*.

28. Here is a more formal definition of entropy,
    1. *Symbol* S For a closed thermodynamic system, a quantitative measure of the amount of thermal energy not available to do work.
    2. A measure of the disorder or randomness in a closed system.
    3. A measure of the loss of information in a transmitted message.
    4. The tendency for all matter and energy in the universe to evolve toward a state of inert uniformity.

http://www.thefreedictionary.com/entropy

29. On entropy as loss of information, see Gange, *Origins*.

happened would be unpredictable and hence difficult, if not impossible, to live in.[30]

But, with entropy's being a fundamental law of nature, the universe and all the organisms therein will inevitably decay. The Sun is using up its fuel and will sometime stop shining. Indeed, if left unchanged, the universe will eventually be nothing but an inactive mass of matter all at the same temperature. However, the sun will take billions of years to die, and the universe may take trillions. In the case of organisms, they inevitably decay and die. Living organisms like human beings are extremely complex things, with many different parts that need to work well together to have a healthy living creature. Because of decay and the fact that most mutations are either neutral or harmful, diseases may develop.

Assuming the truth of all the above, what should we then think about the problem of evil? I wrote above that a proposed theodicy is the idea that humanity, with all its flaws and imperfections, was worth creating. Why, it might be asked, did God not create a race of sentient beings that were smarter, stronger, morally perfect, and better looking than human beings? (Perhaps he did, on other planets or other universes. But it is not an either or. God could have created other races and still thought humanity was worth creating). And, if human beings are created, then it seems plausible to think that a world something like ours is the inevitable result. Even granting this however, one could still make the following simple objection: given the amount of evil and suffering in our world, it was not worth it to create humanity. This is a subjective opinion of course, but so is the response that creating humanity was well worth the amount of evil and suffering.

Does it then come down to a matter of opinion? Perhaps it does, in a sense. However, there is an important caveat here. This is simply, that if God thinks creating humanity was worth the amount of evil and suffering that is existing in our universe, then his opinion is the one that counts. This is not merely because, being omnipotent while we are finite and weak, he simply gets his way because he is stronger than we are. It is also because God is a perfect being, and thus his "opinion" on things is the right one. In this sense, God does not create a world because it is the best. Rather, in some sense the created world may be considered the best possible (or at least no worse than any other world), because God has created it (though if God had created some other world, we would consider that to be the "best world"). It should also be noted that in Christian doctrine, all things work together in the long run for the benefit of those who love God, though we cannot see it now.[31]

---

30. On problems with denying entropy, see Peacock, *Brief History*.
31. See Romans 8:28.

Solution to the Problem of Evil?

By no means do I think that I have here solved the problem of evil. Rather, I think that all that I have done is show that there are some avenues of investigation, and a response that may provide at least a partial answer as to why God has created a universe that contains so much moral evil and suffering. The upshot of all this discussion is that *to try to disprove the existence of God, the argument using the problem of evil is inadequate.*

It should be remembered that the existence of evil is only one of many things that we do not understand. Really, the whole of our existence and that of the universe in which we live is so full of mystery that not only do we not have the answers, but sometimes we do not even know what questions are relevant. These difficult doubts and questions should guarantee job security for philosophers for many centuries to come.

There are a lot of things in the world—in a way, most of them—which we do not understand as to why they are the way that they are. To give one rather silly example, "Why is the island of Great Britain shaped something like a hare standing erect?" (Well, sort of. It looks more like a hare on a small map than on a large one). "Why is the universe such that Mars has the diameter that it has?" "Why is the speed of light 186,282 miles per second?" The fact is that there are a great many things in the universe of which we have very little understanding.

The Problem of Evil and Theism vs Naturalism

What then should be said about *the problem of evil and theism*? Though it is extremely difficult to get an *a priori* estimation of the likelihood of God's existence given evil, it should probably be allowed that one would not expect God to create a universe with so much evil in it.[32] Therefore, this is, indeed, one problem with which theism has to grapple. However, this is only one side of the issue. That is, how likely is it that, before examination, given philosophical naturalism, there exists a universe with so much moral evil and suffering in it? Regarding *philosophical naturalism*, the odds of there being a world with moral evil and deep suffering might seem to be great. However, I will argue that the "odds" may not be as great as they first seem to be. There are at least two quite different reasons for this. Remember that for there to be a problem of evil, at least two different factors must be in

---

32. Assuming that a neutral thought on the issue makes sense, as people holding different worldviews may make different judgments about how much evil a God would allow.

place. First, there must be *a necessarily true standard of good and evil*, and second there must be *evil of a certain quantity or quality*.

True Morality

First, for there to be a problem of evil in the first place, there must be a necessarily *true morality*. Earlier in the chapter, I divided philosophical views into three categories—robust (strong) realism, weak realism, and anti-realism. It seems that *for the problem of evil to 'work,' strong realism must be true*. The reason is simple. If realism regarding ethical truths is false, then there is no thought or act that is right or wrong in itself. If *anti-realism* were true, then ethical statements would be just false, fabricated human beliefs. Given anti-realism, there is nothing right or wrong, there are only things that different people like or dislike—and likes and dislikes do not seem to be strong enough to pose a "problem of evil." If that is all that evil is—things some people dislike, even if they have excellent reason to dislike them—then it poses little threat to theism. That certain things happen which some creatures dislike doesn't gives us any reason to think that God does not exist.

Given *weak realism*, the naturalist is on stronger ground. Here there *are* objective standards of ethical right and wrong. But weak realism still falls short. The ethical standards in weak realism, though objective in some sense, are also based upon contingent facts about human nature. According to naturalism, human nature is what it is because of billions of years of unguided evolution. So, though we do exist in some manner, given a different evolutionary history—say one in a race of sentient beings evolved who had to torture other sentient beings to survive—what the objective standards would be, could be quite different. This being the case, it seems difficult to understand how standards which evolved in such a situation would generate a problem for theism. For, here even weak realism eventually comes down to the following: given that humans are beings with a certain evolved nature, the ethical standards that they have are *contingent*, and hence cannot generate a problem of evil, for the same basic reason that anti-realism cannot. In the final analysis, evil would be *subjective*. So, as far as the problem of the existence of moral evil goes, theism can justify its existence more "naturally" than naturalism can.

Still, this argument, if successful, does not get the theist off the hook. For the anti-theist can still allege that there is an internal contradiction in theism: that the theist says a perfectly good God exists, an objective morality exists, and natural evil and suffering also exist. However, the theist can respond that if there is a problem of evil, there therefore must be a necessarily true morality, which entails the existence of God, and that therefore there must be a solution to the problem of evil. Therefore, the problem of evil is not as damaging to theism as it first appears. If the existence of God and an objective or absolute morality generates the problem of evil, it also entails that there must be an answer to the problem of evil. This is true even if we have no idea of what the answer could be—it must exist.

The "Odds" Question

The second factor is quite different, but, I think, much more damaging to naturalism. This is, given naturalism, what are the 'odds' that a world would develop which would contain suffering? This may not seem at first glance to be a problem for naturalism. Given the existence of the universe and the existence of laws of nature that would allow evolution to work, conscious beings capable of feeling pain need evolve, and then almost inevitably there would develop suffering of some manner and quantity.

However, if the arguments that were given in chapters 3 and 4 are sound, as I believe them to be, none of the above appears likely at all. Given naturalism, in which the natural universe is "just there," there is no reason to think that an orderly universe would exist. Further, given physicalism or materialism, it seems that it is very unlikely that any conscious beings would exist. Therefore, the incompatibility of materialism and consciousness has not been overcome by any naturalist/materialist theory.[33]

Next, it may be stated that even if the right laws of nature had been in place such that sentient life could exist and flourish in the universe, it might still be unlikely that evolution would have created sentient life. In other words, according to evolutionary theory, human beings evolved, to a certain extent, as a matter of *chance*. Certain mutations happened, and certain creatures lived to reproduce, etc. If this is the case, then sentient life such as human beings might not have evolved either, or even conscious life of the higher animals might not have evolved at all. Or, all animals might be "zombies" instead of being conscious.[34] Even if sentient beings evolved, they would still have to also evolve the feeling of pain. The odds that all of these factors and characteristics would have *just happened* in such an organized existence would be at least inscrutable, as there is

---

33. For an up-to-date exposition and discussion of the fine tuning of the laws and constants of the universe, see Lewis and Barnes, *Fortunate Universe*.

34. Philosophically speaking, a zombie is a human being who looks and acts like a normal human being but has no consciousness whatever.

simply no way that human beings can know and evaluate the different probabilities involved in the issue.[35]

The point to all of this is that, though it is of course impossible to calculate probabilities with any exactitude, given philosophical naturalism, it seems probable that there would exist no conscious beings. Then, in the absence of sentient beings there would be no *moral evil*, and if there were no conscious beings, ones that could feel pain, then there would be no *natural evil* either.

For, if there is no conscious life—life that can suffer—then it seems that it would be irrelevant how many natural disasters would happen. That a planet without life might be destroyed doesn't matter to the universe itself. Only sentient beings could care about such a thing. Even in the case of living things, if they are unconscious, like plants are, they do not care when they are being destroyed. Again, only sentient beings would care about the destruction of a world inhabited entirely by unconscious living beings.

Therefore, it seems that *given philosophical naturalism, it would be unlikely that either moral or natural evil would even exist*. Thus, although given perfect being theism, it may seem *initially* unlikely that evil would exist, or at least evil of the quantity and quality that we see, it also seems, given naturalism, that the existence of such evil would also be unlikely. On the other hand, given a revealed religion like Christianity, it is *necessary* that evil exist. So, Christianity predicts the existence of evil and suffering, while it is quite unlikely that philosophical naturalism ever could.

One more point can be made here. That is, not every evil need to lead directly to a good. It just needs to be part of a world that overall is leading to good. Again, given a world with human beings or creatures like them, a world will have many evils that are in themselves unwarranted, but are a necessary part of a world which is not pointless.

Summary of the Problem of Evil

Let me be clear in saying that I do not claim to have solved the problem of evil in any of its varieties. Horrendous things happen frequently in the world that make people conjecture that if they were God, or at least were able to give advice to God, they would prevent those evils from happening. But of course, we are not God, not like him in many important ways, and

---

35. For a discussion on this kind of response to the problem of evil and naturalism, see Ganssle, *Reasonable God*, 151–75. It was Ganssle's book that first brought my attention to the concept that there is a problem for naturalism with the existence of natural evil and human and animal suffering.

can never be like God. So, what we believe we would do is based entirely on the thought of finite creatures, while God, being infinite and knowing all things, thinks differently.

In the conclusion to this examination of the problem of evil, the result in unclear. Though theism may seem to predict that there would be no evil, or at least there would not be the amount and kind that we see around us, Christian theism sees *no contradiction* with evil's existence, though there are questions about the nature and amount of evil.

Atheism in any form does not clearly predict that there would actually be natural evil and suffering. Indeed, considering the sound arguments within chapters 3 and 4, it is extremely unlikely that evil would exist, or at least that the probability of evil, given philosophical naturalism, is either extremely low or else inscrutable. This may seem odd, but only, I think, because *naturalism is so taken for granted today*, especially in academic settings, *that naturalism is usually assumed to be the default position*. Since for many people, philosophical naturalism just *must* be true, serious issues that are problematic for it are sometimes just sort of waved away. Problems that arise from naturalist atheism are simply ignored, as if they are dust bunnies that can be swept under the carpet, or else these problems are bracketed and put aside as things that we do not know now, but that, supposedly, someday will be explained by science.

Therefore, given both theism and naturalism, it seems that on both sides it is unlikely that there would exist so much pain and suffering. So, contrary to what is often or usually thought to be the case, the existence of *natural evil* may be thought of as being something of a standoff in the battle between theism and naturalism, though theism may have the edge. For the issue of *moral evil*, the existence of evil is dependent upon an objective, necessarily true ethical system, which theism can sustain much more plausibly than can naturalism.

Chapter 7

Conclusion

> I know not who put me into the world, nor what the world is, nor what I myself am. I am in terrible ignorance of everything. I know not what my body is, nor my senses, nor my soul, not even that part of me which thinks what I say, which reflects on all and on itself, and knows itself no more than the rest. I see those frightful spaces of the universe which surround me, and I find myself tied to one corner of this vast expanse, without knowing why I am put in this place rather than in another, nor why the short time which is given me to live is assigned to me at this point rather than at another of the whole eternity which was before me or which shall come after me. I see nothing but infinites on all sides, which surround me as an atom and as a shadow which endures only for an instant and returns no more. All I know is that I must soon die, but what I know least is this very death which I cannot escape.
>
> As I know not whence I come, so I know not whither I go. I know only that, in leaving this world, I fall for ever either into annihilations or into the hands of an angry God, without knowing to which of these two states I shall be forever assigned. Such is my state, full of weakness and uncertainty. And from all this I conclude that I ought to spend all the days of my life without caring to inquire into what must happen to me. Perhaps I might find some solution to my doubts, but I will not take the trouble, nor take a step to seek it; and after treating with scorn those who are concerned with this care, I will go without foresight and without fear to try the great event, and let myself be led carelessly to death, uncertain of the eternity of my future state.
>
> Who would desire to have for a friend a man who talks in this fashion? Who would choose him out from others to tell him of his affairs? Who would have recourse to him in affliction? And indeed, to what use in life could one put him?
>
> Blaise Pascal[1]

---

1. Pascal, *Pensées*, #194, 55–56. There are, of course, more imaginable possibilities

IN THE PRECEDING CHAPTERS, I attempted to compare theism and naturalism in three major areas. I will summarize, going through them one at a time showing the responses that the two different philosophies give.[2]

Questions—Set 1: About *Existence*

Existence Question A: *Why* does anything *exist* in the manner that it does?

Why does anything *exist* as it is? Why is there something instead of nothing? Further, why does this particular reality exist? Given that something exists, specifically our universe, why does it exist instead of all the different ways that things seemingly could have been?

Theism's Answer to Existence's "Why?"

For many or most theists, God exists necessarily in every possible world as the Greatest Possible Being and chose to create this rather than any of the infinite number of other plausible worlds for reasons best known to himself. Being omniscient, he can compare every possible world, and being omnipotent, he is able to create the one that he wants. In short, God is sovereign over the rest of reality.

Naturalist Atheism's Answer to Existence's "Why?"

For most naturalists, everything that exists does so ultimately for no reason—in effect by *chance*. There is an infinite number of possible worlds. Of necessity one possible world had to be real, and ours with all that exists in it was the one that was actualized rather than any other, *by chance*. In this case, there is no reason why the universe is orderly or understandable now and yet may cease being so at any moment. This is because, unlike theism, there is no deeper being to choose that possible world and everything in it. Some naturalists think that this is either the only possible world, and that therefore everything that exists does so of logical necessity, or that its beginning was necessary. The basic trouble with this belief

---

than annihilation or an angry God, but the basic point remains.

2. I got the idea for this list from two sources: Cabal, "Naturalism vs Theism"; and Samples, *World of Difference*, 277–79.

is that it seems obvious that things could have been other than they are. So why aren't they?

Existence Question B: Why do things *remain* in existence?

Why do things remain in existence? I think that this is logically just as compelling a question as to the previous query, or perhaps even more so. If something exists, it will remain in existence unless destroyed. We take this for granted (and in these cases, the matter/energy which composed the things also remains in existence). However, there is the question as to why this is the case.

Theism's Answer to Existence's Remaining

God remains in existence because he has necessary existence. The universe remains in existence because God sustains it in existence, for the reasons given under "*Existence's Why.*"

Naturalist Atheism's Answer to Existence's Remaining

The universe and everything in it remain in existence for every moment that this universe exists either as a brute fact, which means by sheer chance repeatedly, or else it *must* remain because its existence is *necessary*, and it could not fail to exist anymore than two plus two could equal five. It is interesting that naturalists have two different answers for this question, which are the exact opposite of each other—and neither is at all plausible.

Existence Question C: Why is the universe *orderly*?

Why is the universe *orderly*? Why do the same laws and constants of nature seem to be in place everywhere and at all time? There are other kinds of order, but this is the most fundamental.

Theism's Answer to Existence's Orderliness

The universe is orderly because God is rational and good, and wanted an orderly universe that is both beautiful and enables creatures to live in it.

Naturalist Atheism's Answer to Existence's Orderliness

Either the universe is orderly over its whole expanse of space and time merely as a brute fact, which means for no reason at all other than just by chance, or else it is contradictory that there be some other order than this one, in which case this is the only possible order—and luckily, the only universe that could exist has us in it. Again, there are two diametrically opposed answers to this with naturalism.

Questions—Set 2: About *Consciousness, Minds (and Persons), Rationality, Intentionality, and Free Will*

Consciousness Questions

Why does consciousness exist at all? Why do conscious beings exist? How did consciousness come into existence in a purely non-conscious universe?

Theism's Answer for Consciousness

God himself is a conscious being, values conscious beings, and in one way or another created conscious beings to live in the universe that he created.

Naturalist Atheism's Answer for Consciousness

Consciousness randomly arose out of an entirely unconscious universe. In other words, there was no consciousness in the universe, and then suddenly there was. For some reason, when a certain kind of brain evolved, consciousness sprang into existence—though it seems entirely arbitrary that it would do so. Some naturalists deny that consciousness exists, or else think that it is nothing more than brain activity being wrongly described.

Mind Questions

Why do *minds* exist? That is, why do beings that can have such attributes as *reason, knowledge, will,* and *emotions* at the center of a subjective awareness exist? How does subjectivity, that of being an "I," exist in a universe of impersonal things?

Theism's Answer for Minds

To put things simply, God is a personal being, and personal beings have minds. Thus, God has a mind. And, because God created finite personal beings to live in the universe, he therefore created beings with minds. Their existence is part of God's purpose in creating the universe.

Naturalist Atheism's Answer for Minds

Persons with minds somehow evolved by chance out of an impersonal universe. Their existence is totally unplanned and purposeless. Further, for most naturalists, persons and minds are somehow identical in some manner with their bodies and brains, which, taken in themselves, are physical objects that are impersonal.

Rationality Questions

Why does *rationality* exist? It is not just the case that consciousness exists, but that it exists in specific forms. One of these is rationality, which is closely related to the ability to use language.

Theism's Answer to Rationality

God is a rational being and created a rational universe and rational creatures to live in it. By using their reason, creatures such as humans can live in and understand the universe. In this, as in other areas, theists think that mankind was made in the image and likeness of God—we are finite analogs of God. Some of what God does infinitely, we do finitely.

Naturalist Atheism's Answer to Rationality

Reason somehow arose by chance out of a purely non-rational universe. By sheer luck, reason arose by pure coincidence out of matter in motion, and reason helps us to understand and live in the universe. Consequentially, human beings have absolute authority, because there is nothing else that has the last word.

Intentionality Questions

Why does *intentionality* exist? Intentionality is another aspect of consciousness. Rational, conscious beings have thoughts that intend toward things. So, when one thinks, one necessarily thinks of something. In other words, how can we relate to anything?

Theism's Answer to Intentionality

God is an intentional being, knowing and thus intending everything that there is to know. He then created other intentional beings to be able to know and relate with things—such as humans (and some animals such as cats and dogs). This is part of being made in his image.

Naturalist Atheism's Answer to Intentionality

As with the other characteristics, intentionality somehow arose by chance out of an entirely non-intentional universe.

Questions of *Free Will*

Why is there *free will*? The existence of free will is controversial, especially as compared to the other characteristics listed above. However, most people believe in free will, and there are good reasons for thinking that some form of it must exist.

Theism's Answer to Free Will

God is a being with free will, and since he desired to create finite beings in his image, he gave them free will. This is made possible because of dualism, wherein human beings are partly immaterial (having consciousness and a soul), and hence humans are not bound by the laws that govern the behavior of matter. There are questions with the definition of free will, and some problems which I will not address here.[3]

---

3. For a couple of brief introductions to the issues, see Basinger, *Predestination*; and Craig, *Only Wise God*.

Naturalist Atheism's Answer to Free Will

Free will either doesn't exist, or else somehow arose by chance out of a purely physical universe. On purely materialistic versions of naturalism, it doesn't seem possible that there could be any free will let alone a mind.[4]

Questions—Set 3: About *Value*

The final questions that were raised at the beginning of the book were about *value*.

Value Question A: Why *Morality?*

Why is there *morality*? Most human beings feel the pull of morality. Those that do not feel this pull seem to be defective. Why is this the case? Do objective moral truths exist, and if so, then *how* and *why* do they exist?

Theism's Answer to Morality

Morality exists because God is purely good and holy. Further, God strongly desires that we lead ethical lives and he can instruct us in a morality for the creatures that he created. With Christianity, God is a trinity of three persons, and the love between the persons is the basis for God's moral principles.

Naturalist Atheism's Answer to Morality

Either morality somehow exists as abstract entities, or else is founded on some contingent aspect of human nature or rationality, or else it doesn't exist at all, being something that we invent. *This has disturbing consequences.*

Value Question B—Why *Beauty?*

Why is there *beauty*? Why is the universe, or most of it anyway, so beautiful? Why do we have the categories of beauty and of art? How and why can we appreciate, let alone sense, beauty?

---

4. For a defense of hard determinism, see Pereboom, *Consciousness*.

Theism's Answer for Beauty

God is an artist and loves beauty, and therefore he created a universe that is full of beauty. Again, this is because God is a personal being, and only personal beings can appreciate beauty.

Naturalist Atheism's Answer for Beauty

Like morality, beauty is somehow either the reflection of abstract entities in an impersonal universe, or else something that human beings are evolved to like but has no objective or necessary basis.

Value Question C: *The Problem of Evil*

Finally, there is the *problem of evil*. Why is there *evil and suffering* in the world, especially the amount that there is?

Theism's Answer to the Problem of Evil

God has created a universe with a great deal of evil and suffering because somehow it results in a greater good, and because creatures such as human beings are worth creating and saving. Moral evil exists because there is an objective moral system based on God's nature, and God, for whatever reason, created the human race with a potential for evil and a propensity to rebel against God.[5] Suffering results both from moral evil, and from the nature of the universe. Human beings need a universe much like the one we live in to survive and flourish, though at the expense of suffering. Evil can be considered real because in a theistic universe there is real goodness.

Naturalist Atheism's Answer to the Problem of Evil

Evil and suffering are just the way that the universe turned out to be, even though a universe that enables the existence of creatures who can understand evil and who can suffer is very rare compared to chaotic or lifeless worlds. It should be noted that with anti-realist theories of morality, there is no such thing as evil. Rather, things happen that most people don't like.

---

5. Which includes some version of free will.

On weak realist theories, things happen that go against some aspect of our human nature or against the nature of rationality itself.

Summary: The Greater Explanatory Power

It can be seen from the above that theism has much greater explanatory power than naturalism. The basic reason for this is that in theism everything, in a sense, is already there: existence, order, consciousness, persons, reason, intentionality, goodness, and beauty. These exist necessarily and are intrinsic to God's nature. God is necessarily existing, orderly, conscious, personal, rational, intentional, good, and beautiful. All these things come naturally with theism.

With naturalist atheism on the other hand, there are two quite different accounts of why the universe is the way that it is: *Brute Fact Theory* and *Necessary Universe Theory*. Given the supposition that the universe and everything in it exist ultimately for *no reason*, the fact that these things exist at all, and continue to exist over time, is sheer luck. Further, given that the universe in which we dwell is physical, then consciousness, persons, reason, and intentionality arose from the physical for no reason.

The other major naturalist option is that everything that exists happens of *logical* or absolute *necessity*. It simply couldn't have happened any other way, on pain of logical contradiction. To restate the major problem with this view is that it simply seems to be false. It doesn't appear at all to be the case that things could *not* have been other than they are. It is certainly interesting that the two naturalist answers are the exact opposite of each other. Either everything that happens is a brute fact and a matter of chance, or else everything happens because it logically cannot be any other way.

Why is naturalism so popular?

The question may be then, "If theism is as superior to naturalism as I have argued, why then is contemporary academia, and indeed society at large, so heavily infused with naturalist ideas?" Why has naturalism been so popular in the modern age, and even become an assumed *"default"* position upon which so many faulty theories rest?

The Problem of Evil

A major reason is that theism has the problem of evil. That is, it is generally agreed that this conundrum is the most difficult challenge that theism faces. I have listed above some responses that theists have given to the problem of

CONCLUSION   225

evil, but none of them tells us how to totally account for the sheer amount and awfulness of evil in the world.

On the other hand, I have argued that *naturalism has more of a problem with evil* than is usually acknowledged. First, the existence of evil implies that there is some necessarily existing standard by which something evil can be judged. Naturalism has a problem accounting for the existence of such a standard. Second, given the random nature of reality in most naturalist theories, it seems that the existence of creatures such as human beings, or even the higher animals in general, is quite unlikely. So, if theism has a problem with accounting for the scope of the existence of evil, so, for quite different reasons, does naturalism.

Science and a false claim of its ownership

There are, however, other reasons for the popularity of naturalism in modern times. One of these is the tremendous success of science in explaining the universe. *Naturalists have often identified their position with science, and thus garnered much of the prestige associated with science. Naturalists have quite successfully claimed a link between their views and science, in both academic and popular minds.*

Naturalism does *not* deserve this linkage and support. *Science can be as easily developed in theism as in naturalism, and historically was largely developed by theists, a fact which is often unknown or ignored.*[6] Indeed, I have argued that theism can account for the order and understandability of nature and that naturalism cannot. So, naturalism has no real advantage when it comes to science as far as explanatory powers go, though this seems strictly to be a minority opinion at present. There seems to have been very successful marketing of the concept of the naturalists' ownership of "science"—especially in the narrow halls of academia.

There is another reason sometimes given that naturalism has the edge with science over theism. This is the idea that if a God exists who can work

---

6. For book outlining the theistic origins of modern science, see for example the ones listed in chapter 1, note 36. Rodney Stark writes this about the matter, "*Christian theology was essential for the rise of science* . . . I show that the leading scientific figures in the sixteenth and seventeenth centuries overwhelmingly were devout Christians who believed it their duty to comprehend God's handiwork. Turning to an assessment of the 'Enlightenment,' I show it to have been conceived initially as a propaganda ploy by militant atheists and humanists who attempted to claim credit for the rise of science. The falsehood that science required the defeat of religion was proclaimed by such self-appointed cheerleaders as Voltaire, Diderot, and Gibbon, who themselves played no part in the scientific enterprise—a pattern that continues." [Italics in the original]. Stark, *For the Glory*, 123–24.

miracles, then nature becomes unknowable, because one could never be sure that God would not be working a miracle.

This is a very weak argument. A rational God does not just throw miracles into the universe at random, especially during scientific experiments, just to make the lives of scientists difficult. A rational God, such as the one that I have been describing, runs the universe according to natural law almost all of the time. Miracles are done to help people or confirm the credentials of prophets, not to make science hard to do. *On the contrary, it is naturalism with its brute fact universe that makes science impossible*, because one could never be sure when or where the laws of nature might change, or the universe cease to be describable by laws at all.

Naturalism is no utopia

Given all of this, what should we make of the case for atheism? Although I can scarcely claim to have investigated every possible argument that might be given for the truth of naturalist atheism, as far as I can see, there are no good reasons for thinking that naturalism is true. More specifically, I argue that the evidence from cosmology (science), the nature of existence, the existence and nature of mind, and the existence and nature of value provide no evidence for the truth of naturalism, and indeed count strongly against its being true.

Taking naturalism seriously, human beings are creatures randomly thrown up by a mindless process of evolution, bereft of free will, any sort of real or absolute value, an afterlife, and even, if one is consistent, rationality. We evolved to survive and reproduce, not to be able to create utopia. Why should one be optimistic about humanity in this case?[7]

To sum up: it seems that the case against atheism and naturalism is overwhelming. Things such as order, consciousness, and robustly real values flow naturally from a theistic worldview. They do not fit well at all in an atheistic and naturalistic one, let alone flow from it. Atheism cannot account for the existence of reality as we find it. When one sees the inadequacy of naturalism to answer these questions logically, at its core, it appears that it actually takes much more "faith" to hold to naturalism than to believe in a Creator God. Therefore, rationally, no one should be an atheist.

---

7 Yet historically, atheists have often been very optimistic and vigorous in attempts to create what they think is a perfect or at least a very good society. This seems to an example of the wish guiding the thought.

Appendix 1

Atheism and Ideology

> The Cosmos is all that is or ever was or ever will be.
>
> CARL SAGAN[1]

> Nature is both beneficent and truth its work; it retains all the properties of the Supreme Being.
>
> JOHN DEWEY[2]

> [T]he attributes of the Christian God are, as it were, unavoidable categories of thought. If the attributes of God are not regarded as his, they are regarded as belonging to some part or the whole of his creation.
>
> JOHN W. ROBBINS[3]

History of the Coming of Atheism in the West

Ancient Times

PHILOSOPHICALLY, MOST OF THE ancient world was both theistic and naturalistic. Most people believed in God or gods, but for the most part the gods were considered to exist within the natural world.[4] Toward the end of the Roman Empire era, many intellectuals had become convinced of the truth of some version of Monotheism.[5] This is one reason that Christianity could

---

1. Carl Sagan, *Cosmos*, 4.
2. Edmondson, *John Dewey*, 21.
3. Robbins, *Answer to Ayn Rand*, 73.
4. Which does not mean that there were no atheists at all.
5. Brown, *Augustine of Hippo*, 79–93. This was mainly a neo-Platonic view of God. However, this monotheism was sometimes mixed with belief in lesser gods, especially at the popular level. Again, the problem of definition arises. As Adrian Goldsworthy

take root in the empire, and then establish itself as the accepted religion and worldview in the West for the next one thousand years or so. In doing so, it changed civilization.

Middle Ages

A major story of modern times in the West is the movement away from religions, especially Christianity, and towards various secular ideologies. This should not be overstated. During the Middle Ages, which are sometimes called the Age of Faith, there was less Christian belief and practice than is sometimes thought. Especially at the popular level, Christianity was frequently mixed with pagan folk beliefs.[6] Nonetheless, the countries of the West were officially Christian, and there was always a minority who were devout. There were, however, alternatives. There was Judaism and Islam, and heretical Christian movements such as the Cathars.[7] None of these denied the existence of the supernatural and can thus be counted as religions by my standards. Virtually all philosophy and intellectual thought was theistic.

Renaissance and Enlightenment

The latter Middle Ages and Renaissance saw the beginning of the return of naturalism. Small at first, it began to grow in strength as allegiance to Christianity among the elite of society began to wane. Why it waned is a long story and includes many factors. Some of these were the wars of religion,[8] corruption in the churches, the cruelty with which heresy was punished,[9]

---

writes, "Throughout the third century there was a tendency amongst many pagans toward a form of monotheism, revering one deity above all others, and perhaps seeing the various gods and goddesses as merely manifestations of a single divine being." Goldsworthy, *How Rome Fell*, 181.

6. See for example Stark, *Triumph of Christianity*, 255–72.

7. On the Cathars, see for example van den Broek, "Cathars," 87–108. He describes Catharism as a medieval form of Gnosticism, 102.

8. Which were more about the rise of the modern nation state, than strictly about religion as such. See Cavanaugh, *Myth*, 164.

9. A classic exposition of how Protestants were treated is in Foxe, *New Foxes Book of Martyrs*, especially 55–319. One thing that is especially horrifying is that so many "heretics" were put to death by being burned alive, which is one of the most painful ways to die. On various matters regarding persecution during the Christian era, see Kamen, *Spanish Inquisition*; for the witch trials see Kamen and Samson, *6 Modern Myths*, 130–50; and Stark, *For the Glory of God*, 201–88. For books that argue that much of the impulse for religious toleration came inside Christianity rather than from without, see Barnett, *Enlightenment and Religion*; Zagorin, *How the Idea of Religious Toleration*

the exploration of the world (which exposed Europeans to other religions and ways of thinking), and the rise of science that upset many previously strongly held ideas. In the eighteenth century, especially, non-Christian ideas grew. At the beginning of this apostasy, the reigning idea was not atheism but *deism*. Deists generally denied revealed religion, such as Christianity claims, but accepted that there was a deity, a God.

Darwin

At the time of deistic development, naturalism and atheism began to grow, too. In the nineteenth century atheism expanded rapidly. They received a large boost in the middle of the century with the publication of Darwin's *Origin of Species*, which most scientists came to believe outlined a way to explain how complicated organisms like human beings could arise without divine intervention. Most of the intelligentsia moved away from Christianity and accepted a secular ideology. This has continued throughout the twentieth century and into the twenty-first.[10]

Secular Worldviews

In place of Christianity, there therefore arose several secular worldviews. Among these secular worldviews are secular humanism, Marxism, fascism, progressivism, nationalism, and objectivism. It should be noted that secular is not necessarily philosophically naturalistic or atheistic. Rather, it merely places an emphasis on this world—as God or gods are considered irrelevant for ordering public life here on this earth.[11] *Secular humanism* is, of course, atheistic; *Marxism* is militantly anti-God; *fascism* is normally atheistic;[12] and Ayn Rand's *objectivism* is also strongly anti-theistic. This does not mean that every member of these movements was an atheist, but rather the movements themselves were either explicitly or implicitly atheistic.

Came; Evans, *Theme is Freedom*; and Van Til, *Liberty of Conscience*.

10. It should be noted that there are different definitions of secularism, and by no means are all of them necessarily anti-Christian. One version is simply the idea that true faith must be a matter of choice rather than coercion. Historically this insight came from Christianity. See Siedentop, *Inventing*, 349–63.

11. For more on the distinction between atheism and secularism, see Beckwith and Parrish, *See the gods Fall*, 136–38. On what may be called the Religion of Humanity, where human beings are elevated to gods, see Mahoney, *Idol of Our Age*.

12. As noted above, Stanley Payne writes, "They [Fascist ideas] represented a specific attempt to achieve a modern normally atheistic form of transcendence." Payne, *Fascism*, 11.

As mentioned, not all secular movements are necessarily atheistic. *Nationalism* and *progressivism* are not intrinsically atheistic, though they are not intrinsically theistic either. However, these movements are quite secular, in the sense that they are primarily concerned with this world, not with God or an afterlife.

From Theistic to Political "Religions"

Over the last few hundred years, therefore, the dominant "religion" or worldview in the West, at least among intellectuals, has moved from Christianity to various secular ideologies. In other words, the West has moved from being based on a *theistic* religion to being based on a *political* religion. Some of these political movements tolerated Christianity fairly well; others did not. The *Jacobins* and *communists*, for example, brutally attacked the churches.[13] In other places in the world, such as contemporary America, Christianity and other traditional religions have remained legal and relatively free from persecution. However, much modern thinking on the subject is that traditional theistic religion, which of course is mainly Christianity, is a purely private matter, acceptable when kept in the home or in church, but which should have no influence in public affairs.[14] On the other hand, some

---

13. For the Jacobins, see for example see Schama, *Citizens*; and Winik, *Great Upheaval*. One thing that is interesting is that the Jacobins and other anti-Christians promptly set about persecuting other people themselves. Writes Alan Schom about the Terror in Lyons, "On one afternoon the execution of a twenty-six year old nun did not go according to schedule, when the good wives of Lyon's working classes slashed at her bloodied head with their meat cleavers several times before succeeding in beheading the young woman, whose only crime had been refusing to stop praying to God when ordered to do so by 'the people.' Clearly democracy and freedom were on the march." Schom, *Napoleon Bonaparte*, 254. On the French Revolution, see also McPhee, *Liberty or Death*. On the communist persecution of religion, see Froese, *Plot*; Zugger, *Forgotten*; and Peris, *Storming the Heavens*. For a brief history of secularist persecution of Christians, see Stark, *Bearing False Witness*, 186–207. According to Stark, the Soviet Union murdered about 200,000 clergy because of the ruler's atheism, and over twenty million of its own religious citizens. Quoting Alexander Yakovlev, who chaired a Russian commission on such matters, "Metropolitan Vladimir of Kiev was mutilated, castrated, and shot, and his corpse was left naked for the public to desecrate. Metropolitan Veniamin of St. Petersburg . . . was turned into a pillar of ice: he was doused with cold water in the freezing cold. Bishop Germogen of Tobolsk . . . was strapped alive to the paddlewheel of a steamboat and mangled by the rotating blades. Archbishop Andronnik of Perm . . . was buried alive. Archbishop Vasily was crucified and burned." Stark, *Bearing False Witness*, 201. See Luxmoore, *God of the Gulag, vol 1*, and *God of the Gulag, vol. 2*.

14. Yancey, *Hostile Environment*, and *Dehumanizing Christians*. This is the same attitude that Hitler had. Richard Weikart writes, "In Hitler's view, morality was the purview of the state and its political leaders, not religious institutions and religious leaders.

political religions and ideologies are thought to legitimately be able to influence and even determine public affairs.[15]

Minimizing Religion

In effect, Christianity and other traditional religions, like Judaism, have been reduced to something like stamp collecting; it's alright if one does it on one's own, but it should not be forced on anyone else. Many people aren't interested in stamp collecting, and don't want to have stamp collectors telling them what to do. The same basic thought is applied to Christianity. This would have amazed people in western civilization in many previous centuries, who took it for granted that theirs was a Christian civilization and that public policy ought to reflect the teachings of the churches. Instead, in the public arena today Christianity is mainly excluded and restricted to the private sphere. In fact, the private sphere of Christians is often invaded by law-making public policy.

Why has this happened? Besides the failure of the Christian churches mentioned above, there are other reasons. Obviously, when talking about major civilization shifts taking place over centuries, there have been a great number of influencing factors. One is this: outside of some Christian circles, it is now often assumed that believing in Christianity or some other traditional religion is a non-rational or even an irrational thing to do. It is often held by secularists of different varieties that there is no good reason to believe in God or other traditional doctrines. It is, in effect, a matter of blind faith.[16] When I started graduate studies in philosophy, I was told that the reason for the atheism or agnosticism of the faculty was due to there being no good arguments for God's existence, while the problem of evil provided a strong argument against God's existence.

To believe something for no good reason is considered at best to be foolish, and at worst, a matter of intellectual dishonesty. Since, it is held that religions like Christianity have no rational support, it is said to be either foolish or intellectually dishonest to hold to them. However, since most people do not want to persecute others, *it is thought to be best to make religion harmless*

Any pastor or priest teaching his congregation morality contrary to Nazi policy or ideology could be labeled a political oppositionist, even if he was simply teaching moral precepts that Christians had been teaching for centuries." Weikart, *Hitler's Religion*, 12.

15. Baker, *End of Secularism*.

16. Contrary to what is often said, most religious believers do not think that they are accepting their beliefs blindly. See Stark, *Triumph of Faith*, 206–10.

by pushing it to the margins of society where it does less damage.[17] Even better, bringing the various religious organizations in line to support whatever goals the secular intellectuals have at the moment would be considered to be ultimately preferred—for example, getting them to support abortion rights. In the meantime, rational people will work to bring into existence the good society, however that is to be defined by those in power.

This is a widely-held view. The notion that religious people think that they "should believe in God and religion purely out of faith without any rational support" is not totally false. There are religious people, including some Christians, who hold to this view. Some go so far as to think that not only is it unnecessary that one use reason in establishing the truth of religious beliefs, but that it is *wrong* to use reason or evidence to establish the truth of religious beliefs. This is a doctrine known as *fideism*.

Blind Faith

What can be said about this "blind faith"? Much, but here I will simply make two points. First, I think that fideism or belief without any reason, whatever opponents may say, is *not* the basis of *most* people's credence, because the human mind doesn't work that way. As was argued in chapter 1, people normally believe things because they seem true, and what seems to be true is normally what we have reason to believe, though of course the reasons we have may not always be good reasons.

The second point is that in today's intellectual climate, adopting *fideism* is the equivalent to fighting a major war without using any weapons. For example, I think that one explanation (though far from the only one) that so many people have left their churches in the last few generations, and no longer think that Christianity is true, is that they have not been given any reason to *think* that Christianity is true. Even though *fideism* is, and has always been, a minority position in the church at large, many people act as if it is true, whether they believe it or not. In short, *fideism* has been a disaster. After all, if you say that there is no reason to think that the beliefs that one holds are true, then why should one pay any attention to those beliefs?

---

17. Of course, not all secularists think this way. Secular but conservative intellectuals usually find value in supernatural religion. "Less [or some non-] religious conservatives will say that religion is an essential and inexpensive form of crowd control, and that everyday secular morality survives still only because it expresses the moral surplus of a former religious morality." Gairdner, *Great Divide*, 40. For an earlier exposition of this idea, see Stephen, *Liberty, Equality*.

The Shoe is on the Other Foot

What I find ironic is that actually, in various ways, the shoe is on the other foot. In intellectual discussions, naturalist atheism is often *assumed* to be true, and any assumptions required to make the concept work are adopted without strain, whether there is any *evidence* for them or not. Some of these assumptions or ideas seem quite absurd, at least to me. For example:

- Things come into existence for no reason and remain in existence for no reason.
- Physical states are assumed to exist out of their own absolute necessity; mind and matter are identical even though they seem almost completely different (or even that consciousness doesn't exist).
- We can have theories without minds.
- Though they are ultimately only organizations of matter in motion, human beings can discover universal truths.
- Reason comes from non-reason, consciousness from the non-conscious, persons from the impersonal, and order comes from pure chance.
- There is no free will of either kind and all that we really are, are machines.

All sorts of strange theories can be and are propounded and are even respected in academia—if they are in accordance with atheism.

Atheism is Ungrounded

There is a significant problem for naturalism, mentioned in the first chapter. This is simply that *in naturalism, human beings are just another part of nature.* Usually, they are entirely material, and thus governed by the laws of nature, the same as everything else. Yet, at the same time, humanity is the highest form of life in the universe, unless there are more highly evolved aliens somewhere, which is unknown.

As the highest form of existence then, with no superior being like God to answer to, humanity is, on the account given by naturalism, its own legislator. We make the rules governing ourselves in accordance with our own reason and desires. Humanity collectively, or each individual by himself or herself, becomes, in effect, a sort of terrestrial god. We are thus the highest authority there is.[18]

Yet at the same time, we are machines. Consistent naturalists are, I think, materialists, and consistent materialists should deny the existence of free will, in either of its two basic varieties. On this thinking, we have no freer will than that of a can opener or a car's transmission. We do have, with some versions of materialism, consciousness, reason, and intentionality.

The Central Paradox of Naturalist Atheism

With naturalism, human beings are gods and human beings are machines. We transcend nature by our reason, with no lawgiver higher than ourselves, but at the same time remain just another part of nature, only a cog in the machine, so to speak. We pride ourselves on being rational, but our reason supposedly developed by, and is caused by, non-rational things by chance mutation and natural selection. This does not seem to me to be a very logical or appealing picture, yet many people are attracted to it.

The Rise of Atheistic Worldviews

Given naturalism, we are in effect here by sheer luck. There is no one who listens to prayers, no God that cares about human beings. Worse, the whole human race, and indeed the universe itself, are doomed to extinction. Life is short, often consists of one stupid thing after another, and for the naturalist, it is the end of personal existence. Why then do so many people find naturalism so attractive?

There are several reasons, but I think that for some people, especially intellectuals, they basically come down to the following issues: Authority, Meaning, and the Nature of human beings.

---

18. See McKnight, *Sacralizing the Secular*, for an exposition of how the notion of human beings as terrestrial gods arose. According William Gairdner, this whole idea of humanity as the ultimate authority has been the source of the institutionalization of abortion on demand. "The source of such an existential transformation is only the naked will of the mothers . . . whereby human life is created *ex nihilo*, or extinguished, not by God or biology, but by human will alone. Which is why I say we fancy ourselves godlets now." Gairdner, *Great Divide*, 226.

Authority

In Christianity there is a being, God, who is vastly (one might say infinitely) more powerful and smarter than we are, and to whom we owe obedience. The locus of authority and meaning is God, and human nature is intrinsically flawed in the sense that all existing human beings, save one, are innately sinful. It is not that being a human is bad. It is rather that every human being, except for Christ,[19] is a being who is inherently sinful and rebellious. In Christianity we cannot save ourselves—God through Christ must do that. Human beings are definitely inferior to God.

However, there is another side to this. For with Christianity, human beings are made in the image of God, they are finite copies of God, only a little lower than heavenly beings as the Psalmist writes, and they are of such worth that God himself made the ultimate sacrifice to save them.[20] Thus, because God has ultimate value and human beings are in some ways like God, human beings also have great intrinsic worth. But, in Christianity, human beings are not in charge. God is, which many people find unattractive. Therefore, they reject Christianity, so as not to be under God's authority.[21]

Meaning

Another area of difference is that of meaning. In theistic theories, meaning is provided by God. We exist because he wants us to, and because we are part of his plan. But in naturalism, we are here by chance. Any meaning we have we must provide ourselves. One way that human beings attempt to live in a meaningless universe is by living only for one's own pleasure (*hedonism*). Another way is throw one's self into some secular ideology, finding meaning in its tenets and activities.

The psychologist Viktor Frankl, who had been in a Nazi concentration camp, argued that the search for meaning is the most important drive that human beings have. With no God to give us guidance, we must make our own meanings. And for godless human beings, what greater meaning could there be than creating a heaven on earth by our own efforts, rather than one in the next life given to us by God? But to be able to do

---

19. According to Roman Catholic teaching, Mary is also considered sinless.
20. Psalm 8: 3–5 states, "When I consider Your heavens, the work of Your fingers, the moon and the stars, which You have ordained, what is man that You are mindful of him, and the son of man that You visit him? For You have made him a little lower than the angels, and You have crowned him with glory and honor."
21. See quote of Nagel in the beginning of the Preface.

this, human beings must not be irretrievably flawed, but rather creatures capable of achieving perfection.

The issue here stems from the fact that most naturalists alive today are not *just* naturalists—that is, the only beliefs that they have is that the natural world is the only existing concrete thing, and that human beings are just the unplanned product of an evolutionary process within the physical universe. There would seem to be no reason why this would produce creatures who can obtain perfection.

There are intellectual forces beyond just pure naturalism that are guiding the development of contemporary secular thought. As was explained above, many of them also hold to a secular ideology. And most of these ideologies are devoted to creating a *utopia*, or at least a very good society. There are reasons for this. Pure naturalism is, by itself, rather depressing. We merely live for a while and then we die and that's all there is. The whole idea can make for a rather meaningless life. But as Frankl argues, there is a strong human need for meaning.[22] Secular ideologies give a meaning to life that pure naturalism does not. Having gotten rid of God, human beings, or least some of them, now must become gods themselves.

Human Nature

As has been said, in some theistic theories, especially in Christianity, human beings are held to be innately flawed. In most secular philosophies (though it doesn't seem to follow inevitably from naturalism), human beings are naturally good, or at least neutral, and "trainable." Further, in theistic systems, there is usually a belief in life after death. One implication of this is that there is in theism, thus, a delayed satisfaction to be found in heaven. In secular naturalism, there is no heaven, so any heaven must be built by us here on earth. Human perfectibility is a necessary doctrine for this; any flaws in humanity are *not* innate, but rather, are caused by a bad society. Since meaning for many naturalists depends upon creating the perfect, or at least a very good society, it follows that human beings must be perfectible.

Eric Voegelin argued that modern ideologies are, in effect, forms of the ancient religious system known as *Gnosticism*.[23] This seems odd, for the

22. Frankl, *Man's Search*.

23. "All gnostic movements are involved in the project of abolishing the constitution of being, with its origin in divine, transcendent being, and replacing it with a world-immanent order of being, the perfection of which lies in the realm of human action. This is a matter of so altering the structure of the world, which is perceived as inadequate, that a new, satisfying world arises. The variants of immanentization, therefore, are the controlling symbols, to which the other complexes are subordinated as secondary ways

ancient Gnostics believed that the physical universe was evil, and that salvation came from escaping it. The modern secular ideologies think that all that exists is the physical universe, and the goal is to reform it. But Voegelin thought that the underlying mentality was the same. He writes of the Gnostics, whether ancient or modern, as follows:

1. It must first be pointed out that the Gnostic is dissatisfied with his situation. This, in itself, is not especially surprising. We all have cause to be not completely satisfied with one aspect or another of the situation in which we find ourselves.

2. Not quite so understandable is the second aspect of the Gnostic attitude: the belief that the drawbacks of the situation can be attributed to the fact that the world is intrinsically poorly organized. For it is likewise possible to assume that the order of being as it is given to us men (wherever its origin is to be sought) is good and that it is we human beings who are inadequate. But gnostics are not inclined to discover that human beings in general and they themselves in particular are inadequate. If in a given situation something is not as it should be, then the fault is to be found in the wickedness of the world.[24]

The idea that the world itself is evil, or at least poorly organized, sometimes goes along with the concept that what we perceive is not the "real" world; it is somehow an illusion that is hiding the genuine perfect world.

---

of expressing the will to immanentization." Voegelin, *Science, Politics*, 99–100.

24. He goes on to write, "3) The third characteristic is the belief that salvation from the evil of the world is possible. 4) From this follows the belief that the order of being will have to be changed in an historical process. From a wretched world a good one must evolve historically. This assumption is not altogether self-evident, because the Christian solution might also be considered—namely, that the world throughout history will remain as it is and that man's salvational fulfillment is brought about through grace in death. 5) With this fifth point we come to the gnostic trait in the narrower sense—the belief that a change in the order of being lies in the realm of human action, that this salvational act is possible through man's own effort. 6) If it is possible, however, so to work a structural change in the given order of being that we can be satisfied with it as a perfect one, then it becomes the task of the gnostic to seek out the prescription for such a change. Knowledge—gnosis—of the method of altering being is the central concern of the gnostic. As the sixth feature of the gnostic attitude, therefore, we recognize the construction of a formula for self and world salvation, as well as the gnostic's readiness to come forward as a prophet who will proclaim his knowledge about the salvation of mankind." Voegelin, *Science, Politics*, 86–87. The gnostic thinks we must save ourselves: for the Christian salvation is the free gift of God. See also Minogue, *Alien Powers*; and Walsh, *After Ideology*, especially 93–130.

Whatever exists then must either be destroyed or at least transformed, so that the "real" world may appear.[25]

This impulse has led to the attempt to create utopia, and was one of the, if not the main, driving forces in history in the twentieth century, and the cause of deaths in the tens of millions.

The Secularization Thesis

Secularization thesis is a notion, much discussed and debated in the last few decades, claiming that as societies progress into a modern, scientific understanding of the world, inevitably religious beliefs will fade. This has happened to a great extent in the modern world, especially in Europe, but also to a certain extent in North America and Japan.

Here I will not attempt to evaluate the thesis *per se*, but rather I will simply highlight an important point. This is simply that although in some modern highly developed societies "religion" has faded (though certainly not disappeared), it has not been replaced by a void, but rather by secular ideologies and political religions.

So, instead of believing, or at least being primarily motivated, by supernatural religions such as Christianity, many people in highly secularized countries now believe in, or at least are primarily motivated by, the concerns of a secular ideology. In some sense, therefore, people are, in this extended sense, just as "religious" as ever, but what is meant by the "religion" they adhere to is different. Indeed, what *genre* of religion they believe in is different.

---

25. About this Richard Pipes writes, "This kind of thinking led to a progressive estrangement from life . . . It is only with the help of this insight that we can understand the seeming paradoxes in the mentality of the genus intelligentsia, and especially its more extreme species, the Russian intelligentsia. Theories and programs, on which Russian intellectuals spent their waking hours, were indeed evaluated in relation not to life but to other theories and programs: the criterion of their validity was consistency and conformity. Live reality was treated as a perversion or caricature of 'genuine' reality . . . " Pipes, *Russian Revolution*, 130–31. Joyce Milton states about the coming of this new view of people and the world, "To maximize one's potential, one had to throw off the distorting influences of society and discover and nurture one's innate good self. While psychology and psychiatry as taught in the universities would remain splintered, the new concept of the self quickly gained popular acceptance, filling the void left by the erosion of traditional religious values and disillusionment with Marxism. The new theory described human nature as it ought to be, not necessarily as it was. Supposedly, once the detritus of repressive social institutions and moral codes was swept away, people would be free to develop their inborn goodness. 'Authentic' human beings would build a society without hypocrisy, prejudice or exploitation." Milton, *Road to Malpsychia*, 8–9. Similarly, David Horowitz writes, "The utopian longing—the need for an alternate reality to supply values that are 'truly human' and social orders that are 'socially just'—is the religious wellspring of the Communist Left and of its Neo-Communist successor. It underpins their hope for a world informed by these ideals and contempt for the actual world that lacks them." Horowitz, *Unholy Alliance*, 67.

APPENDIX 1: ATHEISM AND IDEOLOGY

Political religions take the place of theistic ones. People try to find salvation on earth, by their own efforts.

The situation is further confused by the fact that many secular people still hold on to some concepts from Christianity or Judaism—like the belief in a God, or an afterlife. But their primary focus and loyalty is to secular thinking. The fact is that people can hold different, inconsistent beliefs without even noticing it. However, in the end, the ones that are held most strongly are the ones that are in control. In a very real sense, various secular ideologies are the most successful "religions" in the world today. In the 1700s, very few people held to some secular ideology; now these ideologies have infiltrated most of the globe and are held by hundreds of millions of people.

I consider this to be largely the result of a rejection of the notion of transcendence—that there is anything beyond the natural world.[26] With the idea of a transcendent God—either denied, considered to be unknowable, or else thought to be irrelevant to what is important in life—intrinsic *things* become the ultimate value. To theists, this is idolatry.[27] Something in this world—nation, race, class, personal or societal pleasure, human equality and/or liberty, nature itself, or something else—is held to be the most important value, and society is to be restructured in an attempt to achieve the instantiation, the realization, of this value.

As to why society has become secularized, I believe the main reason is that most intellectuals have become secularized and have influence clearly out of proportion to their numbers.

Utopia

> I am convinced that the battle for mankind's future must be waged and won in the public school classroom by teachers who correctly perceive their role as proselytizers of a new faith: a religion of humanity that recognizes and respects the spark of what theologians call divinity in every human being . . . The classroom must and will become an arena of conflict between the old and the new—the rotting corpse of Christianity, together with all its adjacent evils and misery, and the new faith of humanism, resplendent with its promise of a world in which the never-realized Christian ideal of "love they neighbor" will finally be achieved.
>
> JOHN DUNPHY[28]

---

26. See Kurtz, *Transcendental Temptation*, for a defense of this view.

27. See Pearcey, *Finding Truth*. See also Schlossberg, *Idols*, for an extended discussion of such idolatry.

28. Quoted in Gairdner, *Great Divide*, 181–82.

> Utopia follows secularization as a shadow follows a body.
>
> TAGE LINDBOM[29]

> Half the harm that is done in this world is due to people who want to feel important. They don't mean to do harm—but the harm does not interest them. Or they do not see it, or they justify it, because they are absorbed in the endless struggle to think well of themselves.
>
> T. S. ELIOT[30]

Erik J. Wielenberg argues that, under the right (or wrong) circumstances, theism can be a force for evil. Identifying four strands of thought, he writes,

> Together, the four strands of thought I have identified form the view that *there is a God who has selected a particular group of people to be His chosen people, whose commands trump all other considerations, and who sometimes commands invasion, killing, and sacrifice—sometimes when there is no apparent justification for such actions other than that they have been commanded by God. Furthermore, human beings sometimes can have the authority to order such actions on God's behalf.*[31]

He goes on to write, "Naturalism is devoid of these dangerous ideas."[32] Further, "The naturalist rejects the divisive cry of 'no God but ours' (which always excludes more people than it includes) and replaces it with a cry of 'there is no God to help us; we're all in this together . . . .'"[33]

Without a doubt, theists of various sorts have committed atrocities, and certain theological beliefs lend themselves more to atrocities than others. It is, however, rather strange to see Wielenberg write that naturalists think of humanity as one, as being all in things together. Naturalists of various sorts have been among the biggest killers in history. Some of the Jacobins, the Spanish Anarchists, the Fascists and National Socialists, and the Marxist communists have had no problem in dividing humanity into "us and them," and murdering large numbers of "them." The Marxists

---

29. Lindbom, *Tares*, 11.
30. Quoted in *Daily Dose of Knowledge*, 53. For more on this, see Sowell, *Vision*.
31. Wielenberg, *Value*, 148.
32. Wielenberg, *Value*, 150.
33. Wielenberg, *Value*, 151.

killed members of the "wrong" class, the Nazis killed members of the "wrong" race, and so on.[34]

Indeed 9,121,000 Christians had been martyred by Muslims by the year 2000, while 31,689,000 Christians had been murdered by atheists.[35] This is in spite of the fact that Muslims have been killing Christians for nearly fourteen centuries, while atheists have only been killing them for a little over two centuries, with the vast majority of the killing happening in the twentieth century.

Naturalist atheism itself is not sufficient to form an ideology. All that it states is: 1) the universe is here either by chance or necessity; and 2) human beings themselves are the product of a completely unplanned evolutionary process. These beliefs by themselves are not enough to find a plan of action for reforming humanity. Indeed, taken seriously, it seems rather incompatible with any grand ideology.

What naturalism *does* do is get rid of a creator God, and thus, almost always in modern naturalist thought, any personal god at all. This removes any higher authority. It exalts the natural sciences, because if they are the disciplines that study the natural world, and the natural world is all that there is, then they have pride of place. Besides the rejection of God, there is also a rejection of any idea of an afterlife. Any happiness that people are to get must be acquired in this world.

Though not implied by naturalism, indeed, I think somewhat in tension with it, the doctrine of the natural goodness of mankind, or at least the *perfectibility of mankind*, is also often accepted. This is the rejection of the Christian doctrine of original or innate sinfulness. With the rejection of Christianity, Christian doctrines like *original sin* are jettisoned.

Utopianism

This concept of "Heaven on Earth" is a major result of the belief in the goodness of mankind, the search for meaning, and the concept that any happiness to be had is to be had here on earth. Although more traditional religious groups have not been free of utopianism,[36] it was prevalent in some

---

34. As was argued above, Hitler and some of the National Socialist leadership were pantheists. But this was a pantheism very close to philosophical naturalism.

35. See Barrett and Johnson, *World Christian Trends*, 229. On the supposed tolerance of atheists, see Hitchens, *Rage*.

36. See for example, Shaferivich, *Socialist Phenomenon*, 18–79; and Cohn, *Pursuit*, for a history of utopianism in (usually) theistic, supernatural religions in the Middle Ages. See also, Gellately, *Lenin, Stalin, and Hitler*. Hayek argues that lack of information will always prevent utopia from being constructed, apart from any other problems. See

secular theories—Marxism is one very influential theory. Although it might be thought that utopianism, the desire to create a perfect or at least very good society, might be the cause of great improvements, it can be strongly argued that the pursuit of *utopia* has been the greatest cause of suffering and destruction in modern times.

First, to create utopia means that everything in society must be perfect—or at least as good as possible. To do this means that the creators must have total control over society, which is *totalitarianism*.[37] They must be able to remold or destroy everything—a total transformation—to create what they think will be heaven on earth.[38]

It takes a god to create a heaven, and there has been no lack of people who considered themselves terrestrial gods, bringing a new perfect world to this troubled and disordered world of ours.[39] This is sometimes thought of as Man's or Humanity's taking charge and creating a new much better world. In practice, this means that some people will take charge of all the others.[40]

Second, most utopians will of necessity adopt an ethical theory that is *consequentialist*. They will think that they must do whatever it takes to create utopia. Everything that exists at the present will be considered to be infected

---

his *Fatal Conceit*. See also Goldman, *How Civilizations Die* on the effect of secularism on Europe.

37. On totalitarianism, see Taylor, *Great Lie*.

38. In a famous passage, Marx writes about what his future communist utopia would be like. "[W]hereas in communist society, where nobody has one exclusive sphere of activity but each can become accomplished in any branch he wishes, society regulates the general production and thus makes it possible for me to do one thing today and another tomorrow, to hunt in the morning, fish in the afternoon, rear cattle in the evening, criticize after dinner, just as I have a mind . . . " Marx, *German Ideology*, 53. To put it more modern terms, one might work at McDonald's in the morning, do brain surgery in the afternoon, design video games in the evening, and run a factory after dinner. This passage is simply one example of magical thinking on Marx's part. For an exposition of communist beliefs in this matter, see Heller, *Cogs*; and Tucker, *Marxian Revolutionary Idea*.

39. "At the root of the Marxian idea we find the spiritual disease, the gnostic revolt . . . Marx knew that he was a god creating a world. He did not want to be a creature . . . There are a good number of men who want to be gods." Voegelin, *From Enlightenment*, 298–99. To be a god, men try to destroy the order and laws that God has made and replace them with ones of one's own desires. As Bellinger puts it, relying on the work of Voegelin, "Human beings typically suffer from spiritual sickness, a pneumopathology, that prevents them from inhabiting reality with integrity. They develop a need to create a 'second reality,' an ideologically constructed worldview, that provides a comfortable living space for their immature psyche. In this mindset, the uses of 'autonomy' as rhetorical device is not an *idea*, it is a symptom of the pneumopathology." Bellinger, *Jesus v. Abortion*, 304. For more on this, see Aikman, *Role of Atheism*.

40. "Man's power over nature turns out to be a power exercised by some men over other men with Nature as its instrument." Lewis, *Abolition*, 69.

with old ways of thinking. A fresh start must have total control. In short, for the utopia there must be a total transformation. What this means is that what makes an action ethically right and good are the *consequences* of the action. In practice, what this does is legitimizes an end-justifying-the-means morality, where anything can be done if it leads to the desired outcome. In practice this has meant killing large numbers of human beings.

This disregard for human life has been made easier by the fact that in naturalist atheism, there is no hard break between humanity and the rest of nature—human beings are merely part of the natural world.[41] For totalitarians, the individual is not important, only the collective—whether this is thought of as humanity or merely one race or class or any other grouping.[42]

Based on the above beliefs, the toll of human life in the attempt to create a heaven on earth has been staggering—probably at least one hundred million dead.[43] Yet despite the horrendous toll, the impulse of the attempt to create utopia, for human beings to create heaven on earth, is still very much with us.

No matter how many failures they have, no matter how many disasters they produce, no matter how many bodies pile up, the concept that human beings can produce heaven on earth by their own efforts refuses to die.

It must be said that the desire to make a heaven on earth need not result in a totalitarian society. There are softer versions, wherein people seek utopia within themselves in the form of hedonism—seeking pleasures.[44] In the last few decades American society has embraced a kind of utopianism involving sexual hedonism. This sexual libertinism has been accomplished by attacking Christian morality, and it has badly damaged marriage, with untold negative effects on children, and has caused much suffering via STDs (including infertility, cancer, and death).[45] The idea is still popular that somehow, after destroying the basic structures of society, a perfect or at least vastly better society will somehow emerge. Though perhaps not as bloody as the French, fascist, or communist revolutions, in the long run the sexual revolution may be as damaging to civilization.[46]

41. Robbins, *Without a Prayer*, 141.
42. Weikart, *Death of Humanity*, 4–5.
43. For a list of the mass murders of the 20th century described in some detail, see Rummel, *Death by Government*. Rummel's middle estimate is that during the 20th century, 169,198,000 people were murdered by governments (i.e., not as combatants in war). Most of these murders were done in pursuit of creating a utopia—a heaven on earth. See also Rummel, *Power Kills*.
44. On this, see Goldberg, *Suicide*, 331–51.
45. See Kuby, *Global Sexual Revolution*.
46. Though the sexual revolution has not produced concentration camps like the

Conclusion

To sum up, naturalist atheism is the reigning philosophy among the elite today, especially in Western societies. From the elite, the basic tenets and conclusions of naturalism are flowing down into the rest of society. Naturalism by itself does not imply how either individuals or societies should be ordered. In practice, however, many, if not most, intellectuals have adopted some philosophy that promotes the idea that either a utopia or at least a far better society can be constructed by human efforts. This, although certainly not entailed by naturalism, is attractive for many naturalists, for one reason—because it gives them an authority that had previously been had only by gods or God.

For utopia to be possible, human beings must be naturally good or at least plastic enough so that they can be trained to be completely good. Indeed, I would say that one reason for the modern revolt against Christianity has been the rejection of the doctrine that we are all sinners whose only hope is to trust in and obey God. The concept of human beings' being naturally good does not follow from naturalism but is especially appealing to the many who think that the Christian concept of God and mankind puts human beings into too low of a position. From this comes the concept, which has been repeated throughout the history of the last few centuries, that an elite will take political power and use it to reconstruct society.

To construct utopia, however, one must have total control. To be successful, every institution, and indeed, every individual must be under the control of the elite, which is *totalitarianism*. Further, since every institution and custom that exists is part of the corrupt present which prevents people from realizing their natural goodness, everything that exists is considered corrupt and must be destroyed or altered. Even softer utopian efforts like that involved in the sexual revolution have involved changing the laws in major areas of society.

The desire to improve the world in some way is a good one. Without that desire, civilization would never have been built. However, to think that one can create perfection, a heaven on earth, is a delusion, flowing from a spiritual disorder.[47] It is a desire to escape from the human condition, from the difficulties of life. In modern times it has been a desire to escape from God, who realistically is the only being who *could* create a perfect world. There is a desire to be at once a god creating a world, and at the same time an

---

Gulag or as the Holocaust did, the legalizing of abortion on demand in the United States has resulted in the deaths of nearly 60 million unborn babies. So far.

47. Franz, *Ideology*. I disagree with some of Voegelin's analysis, specifically about the prophet Isaiah, and the apostle Paul.

infant upon whom no demands are made and whose every wish someone else rushes to fulfill. Our society today is in a state of high spiritual disorder; fulfilling people's appetites is held to the greatest value, no matter how irrational or destructive these appetites are.

It is from these widely-held theses that much of the suffering of humanity in the last few centuries have come. On this view, there are no limits save the ones we create for ourselves, and which we can change any time. Because there is considered to be no God, government is only limited by the desires of those in charge. In Christianity, government is limited by God, and all the individuals and institutions of society are under God's law and are subject to his judgment. By getting rid of God, the Christian doctrines of original sin, and the limitation of state power, naturalism enables utopianism and the resulting totalitarianism and mass death that inevitably goes with it.[48]

---

48. See Clark, *Christian View*, 97–147; Berman, *Created Equal*; Lindberg, *Political Teachings*; and Unterman, *Justice*.

Appendix 2
Social Effects of Atheism

> I call Christianity the one great curse, the one great intrinsic depravity, the one great instinct for revenge for which no expedient is sufficiently poisonous, secret, subterranean, *petty*—I call it the one immortal blemish of mankind . . .
>
> And one calculates *time* from *dies nefastus* [unlucky day] on which this fatality arose—from the first day of Christianity!—*Why not rather from its last?*—*From today?*—Revaluation of all values!
>
> FRIEDRICH NIETZSCHE[1]

> Their skepticism about values is on the surface: it is for use on other people's values: about the values current in their own set they are not nearly skeptical enough.
>
> C. S. LEWIS[2]

> The more I study the history of intellectuals, the more they seem like a wrecking crew, dismantling civilization bit by bit—replacing what works with what sounds good.
>
> THOMAS SOWELL[3]

THIS APPENDIX ADDRESSES THE practical question of who leads more moral lives, religious believers or secularists.

I originally had no intention of putting information like this in the book. However, since both Oppy and Wielenberg do include such information in their books defending atheism, I decided to give a brief response.

1. Nietzsche, *Twilight,* Topic 62, 42. Italicized words as in the original.
2. Lewis, *Abolition,* 41.
3. https://www.creators.com/read/thomas-sowell/12/12/random-thoughts-12-12-25. On this theme, see Sowell's *Intellectuals.*

Both of them argue that the evidence shows that secularists are at least as moral as religious believers, though they agree that the evidence is mixed, and that more study needs to be done in the area.

I have a couple of caveats. First, what is *moral* is itself a matter of some dispute. This is true especially in the area of sexual morality, where religious people tend to hold to stricter rules than secularists do. For example, the traditional Christian teaching is that all sex outside of marriage is immoral, while most secularists would disagree.

Second, in giving comparisons one must be careful to compare apples to apples and oranges to oranges, so to speak. In his book *The Best Argument against God*, Oppy gives a chart for four different countries—Ireland, the US, Australia, and Denmark—and compares their church attendance and crime rates. Their religiosity (measured in terms of church attendance) does not seem to have much correlation to lower crime rates and other social problems.[4] Secular Denmark seems to be at least no worse than, and in some cases, better than, the more religious US.

However, one must be careful here. Countries differ from each other in many more ways than just church attendance. Denmark is a small, fairly homogenous country, while the US is a vast and heterogeneous one. It seems obvious that there are many factors involved in a society's function or dysfunction besides religion. There are many more factors here, both in the different societies, and in how the data is collected, as indeed Oppy agrees.[5] In any studies with so many variables, without allowing for differences in measurement of the multiple factors, any conclusions would be seriously undermined.

Further, even with a country, there are differences in religious beliefs between ethnic groups, classes, and so on. For example, a definite belief in philosophical naturalism tends to be concentrated in areas of society such as academia. Since academics tend to be overall more intelligent and educated than the population at large (although I must admit, there are times that I have had my doubts about their intelligence, especially recently), and since both intelligence and education are correlated with lower levels of social dysfunction, this factor by itself would give a boost to the scores of secularists.

To do this, Rodney Stark gathers a vast amount of data about society.[6] Many of his charts distinguish between those people who attend church

---

4. Oppy, *Best Argument against God*, 47.
5. Oppy, *Best Argument*, 48.
6. Stark, *America's Blessings*. Writes Steven Pinker, who is an atheist, "The numbers show that it is not the rich, privileged, robust, or good-looking who are happy; it is those who have spouses, friends, religion, and challenging, meaningful work." *How the*

weekly, those who sometimes attend, and those who never attend. In almost every case, people who attend weekly show less social dysfunction than those who attended only sometimes or never. The point being that it is not mere belief in some theistic religion that causes an increased social functionality, but a lived commitment to it. For example, Stark writes,

> At all ages, religious people are much less likely to commit crimes.[7]

> Religious Americans are far more likely to contribute even to secular charities, to volunteer their time to socially beneficial programs, and to be active in civic affairs.

> Religious Americans enjoy superior mental health—they are happier, less neurotic, and far less likely to commit suicide.

> Religious Americans also enjoy superior physical health, having an average life expectancy more than seven years longer than that of the irreligious. A very substantial difference remains even after the effects of 'clean living' are removed.

> Religious people are more apt to marry and less likely to divorce, and they express higher degrees of satisfaction with their spouses. They are also more likely to have children.

> Religious husbands are substantially less likely to abuse their wives or children.

> Religious American couples enjoy their sex lives more and are far less likely to have extramarital affairs.

> Religious students perform better on standardized achievement tests.

> Religious Americans are far less likely to have dropped out of school, which is especially true for African Americans and Hispanics.

> Religious Americans are more successful, obtaining better jobs and far less subject to being on unemployment or welfare; this is true not only for whites but for African Americans.

> Although portrayed as ignorant philistines, religious Americans are more likely to consume and sustain high culture.

Mind Works, 1999.

7. On this, see also Johnson, *More God*.

Religious people are far less likely to believe in occult and paranormal phenomena such as Bigfoot, UFOs, Atlantis, ghosts, haunted houses, and astrology.[8]

One common thing that secularists appeal to is Scandinavia. Scandinavia is said to be a very well-functioning region of the world, and it is highly secular, showing that secularism can produce societies with a high level of well-being. There is some truth in this, but there are several caveats.

The Scandinavian countries, which include Iceland, Norway, Denmark, Sweden, and Finland, are indeed secular. It is even sometimes claimed that they are atheistic. However, as far as outright declared atheists are concerned (people who *claim* that they are atheists), most Scandinavians are not atheists. One must be careful here, for different samplings will give different readings, but here is one chart for these five nations.[9]

Country	% Atheist
Iceland	3.5%
Norway	6.8%
Denmark	5.0%
Sweden	16.8%
Finland	3.1%

Even in Sweden, the most secular of these countries, atheists, strictly defined, make up only about one sixth of the population. Indeed, according to the same source, the country with the highest proportion of atheists in Europe is France, with 17.1 percent.

As I mentioned previously, one must take these polls with a grain of salt. For one thing, the numbers change over time. In addition, even if someone does not claim to be an atheist, this does not automatically mean that he or she believes in God. The person may be an agnostic or a believer in some sort of impersonal cosmic life force, or something similar.[10]

Still, whatever the truth of the matter, it must be admitted that Scandinavia is highly secular. (So is the rest of western civilization). However, it must also be pointed out that before the coming of Christianity, Scandinavia

---

8. Stark, *America's Blessings*, 4–5.
9. Stark, *Triumph of Faith*, 31–33.
10. As is shown by Zuckerman in "Atheism," 47–65.

was in many ways pretty awful.[11] Further, for the most part, Scandinavia still follows Christian ethics, even though many have dropped Christian theological beliefs.[12]

The following data should also be noted. According to Rodney Stark,

> Denmark has nearly two-and-a-half times as many burglaries per 100,000 population as does the United States . . . Comparing theft rates, the table shows that Sweden has a rate twice as high as that of the United States and that Denmark, the United Kingdom, Norway, Germany, and Finland also have higher theft rates. As for "violent America," the assault rate in Sweden is about three-and-a-half times that of the United States.[13]

Granted, the US *homicide* rate is much higher. Still, the point is that Scandinavia is not paradise, and it is doubtful that the good things about it are the result of secularism.[14] As Nima Sanandaji argues, the good things that Scandinavia has were present there before the coming of secularism.[15] Most of the seeds were planted long ago by Christianity.[16]

Further, it should be pointed out that secularization does not ensure lack of superstition. For example, "[M]ore than 20 percent of Swedes say they believe in reincarnation; half believe in mental telepathy; and nearly one in five believes in the power of lucky charms. A third believe in New Age medicine such as 'healing Crystals'; 20 percent would consider purchasing their personal horoscope; 10 percent would consult a medium; and nearly

---

11. For a quick look at this, see Marshall, *How Jesus Passes*, 93–95.

12. Marshall, *How Jesus Passes*, 95–97, for several quotations to this effect. Writes Marshall, "Modern secularized society still faces grave challenges: high debt burdens, loss of hope for the future, demographic implosion, the growth of radical Islam. Zuckerman also admits that religious faith encourages parents to have more children, which helps solve such problems." Marshall, *How Jesus Passes*, 97.

13. Stark, *America's Blessings*, 39. See also Johnson, *More God*.

14. For an interesting take on Scandinavia, see Booth, *Almost Nearly Perfect People*. Booth is quite positive about Scandinavia overall, but he does point out that there are problems.

15. The Scandinavian countries, though often called socialist, are capitalist economies combined with large welfare states.

16. Relevant to this is the study done by Robert D. Woodberry which shows that the strongest factor in the spread of democracy around the world has been the number of Protestant missionaries in a country, as well as having performed several other services. See Stark, *How the West Won*, 367–68, and Sanandaji, *Debunking Utopia*. Although Sanandaji's book is primarily about economics and welfare, he argues out that the good things in society that people attribute to Scandinavian socialism and secularism in fact predate them.

two out of five believe in ghosts."[17] Also, "55 percent of Icelanders believe in the existence of *huldufolk*, or hidden people, such as elves, trolls, gnomes, and fairies."[18] All of these factors do not sound much like Scandinavia is a beacon of rationality. I really don't want to heap ontoward criticisms on Scandinavia, which does have much going for it. But the region is not Utopia or a paradise of pure rationality.

To reiterate, I am not an expert by any means on these subjects, and doubtless much more can and should be said about them. However, a strong case can be made that secularism does not ensure either rationality or social health better than Christianity can. Indeed, it can be argued that what social health secular societies have is left over from the previous Christian society.[19]

17. Stark, *Triumph of Faith*, 48.

18. Stark, *Triumph of Faith*, 6. Actually, I think that it would be rather cool if elves, trolls, etc. existed. Sadly, however, I don't think they do.

19. Goldman, *How Civilizations Die*, 115–36. For books on the positive influence of Christianity see, the ones listed in chapter 5, note 48.

Bibliography

Adamson, Peter. *Classical Philosophy: A History of Philosophy Without Any Gaps*, vol. 1. New York: Oxford University Press, 2014.
———. *Philosophy in the Hellenistic and Roman Worlds: A History of Philosophy Without Any Gaps*, vol. 2. New York: Oxford University Press, 2015.
———. *Philosophy in the Islamic World: A History of Philosophy Without Any Gaps*, vol. 3. New York: Oxford University Press, 2016.
Aikman, David Barr. *The Role of Atheism in the Marxist Tradition*. Ann Arbor: University of Michigan Press, 1980.
Alexander, David E., and Daniel M. Johnson, eds. *Calvinism and the Problem of Evil*. Eugene: Pickwick, 2016.
Almeida, Michael J. *Freedom, God, and Worlds*. Oxford: Oxford University Press, 2012.
———. *The Metaphysics of Perfect Beings*. New York: Routledge, 2014.
Alston, William P. *The Reliability of Sense Perception*. Ithaca: Cornell University Press, 1993.
Andersen, David. *Martin Luther—The Problem of Faith and Reason*. Bonn: Verlag fur Kultur and Wissenschaft, 2009.
Anselm, Saint. *Basic Writings*. Translated by S. N. Deane. LaSalle: Open Court, 1968.
Applebaum, Anne. *Gulag: A History*. New York: Anchor, 2004.
———. *Red Famine: Stalin's War on Ukraine*. New York: Doubleday, 2017.
Armstrong, David M. *A Materialist Theory of the Mind*. Rev. ed. New York: Routledge, 1993.
———. *What is a Law of Nature?* Cambridge: Cambridge University Press, 1983.
Aron, Raymond. *The Opium of the Intellectuals*. Translated by Terence Kilmartin. New York: Norton, 1962.
Audi, Robert. *Epistemology: A Contemporary Introduction to the Theory of Knowledge*. 2nd ed. New York: Routledge, 2004.
———. *The Good in the Right: A Theory of Intuition and Intrinsic Value*. Princeton: Princeton University Press, 2004.
———. *Moral Perception*. Princeton: Princeton University Press, 2013.
Augustine. *Saint Augustine's Contra Academicos: Answer to Skeptics*. Translated by Denis J. Kavanagh. New York: Cosmopolitan Science & Art, 1943.
Baggett, David, and Jerry L. Walls. *God and Cosmos: Moral Truth and Human Meaning*. New York: Oxford University Press, 2016.
———. *Good God: The Theistic Foundations of Morality*. Oxford: Oxford University Press, 2011.

Baggini, Julian. *Atheism: A Very Short Introduction*. New York: Oxford University Press, 2003.
Baker, Hunter. *The End of Secularism*. Wheaton: Crossway, 2009.
Baker, Lynne Rudder. *Naturalism and the First-Person Perspective*. New York: Oxford University Press, 2013.
———. *Persons and Bodies: A Constitution View*. New York: Cambridge University Press, 2000.
Baker, Mark C., and Stewart Goetz, eds. *The Soul Hypothesis: Investigations into the Existence of the Soul*. New York: Continuum, 2011.
Balfour, Arthur James. *Theism and Humanism: The Book that Influenced C.S. Lewis*. Seattle: Inkling, 2000.
Barfield, Kenny. *Why the Bible is Number 1: The World's Sacred Writings in the Light of Science*. Grand Rapids: Baker, 1988.
Barnett, Paul. *Jesus & the Rise of Early Christianity: A History of New Testament Times*. Downers Grove: InterVarsity, 1999.
Barnett, S. J. *The Enlightenment and Religion: The Myths of Modernity*. New York: Manchester University Press, 2003.
Barr, Stephen M. *The Believing Scientist: Essays on Science and Religion*. Grand Rapids: Eerdmans, 2016.
———. *Modern Physics and Ancient Faith*. Notre Dame: University of Notre Dame Press, 2003.
Barrett, David B., and Todd M. Johnson, eds. *World Christian Trends AD 30–AD 2200*. Pasadena: William Carey, 2001.
Barrett, Justin L. *Why Would Anyone Believe in God?* Lanham: AltaMira, 2004.
Bartlett, Jonathan, and Eric Holloway, eds. *Naturalism and Its Alternatives in Scientific Methodologies*. Broken Arrow: Blyth Institute Press, 2017.
Basinger, David, and Randall Basinger, eds. *Predestination & Free Will: Four Views of Divine Sovereignty & Human Freedom*. Downers Grove: InterVarsity, 1986.
Becker, Carl. *The Heavenly City of the Eighteenth Century Philosophers*. New Haven: Yale University Press, 1960.
Beckwith, Francis J., Carl Mosser and Paul Owen, eds. *The New Mormon Challenge: Responding to the Latest Defenses of a Fast-Growing Movement*. Grand Rapids: Zondervan, 2002.
Beckwith, Francis J., and Stephen E. Parrish. *The Mormon Concept of God: A Philosophical Analysis*. Lewiston: Mellen, 1991.
———. *See the gods Fall: Four Rivals to Christianity*. Joplin: College, 1997.
Becker, Jasper. *Hungry Ghosts: Mao's Secret Famine*. New York: The Free Press, 1996.
Beilby, James, ed. *Naturalism Defeated?* Ithaca: Cornell University Press, 2002.
Bellinger, Charles K. *Jesus v. Abortion: They Know Not What They Do*. Eugene: Cascade, 2016.
Berman, Harold J. *Law and Revolution: The Formation of the Western Legal Tradition*. Cambridge: Harvard University Press, 1983.
———. *Law and Revolution II: The Impact of the Protestant Reformations on the Western Legal Tradition*. Cambridge: Belknap of Harvard University Press, 2003.
Berman, Joshua A. *Created Equal: How the Bible Broke with Ancient Political Thought*. New York: Oxford University Press, 2008.
Billington, James H. *Fire in the Minds of Men: Origins of the Revolutionary Faith*. New York: Basic, 1980.

Blackburn, Simon. *Essays in Quasi-Realism*. New York: Oxford University Press, 1993.
Blanshard, Brand. *Reason and Analysis*. LaSalle: Open Court, 1964.
Bloomfield, Paul. *Moral Reality*. New York: Oxford University Press, 2001.
Boghossian, Paul. *Fear of Knowledge: Against Relativism and Constructivism*. New York: Oxford University Press, 2006.
BonJour, Laurence. *In Defense of Pure Reason*. Cambridge: Cambridge University Press, 1997.
Booth, Michael. *The Almost Nearly Perfect People: The Truth About the Nordic Miracle*. London: Random House, 2014.
Bormann, Martin. "Circular on the Relationship of National Socialism and Christianity." In *The Nazi Persecution of the Churches 1933–45*, by John S. Conway, 384. Toronto: Ryerson, 1968.
Bradley, F. H. *Appearance and Reality: A Metaphysical Essay*. 2nd ed. Oxford: Oxford University Press, 1978.
Brady, Michael, ed. *New Waves in Metaethics*. New York: Palgrave Macmillan, 2011.
Brandon, Nathaniel, and Barbara Brandon. *Who is Ayn Rand?* New York: Paperback, 1967.
Brandt, Richard B. *A Theory of the Good and the Right*. Amherst: Prometheus, 1998.
Brent, Joseph. *Charles Sanders Peirce: A Life*. Revised and enlarged ed. Bloomington: Indiana University Press, 1993.
Brown, Nancy Marie. *The Abacus and the Cross: The Story of the Pope Who Brought the Light of Science to the Dark Ages*. New York: Basic, 2010.
Brown, Peter. *Augustine of Hippo: A Biography*. Berkeley: University of California Press, 2000.
Bruce, F. F. *The Book of Acts*. Grand Rapids: Eerdmans, 1977.
Buckley, Michael J. *At the Origins of Modern Atheism*. New Haven: Yale University Press, 1987.
Bullock, Alan. *Hitler and Stalin: Parallel Lives*. New York: Vintage, 1993.
Burke, Edmund. *A Philosophical Enquiry into the Origin of our Ideas of the Beautiful and Sublime*. New York: Oxford University Press, 1992.
Burkitt, F. Crawford. "The Religion of the Manichees." *The Journal of Religion* 2:3 (May 1922) 263–76.
Burleigh, Michael. *Earthly Powers: The Clash of Religion and Politics in Europe from the French Revolution to the Great War*. New York: Harper Collins, 2006.
———. *Sacred Causes: The Clash of Religion and Politics, From the Great War to the War on Terror*. New York: Harper Collins, 2007.
———. *The Third Reich: A New History*. New York: Hill and Wang, 2000.
Bussey, Peter. *Signposts to God: How Modern Physics and Astronomy Point the Way to Belief*. Downers Grove: InterVarsity, 2016.
Butchvarov, Panayot. *Skepticism about the External World*. New York: Oxford University Press, 1998.
Cabal, Ted, ed. *The Apologetics Study Bible*. Nashville: Holman Bible, 2007.
———. "Naturalism vs Theism: Which Context Best Explains the Phenomena We Observe?" In *The Apologetics Study Bible*, edited by Ted Cabal, Appendix. Nashville: Holman Bible, 2007.
Cassirer, Ernst. *The Philosophy of the Enlightenment*. Translated by Fritz C. A. Koellin and James P. Pettegrove. Princeton: Princeton University Press, 1979.

Cavanaugh, William T. *The Myth of Religious Violence: Secular Ideology and the Roots of Modern Conflict.* New York: Oxford University Press, 2009.

Chalmers, David. *The Conscious Mind: In Search of a Fundamental Theory.* New York: Oxford University Press, 1996.

Chamberlain, Lesley. *Nietzsche in Turin: An Intimate Biography.* New York: Picador, 1996.

Chambers, Whittaker. *Witness.* New York: Random House, 1952.

Chapman, Allan. *Gods in the Sky: Astronomy, Religion and Culture from the Ancients to the Renaissance.* London: Channel 4, 2001.

———. *Slaying the Dragons: Destroying Myths in the History of Science and Faith.* Oxford: Lion Hudson, 2013.

Churchland, Patricia Smith. *Neurophilosophy: Toward a Unified Science of the Mind-Brain.* Cambridge: Bradford, 1996.

Churchland, Paul M. *Matter and Consciousness.* 3rd ed. Cambridge: Bradford, 2013.

Clark, Gordon H. *Ancient Philosophy.* Jefferson, MD: The Trinity Foundation, 1997.

———. *A Christian View of Men and Things: An Introduction to Philosophy.* Grand Rapids: Baker, 1981.

———. *Selections from Hellenistic Philosophy.* New York: Irvington, 1975.

———. *Thales to Dewey: A History of Philosophy.* Grand Rapids: Baker, 1980.

———. *The Trinity.* Jefferson, MD: The Trinity Foundation, 1985.

Clark, Kelly James, ed. *The Blackwell Companion to Naturalism.* Malden: Wiley Blackwell, 2016.

Clouser, Roy A. *The Myth of Religious Neutrality: An Essay on the Hidden Role of Religious Belief in Theories.* Rev. ed. Notre Dame: University of Notre Dame Press, 2005.

Cohn, Norman. *The Pursuit of the Millennium: Revolutionary Millenarians and Mystical Anarchists of the Middle Ages.* Rev. ed. New York: Oxford University Press, 1970.

Colimore, Edward. "Papers Reveal Nazi Aim: End Christianity." In *The Philadelphia Inquirer*, 9 Jan. 2002. In *The Irrational Atheist*, by Vox Day, 212. Dallas: Ben Bella, 2008.

Collins, C. John. *Did Adam and Eve Really Exist?: Who They Were and Why You Should Care.* Wheaton: Crossway, 2011.

Collins, Paul. *The Birth of the West: Rome, Germany, France, and the Creation of Europe in the Tenth Century.* New York: Public Affairs, 2013.

Collins, Robin. "The Energy of the Soul." In *The Soul Hypothesis: Investigations into the Existence of the Soul,* edited by Mark C. Baker and Stewart Goetz, 123–33. New York: Continuum, 2011.

Conway, J. S. *The Nazi Persecution of the Churches 1933–45.* Toronto: Ryerson, 1968.

Cooper, John. "'Absent from the Body . . . Present with the Lord': Is the Intermediate State Fatal to Physicalism?" In *Christian Physicalism?*, edited by R. Keith Loftin, et al., 319–39. Lanham: Lexington, 2018.

———. *Body, Soul, & Life Everlasting: Biblical Anthropology and the Monism-Dualism Debate.* Grand Rapids: Eerdmans, 1989.

———. *Panentheism—The Other God of the Philosophers.* Grand Rapids: Baker Academic, 2013.

———. "Whose Interpretation? Which Anthropology?" In *Neuroscience and the Soul: The Human Person in Philosophy, Science, and Theology,* edited by Thomas M. Crisp, 258–68. Grand Rapids: Eerdmans, 2016.

Copan, Paul and William Lane Craig. *Creation Out of Nothing: A Biblical, Philosophical, and Scientific Exploration*. Grand Rapids: Baker Academic, 2004.
Copan, Paul, and Ronald K. Tacelli. *Jesus' Resurrection: Fact or Figment? A Debate between William Lane Craig and Gerd Lüdemann*. Downers Grove: InterVarsity, 2000.
Copan, Paul, ed. *Will the Real Jesus Please Stand Up? A Debate Between William Lane Craig and John Dominic Crossan*. Grand Rapids: Baker, 1998.
Copleston, Frederick. *A History of Philosophy: vol. 1, Greece and Rome, part I*. Garden City: Image, 1962.
———. *A History of Philosophy: vol. 1, Greece and Rome, part II*. Garden City: Image Books, 1962.
———. *A History of Philosophy: vol. 7, Modern Philosophy, part I, Fichte to Hegel*. Garden City: Image, 1965.
———. *A History of Philosophy: vol. 7, Modern Philosophy, part II, Schopenhauer to Nietzsche*. Garden City: Image, 1965.
———. *A History of Philosophy: vol. 8, Modern Philosophy, part II, Bentham to Russell*. Garden City: Image, 1967.
Corduan, Winfried. *In the Beginning God: A Fresh Look at the Case for Original Monotheism*. Nashville: B&H Academic, 2013.
Couper, Heather, and Nigel Henbest. *The History of Astronomy*. Buffalo: Firefly, 2007.
Courtois, Stephane, et al. *The Black Book of Communism: Crimes, Terror, Repression*. Translated by Jonathan Murphy and Mark Kramer. Cambridge: Harvard University Press, 1999.
Craig, William Lane, and J. P. Moreland, eds. *The Blackwell Companion to Natural Theology*. Malden: Blackwell, 2009.
———. *Naturalism: A Critical Analysis*. New York: Routledge, 2000.
Craig, William Lane. *The Cosmological Argument from Plato to Leibniz*. New York: Barnes and Noble, 1980.
———. *God Over All: Divine Aseity and the Challenge of Platonism*. New York: Oxford University Press, 2016.
———. *The Kalam Cosmological Argument*. New York: Barnes and Noble, 1979.
———. *The Only Wise God: The Compatibility of Divine Foreknowledge and Human Freedom*. Grand Rapids: Baker, 1987.
Craig, William Lane, and Walter Sinnott-Armstrong. *GOD?: A Debate Between a Christian and an Atheist*. New York: Oxford University Press, 2004.
Craig, William Lane, and James D. Sinclair. "The Kalam Cosmological Argument." In *The Blackwell Companion to Natural Theology*, edited by William Lane Craig, et al., 101–201. Malden: Blackwell, 2009.
Craig, William Lane, and Quentin Smith. *Theism, Atheism, and Big Bang Cosmology*. Oxford: Oxford University Press, 1993.
Crisp, Thomas M., et al., eds. *Neuroscience and the Soul: The Human Person in Philosophy, Science, and Theology*. Grand Rapids: Eerdmans, 2016.
Cuneo, Terence. *The Normative Web: An Argument for Moral Realism*. New York: Oxford University Press, 2007.
———. *Speech and Morality: On the Metaethical Implications of Speaking*. New York: Oxford University Press, 2014.
Daily Dose of Knowledge: Brilliant Thoughts. Lincolnwood: Westside, 2008.

Darwish, Nonie. *Wholly Different: Why I Chose Biblical Values Over Islamic Values.* Washington, DC: Regnery Faith, 2017.
Davies, Paul. *Cosmic Jackpot: Why Our Universe Is Just Right for Life.* Boston: Houghton Mifflin, 2007.
———. *God and the New Physics.* New York: Touchstone, 1983.
Davis, Ted. "Did Newton's God Vanish with the "Gaps" in His Science?" www.biologos.org.
de Lubac, Henri. *The Drama of Atheist Humanism.* San Francisco: Ignatius, 1995.
Day, Vox. *The Irrational Atheist: Dissecting the Unholy Trinity of Dawkins, Harris, and Hitchens.* Dallas: Benbella, 2008.
Dembski, William, and Jonathan Wells. *The Design of life: Discovering Signs of Intelligence in Biological Systems.* Dallas: Foundation for Thought and Ethics, 2008.
Dennett, Daniel. *Consciousness Explained.* New York: Little, Brown, 1991.
———. *Sweet Dreams: Philosophical Obstacles to a Science of Consciousness.* Cambridge: A Bradford, 2005.
Dictionary. http://www.dictionary.com/browse/.
Dikötter, Frank. *Mao's Great Famine: The History of China's Most Devastating Catastrophe, 1958–1962.* New York: Walker, 2010.
Dolezal, James E. *God without Parts: Divine Simplicity and the Metaphysics of God's Absoluteness.* Eugene: Pickwick, 2011.
Dombrowski, Daniel A. *Analytic Theism, Hartshorne, and the Concept of God.* Albany: State University of New York Press, 1996.
Dooyeweerd, Herman. *In the Twilight of Western Thought: Studies in the Pretended Autonomy of Philosophical Thought.* Nutley: Craig, 1972.
———. *A New Critique of Theoretical Thought*, 4 vols. Translated by David H. Freeman and William S. Young. Phillipsburg: Presbyterian and Reformed, 1969.
Dore, Clement. *Theism.* Boston: Reidel, 1984.
Dostoevsky, Fyodor. *The Brothers Karamazov.* Translated by Constance Garnett. New York: Barnes and Noble Classics, 2004.
Drier, James, ed. *Contemporary Debates in Moral Theory.* Malden: Blackwell, 2006.
Dulles, Avery Robert. *A History of Apologetics.* 2nd ed. San Francisco: Ignatius, 2005.
D'Souza, Dinesh. *Life After Death: The Evidence.* Washington, DC: Regnery, 2009.
Edmonson, Henry T., III. *John Dewey and the Decline of American Education: How the Patron Saint of Schools has Corrupted Teaching and Learning.* Wilmington: ISI, 2006.
Ehlke, Roland Cap. *Like a Pelting Rain: The Making of the Modern Mind.* Abridged version. Milwaukee: Ehlkeworks, 2013.
Eire, Carlos M. N. *War Against the Idols: The Reformation of Worship from Erasmus to Calvin.* New York: Cambridge University Press, 1989.
Engels, Frederick (Friedrich). *Socialism: Utopian and Scientific.* New York: International, 1935.
Enoch, David. *Taking Morality Seriously: A Defense of Robust Realism.* Oxford: Oxford University Press, 2011.
Epstein, Joseph, and Gail Kennedy. *The Process of Philosophy: A Historical Introduction.* New York: Random House, 1967.
Evans, C. Stephen. *God & Moral Obligation.* Oxford: Oxford University Press, 2013.
Evans, M. Stanton. *The Theme is Freedom: Religion, Politics, and the American Tradition.* Washington, DC: Regnery, 1994.

Evans, Richard J. *The Third Reich in Power.* New York: Penguin, 2005.
Everitt, Nicholas. *The Non-Existence of God.* New York: Routledge, 2004.
Feinberg, John S. *The Many Faces of Evil: Theological Systems and the Problem of Evil.* Grand Rapids: Zondervan, 1994.
Feser, Edward. *Five Proofs of the Existence of God.* San Francisco: Ignatius, 2017.
———. *The Last Superstition: A Refutation of the New Atheism.* South Bend: St. Augustine's, 2010.
———. *Scholastic Metaphysics: A Contemporary Introduction.* Postfach: Editions Scholasticae, 2014.
Finegan, Jack. *Myth and Mystery: An Introduction to the Pagan Religions of the Biblical World.* Grand Rapids: Baker, 1989.
Fisher, Andrew. *Metaethics: An Introduction.* New York: Routledge, 2014.
Fisher, John Martin, et al. *Four Views on Free Will.* Malden: Blackwell, 2007.
Foot, Philippa. *Natural Goodness.* New York: Clarendon, 2001.
Foster, John. *The Divine Lawmaker: Lectures on Induction, Laws of Nature, and the Existence of God.* Oxford: Oxford University Press, 2004.
———. *The Immaterial Self: A Defence of the Cartesian Dualist Conception of the Mind.* New York: Routledge, 1991.
———. "Subjects of Mentality." In *After Physicalism,* edited by Benedikt Paul Goeke, 72–103. Notre Dame: The University of Notre Dame Press, 2012.
Foxe, John. *The New Foxe's Book of Martyrs.* Rewritten and updated by Harold J. Chadwick. New Brunswick: Bridge-Logos, 1997.
Frame, John. *Apologetics: A Justification of Christian Belief.* Phillipsburg: P&R, 2015.
Frankl, Viktor E. *Man's Search for Meaning.* Boston: Beacon, 2006.
Franz, Michael G. *Eric Voegelin and the Politics of Spiritual Revolt: The Roots of Modern Ideology.* Baton Rouge: Louisiana State University Press, 1992.
———. *Ideology and Pneumapathological Consciousness: Eric Voegelin's Analysis of the Spiritual Roots of Political Disorder.* Ann Arbor: University of Michigan Press, 1989.
Freeman, Anthony, ed. *Consciousness and Its Place in Nature: Does Physicalism Entail Panpsychism?* Charlottesville: Imprint Academic, 2006.
Fregosi, Paul. *Jihad in the West: Muslim Conquests from the 7th to the 21st Centuries.* Amherst: Prometheus, 1998.
Froese, Paul. *The Plot to Kill God: Findings from the Soviet Experiment in Secularization.* Berkeley: University of California Press, 2008.
Fumerton, Richard. *Knowledge, Thought, and the Case for Dualism.* Cambridge: Cambridge University Press, 2015.
Gairdner, William D. *The Book of Absolutes: A Critique of Relativism and a Defence of Universals.* Montreal: McGill-Queen's University Press, 2008.
———. *The Great Divide: Why Liberals and Conservatives Will Never, Ever Agree.* New York: Encounter, 2015.
Gange, Robert. *Origins and Destiny.* Waco: Word, 1986.
Ganssle, Gregory E. *A Reasonable God: Engaging the New Face of Atheism.* Waco: Baylor University Press, 2009.
Gasman, Daniel. *The Scientific Origins of National Socialism.* New Brunswick: Transaction, 2004.
Gay, Peter. *The Enlightenment: The Rise of Modern Paganism.* New York: Norton, 1966.
———. *The Enlightenment: The Science of Freedom.* New York: Norton, 1969.

Geisler, Norman, and Winfried Corduan. *Philosophy of Religion*. 2nd ed. Grand Rapids: Baker, 1988.
Geisler, Norman, and William Watkins. *Perspectives: Understanding and evaluating today's Worldviews*. San Bernardino: Here's Life, 1984.
Geivett, R. Douglas, and Gary R. Habermas. *In Defense of Miracles: A Comprehensive Case for God's Action in History*. Downers Grove: InterVarsity, 1997.
Gelernter, David. *The Tides of Mind: Uncovering the Spectrum of Consciousness*. New York: Liveright, 2016.
Gellately, Robert. *Lenin, Stalin, and Hitler: The Age of Social Catastrophe*. New York: Knopf, 2007.
Gerrish, B. A. *Grace and Reason: A Study in the Theology of Luther*. Oxford: Oxford University Press, 1962.
Gibbard, Allan. *Thinking How to Live*. Cambridge: Harvard University Press, 2003.
Gilbert, Martin. *The Holocaust: A History of the Jews of Europe During the Second World War*. New York: Holt, Rinehart, and Winston, 1985.
Gilson, Tom, and Carson Weitnauer. *True Reason: Confronting the Irrationality of the New Atheism*. Grand Rapids: Kregel, 2013.
Glover, Willis B. *Biblical Origins of Modern Secular Culture: An Essay in the Interpretation of Western History*. Macon: Mercer University Press, 1984.
Göcke, Benedikt Paul, ed. *After Physicalism*. Notre Dame: The University of Notre Dame Press, 2012.
Goebbels, Josef. *The Goebbel's Diaries, 1939–1941*. Translated and edited by Fred Taylor. New York: Penguin, 1984.
Goff, Philip. "Experiences Don't Sum." In *Consciousness and Its Place in Nature: Does Physicalism Entail Panpsychism?*, edited by Anthony Freeman, 53–61. Charlottesville: Imprint Academic, 2006.
Goldberg, Jonah. *Liberal Fascism: The Secret History of the American Left from Mussolini to the Politics of Meaning*. New York: Doubleday, 2007.
———. *Suicide of the West: How the Rebirth of Tribalism, Populism, Nationalism, and Identity Politics is Destroying American Democracy*. New York: Crown Forum, 2018.
Goldman, David. *How Civilizations Die: (And Why Islam is Dying Too)*. Washington, DC: Regnery, 2011.
Goldschmidt, Tyron, ed. *The Puzzle of Existence: Why Is There Something Rather Than Nothing?* New York: Routledge, 2013.
Goldsworthy, Adrian. *How Rome Fell: Death of a Superpower*. New Haven: Yale University Press, 2009.
Goodrick-Clarke, Nicholas. *The Occult Roots of Nazism: Secret Aryan Cults and Their Influence on Nazi Ideology*. New York: New York University Press, 1992.
Gordon, Bruce L., and William A. Dembski, eds. *The Nature of Nature: Examining the Role of Naturalism in Science*. Wilmington: Intercollegiate Studies Institute, 2011.
Gould, Paul M., ed. *Beyond the Control of God? Six Views on the Problem of God and Abstract Objects*. New York: Bloomsbury Academic, 2014.
Grant, Edward. *The Foundations of Modern Science in the Middle Ages: Their Religious, Institutional, and Intellectual Contexts*. New York: Cambridge University Press, 1996.
———. *God and Reason in the Middle Ages*. New York: Cambridge University Press, 2001.

Gray, John. *Seven Types of Atheism*. New York: Farrar, Straus and Giroux, 2018.
Gruenler, Royce Gordon. *The Inexhaustible God: Biblical Faith and the Challenge of Process Theism*. Grand Rapids: Baker, 1983.
Grünbaum, Adolf. "No Explanation Needed." In *The Mystery of Existence*, edited by John Leslie, et al., 56–70. Malden: Wiley-Blackwell, 2013.
Habermas, Gary R., and Michael R. Licona. *The Case for the Resurrection of Jesus*. Grand Rapids: Kregel, 2004.
Habermas, Gary R., and Antony Flew. *Did Jesus Rise from the Dead? The Resurrection Debate*. San Francisco: Harper & Row, 1987.
Hadot, Pierre. *Plotinus: or The Simplicity of Vision*. Chicago: University of Chicago Press, 1998.
Hague, William. *William Wilberforce: The Life of the Great Anti-Slave Trade Campaigner*. New York: Harcourt, 2007.
Hale, Bob. *Necessary Beings: An Essay on Ontology, Modality, & the Relations Between Them*. New York: Oxford University Press, 2013.
Hannam, James. *God's Philosophers: How the Medieval World Laid the Foundations of Modern Science*. London: Icon, 2009.
Harrison, Victoria S. *Eastern Philosophy: The Basics*. New York: Routledge, 2013.
Hart, David Bentley. *Atheist Delusions: The Christian Revolution and Its Fashionable Enemies*. New Haven: Yale University Press, 2009.
———. *The Beauty of the Infinite: The Aesthetics of Christian Truth*. Grand Rapids: Eerdmans, 2003.
Hartshorne, Charles. *Creative Synthesis & Philosophic Method*. La Salle: The Open Court, 1970.
———. *The Logic of Perfection*. LaSalle: The Open Court, 1991.
———. *Omnipotence: and Other Theological Mistakes*. Albany: State University of New York, 1984.
Hasker, William. "Do My Quarks Enjoy Beethoven?" In *Neuroscience and the Soul: The Human Person in Philosophy, Science, and Theology*, edited by Thomas M. Crisp, et al., 13–40. Grand Rapids: Eerdmans, 2016.
———. *The Emergent Self*. Ithaca: Cornell University Press, 1999.
Hayek, F. A. *The Fatal Conceit: The Errors of Socialism*. Chicago: The University of Chicago Press, 1988.
Heidegger, Martin. *Introduction to Metaphysics*. 2nd ed. Revised and expanded translation by Gregory Fried and Richard Polt. New Haven: Yale University Press, 2014.
Heller, Mikhail. *Cogs in the Wheel: The Formation of Soviet Man*. New York: Alfred A Knopf, 1988.
Heller, Mikhail, and Aleksandr M. Neckrich. *Utopia in Power: The History of the Soviet Union from 1917 to the Present*. New York: Summit Books, 1986.
Henry, Carl F. H. *God, Revelation and Authority vol. III: God Who Speaks and Shows*. Waco: Word, 1979.
Hesiod. *The Complete Hesiod Collection*. Translated by Hugh G. Evelyn-White. Middletown: First Rate, 2016.
Hick, John. *Evil and the God of Love*. Rev. ed. New York: Harper and Row, 1977.
———. *The Existence of God*. New York: Macmillan, 1964.
Hill, Christopher S. *Sensations: A Defense of Type Materialism*. New York: Cambridge University Press, 1991.

Hill, Daniel J. *Divinity and Maximal Greatness*. New York: Routledge, 2005.
Hinlicky, Paul R. *Divine Simplicity: Christ the Crisis of Metaphysics*. Grand Rapids: Baker Academic, 2016.
Hitchcock, James. *What Is Secular Humanism? How Humanism Became Secular and How It Is Changing Our World*. Ann Arbor: Servant, 1982.
Hitchens, Peter. *The Rage Against God: How Atheism Led Me to Faith*. Grand Rapids: Zondervan, 2010.
Hitler, Adolf. "Monologue on July 11–12, 1941." In *Monologe im Führerhauptquartier 1941–1944: Die Aufzeichnungen Heinrich Heims*, 285–86. In *Hitler's Religion: The Twisted Beliefs that Drove the Third Reich*, by Richard Weikart, 364. Washington, DC: Regnery History, 2016.
Hochschild, Adam. *Bury the Chains: Prophets and Rebels in the Fight to Free an Empire's Slaves*. Boston: Houghton Mifflin, 2005.
Holder, Rodney. *Big Bang, Big God: A Universe Designed for Life?* Oxford: Lion Hudson, 2013.
Holmes, Stephen R. *The Quest for The Trinity: The Doctrine of God in Scripture, History and Modernity*. Downers Grove: InterVarsity Academic, 2012.
Holt, Jim. *Why Does the World Exist? An Existential Detective Story*. New York: Liveright, 2012.
Horowitz, David. *Unholy Alliance: Radical Islam and the American Left*. Washington, DC: Regnery, 2004.
Howard-Snyder, Daniel. *The Evidential Argument from Evil*. Indianapolis: Indiana University Press, 1996.
Huemer, Michael. *Ethical Intuitionism*. New York: Palgrave Macmillan, 2005.
———. *Skepticism and the Veil of Perception*. Lanham: Rowman and Littlefield, 2001.
Huff, Toby. *Intellectual Curiosity and the Scientific Revolution: A Global Perspective*. New York: Cambridge University Press, 2011.
Hughes, Christopher. *On a Complex Theory of a Simple God: An Investigation in Aquinas' Philosophical Theology*. Ithaca: Cornell University Press, 1989.
Humanist Manifestos I and II, The. Buffalo: Prometheus, 1973.
Hume, David. *Dialogues Concerning Natural Religion*. Edited with an introduction by Martin Bell. New York: Penguin, 1990.
Husserl, Edmund. *The Crisis of European Sciences and Transcendental Phenomenology: An Introduction to Phenomenological Philosophy*. Evanston: Northwestern University Press, 1970.
Isaac, Erich and Jean Rael. *The Coercive Utopians: Social Deception by America's Power Players*. Chicago: Regnery Gateway, 1983.
Jaeger, Lydia. *Einstein, Polanyi, and the Laws of Nature*. West Conshohocken: Templeton, 2010.
———. *What the Heavens Declare: Science in the Light of Creation*. Eugene: Wipf and Stock, 2012.
Jaki, Stanley L. *God and the Cosmologists*. Washington, DC: Regnery Gateway, 1989.
———. *The Origin of Science and the Science of Its Origin*. South Bend: Regnery Gateway, 1978.
———. *The Paradox of Olbers' Paradox: A Case History of Scientific Thought*. New York: Herder and Herder, 1969.
———. *The Purpose of It All*. Washington, DC: Regnery Gateway, 1990.

———. *The Road of Science and the Ways to God*. Chicago: The University of Chicago Press, 1978.
———. *The Savior of Science*. Washington, DC: Regnery Gateway, 1988.
———. *Science & Creation: From eternal cycles to an oscillating universe*. Lanham: University Press of America, 1990.
Jaquette, Dale. *The Philosophy of Schopenhauer*. Montreal: McGill-Queen's University Press, 2005.
Johnson, B. C. *The Atheist Debater's Handbook*. Buffalo: Prometheus, 1983.
Johnson, Byron R. *More God, Less Crime: Why Faith Matters and How It Could Matter More*. West Conshohocken: Templeton, 2011.
Jones, Peter. *The Gnostic Empire Strikes Back: An Old Heresy for a New Age*. Phillipsburg: P&R, 1992.
Joyce, Richard. *The Myth of Morality*. New York: Cambridge University Press, 2007.
Junge, Traudl. *Until the Final Hour: Hitler's Last Secretary*, edited by Melissa Muller. New York: Arcade, 2002.
Kamen, Henry. *The Spanish Inquisition: A Historical Revision*. London: Weidenfeld & Nicolson, 1997.
Kant, Immanuel. *Critique of Judgment*. Translated, with an introduction, by J. H. Bernard. New York: Hafner, 1951.
———. *Critique of Pure Reason*. Translated by Norman Kemp Smith. New York: St. Martin's, 1965.
———. *Foundations of the Metaphysics of Morals*. Translated and introduction by Lewis White Beck. Indianapolis: Bobbs-Merrill, 1959.
Keener, Craig. *Miracles: The Credibility of the New Testament Accounts*. 2 vols. Grand Rapids: Baker Academic, 2011.
Kelly, Edward F., et al., eds. *Beyond Physicalism: Toward Reconciliation of Science and Spirituality*. Lanham: Rowman and Littlefield, 2015.
Keown, Damien. *Buddhism: A Very Short Introduction*. Oxford: Oxford University Press, 2013.
Kim, Jaegwon. "Against Cartesian Dualism." In *The Blackwell Companion to Substance Dualism*, edited by Jonathan J. Loose, et al., 152–67. Hoboken: Wiley Blackwell, 2018.
Kinneging, Andreas. *The Geography of Good and Evil: Philosophical Investigations*. Wilmington: ISI, 2009.
Koontz, Dean. *The Husband*. New York: Bantam, 2006.
Koperski, Jeffrey. *The Physics of Theism: God, Physics, and the Philosophy of Science*. Malden: Wiley Blackwell, 2015.
Koran, The Meaning of the Glorious. Translated and explained by Mohammed Marmaduke Pickthall. New York: Mentor, 1963.
Korsgaard, Christine M. *The Sources of Normativity*. New York: Cambridge University Press, 1996.
Kuby, Gabriele. *The Global Sexual Revolution: Destruction of Freedom in the Name of Freedom*. Translated by James Patrick Kirchner. Kettering: LifeSite, 2015.
Kulp, Christopher B. *Knowing Moral Truth: A Theory of Metaethics and Moral Knowledge*. Lanham: Lexington, 2017.
Kurtz, Paul. *Humanist Manifesto 2000: A Call for A New Planetary Humanism*. Amherst: Prometheus, 2000.
———. *Humanist manifestos I and II*. Buffalo: Prometheus, 1984.

———. *In Defense of Secular Humanism*. Buffalo: Prometheus, 1983.

———. *The Transcendental Temptation: A Critique of Religion and the Paranormal*. Buffalo: Prometheus, 1991.

Kvanvig, Jonathan L. *The Possibility of an All-Knowing God*. New York: St. Martin's, 1986.

Lange, Marc. *Laws & Lawmakers: Science, Metaphysics, and the Laws of Nature*. New York: Oxford University Press, 2009.

Lasky, Melvin J. *Utopia & Revolution: On the Origins of a Metaphor*. New Brunswick: Transaction, 2004.

Lavazza, Andrea, and Howard Robinson, eds. *Contemporary Dualism: A Defense*. New York: Routledge, 2016.

Lawhead, William F. *The Voyage of Discovery: A Historical Introduction to Philosophy*. Belmont: Wadsworth, 2007.

LeDrew, Stephen. *The Evolution of Atheism: The Politics of a Modern Movement*. New York: Oxford University Press, 2016.

Lee, Francis Nigel. *Communist Eschatology: A Christian philosophical analysis of the post-capitalistic views of Marx, Engels, and Lenin*. Nutley: Craig, 1974.

Lennox, John C. *God and Stephen Hawking: Whose Design Is It Anyway?* Oxford: Lion Hudson, 2011.

Leslie, John. "The Ethical Requiredness of There Being Something." In *Why Does the World Exist?, An Existential Detective Story*, edited by Jim Holt, 197–215. New York: Liveright, 2012.

———. *Infinite Minds: A Philosophical Cosmology*. New York: Oxford University Press, 2001.

———. *Physical Cosmology and Philosophy*. New York: Macmillan, 1990.

———. *Universes*. New York: Routledge, 1989.

———. *Value and Existence*. Totowa: Rowman and Littlefield, 1979.

Leslie, John, and Robert Lawrence Kuhn, eds. *The Mystery of Existence: Why Is There Anything at All?* Malden: Wiley-Blackwell, 2013.

Levering, Matthew. *Proofs of God: Classical Arguments from Tertullian to Barth*. Grand Rapids: Baker Academic, 2016.

Levine, Joseph. "Naturalism and Dualism." In *The Blackwell Companion to Naturalism*, edited by Kelly James Clark, 209–19. Malden: Wiley Blackwell, 2016.

Levine, Michael P. *Pantheism: A Non-Theistic Concept of Deity*. New York: Routledge, 1994.

Lewis, C. S. *The Abolition of Man*. New York: Macmillan, 1955.

———. *Mere Christianity*: A Revised and Enlarged Edition, with a New Introduction, of the Three Books *The Case for Christianity*, *Christian Behaviour*, and *Beyond Personality*. New York: Macmillan, 1970.

———. *Miracles*. New York: Macmillan, 1978.

———. *The Problem of Pain*. New York: Macmillan, 1971.

Lewis, David. *On the Plurality of Worlds*. Malden: Blackwell, 2001.

Lewis, Geraint F. and Luke A. Barnes. *A Fortunate Universe: Life in a Finely Tuned Cosmos*. Cambridge: Cambridge University Press, 2016.

Licona, Michael R. *The Resurrection of Jesus: A New Historiographical Approach*. Downers Grove: InterVarsity, 2010.

Lindberg, Tod. *The Political Teachings of Jesus*. New York: HarperOne, 2007.

Lindbom, Tage. *The Tares and the Good Grain: or the Kingdom of Man at the Hour of Reckoning*. Translated by Alvin Moore, Jr. Macon: The Mercer University Press, 1983.

Little, Bruce. *God, Why This Evil?* Lanham: Hamilton, 2010.

Loftin, R. Keith, and Joshua R. Farris, eds. *Christian Physicalism? Philosophical Theological Criticisms*. Lanham: Lexington, 2018.

———. *God and Morality: Four Views*. Downers Grove: InterVarsity, 2012.

Loke, Andrew Ter Ern. *God and Ultimate Origins: A Novel Cosmological Argument*. Cham: Palgrave Macmillan, 2017.

Loose, Jonathan J, et al., eds. *The Blackwell Companion to Substance Dualism*. Hoboken: Wiley Blackwell, 2018.

Lucretius. *On Nature*. Translated, with an introduction by Russell M. Geer. New York: Bobbs-Merrill, 1965.

Lund, David H. *The Conscious Self: The Immaterial Center of Subjective States*. Amherst: Humanity, 2005.

———. *Perception, Mind, and Personal Identity: A Critique of Materialism*. Lanham: University Press of America, 1994.

Luther, Martin. "Weimarer Ausgabe, 40, 612. 31; on Isa. ix 1." In *Luther's Works, Volume 34, Career of the Reformer*, 137. In *Grace and Reason: A Study in the Theology of Luther*, by B. A. Gerrish, 17. Oxford: Oxford University Press, 1962.

Luxmoore, Jonathan. *The God of the Gulag, Volume 1: Martyrs in an Age of Revolution*. Leominster: Gracewing, 2016.

———. *The God of the Gulag, Volume 2: Martyrs in an Age of Secularism*. Leominster: Gracewing, 2016.

Mackie, J. L. *The Cement of the Universe: A Study of Causation*. Oxford: Clarendon, 1980.

———. *Ethics: Inventing Right and Wrong*. New York: Penguin, 1977.

———. *The Miracle of Theism: Arguments for and against the Existence of God*. Oxford; Oxford University Press, 1982.

Mahoney, Daniel J. *The Idol of Our Age: How the Religion of Humanity Subverts Christianity*. New York: Encounter Books, 2018.

Mangalwadi, Vishal. *The Book That Made Your World: How the Bible Created the Soul of Western Civilization*. Nashville: Nelson, 2011.

Maritain, Jacques. "System of Philosophic Harmonies." In *The Process of Philosophy: A Historical Introduction*, edited by Joseph Epstein, et al., 233–47. New York: Random House, 1967.

Marozzi, Justin. *Tamerlane: Sword of Islam, Conqueror of the World*. New Edition. Cambridge: Da Capo, 2006.

Marshall, David, and Timothy McGrew. "Faith and Reason in Historical Perspective." In *True Reason*, edited by Tom Gilson and Carson Weitenauer, 148–65. Grand Rapids: Kregel, 2013.

Marshall, David. *How Jesus Passes the Outsider Test: The Inside Story*. Seattle, WA: Kuai Mu, 2015.

Martin, Michael. *Atheism: A Philosophical Justification*. Philadelphia: Temple University Press, 1990.

———. *Atheism, Morality, and Meaning*. Amherst: Prometheus, 2002.

———, ed. *The Cambridge Companion to Atheism*. New York: Cambridge University Press, 2007.

Martin, Michael, and Ricki Monnier, eds. *The Impossibility of God*. Amherst: Prometheus, 2003.

———. *The Improbability of God*. Amherst: Prometheus, 2006.

Marx, Karl, with Friedrich Engels. *The Communist Manifesto*. New York: Pocket, 1964.

———. "Contributions to the Critique of Hegel's Philosophy of Law." In *Marx [and] Engels: On Religion*, 38–52, Rev. ed. Moscow: Progress, 1976.

———. "Forward to Thesis: Difference between the Democritean and Epicurean Philosophy of Nature." In *Marx [and] Engels: On Religion*. Rev. ed. Moscow: Progress, 1976.

Marx, Karl. *The German Ideology: Including: Theses on Feuerbach and the Introduction to the Critique of Political Economy*. Amherst: Prometheus, 1998.

McCall, Thomas H. *Which Trinity? Whose Monotheism? Philosophical and Systematic Theologians on the Metaphysics of Trinitarian Theology*. Grand Rapids: Eerdmans, 2010.

McGinn, Colin. *Inborn Knowledge: The Mystery Within*. Cambridge: The MIT Press, 2015.

———. *The Mysterious Flame: Conscious Minds in a Material World*. New York: Basic, 1999.

McGrew, Timothy, and Lydia McGrew. *Internalism and Epistemology: The Architecture of Reason*. New York: Routledge, 2007.

McKnight, Stephen A. *Sacralizing the Secular: The Renaissance Origins of Modernity*. Baton Rouge: Louisiana State University Press, 1989.

McPhee, Peter. *Liberty or Death: The French Revolution*. New Haven: Yale University Press, 2016.

Meixner, Uwe. "Against Physicalism." In *Contemporary Dualism: A Defense*, edited by Andrea Lavazza, et al., 17–34. New York: Routledge, 2014.

———. *The Two Sides of Being: A Reassessment of Psycho-Physical Dualism*. Paderborn: Mentis, 2004.

Melnyk, Andrew. *A Physicalist Manifesto: Thoroughly Modern Materialism*. Cambridge: Cambridge University Press, 2003.

Menuge, Angus. *Agents Under Fire: Materialism and the Rationality of Science*. New Yok: Rowman and Littlefield, 2004.

Merriam-Webster Collegiate Dictionary. 11th ed. USA: Merriam-Webster, 2003.

Meyer, Stephen C., *Return of the God Hypothesis: Three Scientific Discoveries That Reveal the Mind Behind the Universe*. New York: HarperCollins, 2021.

Miethe, Terry L., ed. *Did Jesus Rise from the Dead? The Resurrection Debate*. San Francisco: Harper & Row, 1987.

Miethe, Terry L. and Antony Flew. *Does God Exist?: A Believer and an Atheist Debate*. San Francisco: HarperSanFrancisco, 1991.

Mill, John Stuart. *Utilitarianism and the 1868 Speech on Capital Punishment*. 2nd ed., edited by George Sher. Indianapolis: Hackett, 2001.

Miller, Barry. *A Most Unlikely God: A Philosophical Enquiry into the Nature of God*. Notre Dame: University of Notre Dame Press, 1996.

Milton, Joyce. *The Road to Malpsychia: Humanistic Psychology and Our Discontents*. San Francisco: Encounter, 2002.

Minogue, Kenneth. *Alien Powers: The Pure Theory of Ideology*. New York: St. Martin's, 1985.

Molnar, Thomas. *God and the Knowledge of Reality*. New York: Basic, 1973.

———. *The Pagan Temptation*. Grand Rapids: Eerdmans, 1987.
———. *Theists and Atheists: A Typology of Non-Belief*. New York: Mouton, 1980.
———. *Utopia: The Perennial Heresy*. Lanham: The Intercollegiate Studies Institute, 1990.
Monk, Ray. *Ludwig Wittgenstein: The Duty of Genius*. New York: The Free Press, 1990.
More, Paul Elmer. *Christ the Word*. Princeton: Princeton University Press, 1927.
Moreland J. P. *Christianity and the Nature of Science: A Philosophical Investigation*. Grand Rapids: Baker, 1994.
———. *The Recalcitrant* Imago Dei: *Human Persons and the Failure of Naturalism*. London: SCM, 2009.
———. *Scientism and Secularism: Learning to Respond to a Dangerous Ideology*. Wheaton: Crossway, 2018.
———. *The Soul: How We Know It's Real and Why It Matters*. Chicago: Moody Publishers, 2014.
———. "Substance Dualism and the Diachronic/Synchronic Unity of Consciousness." In *Christian Physicalism? Philosophical Theological Criticisms*, edited by R. Keith Loftin, et al., 43–73. Lanham: Lexington, 2018.
———. *Universals*. Montreal: McGill-Queen's University Press, 2005.
Moreland J. P., and Kai Nielsen. *Does God Exist? The Great Debate*. Nashville: Thomas Nelson, 1990.
Morey, Robert A. *The New Atheism and the Erosion of Freedom*. Minneapolis: Bethany House, 1986.
Morris, Thomas V. *Anselmian Explorations: Essays in Philosophical Theology*. Notre Dame: University of Notre Dame Press, 1987.
———. *Our Idea of God: An Introduction to Philosophical Theology*. Downers Grove: InterVarsity, 1991.
Muravchik, Joshua. *Heaven on Earth: The Rise and Fall of Socialism*. San Francisco: Encounter, 2002.
Murphy, Mark C. *God & Moral Law: On the Theistic Explanation of Morality*. New York: Oxford University Press, 2011.
Murphy, Nancey, and Warren S. Brown. *Did My Neurons Make Me Do It? Philosophical and Neurobiological Perspectives on Moral Responsibility and Free Will*. New York: Oxford University Press, 2010.
Nagasawa, Yujin. *Maximal God: A New Defence of Perfect Being Theism*. New York: Oxford University Press, 2017.
Nagel, Thomas. *The Last Word*. New York: Oxford University Press, 1997.
———. *Mind & Cosmos: Why the Materialist Neo-Darwinian Conception of Nature Is Almost Certainly False*. New York: Oxford University Press, 2012.
Nash, Ronald H. *The Concept of God: An Exploration of Contemporary Difficulties with the Attributes of God*. Grand Rapids: Zondervan, 1983.
———, ed. *Process Theology*. Grand Rapids: Baker, 1987.
Netland, Harold A. *Christianity & Religious Diversity: Clarifying Christian Commitments in a Globalizing Age*. Grand Rapids: Baker Academic, 2015.
Neusch, Marcel. *The Sources of Modern Atheism: One Hundred Years of Debate Over God*. New York: Paulist, 1982.
Nielsen, Kai. *Naturalism without Foundations*. Amherst: Prometheus, 1996.
———. *Philosophy and Atheism: In Defense of Atheism*. Buffalo: Prometheus, 1985.

Nietzsche, Friedrich. *Beyond Good and Evil: Prelude to a Philosophy of the Future*. Translated by R. J. Hollingdale. New York: Penguin, 1990.

———. *The Dawn of Day*. Translated by John Macfarland Kennedy. Philadelphia: Jefferson, 2015.

———. *The Genealogy of Morals*. Translated by Horace B. Samuel. Mineola: Dover, 2003.

———. *Thus Spoke Zarathustra*. Translated by R. J. Hollingdale. New York: Penguin, 1969.

———. *Twilight of the Idols and The Antichrist*. Translated by R. J. Hollingdale. London: Penguin, 1990.

Noë, Alva. *Out of Our Heads: Why You Are Not Your Brain, and Other Lessons from the Biology of Consciousness*. New York: Hill and Wang, 2009.

Noll, Richard. *The Jung Cult: Origins of a Charismatic Movement*. Princeton: Princeton University Press, 1994.

Nolte, Ernst. *Three Faces of Fascism: Action Francaise; Italian Fascism; National Socialism*. Translated by Leila Vennewitz. New York: New American Library, 1965.

O'Connor, Timothy. *Theism and Ultimate Explanation: The Necessary Shape of Contingency*. Malden: Blackwell, 2008.

Oderberg, David S. *Real Essentialism*. New York: Routledge, 2007.

Olson, Jonas. *Moral Error Theory: History, Critique, Defence*. New York: Oxford University Press, 2014.

Oppy, Graham. *Arguing about Gods*. Cambridge: Cambridge University Press, 2009.

———. *The Best Argument against God*. New York: Palgrave Pivot, 2013.

———. "The Shape of Causal Reality: A Naturalistic Adaption of O'Connor's Cosmological Argument." *Philosophia Christi* 12:2 (2010) 281–287.

———. "Ultimate Naturalistic Causal Explanation." In *The Puzzle of Existence*, edited by Tyrone Goldschmidt, 4663. New York: Routledge, 2013.

Ostler, Blake. *Exploring Mormon Thought*, 3 vols. Salt Lake City: Greg Kofford, 2001–2008.

Padgett, Alan G. *God, Eternity, and the Nature of Time*. Eugene: Wipf and Stock, 2000.

Papineau, David. *Philosophical Naturalism*. Cambridge, MA: Blackwell, 1993.

Parfit, Derek. *On What Matters*, Vol. 1. New York: Oxford University Press, 2011.

———. *On What Matters*, Vol 2. New York: Oxford University Press, 2011.

———. *On What Matters*, Vol 3. New York: Oxford University Press, 2017.

Parrish, Stephen E. "Against a Naturalistic Causal Account of Reality." *Philosophia Christi* 13:2 (2011) 415–26.

———. *God and Necessity: A Defense of Classical Theism*. Lanham: University Press of America, 2001.

———. "God and Objectivism." *The Journal of Ayn Rand Studies* 8 (2007) 169–210.

———. *The Knower and the Known: Physicalism, Dualism, and the Nature of Intelligibility*. South Bend: St. Augustine's Press, 2013.

———. "Rundel on Sustaining the Universe." *Philosophia Christi* 11:2 (2009) 471–77.

———. "Theism, Naturalism, and Worlds: The Puzzle and the Problem." *Philosophia Christi* 18:2 (2016) 433–50.

———. "What's Good for the Goose and Related Matters." *The Journal of Ayn Rand Studies* 9:2 (2008) 395–415.

Parrish, Stephen E., with Carl Mosser. "A Tale of Two Theisms." In *The New Mormon Challenge: Responding to the Latest Defenses of a Fast-Growing Movement*, edited by Francis J. Beckwith, et al., 193-218. Grand Rapids: Zondervan, 2002.

Parrish, Stephen E., and J. W. Wartick. "Coming into Existence, the Universe, and God." *Concordia Theological Journal*, 4 (2016) 71-89.

———. "The Dilemma of Divine Simplicity." *Concordia Theological Journal* 2:1 (2014) 13-24, and 2:2 (2015) 71-84.

Pascal, Blaise. *Pascal's Pensées*. New York: Dutton, 1958.

Passmore, John. *The Perfectibility of Man*. 3rd ed. Indianapolis: Liberty Fund, 2000.

Paulson, David Lamont. *Comparative Coherence of Mormon (Finitistic) and Classical Theism*. Ann Arbor: University Microfilms International, 1975.

Payne, Stanley G. *Fascism: Comparison and Definition*. Madison: The University of Wisconsin Press, 1980.

———. *A History of Fascism, 1914-1945*. Madison: The University of Wisconsin Press, 1995.

Peacock, Roy E. *A Brief History of Eternity*. Wheaton: Crossway, 1990.

Pearcey, Nancy. *Finding Truth: 5 Principles for Unmasking Atheism, Secularism, and Other God Substitutes*. Colorado Springs: David C. Cook, 2015.

Pearcey, Nancy, and Charles B. Thaxton. *The Soul of Science: Christian Faith and Natural Philosophy*. Wheaton: Crossway, 1994.

Peikoff, Leonard. *Objectivism: The Philosophy of Ayn Rand*. New York: Dutton, 1991.

Pereboom, Derk. *Consciousness and the Prospects for Physicalism*. New York: Oxford University Press, 2011.

Perez, N. Jahdiel. "Three Popular Bad Arguments against Atheism." Unpublished Paper. 2016.

Peris, Daniel. *Storming the Heavens: The Soviet League of the Militant Godless*. Ithaca: Cornell University Press, 1998.

Peterson, Michael, et al. *Reason and Religious Belief: An Introduction to the Philosophy of Religion*. 4th ed. New York: Oxford University Press, 2009.

Peterson, Michael, and Michael Ruse. *Science, Evolution, and Religion: A Debate about Atheism and Theism*. New York: Oxford University Press, 2017.

Philipse, Herman. *God in the Age of Science?* Oxford: Oxford University Press, 2012.

———. "Transcendental Idealism." In *The Cambridge Companion to Husserl*, edited by Barry Smith, et al., 239-322. Cambridge: Cambridge University Press, 1995.

Pinkard, Terry. *German Philosophy 1760-1860: The Legacy of Idealism*. Cambridge: Cambridge University Press, 2002.

Pinker, Steven. *The Blank Slate: The Modern Denial of Human Nature*. New York: Penguin, reprint ed. 2003.

———. *How the Mind Works*. New York: Norton, 1999.

Pipes, Richard. *The Russian Revolution*. New York: Knopf, 1990.

Pitre, Brant. *The Case for Jesus: The Biblical and Historical Evidence for Christ*. New York: Image, 2016.

Plantinga, Alvin. "Actualism and Possible Worlds", http://www.andrewmbailey.com/ap/Actualism_Possible_Worlds.pdf.

———. *Does God Have a Nature?* Milwaukee: Marquette University Press, 1980.

———. *Faith and Rationality: Reason and Belief in God*. Notre Dame: University of Notre Dame Press, 1983.

———. *God and Other Minds: A Study of the Rational Justification of Belief in God*. Ithaca: Cornell University Press, 1967.
———. *God, Freedom, and Evil*. New York: Harper Torch, 1974.
———. *Knowledge and Christian Belief*. Grand Rapids: Eerdmans, 2015.
———. *The Nature of Necessity*. Oxford: Oxford University Press, 1978.
———. "Reply to Beilby's Cohorts." In *Naturalism Defeated?*, edited by James Beilby, 204–75. Ithaca: Cornell University Press, 2002.
———. *Warrant and Proper Function*. New York: Oxford University Press, 1993.
———. *Warranted Christian Belief*. New York: Oxford University Press, 2000.
———. *Where the Conflict Really Lies: Science, Religion, and Naturalism*. New York: Oxford University Press, 2011.
Plantinga, Alvin, and Michael Tooley. *Knowledge of God*. Malden: Blackwell, 2008.
Plato. *The Collected Dialogues: including the Letters*, edited by Edith Hamilton and Huntington Cairns. Princeton: Princeton University Press, 1971.
Plotinus. *The Six Enneads of Plotinus*. Translated from The Latin by Stephen McKenna and B. S. Page. London: Forgotten, 2007.
Poewe, Karla. *New Religions and the Nazis*. New York: Routledge, 2006.
Post, John F. *The Faces of Existence: An Essay in Nonreductive Metaphysics*. Ithaca: Cornell University Press, 1987.
Pruss, Alexander R. *Actuality, Possibility, and Worlds*. New York: Continuum, 2011.
———. *The Principle of Sufficient Reason: A Reassessment*. New York: Cambridge University Press, 2006.
———, and Joshua L. Rasmussen, *Necessary Existence*. New York: Oxford University Press, 2018.
Rana, Fazale, et al. *Building Bridges: Presentations on RTB's Testable Creation Model*. Covina: Reasons to Believe, 2018.
Rand, Ayn. *Philosophy: Who Needs It?*, edited, with an introduction by Leonard Peikoff. New York: New American Library, 1982.
Reilly, Robert R. *The Closing of the Muslim Mind: How Intellectual Suicide Created the Modern Islamist Crisis*. Wilmington: Intercollegiate Studies Institute, 2010.
Richards, Jay Wesley. *The Untamed God: A Philosophic Exploration of Divine Perfection, Simplicity and Immutability*. Downers Grove: InterVarsity, 2003.
Richardson, Don. *Peace Child*. Ventura: Regal, 2005.
Rist, John M. *On Inoculating Moral Philosophy Against God*. The Aquinas Lecture, 2000. Milwaukee: Marquette University Press, 1999.
Ritchie, Angus. *From Morality to Metaphysics: The Theistic Implications of our Ethical Commitments*. Oxford: Oxford University Press, 2012.
Robbins, John W. *Answer to Ayn Rand: A Critique of the Philosophy of Objectivism*. Washington, DC: Mount Vernon, 1974.
———. *Christ and Civilization*. Unicoi: The Trinity Foundation, 2003.
———. *Without a Prayer: Ayn Rand and the Close of Her System*. Hobbs: The Trinity Foundation, 1997.
Roberts, Anjeanette. "Why Would a Good God Create Viruses?" In *Building Bridges: Presentations on RTB's Testable Creation Model*, Rana, et al., 59–67. Covina: Reasons to Believe, 2018.
Robinson, Howard. *From the Knowledge Argument to Mental Substance: Resurrecting the Mind*. New York: Cambridge University Press, 2017.

Rogers, Katherin A. *Perfect Being Theology*. Edinburgh: Edinburgh University Press, 2000.
Rosenblum, Bruce, and Fred Kuttner. *Quantum Enigma: Physics Encounters Consciousness*. New York: Oxford University Press, 2006.
Ross, Hugh. *A Matter of Days: Resolving a Creation Controversy*. 2nd ed. Covina: Reasons to Believe, 2015.
———. *Why the Universe Is the Way It Is*. Grand Rapids: Baker, 2008.
Ross, James. *Philosophical Theology*. Indianapolis: Bobbs-Merrill, 1969.
Rowe, William E. *Can God be Free?* New York: Oxford University Press, 2004.
Rucker, Rudy. *Infinity and the Mind: The Science and Philosophy of the Infinite*. Boston: Birkhauser, 1982.
Rummel, R. J. *Death by Government*. New Brunswick: Transaction, 1997.
———. *Power Kills: Democracy as a Method of Non-Violence*. New Brunswick: Transaction, 2009.
Rundle, Bede. *Why there is Something rather than Nothing*. New York: Oxford University Press, 2004.
Russell, Bertrand and F. C. Copleston. "A Debate on the Existence of God." In *The Existence of God*, edited by John Hick, 167–91. New York: Macmillan, 1964.
Ryder, John, ed. *American Philosophical Naturalism in the Twentieth Century*. Amherst: Prometheus, 1994.
Sagan, Carl. *Cosmos*. New York: Random House, 1980.
Samples, Kenneth Richard. *A World of Difference: Putting Christian Truth-Claims to the Worldview Test*. Grand Rapids: Baker, 2007.
Samson, Philip J. *6 Modern Myths: About Christianity and Western Civilization*. Downers Grove: InterVarsity, 2001.
Sanandaji, Nima. *Debunking Utopia: Exposing the Myth of Nordic Socialism*. Washington, DC: WND, 2016.
Sansbury, Timothy N. *Beyond Time: Defending God's Transcendence*. Lanham: University Press of America, 2009.
Sartre, Jean-Paul. *Being and Nothingness*. Translated and with an introduction by Hazel Barnes. New York: Washington Square, 1966.
Satel, Sally, and Scott O. Lilienfeld. *Brainwashed: The Seductive Appeal of Mindless Neuroscience*. New York: Basic, 2013.
Schama, Simon. *Citizens: A Chronicle of the French Revolution*. New York: Knopf, 1989.
Schlossberg, Herbert. *Idols for Destruction: Christian Faith and Its Confrontation with American Society*. Nashville: Thomas Nelson, 1983.
Schmidt, Alvin J. *The Great Divide: The Failure of Islam and the Triumph of the West*. Boston: Regina Orthodox, 2004.
———. *How Christianity Changed the World*. Grand Rapids: Zondervan, 2004.
Schneider, Nathan. *God in Proof: The Story of a Search from the Ancients to the Internet*. Berkeley: University of California Press, 2013.
Schom, Alan. *Napoleon Bonaparte: A Life*. New York: HarperCollins, 1997.
Schopenhauer, Arthur. *The World as Will and Representation*, 3 vols. Mineola: Dover, 1966.
Schroeder, William R. *Continental Philosophy: A Critical Approach*. Malden: Blackwell, 2005.
Schwartz, Jeffrey M., and Sharon Begley. *The Mind and the Brain: Neuroplasticity and the Power of Mental Force*. New York: Regan, 2002.

Scruton, Roger. *Beauty: A Very Short Introduction*. New York: Oxford University Press, 2011.
———. *Spinoza: A Very Short Introduction*. Oxford: Oxford University Press, 2002.
Searle, John R. *The Rediscovery of the Mind*. Cambridge: Bradford, 7th Printing, 1998.
Sebestyen, Victor. *Lenin: The Man, the Dictator, and the Master of Terror*. New York: Pantheon, 2017.
Sesardić, Neven. *When Reason Goes on Holiday: Philosophers in Politics*. New York: Encounter, 2016.
Shafarevich, Igor. *The Socialist Phenomenon*. New York: Harper & Row, 1975.
Shaw, Gregory. "Platonic Siddhas: Supernatural Philosophers of Neoplatonism." In *Beyond Physicalism: Toward Reconciliation of Science and Spirituality*, edited by Edward F. Kelly, et al., 275–313. Lanham: Rowman and Littlefield, 2015.
Shook, John R., and Paul Kurtz, eds. *The Future of Naturalism*. Amherst: Humanity Books, 2009.
Siedentop, Larry. *Inventing the Individual: The Origins of Western Liberalism*. Cambridge: The Belknap Press of Harvard University Press, 2014.
Singer, Peter, ed. *Does Anything Really Matter? Essays on Parfit on Objectivity*. New York: Oxford University Press, 2017.
Singh, Simon. *Big Bang: Origin of the Universe*. New York: Harper Perennial, 2004.
Sinnott-Armstrong, Walter. *Morality Without God*. New York: Oxford University Press, 2009.
Sire, James W. *The Universe Next Door: A Basic Worldview Catalog*. 5th ed. Downers Grove: InterVarsity, 2009.
Sklar, Lawrence. *Space, Time, and Spacetime*. Berkeley: University of California Press, 1977.
Slagle, Jim. *The Epistemological Skyhook: Determinism, Naturalism, and Self-Defeat*. New York: Routledge, 2016.
Smart, J. J. C., and J. J. Haldane. *Atheism & Theism*. Cambridge: Blackwell, 1996.
Smith, Barry, and David Woodruff Smith, eds. *The Cambridge Companion to Husserl*. New York: Cambridge University Press, 1999.
Smith, Barry D. *The Indescribable God: Divine Otherness in Christian Theology*. Eugene: Pickwick, 2012.
———. *The Oneness and Simplicity of God*. Eugene: Pickwick, 2014.
Smith, George H. *Atheism: The Case Against God*. Buffalo: Prometheus, 1979.
Smith, Quentin. *The Felt Meanings of the World: A Metaphysics of Feeling*. West Lafayette: Purdue University Press, 1986.
———. "The Metaphilosophy of Naturalism." *Philo* 4:2 (Fall–Winter, 2001) 195–215.
Snyder, Timothy. *Black Earth: The Holocaust as History and Warning*. New York: Tim Duggan, 2015.
———. *Bloodlands: Europe Between Hitler and Stalin*. New York: Basic, 2010.
Sobel, Jordan Howard. *Logic and Theism: Arguments For And Against Beliefs in God*. Cambridge: Cambridge University Press, 2004.
Sorell, Tom. *Scientism: Philosophy and the Infatuation with Science*. New York: Routledge, 1991.
Sowell, Thomas. *A Conflict of Visions: Ideological Origins of Political Struggles*. New York: William Morrow, 1987.
———. *Intellectuals and Society*. Rev. ed.. New York: Basic, 2011.
———. *The Vision of the Anointed: Self-Congratulation as a Basis for Social Policy*. New York: Basic, 1995.

———. https://www.creators.com/read/thomas-sowell/12/12/random-thoughts-12-12-25
Sperber, Jonathan. *Karl Marx: A Nineteenth Century Life*. New York: Liveright, 2015.
Spinoza, Benedict de. *On the Improvement of the Understanding, the Ethics, Correspondence*. New York: Dover, 1955.
Spitzer, Robert J. *New Proofs for the Existence of God: Contributions of Contemporary Physics and Philosophy*. Grand Rapids: Eerdmans, 2010.
Stapp, Henry. *Mindful Universe: Quantum Mechanics and the Participating Observer*. New York: Springer-Verlag, 2007.
Stark, Rodney. *America's Blessings: How Religion Benefits Everyone, Including Atheists*. West Conshohocken: Templeton, 2012.
———. *Bearing False Witness: Debunking Centuries of Anti-Catholic History*. West Conshohocken: Templeton, 2016.
———. *For the Glory of God: How Monotheism Led to Reformations, Science, Witch-Hunts, and the End of Slavery*. Princeton: Princeton University Press. 2003.
———. *How the West Won: The Neglected Story of the Triumph of Modernity*. Wilmington: Intercollegiate Studies Institute, 2014.
———. *The Triumph of Christianity: How the Jesus Movement Became the World's Largest Religion*. New York: HarperOne, 2011.
———. *The Triumph of Faith: Why the World is More Religious Than Ever*. Wilmington: ISI, 2015.
———. *Why God? Explaining Religious Phenomena*. West Conshohocken: Templeton, 2016.
Stephen, James Fitzjames. *Liberty, Equality, Fraternity*, edited by Stuart D. Warner. Indianapolis: Liberty Fund, 1993.
Steup, Matthias, and Ernest Sosa, eds. *Contemporary Debates in Epistemology*. Malden: Blackwell, 2005.
Stone, David Reuben. *Atheism is False: Richard Dawkins and the Improbability of God Delusion*. www.atheismisfalse.com: David Reuben Stone, 2007.
Swinburne, Richard. *The Coherence of Theism*. Oxford: Oxford University Press, 1995.
———. *The Existence of God*. 2nd ed. Oxford: Oxford University Press, 2004.
———. *Mind, Brain & Free Will*. Oxford: Oxford University Press, 2013.
Taylor, Charles. *A Secular Age*. Cambridge: The Belknap Press of Harvard University Press, 2007.
Taylor, F. Flagg IV, ed. *The Great Lie: Classic and Recent Appraisals of Ideology and Totalitarianism*. Wilmington: ISI, 2011.
Terrell, Richard. *Christ, Faith, and the Holocaust*. Bloomington: WestBow, 2011.
Tolkien, J. R. R. *The Silmarillion*. Boston: Houghton Mifflin, 1977.
Torrance, Thomas F. *Divine and Contingent Order*. Eugene: Wipf & Stock, 2004.
Trevor-Roper, Hugh, ed. *Hitler's Table Talk 1941–1944*. New York: Enigma, 2000.
Trueblood, Elton. *Philosophy of Religion*. Grand Rapids: Baker, 1973.
———. https://answers.yahoo.com/question/index?qid=20070619072059AAc201V.
Tucker, Robert C. *The Marxian Revolutionary Idea*. New York; Norton, 1969.
Tucker, William. *Marriage and Civilization: How Monogamy Made Us Human*. Washington, DC: Regnery, 2014.
Unger, Peter. *All the Power in the World*. New York: Oxford University Press, 2006.
Unterman, Jeremiah. *Justice for All: How the Jewish Bible Revolutionized Ethics*. Philadelphia: The Jewish Publication Society, 2017.

van den Broek, Roelof, and Wouter J. Hanegraaff. *Gnosis and Hermeticism: From Antiquity to Modern Times.* Albany: State University of New York Press, 1998.
van Fraassen, Bas C. *Laws and Symmetry.* Oxford: Oxford University Press, 1989.
van Inwagen, Peter. *Christian Faith and the Problem of Evil.* Grand Rapids: Eerdmans, 2004.
———. *An Essay on Free Will.* Oxford: Oxford University Press, reprinted, 1986.
van Roojen, Mark. *Metaethics: A Contemporary Introduction.* New York: Routledge, 2015.
Van Til, Cornelius. *The Defense of the Faith.* 4th ed., edited by K. Scott Oliphint. Phillipsburg: P&R, 2008.
Van Til, L. John. *The Liberty of Conscience: The History of a Puritan Idea.* Phillipsburg: P&R, 1992.
Varghese, Roy Abraham. *The Missing Link: A Symposium on Darwin's Framework for a Creation-Evolution Solution.* Lanham: The University Press of America, 2013.
Veith, Gene Edward. *Modern Fascism: Liquidating the Judeo-Christian Worldview.* St. Louis: Concordia, 1993.
Vitzhum, Richard C. *Materialism: An Affirmative History and Definition.* Amherst: Prometheus, 1995.
Voegelin, Eric. *From Enlightenment to Revolution.* Durham, NC: Duke University Press, 1975.
———. *Israel and Revelation*, vol. 1 of Order and History. Baton Rouge: Louisiana State University Press, 1986.
———. *Modernity Without Restraint*, edited and with an introduction by Manfred Henningsen. The Collected Works of Eric Voegelin, vol. 5. Columbia: University of Missouri Press, 2000.
———. *Science, Politics, and Gnosticism: Two Essays.* Chicago: Regnery Gateway, 1968.
von Mises, Ludwig. *Human Action.* 3rd rev. ed. Chicago: Henry Regnery, 1966.
Wallace, Stan W., ed. *Does God Exist?: The Craig-Flew Debate.* Burlington: Ashgate, 2003.
Walls, Jerry L, and Trent Dougherty, eds. *Two Dozen (or So) Arguments for God: The Plantinga Project.* New York: Oxford University Press, 2018.
Walsh, David. *After Ideology: Recovering the Spiritual Foundations of Freedom.* San Francisco: HarperSanFrancisco, 1990.
Ward, Bruce K. *Redeeming the Enlightenment: Christianity and the Liberal Virtues.* Grand Rapids: Eerdmans, 2010.
Ward, Keith. *Christ and the Cosmos: A Reformulation of Trinitarian Doctrine.* New York: Cambridge University Press, 2015.
Weaver, Richard M. *Ideas Have Consequences.* Chicago: University of Chicago Press, 1984.
Weikart, Richard. *The Death of Humanity: And the Case for Life.* Washington, DC: Regnery Faith, 2016.
———. *From Darwin to Hitler: Evolutionary Ethics, Eugenics, and Racism in Germany.* New York: Palgrave Macmillan, 2004.
———. *Hitler's Ethics: The Nazi Pursuit of Evolutionary Progress.* New York: Palgrave Macmillan, 2011.
———. *Hitler's Religion: The Twisted Beliefs that Drove the Third Reich.* Washington, DC: Regnery History, 2016.
Welty, Greg. "Theistic Conceptual Realism." In *Beyond the Control of God?: Six Views on the Problem of God and Abstract Objects*, edited by Paul M. Gould, 81–111. New York: Bloomsbury Academic, 2014.

———. *Why is There Evil in the World (And So Much Of It?)*. Glasgow: Christian Focus, 2018.
Whitehead, Alfred N. *Process and Reality*. New York: Macmillan, 1941.
Whitmarsh, Tim. *Battling the Gods: Atheism in the Ancient World*. New York: Knopf, 2015.
Wielenberg, Erik J. *Robust Ethics: The Metaphysics and Epistemology of Godless Normative Realism*. New York: Oxford University Press, 2014.
———. *Value and Virtue in a Godless Universe*. New York: Cambridge University Press, 2005.
Wiker, Benjamin, and Jonathan Witt. *A Meaningful World: How the Arts and Sciences Reveal the Genius of Nature*. Downers Grove: InterVarsity Academic, 2006.
Wiker, Benjamin. *Worshipping the State: How Liberalism Became Our State Religion*. Washington, DC: Regnery, 2013
Wikipedia. "Toledo War." http://en.wikipedia.org/wiki/Toledo_War.
Wilczek, Frank. *A Beautiful Question: Finding Nature's Deep Design*. New York: Penguin, 2015.
———. *The Lightness of Being: Mass, Ether, and the Unification of Forces*. New York: Basic, 2008.
Wilkens, Steve. *Beyond Bumper Sticker Ethics: An Introduction to Theories of Right and Wrong*. 2nd ed. Downers Grove: InterVarsity Academic, 2011.
Williams, John F. *Hating Perfection: A Subtle Search for the Best Possible World*. Amherst: Humanity, 2013.
Williams, Richard M., and Daniel N. Robinson, eds. *Scientism: The New Orthodoxy*. New York: Bloomsbury, 2015.
Winik, Jay. *The Great Upheaval: America and the Birth of the Modern World, 1788–1800*. New York: HarperCollins, 2007.
Wittgenstein, Ludwig. *The Blue and Brown Books: Preliminary Studies for the 'Philosophical Investigations'*. New York: Harper Torch, 1965.
———. *Tractatus Logico-Philosophicus*. Translated by D. F. Pears and B. F. McGuinness. New Jersey: Humanities, 1974.
Wood, W. Jay. *God*. Montreal: McGill's-Queens University Press, 2011.
Wright, Edmond, ed. *The Case for Qualia*. Cambridge: Bradford, 2008.
Wright, N. T. *The Resurrection of the Son of God*. Minneapolis: Fortress, 2003.
Wynn, Mark. *God and Goodness: A Natural Theological Perspective*. New York: Routledge, 1999.
Yancey, George. *Dehumanizing Christians: Cultural Competition in a Multicultural World*. New Brunswick: Transaction, 2014.
———. *Hostile Environment: Understanding and Responding to Anti-Christian Bias*. Downers Grove: InterVarsity, 2015.
Yandell, Keith E., and Harold Netland. *Buddhism: A Christian Exploration and Appraisal*. Downers Grove: InterVarsity, 2009.
Yandell, Keith E. *Christianity and Philosophy*. Grand Rapids: Eerdmans, 1984.
Zagorin, Perez. *How the Idea of Religious Toleration Came to the West*. Princeton: Princeton University Press, 2003.
Zuckerman, Phil. "Atheism: Contemporary Numbers and Patterns." In *The Cambridge Companion to Atheism*, edited by Michael Martin, 47–65. New York: Cambridge University Press, 2007.
Zugger, Christopher Lawrence. *The Forgotten: Catholics of the Soviet Empire from Lenin to Stalin*. Syracuse: Syracuse University Press, 2001.

Index

Abortion, 183, 232, 234n182, 242n39, 244n46
"Absolute", 64, 68–72, 108, 128
Abstracta (Abstract objects), 42, 73–74, **96–98**, 107, 110, 116n43, 127, 133–36, 169, 172, 192, 194, 222–23
Aesthetics, 14, 57–58, 168, 180, 197n3
Agnosticism, 7, 11, **88–91**, 231, 249
Allah, 37, 63–64
Analogical Knowledge, **79–81**
Anselm, Saint, 2n3, 72, 108
Anti-Realism, see Metaethics
Aristotle, 10, 17, 26, 70
Augustine, Saint, 227n5
Austere Theism, **206–8**
Axiarchism, 134n70, 172
Axioms, **174–75**, 176, 189–90

Barr, Stephen, 114n38, 132, 162n40
Beauty, 1, 14n37, 57, 111n27, 180–81, **197–200**, 222–24
Begging the Question, 39–40, 54, 77, 123, 132, 191n51
Bentham, Jeremy, 174
Blind Faith, 41, **45–47**, 50–51, 231–32
Bob the Proton, 119–22, 125, 128
Bobbin, 126
Bradley, F. H., 69, 109
Brady, Tom, 129
Brahman, 62, 64
Broxable, 80–81

Brute Fact Theory, 12, 105–6, 109–10, **111–25**, 133, 136, 193, 218–19, 224, 226
Bubonic plague, 202
Burden of Proof, xix, 41, **89–91**, 126

Cartesian, xviii n4, 140, 162n41
Cat, 34n48, 79–80, 94–95, 97, 104, 126, 129–30, 142, 208, 221
Categorical Imperative, 175, **179–80**, 186, 192, 195
Chance, 5, 37, 75n49, 102, **105–10**, 113, **115–20**, 121–25, 133, 135, 146, 165, 168, 193, 213, 217–24, 233–35, 241, 250
Chapman, Allan, 18 n8, 93
Chemical scum, 166
Churchland, Patricia, 137, 139n8, 148n24
Churchland, Paul, 139n8, 148n24, 163
Civil War, 76, 113
Clark, Gordon H., xix, 3n6, 14n38, 60, 83n66, 245n48
Clouser, Roy, 60n3, 79n59, 99, 134n69
Collingwood, R. G., 25
Concrete Objects, **96–98**, 104–5, 110, 113, 121, 134, 139–40
Constructivism, 173
Contingent, xviii, 92, 99n95, 100, 103, 105, **120–25**, 127, 130–31, 136, 146–47, 171, 193, 212, 222
Contractualism, 173, 185
Copleston, Frederick, 9n25, 10n26, 17n5, 69, 105

277

INDEX

Cornell Realism, 173
Cosmological Argument, 58n82, 108

D'Souza, Dinesh, 148n24
Davies, Paul, 25
Dennett, Daniel, 137, 139n8
Descartes, René, 120, 140
Detroit Lions, 76, 156
Dewey, John, 14n38, 60n4, 227
Divine Command, 172
Divine Simplicity, 73, **83–86**
Dostoevsky, Fyodor, 200
Dualism, 4n8, 9n23, 20, 89n79, **95**, 138–40, 145, 153, 158, **161–66**, 221
Dunphy, John, 239–40

Egoism, 173, 184, 186, 190–91
Einstein, Albert, 69–70, 103n5
Eliminativism, 140–49, 167
Eliot, T. S., 240
Emotivism, 173
Engels, 18n9, 28
Ethics, 7, 10, 56, 60, 62n10, 65n16, 92–93, 133–35, **168–96**, 197–98, 212–13, 215, 222, 243
Euthanasia, 188
Euthyphro Objection, **194–95**
Evil, 22n20, 23, 26n35, 57–58, 71, 76, 88n77, 106, 180, 194, 214–15, 239–40
    Moral Evil, 87n74, 194, 212–13
    Natural Evil, 10, 209–10, 237
    Problem of, **200–15**, 223–25, 231
Explanatory Gap, 185

Faith, 16, 34, 36, **44–56**, 98–99, 226, 229n10, 231–32, 239, 250n12
Faith Commitment, 51, 98–99
Fichte, Johann Gottlieb, 69
Fictionalism, 173–74, 177
Fideism, 47, 50, 232. Also see Blind Faith
Fisher, Andrew, 169
Frankl, Viktor, 235–36
Functionalism, 140–41, 143

Gnosticism, 10, 31, 228n7, 236–37, 242n39
Goldbach's Conjecture, 78

Goldschmidt, Tyron, 59, 104n8, 113n33, 121
God of Classical Theism, 61, 64–65, 72–86, 107
Goebbels, Joseph, 66
Greeks, 3, 9–10, 18, 26, 62, 64, 91
Grünbaum, Adolf, 120–21

Haeckel, Ernst, 69
Hart, David Bentley, 26n35, 111, 190n48, 197
Hawking, Stephen, 166
Hegel, Georg, 69
Hesiod, 112
Hitler Youth Song, 22 (see note 20 also)
Hitler, Adolph, 22, **65–69**, 93, 170, 231n14, 241n34
Hobbits, 62, 134
Holocaust, 176, 201, 244n46
Holodomor, 201
Holt, Jim, 77

Identity
    Law of, 53
    Numerical, 86
    Theory, 140–43
Immanence, 68, 73, **82**
Incomprehensible, 73, **78–79**
Incredulous Stare, 204
Infinite (Attribute of God), 73, **82**, 100, 129–30, 136, 161, 165, 197n2, 205, 215, 220, 235
Intentionality, 57, 141, 148–49, 151, 161, 165–66, 219, **221–24**, 234
Intuitionism, 172
Inwagen, Peter van, 158
Islam, 13–14, 24, 37–38, 63–65, 70, 85n71, 184, 194, 196, 228, 241, 250n12

James, William, 102
Jihad, 24
Junge, Traudl, 66, 67n23

Kalam Cosmology, 58n82, 108–9
Kant, Immanuel, 102, 175, 179, 197n2
Kantianism, 173, 185–86, 191
Kent, Clark, 86
Klingon, 62, 134, 170

Koontz, Dean, 201
Korsgaard, Christine, 172n14, 184, 187
Kung, Hans, 201
Kurtz, Paul, 2n2, 7n15, 23n27, 93, 239n26

Lavoisier, Antoine, 120
Law of Non-Contradiction, 53, 74, 91, 126, **175-76**
Laws of Logic, **53-54**, 74, **125-36**, 180
Laws of Physics (Nature), 43n61, 56, 58n83, 102, 114-27, 141, 146, 204-5, 218, 226
Leibnizian Cosmology, 108-9
Leslie, John, 59n2, 133-34
Lewis, C. S., 140n9, 172n12, 184n36, 202n17, 242n40, 246
Lewis, David, 103n7, 116n42, 132n65, 204
Linbom, Tage, 240
Lord of the Rings, 170n8
Luther, Martin, 33, 50n76

Mackie, J. L., 87n73, 109, 173n16, 181-82
Mao Tse Dung, 201
Maritain, Jacques, 102
Marks, Joel, 181
Marx, Karl, 16, 28, 87
Marxism, 8, 12, 14, 17-18, 20, 22-24, 54, 68, 229, 238n25, 241-42
Meixner, Uwe, 138, 140n9
Mencken, H. L., 44
Metaethics, 149, 172n12, 173n15-16, 174, 176, 184n38
   Anti-Realism, 43n62, 168, **171-74**, 178, 181-85, 189, 212, 223
   Strong Realism, 168, **171-72**, **176-78**, 181-83, 185, **192-96**, 212-13
   Weak Realism, 7, 171-74, **184-92**, 212
Metaphysics, 25n33, 42, 59n1, 111, 120, 169
Methodological Naturalism, 42-44
Mill, John Stuart, 174-75
Miracles, 21, 26n35, 31-32, 36-40, 44, 58n83, 65, 70, 205-6, 226

Modal Realism, 131-33, 135
Molnar, Thomas, 7n17, 63n12, 88, 90n82, 99n95
Monotheism, 2-3, 8-15, 92, 227
Moral Error Theory, **173-74**, 182n30-31
Moral Truths, 57, 78, **169-81**, 212-13, 222
Morality, **168-96**, 212-13, 222-23, 231n14, 232n17, 243, 247
Mormonism, 21-22, 61-62, 65, 67n22, 72, 96
Morris, Thomas V., 108
Mysterianism, **141-42**, 145, 167

Nagel, Thomas, xvii-xviii, 47n72, 133n67
Natural Law Ethics, 172
Nazism, 65-68, 231n14, 235, 241
Necessary Deity Theory, **105-112**, 125, 136
Necessary World Theory, **105-6**
Necessarily Existent, 8, 77-78, 92, 96, 105-10, 218
Nietzsche, Friedrich, 33, 87, 168-69, 181, 246
Nihilism, 8, 173-74, 190-91
Noë, Alva, 137

Omnibenevolence, 64, 73, **78**, 84
Omnipotence, 25, 63-65, **74**-75, 82-86, 210
Omnipresence, 73, **75**, 82
Omniscience, 64, 73-75, 82, 84-86, 100, 130, 135, 165, 194, 217
"One", The, 62-64, 68, 128
Ontological Argument, 77, 111
Oppy, Graham, xix, 76n51, **130-31**, **164-65**, 246-47

Panentheism, 55, 61, 71-72, 81
Pantheism, 3, 6, 55-56, **61**, 63-72, 81, 90n82, 129-30, 135-36, 241n34
Pascal, Blaise, 16, 137, 216
Perfect Being Theism, xix, 8, 60-61, 64, **72-73**, 77, 84, 92, 107-9, 130, 135-36, 155-56, 165, 168, 194, 214

Phenomenality, 141–42, 161–62, 166, 178–79
Philipse, Herman, 98n92, 124
Philosophical Naturalism, xix, 2n2, 11, 31–32, 40–41, 90, **93–99**, 124, 136, 145, 164, 211, 214–15, 241n34, 247
Plantinga, Alvin, xix, 11n32, 48n73, 51n78, 75n50, 76n52, 79n60, 106n11, 112, 113n32, 204n18, 206, 209n27
Plato, 10, 97
Platonism, 74, 107, 172, 193, 227n5
Plausibility Structures, **35–40**, 52–54
Plotinus, 62, 83, 108, 129
Polytheism, 3, 61–62, 65, 92, 183n34
Possible Worlds, 75–77, 81, **103–5**, 106, 108, **112–15**, 125, 130–35, 164, 207–8, 217
"Positive Christianity", 66
Prescriptivism, 173
Problem of Evil, see Evil
Problem of the One and the Many, 83
Property Dualism, 89n79
Pythagoreans, 133

Qur'an, 37, 64

Rationality, 34, 38, 44, 51, 57, 62, 69–70, 124, 136, 141, 149, 157, 161, 165–66, 173, **187–89**, 219–22, 224, 226, 251
Realization Materialism, 140–43
Reason, 33–44, and throughout the book
Relativism, 173, 190
Ritchie, Angus, 7n16, 172n12, **185**
Robbins, John W., 24n30, 190n48, **227**
Roman Empire, 76, 227
Russell, Bertrand, xvii–xviii, 105, 111–12

Sagan, Carl, 227
Sanandaji, Nima, 250
Sankara, 63–64
Sartre, Jean-Paul, 87, 111
Scandinavia, 64, 249–51
Schelling, Friedrich, 69

Schopenhauer, Arthur, 69
Science, xix, 6–7, 12, 15n39, 16, 21, **25–33**, 40–44, 51, 58, 63n13, 90n82, 93–95, 102–3, 118, 120, 138–39, 163, 215, 225–26, 229, 241
Scientism, 28–30
Searle, John R., 166
Sellars, Wilfred, 25
Shook, John R., 93
Sinnott-Armstrong, Walter, 190
Slavery/Slave Trade, 11, 173, 176, 179n25, 202
Smith, Quentin, 11n32, **123–24**
Sovereign (Attribute of God), 82, 109–10, 217
Sowell, Thomas, 35–36n50, 240n30, **246**
Spinoza, Benedict, 62, **69–71**, 125, 129–30
Star Trek, 42, 170n8
Star Wars, 62, 170n8
Stark, Rodney, 20n18, 225n6, 228n6&9, 230n13, 231n16, 247–51
Stoics, 3, 69
Strangeness Argument, 181–82
Strong Realism, see Metaethics
Subjectivism, 173, 190
Superman, see Clark Kent
Supervenience, **140–43**

Tamerlane, 189, 201
Tautology, 77n55
Theodicy, 203, 210
Thomist Cosmology, 108–9, 124
Tolkein, J. R. R., 201
Transcendence, 23, 63n12, 68n27, 73, 81, 92, 128, 229n12, 236n23, 239
Transcendental Test, 55
Trinity, 63, 66, **83**, 86, 196, 222
Trueblood, Elton, 45, 176

Ultimate Reality, xviii, 1–2, 4, 8, 20, **59–60**, 61, 63, 83, 92–93, 96, **99–100**, 165, 168, 196
Univocal Knowledge, **79–80**
Utilitarianism, 173–75, **184–87**, 210–11
Utopia, 7–8, 16n1, 18n9, 226, 236, 238–45

Van Til, Cornelius, 83n68, 122n50, 123n54, 125n56, 136
Vikings, 189
Virtue Ethics, 173, 185
Voegelin, Eric, 18n10, 22, 236–37, 242n39, 245n47
Voluntarism, 194

Weak Realism, see Metaethics
Wielenberg, Erik J., 192, 240, 246
Wilczek, Frank, 94, 197

Williams, John F., 133
World, Actual, 75, 103–6, 112, 127, 131, 208, 238n25
World, Possible, 75–77, 81, **103–15**, 125, 130–35, 164
World, "Sue", 105–6, 113–14, 120–21, 207–8, 217
Worldviews, 1–3, 5–6, 12–15, 17, 21–24, 27–41, 48, 50–60, 98–99, 183, 211n32, 226–29, 234, 242n39

www.ingramcontent.com/pod-product-compliance
Lightning Source LLC
Chambersburg PA
CBHW070235230426
43664CB00014B/2306